Lecture Notes in Computer Science 4846

Commenced Publication in 1973
Founding and Former Series Editors:
Gerhard Goos, Juris Hartmanis, and Jan van Leeuwen

Iliano Cervesato (Ed.)

Advances in Computer Science – ASIAN 2007

Computer and Network Security

12th Asian Computing Science Conference
Doha, Qatar, December 9-11, 2007
Proceedings

 Springer

Volume Editor

Iliano Cervesato
Carnegie Mellon University
Doha, Qatar
E-mail: iliano@cmu.edu

Library of Congress Control Number: 2007939450

CR Subject Classification (1998): F.3, E.3, D.2.4, D.4.6-7, K.6.5, C.2

LNCS Sublibrary: SL 1 – Theoretical Computer Science and General Issues

ISSN	0302-9743
ISBN-10	3-540-76927-7 Springer Berlin Heidelberg New York
ISBN-13	978-3-540-76927-9 Springer Berlin Heidelberg New York

Springer is a part of Springer Science+Business Media

springer.com

© Springer-Verlag Berlin Heidelberg 2007
Printed in Germany

Typesetting: Camera-ready by author, data conversion by Scientific Publishing Services, Chennai, India
Printed on acid-free paper   SPIN: 12195626   06/3180   5 4 3 2 1 0

Preface

The ASIAN conference series provides a forum for researchers throughout Asia to present cutting-edge results in yearly-themed areas of computer science, to discuss advances in these fields, and to promote interaction with researchers from other continents. Accordingly, the conference moves every year to a different center of research throughout Asia: previous editions were held in Tokyo, Kunming (China), Bangkok, Mumbai, Hanoi, Penang (Malaysia), Phuket (Thailand), Manila, Kathmandu, Singapore, and Pathumthani (Thailand) where ASIAN was initiated by AIT, INRIA and UNU/IIST in 1995. The 12th edition took place in Doha, Qatar, during December 9–11, 2007.

Each year, the conference focuses on a different theme at the cutting edge of computer science research. The theme of ASIAN 2007 was "Computer and Network Security". It has been a tradition of ASIAN to invite three of the most influential researchers in the focus area, one from Asia, one from Europe and one from the Americas, to discuss their work and their vision for the field. This year's distinguished speakers were Andrei Sabelfeld (Chalmers University, Sweden), Joshua Guttman (MITRE, USA) and Kazuhiko Kato (University of Tsukuba, Japan).

Following the call for paper, ASIAN 2007 received 112 submissions, of which 65 were eventually reviewed. Of these, the Program Committee selected 15 regular papers and 10 short papers. This volume contains the abstracts of the invited talks and the revised versions of the regular papers and the short papers. I wish to thank the members of the Program Committee and the external reviewers for doing an excellent job at selecting the contributed papers under severe time pressure. *EasyChair* proved an egregious platform for smoothly carrying out all aspects of the program selection and finalization.

The conference was held in Doha, Qatar, where Carnegie Mellon University recently established a branch campus with the goal of promoting the same high standards of research and education for which its original campus in Pittsburgh, USA, is internationally recognized. Carnegie Mellon Qatar is located in Education City, a 2,500-acre campus which provides state-of-the-art research and teaching facilities to branches of five of the world's leading universities. It is part of an unprecedented commitment of resources made by the Qatari leadership to position Qatar as a world-class center of education and research.

Many people were involved in the organization of this conference. In particular, I wish to thank the General Chair, Kazunori Ueda, for his support, and the Steering Committee for endorsing the candidacy of Doha for this year's edition of ASIAN. This conference would not have been possible without the hard work of the many people who relentlessly handled the local arrangements, especially Thierry Sans and Kara Nesimiuk. We greatly appreciate the generous support of our sponsors, Carnegie Mellon University in Qatar and QCERT. Finally we are grateful to the authors, the invited speakers and the attendees who made this conference an enjoyable and fruitful event.

September 2007   Iliano Cervesato

Conference Organization

Steering Committee

Philippe Codognet (French Embassy, Japan)
Joxan Jaffar (National University, Singapore)
Mitsu Okada (Keio Univerity, Japan)
R.K. Shyamasundar (Tata Institute of Fundamental Research, India)
Kazunori Ueda (Waseda University, Japan)

General Chair

Kazunori Ueda (Waseda University, Japan)

Program Chair

Iliano Cervesato (Carnegie Mellon University, Qatar)

Program Committee

Michael Backes (Saarland University, Germany)
Anupam Datta (Stanford University, USA)
Mourad Debbabi (Concordia University, Canada)
Sven Dietrich (CERT, USA)
Masami Hagiya (University of Tokyo, Japan)
Yassine Lakhnech (VERIMAG, France)
Ninghui Li (Purdue University, USA)
Catherine Meadows (Naval Research Lab, USA)
R. Ramanujam (Institute of Mathematical Sciences, India)
Takamichi Saito (Meiji University, Japan)
Dheeraj Sanghi (IIT Kanpur, India)
Thierry Sans (Carnegie Mellon University, Qatar)
Andre Scedrov (University of Pennsylvania, USA)
Vitaly Shmatikov (University of Texas-Austin, USA)
Duminda Wijesekera (George Mason University, USA)
Yuqing Zhang (Chinese Academy of Sciences, China)
Jianying Zhou (Institute for Infocomm Research, Singapore)

Local Organization

Thierry Sans (Carnegie Mellon University, Qatar)

External Reviewers

Kumar Avijit
Vishwas B.C.
Adam Barth
A. Baskar
Justin Brickell
Judicaël Courant
Shruti Dubey
Markus Dürmuth
Jason Franklin
Yoshinobu Kawabe
Dilsun Kaynar
Ken Mano
Azzam Mourad
Hadi Otrok
Iosif Radu
Arun Raghavan
Arnab Roy
Hideki Sakurada
Mohamed Saleh
Satyam Sharma
S.P. Suresh
Yasuyuki Tsukada

Table of Contents

Invited Speaker: Joshua Guttman

Session 4: Protocols

Invited Speaker: Kazuhiko Kato

Session 5: Intrusion Detection

Session 6: Short Papers on Network Security

Session 7: Safe Execution

Dimensions of Declassification in Theory and Practice

Andrei Sabelfeld

Dept. of Computer Science and Engineering, Chalmers University of Technology
412 96 Gothenburg, Sweden

Abstract. Computing systems often deliberately release (or declassify) sensitive information. A principal security concern for systems permitting information release is whether this release is safe: is it possible that the attacker compromises the information release mechanism and extracts more secret information than intended? While the security community has recognized the importance of the problem, the state-of-the-art in information release is, unfortunately, a number of approaches with somewhat unconnected semantic goals. We provide a road map of the main directions of current research, by classifying the basic goals according to *what* information is released, *who* releases information, *where* in the system information is released, and *when* information can be released. We apply this classification in order to evaluate the security of a case study realized in a security-typed language: an implementation of a non-trivial cryptographic protocol that allows playing online poker without a trusted third party. In addition, we identify some prudent principles of declassification. These principles shed light on existing definitions and may also serve as useful "sanity checks" for emerging models.

The talk is based on joint work, in part, with David Sands, and, in part, with Aslan Askarov.

I. Cervesato (Ed.): ASIAN 2007, LNCS 4846, p. 1, 2007.

A Static Birthmark of Binary Executables Based on API Call Structure*

Seokwoo Choi, Heewan Park, Hyun-il Lim, and Taisook Han

Division of Computer Science and
Advanced Information Technology Research Center(AITrc).
Korea Advanced Institute of Science and Technology
{swchoi,hwpark,hilim}@pllab.kaist.ac.kr, han@cs.kaist.ac.kr

Abstract. A software birthmark is a unique characteristic of a program that can be used as a software theft detection. In this paper we suggest and empirically evaluate a static birthmark of binary executables based on API call structure. The program properties employed in this birthmark are functions and standard API calls when the functions are executed. The API calls from a function includes the API calls explicitly found from the function and its descendants within limited depth in the call graph. To statically identify functions, call graphs and API calls, we utilizes IDAPro disassembler and its plug-ins. We define the similarity between two functions as the proportion of the number of all API calls to the number of the common API calls. The similarity between two programs is obtained by the maximum weight bipartite matching between two programs using the function similarity matrix. To show the credibility of the proposed techniques, we compare the same applications with different versions and the various types of applications which include text editors, picture viewers, multimedia players, P2P applications and ftp clients. To show the resilience, we compare binary executables compiled from various compilers. The empirical result shows that the similarities obtained using our birthmark sufficiently indicates the functional and structural similarities among programs.

Keyword: software piracy, software birthmark, binary analysis.

1 Introduction

Recently a large amount of software is developed in the form of open source projects. Most open source projects contain software licenses. A widely used software license for open source software is the GNU Public License(GPL). The GPL allows developers to use software freely, but requires new projects using the original work to be licensed under the GPL. There are also more permissive software licenses like the MIT license and the BSD licenses which allow the original source code to be combined in commercial software. The permissive licenses, however, require the copyright notice of the original software to be included.

---

* This work was supported by the Korea Science and Engineering Foundation (KOSEF) through the Advanced Information Technology Research Center(AITrc).

I. Cervesato (Ed.): ASIAN 2007, LNCS 4846, pp. 2–16, 2007.

There have been reported that many companies use open source software for commercial purpose without permission. To detect code theft when source code is available, we can utilize well-known plagiarism detection tools like MOSS, JPlag and YAP [1,2,3]. Suppose that source code under the GPL is contained in commercial software, which is distributed in compiled binaries without indicating the copyright notice of the original software. In this case, we need to prove whether the open source code is used or not in the binary executables. Software birthmarking is one of the techniques to solve such software theft problems.

A software birthmark is unique characteristics of a program that can be used to identify the program. If program p and q have the same or very similar birthmark, q is very likely to be a stolen copy of p (and vice versa). Comparing the strings analyzed from binary executables can be a easy birthmarking technique. In this case, a set of strings is a birthmark. Sometimes comparing the structures of binaries can be a good birthmark technique. For example, SabreSecurity Bin-Diff effectively found similarities between two MacOS emulators named CherryOS and PearPC[4,5]. Tamada et al. suggested a dynamic software birthmark for Windows applications using Win32 API function call sequences [6,7]. Dynamic birthmarks extract program properties from a program execution trace when a sequence of input is given, while static birthmarks extract properties only from the program itself.

In this paper we propose a new static birthmarking technique that can help to identify ownership and similarity of binary executables. Program properties used as our birthmark are summaries extracted from each binary function in a program. The summary of each function is a set of possible standard API calls when the function is executed. We statically identify API function calls by analyzing disassembled code which is generated by IDAPro disassembler[8]. A similarity between two functions is calculated by comparing API call sets of two functions. A similarity between two programs is obtained by matching problem.

We evaluate the proposed birthmark by comparing various categories of Windows applications. To show the credibility, the same applications with different versions are compared. To show the resilience, we compare binary executables compiled from various compilers. The empirical result shows that the similarities obtained using our birthmark sufficiently indicate the functional and structural similarities among programs.

2   Related Work

There are three major threats against the intellectual property contained in software. *Software piracy* is the illegal use, duplication or reselling of legally protected software. *Software tampering* is the illegal modification of software to gain control over restricted code or digital media protected by the software. *Malicious reverse engineering* is the extracting of a piece of a program in order to reuse it in one's own. To deal with these threats, several techniques have been explored, for example, software watermarking to deal with piracy, code obfuscation to deter reverse engineering, and software tamper-proofing [9].

Software watermarking is a well-known technique used to provide a way to prove ownership of stolen software. Software watermarking systems embed watermarks in software and recognize the watermarks. Software watermark can be either static or dynamic [10,11]. Unfortunately, watermarking is not always feasible because it requires software developers to embed a watermark before releasing the software.

Software birthmarking is a technique that identifies the inherent characteristics occurring in a program by chance. Unlike software watermarks, software birthmarks do not embed additional code or identifier. Instead a birthmark relies on an inherent characteristic of the application to show that one program is a copy of another. The result of comparing two programs with software birthmarking is similarities between two programs. With the similarities, we are able to say that one program is a copy of another, totally or in part.

Tamada et al. [12,13] suggested the first practical application of static software birthmarks to identify the theft of programs. This technique is specific to Java class files which is a combination of four individual birthmarks: constant values in field variables(CVFV), sequence of method calls(SMC), inheritance structure(IS), and used classes(UC). These four birthmarks could be used individually but the combination makes this technique more reliable. Their experiment with several sample programs shows that the proposed birthmarks identify a class within a program with high precision, but can easily be confused by several obfuscation techniques.

Tamada et al. [6,7] introduced dynamic birthmarks and proposed two birthmarks based on the trace of system calls for Windows programs. The dynamic birthmarks are the sequence and frequency of API function calls during execution of software. They claim that these birthmarks are reasonably robust against program transformations. The credibility of this birthmark highly relies on user interactions, inputs and system environments. To avoid this weakness, they highly restricted inputs and user interactions in the experiments.

Myles et al. proposed a k-gram based static birthmark [14]. They adopted k-gram, which have been previously used to detect similarity between documents, as their birthmark for Java applications. The k-gram birthmark is the set of unique opcode sequence of length k. For each method in a module they compute the set of unique k-grams by sliding a window of length k over the static instruction sequence. k-gram based birthmark is precise, but highly susceptible to program transformations. They evaluated this birthmarking techniques with several tiny Java programs.

Myles et al. [15,16] proposed the concept of another dynamic birthmark known as Whole Program Path(WPP) birthmark. A WPP is a directed acyclic graph(DAG) representation of a context-free grammar that generates a program's acyclic path [17]. To get WPP, dynamic trace of a program is obtained by instrumentation, and the trace is compressed into a DAG using SEQUITUR algorithm. They used WPP as their birthmarks and computed similarity between two birthmarks using a graph distance for maximal common subgraph [18]. They experimented WPP birthmarking technique with a few tiny Java programs. The result shows that the credibility and the resilience of the WPP birthmark is between the static Java birthmark of Tamada et al. and k-gram birthmark.

Shuler and Dallmeier[19] presented a dynamic birthmarking technique based on the API call sequence sets during program execution. The result of this birthmark, like Tamada's, is also highly dependent on user interactions, inputs and environments. They improved their reliability by limiting windows length to 5, like k-gram. They evaluated this birthmark on image processing programs and XML processors. This birthmarking technique can be applied to more realistic applications compared to Myles's birthmarking technique.

3 Static API Call Structure Birthmark

3.1 Software Birthmarks

Tamada et al.[13] and Myles et al.[14] formally defined a birthmark of a software using copy relations. The followings are the definition of birthmark by Myles et al.

Definition 1 (Birthmark). *Let p, q be programs. Let f be a method for extracting a set of characteristics from a program. Then $f(p)$ is called a birthmark of p iff:*
1. $f(p)$is obtained only from p itself (without any extra information), and
2. q is a copy of $p \Rightarrow f(p) = f(q)$.

Condition 1 explains the main difference between watermarking and birthmarking. A birthmark extracts characteristics only from the program itself, while a watermark extracts extra copyright information which is previously embedded by authors or program distributors. Condition 2 means that if p and q are in copy relation, the birthmark of p and the birthmark of q is the same. In this definition, the meaning of *copy* implies not only the exact duplication but also the semantics preserving transformation. But when we say the semantics are preserved, we do not mean that the two implementations with the same specification have the same birthmark. The terms are introduced to require the birthmark to be resilient to the obfuscation transformation to avoid theft detection. Thus a good birthmark value should not change after a slight semantics preserving modification of the program.

The following properties are restatements of those of Tamada et al. [13] and Myles[15]. These properties suggest two evaluation criteria which a birthmark should meet.

Property 1 (Distinction). Let p and q be programs with the same functionality. If p and q are implemented independently, then $f(p) \neq f(q)$.

Property 2 (Preservation). For p' obtained from p by any program transformation, $f(p) = f(p')$ holds.

Property 1 explains the distinction property. The distinction property complements Condition 2 of the birthmark definition. It is a criteria related to the possibility of false positives. It means that a good birthmark should catch copy relations well, while it should not falsely say two independently implemented programs with the same functionality are copy.

Property 2 is concerned with the resilience of a birthmark. If a copied code is transformed by compilers, optimizers or obfuscators, the appearance of the transformed code, which is in binary executables in this work, is different from the original code. If a birthmark is resilient to program transformations, it should only catch the inherent properties of the programs.

3.2 Proposed Birthmark

Microsoft Windows applications normally use the Windows API which offers essential libraries for developing Windows applications. The Windows API consists of functional categories which are system managements, diagnostics, graphics, multimedia, networking, security, system services, and user interfaces. Since Windows applications exploit Windows OS capabilities via the Windows API calls, the API calls are hard to be replaced. The API calls reflect the functionalities of a program, that is, the inherent characteristics of the program. If we can analyze the API call patterns correctly, we can use the patterns as a good birthmark of a program.

Previous birthmark research on Windows binaries [6,7] utilized dynamic API call sequences by hooking the executable file. The dynamic API call sequence only shows API call patterns for a given execution trace. The resulting birthmarks are dependent on inputs, user interactions and system environments. Furthermore it cannot cover whole program path. If given inputs do not lead the execution to the theft codes, the dynamic birthmarking cannot give us a meaningful answer. We here suggest a static birthmarking using Windows API calls. The proposed birthmarking technique analyzes whole part of given programs. Therefore it can catch the containment of the theft code. To compare two binaries we use assembly codes generated by IDAPro disassembler. We can also get function information, branch instructions and external calls from IDAPro.

Our birthmark is defined using API call set. We can also consider multisets instead of API call set since we have call graphs. Multisets reflects API call structure more precisely, while they are vulnerable to program transformation like inlinng or wrapping of functions. Inlining occurs when compiler optimizes, and wrapping often occurs when compiled with debug option. For this reason, we currently considers only sets of API calls.

Definition 2 (API Call Set). *API call set of a function is a collection of possible standard API calls that the function can invoke when the function is executed.*

According to the definition of API call set, the API call set of the main function covers all API calls that the program can reach. We simplify the API call set using call depth.

Definition 3 (k-depth API Call Set). *Let k be a integer (with $k \geq 0$). The k-depth API call set of a function is a collection of all possible standard API calls gathered from functions having call depths within k.*

A k-depth API call set of a function is a subset of *API call set* of the function. By limiting call depths, though we lose a little precision, we can calculate API call sets in reasonable time. Our experiment showed that the call depth as small as 2 or 3 sufficiently estimates the properties of functions.

Our static API call structure birthmark for a program is defined as follows.

Definition 4 (Static API Call Structure Birthmark). *Given API call sets for each function of a program, a static API call structure birthmark of the program is the collection of all API call sets.*

3.3 Calculating Similarity

To calculate similarity by the proposed birthmark, we first calculate all similarities between functions. A Similarity between two functions is defined as follows.

Definition 5 (Function Similarity). *Let S_A and S_B be sets of standard API call sets of function A and function B. Similarity between two functions is defined as*

$$sim_f(A, B) = \frac{2\ |S_A \cap S_B|}{|S_A| + |S_B|}$$

where $|S_A|$ is the cardinality of S_A, $|S_B|$ is the cardinality of S_B, and $|S_A \cap S_B|$ is the cardinality of common API calls of S_A and S_B.

The similarity function measures the fraction of common calls over all standard API calls. If two functions are identical, the similarity between the functions becomes 1. If the two functions have no API calls in common, the similarity value become 0. Figure 1 illustrates matching between functions. According to Definition 5, the similarity between foo and joo is 2/3, and the similarity between goo and koo is 3/4.

We want to match functions between two programs such that the grand total of the similarities has a maximum value. We compute similarities between all possible pairs of functions between two programs. After the similarity calculation, we can get a $|A|$ by $|B|$ similarity matrix where A and B are the set of functions in each program. With the similarity matrix, we compute the program similarity. We define a program similarity as follows.

Definition 6 (Program Similarity). *Let P_1, P_2 be programs, $|P_1|$ and $|P_2|$ be numbers of functions in P_1 and P_2. We define the program similarity between P_1 and P_2 as*

$$sim_p(P_1, P_2) = \frac{2 \sum_{(A,B) \in match(P_1, P_2)} sim_f(A, B)}{|P_1| + |P_2|}$$

where $match(P_1, P_2)$ is a set of matched functions between P_1 and P_2.

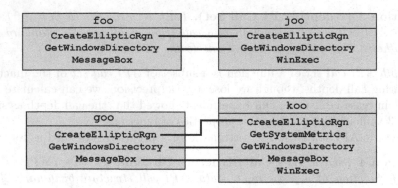

Fig. 1. Matching functions to compute similarity

The program similarity we defined is the maximum value among all possible function matching configurations. The problem maximizing the sum of similarities between the functions from program P_1 and the functions from program P_2 is isomorphic to the weighted $X - Y$ bipartite matching problem. Each function corresponds to each node. The functions from P_1 belong to the partition X of the bipartite graph, and the functions from P_2 belong to Y. Matching from a function from P_1 with a function from B corresponds to inserting an edge from a node in X to a node in Y. Similarities between two functions correspond to weights of edges. To find a maximum matching, we use the Hungarian algorithm[20] which solve the problem in polynomial time. The time complexity of the Hungarian algorithm is $O(n^3)$. Since the algorithm by default performs minimization, we use the difference matrix of which each element has a difference value instead of a similarity. A difference value is $1 - similarity$. The program similarity obtained by the Hungarian algorithm is the maximal similarity between two programs.

4   Implementation

Figure 2 shows the structure of the static API Call birthmark system. This system operates as follows.

Step1: Generating idb file

IDAPro generates the IDA database file(.idb) by disassembling and analyzing the binary executable of sample program. We use IDAPro 5.1 for front-end.

Step2: Generating database file

Database file(.db) is generated from idb file using IDA2SQLite3 plug-in. This plug-in stores initial analysis result from IDAPro in sqlite3 database format for future use. Stored item includes program information such as function name, start address of that function, call graphs, assembly codes, etc.

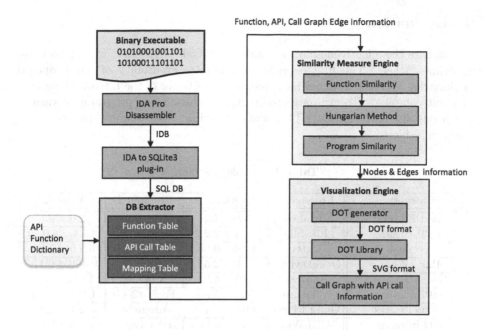

Fig. 2. The architecture of static API call structure birthmark system

Step3: Extracting function, API call, and Mapping table

Function table, API call table and function mapping table are obtained from the sqlite3 database file. Function table contains information about the function name, start address of the function, and library flag, etc. API call table contains API call instructions used in each functions. Mapping table contains the call relation between functions in the program. This program is developed with python 2.5 and pysqlite 2.3.3.

Step4: Calculating program similarity

This routine calculates program similarities using the information of function table, API call table, and function table. From the information of tables, function call graph is generated and set of API calls which can be used in each function is collected. As function call depth increases, each function collects API names of functions that are reachable from the function in the call graph. In this way, as function call depth increases, the number of APIs included in function is also increased. After forwarding APIs by predefined call depth k, API differences between every function in each program are calculated and API difference matrix is constructed. The maximum similarity value is calculated from this matrix using the Hungarian method. Similarity calculation program is implemented in C++. To check function matching result, call graphs with matching information is generated in DOT format. DOT file is translated into SVG(scalable vector graphic) format. Resulting SVG file can be displayed using SVG Viewers.

5   Evaluation

To evaluate the effectiveness of our static API Call birthmark, we conduct two experiments here. The first experiment evaluates credibility of our proposed birthmarks. The second experiment measures resilience of the birthmark against different compilers. To evaluate credibility, we chose some programs in various categories like text editors, FTP clients, Terminals, etc. Sample programs are listed in Table 1.

Table 1. Sample programs

Category	Program 1	Versions	Program 2	Versions
Text Editors	UltraEdit	7.0 / 7.2	Edit Plus	2.0 / 2.1
FTP clients	FileZilla	2.2.14 / 2.2.26	CuteFTP32	3.5.4 / 4.0.19
Terminals	Putty	0.56 / 0.58	SecureCRT	5.5.0 / 5.5.1
P2P clients	Dongkeyhote	2.40 / 2.54	Emule	0.45b / 0.47c
Graphic Tools	ACDSee	4.01 / 4.02	xnView	1.21 / 1.25a
MP3 Players	Winamp	5.23 / 5.35	Foobar2000	0.9.1 / 0.9.4
Video Players	GOM Player	2.0.0 / 2.1.6	Adrenalin	2.1 / 2.2
CD Burners	CDRWin	3.8 / 3.9	DVDCopy	2.2.6 / 2.5.1
Download Managers	Flashget	1.6.5 / 1.7.2	NetTransport	2.3.0 / 2.4.1
Disk Image Emulators	Daemon	4.3.0 / 4.9.0	CD Space	5.0

To evaluate resilience, we chose open source hex editor *frhed*[21] and *Microsoft Visual C++ 6.0, .NET 2003 and .NET 2005* compilers.

To verify the effectiveness of our static API call structure birthmark, we examined API call distributions of sample programs. Figure 3 shows that more than 100 functions have at least one API calls. z-axis represents each program. This result shows that the API call structure reflects the unique characteristics of programs.

Table 2 shows that the similarities of programs are changed by call depth. As call depth increases, the similarity decreases in most cases while the accuracy increases. We should limit call depth to compute API call set in reasonable time. Given the call depth k and the number of nodes n, the time complexity to find k-depth API call set for all functions is $O(k\,n^2)$. Our experiment showed that the call depth as small as 2 or 3 will sufficiently estimates the properties of functions. Hereafter our experiments are evaluated using 3-depth API call sets.

5.1   Credibility

Different Versions of Same Programs. To evaluate credibility of our birthmark, we compared different versions of same programs. Figure 5 shows that similarities between the same programs with a little different versions are over 0.7. In general a minor upgraded version of software shares almost all code from the previous version. This can be restated that the new version copied most

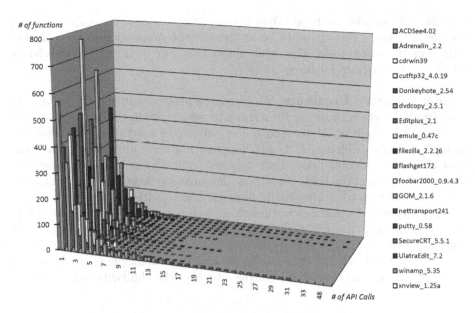

Fig. 3. API call distributions of sample programs

Table 2. Similarities with various call depth

	0	1	2	3	4	5
cutftp32_3.5.4 / cutftp32_4.0.19	0.9180	0.8993	0.8959	0.8948	0.8960	0.8969
filezilla_2.2.14 /filezilla_2.2.26	0.9058	0.8755	0.8522	0.8400	0.8340	0.8323
UltraEdit_7.0 / UltraEdit_7.2	0.9704	0.9151	0.8537	0.8464	0.8381	0.8278
filezilla_2.2.26 / cutftp32_4.0.19	0.4875	0.3865	0.3278	0.3186	0.3115	0.3091
filezilla_2.2.26 / UltraEdit_7.2	0.3574	0.3079	0.2773	0.2710	0.2702	0.2676

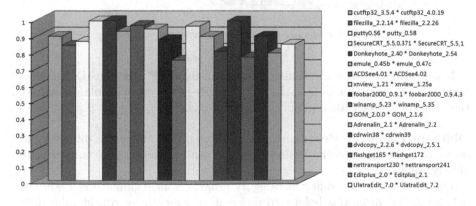

Fig. 4. Similarities between same programs with different versions

part from the previous version. Then the similarity between the old version and the new version is considered to be as large as the proportion of the common code over the whole code. The result shows that our birthmark is sufficiently reflecting the program functionalities.

Similar Category Programs. We compared programs in same categories to prove the distinction property. Even if two programs are in similar category, the similarity is not always high enough. The number of functions is different and each program uses different API calls. Suppose that there are different programs with the same functionalities. They may use almost same APIs because they have the same functionalities. The distinction property says that the similarities should be different when they are implemented independently.

Figure 5 supports that our birthmarking technique suffices distinction property. For example, the multimedia players Gom and Adrenalin have very similar functionalities, but the similarity is very low. And the text editors EditPlus and UltraEdit have almost the same functionalities, similar file sizes and similar numbers of functions extracted from the binaries. The similarity is near 0.5.

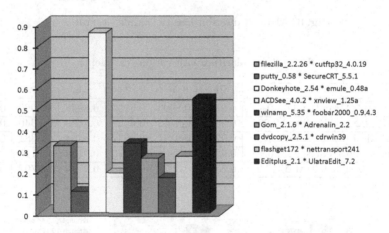

Fig. 5. Similarities between programs with the same category

It is remarkable that the similarity between two P2P programs Dongkeyhote and Emule is very high. In fact, the Dongkeyhote is a clone of Emule. It borrowed the Emule's source code and only modified GUIs.

Different Category Programs. We compared programs with different categories to show that the similarities between totally different programs are sufficiently small.

Figure 6 shows that different category programs have similarities lower than 0.4. Since the programs belong to different category have considerably lower similarities. We can observe that totally different programs have a small size of

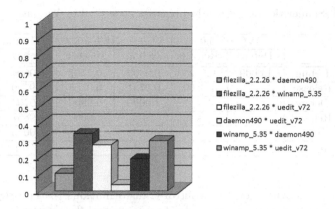

Fig. 6. Similarities between different category programs

similarity. The reason is that Windows applications should use common features like GUI, file management and networks.

5.2   Resilience

To evaluate resilience of our birthmark, we compiled an open source free hex editor, fr-hed with Microsoft Visual C++ 6.0 .NET 2003 and .NET 2005 compilers. Table 3 explains that even if compiler changes or compile option changes, used API calls are almost the same. The number of functions excluding library is different but the number of functions with API calls is nearly equal.

Table 3. Binaries compiled with various versions of compilers

Compilers and options		File size (bytes)	Number of Functions excluding Library	Number of Functions with API Calls
VC++ 6.0	Debug	409,668	441	218
	Release	317,952	479	221
VC++ .NET 2003	Debug	446,464	432	215
	Release	331,776	440	212
VC++ .NET 2005	Debug	716,800	534	218
	Release	377,344	453	215

Table 4 shows the similarity results of the resilience experiment using various compilers. Similarity is always over 0.95 in each combination. So, we concluded that our birthmark is very resilient to different compilers.

This is not enough to conclude that our birthmark is resilient to the program transformation. As far as we know, there is one available commercial C/C++ obfuscator named CloakWare security suite[22]. The CloakWare security suite

Table 4. Similarities between fr-hed binaries generated by various compilers

		VC++ 6.0		VC++ .NET 2003		VC++ .NET 2005	
		Debug	Release	Debug	Release	Debug	Release
VC++ 6.0	Debug	1.0000	0.9823	0.9809	0.9767	0.9694	0.9797
	Release	-	1.0000	0.9751	0.9755	0.9590	0.9780
VC++ .NET 2003	Debug	-	-	1.0000	0.9900	0.9793	0.9924
	Release	-	-	-	1.0000	0.9857	0.9977
VC++ .NET 2005	Debug	-	-	-	-	1.0000	0.9881
	Release	-	-	-	-	-	1.0000

applies data transformations and control transformations to the original code. The control transformation used by this tool is control-flow flattening[23] which makes static analysis of the code almost impossible. But our birthmark is resilient to the control-flow flattening, because control-flow flattening cannot remove the API calls.

5.3 Limitations

Our birthmark relies on the API call set. The birthmark of applications which rarely use the standard API calls like encoders, decoders, scientific application, etc may be very inaccurate. Birthmarks of these applications should catch the algorithmic structure of the program. If WPP birthmark [15] could be applied to binary programs, it will be a good option.

The weak link of our birthmark system is the analysis phase of the binary executables. We rely on IDAPro about function identification. Since IDAPro cannot generate precise call graphs if the binary contains function pointers and virtual calls. It is very hard to resolve virtual calls in binaries. If an unresolved indirect call like virtual calls exists in a function, the function can point to all possible functions. Then the API call set of a function may contain almost all API calls. Virtual call resolution method for binary executables suggested by Balakrishnan et al.[24] may help to improve the accuracy of our birthmark.

6   Conclusion

In this paper we proposed a novel static birthmarking technique that can help to identify ownership and similarity of binary executables. We defined the static API call birthmark of a program as the collection of the k-depth API call set. The program similarity we defined is the maximum value among all possible function matching configurations. The problem maximizing the sum of similarities between the functions from program A and the functions from program B is isomorphic to the weighted X-Y bipartite matching problem. Thus the similarity between two programs was able to be obtained by applying the Hungarian algorithm.

We evaluated the proposed birthmark by comparing various categories of Windows applications. To show the credibility, the same applications with different versions are compared. To show the resilience, we compare binary executables compiled from various compilers. The empirical result shows that the similarities obtained using our birthmark sufficiently indicates the functional and structural similarities among programs.

In the future, we are planning to extend our method by applying indirect call resolution. The proposed method could be also applied to Java class files.

References

1. Schleimer, S., Wilkerson, D., Aiken, A.: Winnowing: local algorithms for document fingerprinting. In: Proceedings of the 2003 ACM SIGMOD international conference on Management of data, pp. 76–85. ACM Press, New York (2003)
2. Wise, M.: YAP3: improved detection of similarities in computer program and other texts. In: Proceedings of the twenty-seventh SIGCSE technical symposium on Computer science education, pp. 130–134 (1996)
3. Prechelt, L., Malpohl, G., Philippsen, M.: Finding plagiarisms among a set of programs with JPlag. Journal of Universal Computer Science 8(11), 1016–1038 (2002)
4. SABRE BinDiff, http://www.sabre-security.com/products/bindiff.html
5. Using BinDiff for Code theft detection, http://www.sabre-security.com/products/CodeTheft.pdf
6. Tamada, H., Okamoto, K., Nakamura, M., Monden, A., Matsumoto, K.: Dynamic Software Birthmarks to Detect the Theft of Windows Applications. International Symposium on Future Software Technology 20(22) (2004)
7. Okamoto, K., Tamada, H., Nakamura, M., Monden, A., Matsumoto, K.: Dynamic Software Birthmarks Based on API Calls. IEICE Transactions on Information and Systems 89(8), 1751–1763 (2006)
8. The IDA Pro Disassembler and Debugger, http://www.datarescue.com/idabase
9. Collberg, C., Thomborson, C.: Watermarking, tamper-proofing, and obfuscation-tools for software protection. Software Engineering, IEEE Transactions on 28(8), 735–746 (2002)
10. Collberg, C., Thomborson, C.: Software watermarking: models and dynamic embeddings. In: Proceedings of the 26th ACM SIGPLAN-SIGACT symposium on Principles of programming languages, pp. 311–324. ACM Press, New York (1999)
11. Collberg, C., Myles, G., Huntwork, A.: Sandmark-A tool for software protection research. Security & Privacy Magazine, IEEE 1(4), 40–49 (2003)
12. Tamada, H., Nakamura, M., Monden, A., Matsumoto, K.: Design and evaluation of birthmarks for detecting theft of java programs. In: Proc. IASTED International Conference on Software Engineering (IASTED SE 2004), pp. 569–575 (2004)
13. Tamada, H., Nakamura, M., Monden, A., Matsumoto, K.: Java Birthmarks–Detecting the Software Theft–. IEICE Transactions on Information and Systems 88(9), 2148–2158 (2005)
14. Myles, G., Collberg, C.: K-gram based software birthmarks. In: Proceedings of the 2005 ACM symposium on Applied computing, pp. 314–318. ACM Press, New York (2005)
15. Myles, G., Collberg, C.: Detecting software theft via whole program path birthmarks. Information Security Conference, 404–415 (2004)

16. Myles, G.M.: Software Theft Detection Through Program Identification. PhD thesis, Department of Computer Science, The University of Arizona (2006)
17. Larus, J.: Whole program paths. In: Proceedings of the ACM SIGPLAN 1999 conference on Programming language design and implementation, pp. 259–269. ACM Press, New York (1999)
18. Bunke, H., Shearer, K.: A graph distance metric based on the maximal common subgraph. Pattern Recognition Letters 19(3-4), 255–259 (1998)
19. Schuler, D., Dallmeier, V., Lindig, C.: A Dynamic Birthmark for Java. In: Proceedings of the 22nd IEEE/ACM International Conference on Automated Software Engineering
20. Kuhn, H.: The Hungarian method for the assignment problem. Naval Research Logistics 52(1), 7–21 (2005)
21. Kibria, R.: frhed - free hex editor, http://www.codeproject.com/tools/frhed.asp
22. Cloakware security suite, http://www.cloakware.com/products_services/security_suite
23. Wang, C.: A Security Architecture for Survivability Mechanisms. PhD thesis, University of Virginia
24. Balakrishnan, G., Reps, T.: Recency-abstraction for heap-allocated storage. Static Analysis Symp. (2006)

Compiling C Programs into
a Strongly Typed Assembly Language

Takahiro Kosakai, Toshiyuki Maeda, and Akinori Yonezawa

Department of Computer Science,
Graduate School of Information Science and Technology,
The University of Tokyo,
7-3-1 Hongo, Bunkyo-ku, Tokyo, Japan
{tkosakai, tosh, yonezawa}@is.s.u-tokyo.ac.jp

Abstract. C is one of the most popular languages in system programming, though its unsafe nature often causes security vulnerabilities. In the face of this situation, many tools are developed to ensure safety properties of C programs. However, most of them work at the source code level, and conventional compilers lose safety guarantee as they translate source code into assembly code. In this paper, we present $CTAL_0$, a strongly typed assembly language that is aimed at certifying the memory safety of assembly code compiled from C programs. $CTAL_0$ is expressive enough to implement potentially unsafe ANSI C features including pointer arithmetics and casts. We have also implemented a type-checker and an experimental C compiler that produces safe $CTAL_0$ assembly code by performing several transformations on given programs to avoid dangerous operations.

Keywords: typed assembly language, memory safety, C.

1 Introduction

Although the C programming language [1] is a classical language developed in 1972, it is one of the most frequently used languages in the field of system programming even today, thanks to its high flexibility and expressiveness. Unfortunately, these desirable properties are realized at the cost of the safety, especially the memory safety. Indeed, even a single mistake in handling a memory access can completely destroy the consistency of a program. This often leads to severe vulnerabilities that violate security; for example, about 40% of the security vulnerabilities of the Linux kernel reported in the first half of 2007 were caused by memory-related bugs [2]. Therefore, in order to ensure the security of programs, it is crucial to ensure their memory safety.

In the face of this situation, many instrumentation tools are developed which slightly modify original programs and make them safer. For example, CCured [3] and Fail-Safe C [4] can transform C programs into new C programs that have almost the same functionality as the original ones but are certified to be memory safe, i.e., not to perform any dangerous memory accesses.

I. Cervesato (Ed.): ASIAN 2007, LNCS 4846, pp. 17–32, 2007.

One problem with the tools is that they are actually source-to-source translators, and after the transformed programs are compiled into assembly code by conventional compilers, there is no way to check whether they are safe. We are therefore required to trust that the compilers always work correctly.

A solution to this problem is to certify safety properties at the level of assembly code. The main advantage of the assembly-level certification over the source-level one is that we do not need to trust compilers, because even if they mistakenly produced unsafe assembly code, the assembly-level certifier will point out that unsafety. In addition, certification of assembly code does not require the source code of the programs to be checked, thus it is applicable to closed-source product software.

In order to realize the assembly-level certification, we selected Typed Assembly Language (TAL) [5] as our starting point. TAL is an assembly language equipped with a firm static type system that enables us to prove several safety properties of well-typed programs, including the memory safety. TAL has been extended in various directions including the support of dependent types (DTAL [6]) and stacks (STAL [7]). However, it is difficult to express within them the features of the C language because C is essentially an "untyped" language which allows arbitrary casts from one type to another.

In this paper, we present our extension of TAL, called $CTAL_0$. Its main design goal is to be a target language into which C programs can be compiled. In order to achieve the goal, we incorporated into $CTAL_0$ the notions of byte addressing and simple dependent types. Furthermore, in order to fill the gap between essentially untyped C and strongly typed $CTAL_0$, the type system of $CTAL_0$ allows several fragments of data structures to be left untyped or weakly typed, by employing *untyped array types* which represent completely untyped memory blocks, and *guarded types* which represent values whose types can be determined only if certain conditions provably hold.

We have implemented a type-checker for $CTAL_0$ and an experimental compiler that compiles C programs into $CTAL_0$ assembly code. Our compiler supports a lot of C language features including arbitrary casts from integers to pointers and vice versa, arrays, structures, unions, and function pointers. In order to compile possibly unsafe C programs into safe $CTAL_0$ programs, the compiler automatically performs several program transformations.

The remainder of this paper is organized as follows. In Sect. 2, we informally explain the ideas of $CTAL_0$, and in Sect. 3, we present $CTAL_0$ in more detail. We describe our implementations of a type-checker and a compiler in Sect. 4, and an extension for supporting function pointers in Sect. 5. In Sect. 6, we discuss existing related work. We conclude and mention our future work in Sect. 7.

2   Overview of $CTAL_0$

In this section, we introduce the key ideas of our proposed language $CTAL_0$. For the sake of clarity, we use informal notations here; more formal arguments are in Sect. 3. We use the C program shown in Fig. 1 as a motivating example.

```
1:  void f(int *p) {      /* argument p is a pointer to int */
2:    char buf[5];        /* declare buf as a 5-element array of char */
3:    *(int *)buf = *p;   /* store integer pointed by p into head of buf */
4:    /* ··· */
5:  }
```

Fig. 1. A motivating example of C program

2.1 Untyped Array Types

The second line of the example program in Fig. 1 declares a variable buf as an array of char. In order to compile this program into a strongly typed assembly language, we must decide what assembly-level type the array buf should have.

If the target assembly language was TAL [5] or many of its variants, we would have no choice but an array type Array(char, 5), which denotes an array of length 5 whose elements have type char. This might be a good choice if C was a type-safe language, but in fact its unsafe cast mechanism gives rise to a difficulty. In the example program, the third line stores the value *p into the head of the array buf via a cast. Since the stored value *p has type int, at the point of this store operation buf should have type Array(int, 1) or such. It is however impossible because we had chosen Array(char, 5) as buf's type.

To solve the problem, CTAL_0 provides new sort of array types: *untyped array types*. An untyped array type Array(i) represents an array of i bytes, whose contents are untyped (i.e., not tracked by the type system of CTAL_0). Since the type system allows any values of any types to be stored in untyped arrays, using CTAL_0 we can give a type Array(5) to the array buf and the store operation at the third line will be accepted without difficulty.

2.2 Dependent Types

Next, let us examine what the assembly-level representation of p's type should be. Because p is declared as a pointer to int at the first line of Fig. 1, it might seem that a pointer type like Ptr(int) is suitable. However, such type cannot describe the relation between pointers and integers. Pointers are actually integer addresses in most C implementations, and indeed several C programs rely on the assumption that pointers can be converted to integers and vice versa.

In order to capture the relation, CTAL_0 uses ordinary integer types for representing pointers, by combining the notions of *heap types* [8] and *dependent integer types* [6] (this approach was adopted from [9]). A heap type Ψ is a map from integer addresses to types, describing the currently accessible values in the heap. To establish the memory safety, the CTAL_0 type system allows a memory access only if the accessed address is known to be inside Ψ. For example, a heap type $\{x \mapsto \text{int}, y \mapsto \text{char}\}$ says that a value of type int is at address x and another of char is at y, preventing memory accesses other than at x or y. At this point, a pointer to the latter char value can be expressed by a dependent integer type Int(y), which denotes an integer whose value is exactly y.

Reasoning similarly, one might think that the pointer p can be represented by, say, type $\text{Int}(x_p)$ while the heap type Ψ containing $x_p \mapsto \texttt{int}$. Yet there are two problems. First, adopting such representation requires every value pointed by some pointers to be inside Ψ, which is clearly impossible. This problem can be solved by packing the integer type, along with a part of Ψ, in an existential type: $\exists(x_p \,|\, \{x_p \mapsto \texttt{int}\}). \text{Int}(x_p)$. This type not merely denotes an integer of some abstract value x_p, but also states that an $\texttt{int}$-type value is at that address.

The second problem with the representation arises when null pointers are involved. The next section describes this further.

2.3 Guarded Types

The C language treats null pointers as normal pointers, thus the function f in the example program (Fig. 1) could be given a null pointer as its argument p. In this situation, the type for p mentioned above, namely $\exists(x_p \,|\, \{x_p \mapsto \texttt{int}\}). \text{Int}(x_p)$, becomes problematic because $x_p \mapsto \texttt{int}$ is not really correct.

To solve this problem, CTAL$_0$ provides *guarded types*, which is a mechanism for specifying types conditionally. More concretely, a guarded type $\phi \,?\, \tau_1 : \tau_2$ denotes a value of type τ_1 if the condition ϕ is true, or a value of type τ_2 if ϕ is false. Utilizing the guarded types, we can express the pointer p as $\exists(x_p \,|\, \{x_p \mapsto (x_p \neq 0) \,?\, \texttt{int} : \langle\rangle\}). \text{Int}(x_p)$, where $\langle\rangle$ denotes a zero-length memory block. This type reads: this is an integer of some value x_p, and if x_p is not zero then an $\texttt{int}$-type value will be at address x_p—in short, it is a "maybe-null" pointer to $\texttt{int}$. Note that we assumed here null pointers are represented by integer zeroes, but other representations could be adopted without problems.

After ensuring p is not null, we can promote it from a maybe-null pointer to a definite pointer. This is done by executing a special pseudo-instruction named **unguard** that extracts either τ_1 or τ_2 from guarded type $\phi \,?\, \tau_1 : \tau_2$, according to the validity of ϕ. To illustrate, consider the following assembly program, where the register r1 is assumed to have type $\text{Int}(x_p)$ and the heap type contains $x_p \mapsto (x_p \neq 0) \,?\, \texttt{int} : \langle\rangle$. This would be a situation after the existential type of p is opened.

```
beq r1, 0, abort    # null-check: go to abort if x_p = 0
unguard x_p         # unseal the guarded type at address x_p
```

Since x_p was checked to be non-zero by the first conditional branch instruction, the second **unguard** instruction will produce $x_p \mapsto \texttt{int}$ into the heap type, which enables p to be used as a definite pointer.

2.4 Byte Addressing

Memory operations in C are based on the byte addressing scheme; that is, the minimum unit of memory accesses and allocations is a byte. Therefore, although many strongly typed assembly languages including TAL employ word addressing, CTAL$_0$ employs byte addressing. For example, an array type $\text{Array}(\texttt{int}, 5)$ represents a 5-*byte* (not 5-*element*) array of integers, and memory access instructions take an extra argument which specifies the number of bytes to access.

Program states $\qquad P \quad ::= (R, H, I)$
Register files $\qquad R \quad \in Registers \rightarrow Integers$
Heaps $\qquad H \quad \in Integers \rightharpoonup ByteVectors$
Instruction sequences $\quad I \quad ::= \texttt{halt} \mid \texttt{jmp } v \mid \iota; I$
Instructions $\qquad \iota \quad ::=$
    arithmetics $\qquad \texttt{add } r, v \mid \texttt{sub } r, v \mid \texttt{mul } r, v \mid \texttt{div } r, v \mid \texttt{mod } r, v \mid$
$\qquad\qquad\qquad\qquad \texttt{mov } r, v \mid$
    memory access $\quad \texttt{load<}k\texttt{> } r, v_o (v_b) \mid \texttt{store<}k\texttt{> } v, v_o (v_b) \mid$
    branch $\qquad\quad \texttt{beq } v_1, v_2, v_d \mid \texttt{ble } v_1, v_2, v_d \mid$
    coercion $\qquad\quad \texttt{pack}_h \ i \text{ as } \tau^h \text{ using } \vec{i} \mid \texttt{unpack}_h \ i \text{ as } \vec{x} \mid$
$\qquad\qquad\qquad\qquad \texttt{pack}_r \ r \text{ as } \tau^w \text{ using } \vec{i} \mid \texttt{unpack}_r \ r \text{ as } \vec{x} \mid$
$\qquad\qquad\qquad\qquad \texttt{roll}_h \ i \text{ as } \tau^h \mid \texttt{unroll}_h \ i \mid \texttt{roll}_r \ r \text{ as } \tau^w \mid \texttt{unroll}_r \ r \mid$
$\qquad\qquad\qquad\qquad \texttt{guard}_h \ i \text{ as } \tau^h \mid \texttt{unguard}_h \ i \mid \texttt{guard}_r \ r \text{ as } \tau^w \mid \texttt{unguard}_r \ r \mid$
$\qquad\qquad\qquad\qquad \texttt{apply } i, \theta$
Registers $\qquad\qquad r \quad \in Registers = \{\texttt{r1}, \cdots, \texttt{rN}\}$
Operands $\qquad\qquad v \quad \in Integers \cup Registers$
Integers $\qquad\qquad n, m, k \in Integers = \{\dots, -2, -1, 0, 1, 2, \dots\}$
Substitutions $\qquad\quad \theta \quad : \text{ Partial function from type and index variables}$
$\qquad\qquad\qquad\qquad\qquad \text{to types and indices, respectively}$
Bytes $\qquad\qquad\qquad b \quad \in Bytes = \{0, 1, 2, \dots\}$
Byte vectors $\qquad\quad \vec{b} \quad \in ByteVectors = \bigcup_{k \geq 0} Bytes^k$

Fig. 2. Program states of CTAL$_0$

3   Proposed Language: CTAL$_0$

In this section, we present the program states and a part of the typing rules of CTAL$_0$. The operational semantics is omitted for space reasons, but it follows that of TAL [5] and mostly straightforward.

3.1   Program States

Figure 2 gives the definitions of *program states* of CTAL$_0$, including the list of the assembly instructions. We assume that there are N 4-byte registers ($\texttt{r1}, \cdots, \texttt{rN}$). We use the notation $\vec{a}$ to denote an ordered sequence consisting of a.

A program state P is a triple consisting of the state of the registers (R) which is a map from the register names to integers, the state of the heap (H) which is a map from integer addresses to byte vectors of arbitrary length, and the instruction sequence to be executed hereafter (I).

Instructions of CTAL$_0$ are divided into two groups: ordinary instructions and coercion instructions.

Ordinary instructions consist of arithmetic, memory access, and branch instructions. Arithmetic instructions are designed after the IA-32 architecture [10]. They take two operands and return the result in the first operand (for example, $\texttt{sub } \texttt{r1}, 3$ decrements the value of register $\texttt{r1}$ by 3). The $\texttt{mov}$ instruction simply copies the value of the second operand into the first one. Memory load instruction $\texttt{load<}k\texttt{> } r, v_o (v_b)$ fetches k bytes from address $v_b + v_o$ (v_b indicates the

Basic types	τ ::= $\tau^w \mid \tau^h$
Word-value types	τ^w ::= $\alpha^w \mid \text{Int}(i) \mid$
	$\exists(\vec{x} \mid \Psi; \phi).\tau^w \mid \mu(\alpha^w).\tau^w \mid \phi ? \tau_1^w : \tau_2^w$
Heap-value types	τ^h ::= $\alpha^h \mid \langle A_1, \cdots, A_n \rangle \mid \forall(\vec{\alpha}; \vec{x}).\text{code}(\Gamma; \Psi; \phi) \mid$
	$\exists(\vec{x} \mid \Psi; \phi).\tau^h \mid \mu(\alpha^h).\tau^h \mid \phi ? \tau_1^h : \tau_2^h$
Array types	A ::= $\text{Array}(i) \mid \text{Array}(\tau^w, i)$
Register file types	Γ ::= $\{\text{r1} \mapsto \tau_1^w, \cdots, \text{rN} \mapsto \tau_N^w\}$
Heap types	Ψ ::= $\{i_1 \mapsto \tau_1^h, \cdots, i_n \mapsto \tau_n^h\}$
Indices	i, j ::= $n \mid x \mid$
	$i_1 + i_2 \mid i_1 - i_2 \mid i_1 \times i_2 \mid i_1 \div i_2 \mid i_1 \bmod i_2$
Constraints	ϕ ::= $\top \mid \phi_1 \wedge \phi_2 \mid \phi_1 \vee \phi_2 \mid \neg\phi \mid i_1 = i_2 \mid i_1 \leq i_2$
Word-value type vars.	α^w
Heap-value type vars.	α^h
Index variables	x, y
Typing contexts	Δ : Set of type and index variables

Fig. 3. Types of CTAL0

base address and v_o the offset) and puts the result into register r. The store instruction, which stores a value into memory, is similar. Unconditional jumps are performed by jmp, while conditional jumps are done by beq (which jumps if its first operand v_1 is equal to its second operand v_2) and ble (which jumps if $v_1 \leq v_2$). A program will be terminated when it executes the halt instruction.

Coercion instructions manipulate the types of the heap or the registers. These are pseudo-instructions: they have effects only at type-checking, not at run-time. Instructions pack$_h$ and pack$_r$ create existential types, while unpack$_h$ and unpack$_r$ destruct them, in a similar fashion to [5,9]. Here, the suffix h or r indicates that the instruction operates on the type of a heap value or a register, respectively. The roll and unroll families create and destruct recursive types. The guard and unguard families manipulate guarded types, which were introduced briefly in Sec. 2.3. Lastly, the apply instruction instantiates a polymorphic type with concrete values according to the second operand θ.

3.2 Types

Figure 3 gives the syntax of types of CTAL0.

Basic types are classified into two kinds: *word-value types* (τ^w) which are assigned to values that can be held in a register, and *heap-value types* (τ^h) whose values are kept in the heap. A register file type Γ specifies the types of values in the registers, while a heap type Ψ specifies the types of heap values.

Among others, the characteristic types of CTAL0 are the untyped array types and the guarded types, as mentioned in Sect. 2. An untyped array type $\text{Array}(i)$ denotes an i-byte memory block whose contents are not tracked by the type system of CTAL0, and a guarded type $\phi ? \tau_1 : \tau_2$ denotes a value which can be assumed to have type τ_1 when ϕ is valid and τ_2 when ϕ is not satisfiable. Here i, an *index*, is a simple integer expression and ϕ, a *constraint*, is a simple logical formula over integers, both defined in Fig. 3.

Other types are more or less standard. An integer type $\text{Int}(i)$ denotes a one-word integer whose value is exactly i. A typed array type $\text{Array}(\tau, i)$ denotes an i-byte memory block filled with values of type τ. A tuple type $\langle \tau_1, \cdots, \tau_n \rangle$ denotes a sequence of values of types $\tau_1, \cdots, \tau_n$. A code type $\forall(\vec{\alpha}; \vec{x}).\,\text{code}(\Gamma; \Psi; \phi)$, which is polymorphic in type variables $\vec{\alpha}$ and index variables $\vec{x}$, denotes an instruction sequence that can be executed when the current state *entails* Γ, Ψ, and ϕ. Roughly speaking, the entailment relation requires that Γ is exactly the same as the current register type, that each value in Ψ exists in the current heap type unless the value is zero-sized, and that ϕ is valid under the current constraint. An existential type $\exists(\vec{x} \mid \Psi; \phi).\,\tau$ means that there exist some indices $\vec{x}$ such that Ψ is a part of the current heap and ϕ is valid. Lastly, a recursive type $\mu(\alpha).\,\tau$ binds the type variable α to the recursive type itself.

Although omitted for brevity in this paper, our implementation also supports linear types [11,8] and dynamic memory allocation facilities. Linear types include stack types that are used to deal with the stack in a similar manner to STAL [7], and linear tuple types that are used for initializations of dynamically allocated memory blocks.

3.3   Typing Rules

We have designed the type system of CTAL$_0$ so that well-typed programs never perform wrong memory accesses and jumps. This property is formalized as the following theorem of type safety, where $\vdash P$ means that the program state P is well-typed and $P \rightsquigarrow P'$ means that P' is the next state of P according to the operational semantics (which is omitted in this paper).

Theorem. *Let P be (R, H, I). If $\vdash P$ and $I \not\equiv \mathtt{halt}$, then there exists some P' such that $P \rightsquigarrow P'$ and $\vdash P'$.*

The definition of $\vdash P$ relies on several typing judgments. Among them, the most important is the instruction typing judgment, written $\Delta; \Gamma; \Psi; \phi \vdash I$, which states that the instruction sequence I is well-typed if the type and index variables Δ are in scope, the registers have type Γ, the heap has type Ψ, and the constraint ϕ is valid. Due to space limitations, we only describe the most interesting typing rules for instructions.

Memory Access. The instruction $\mathtt{load}\texttt{<}k\texttt{>}\ r, v_o\,(v_b)$ requires a tuple is at the base address v_b, and loads k bytes from the offset v_o of that tuple. As shown below, there are two typing rules for $\mathtt{load}$, one is for loading from a typed array and the other is for loading from an untyped array. The former assigns the array's element type to the loaded value, while the latter always assigns an Int type. The typing rules for $\mathtt{store}$ instruction are similar.

$$\frac{\begin{array}{c} \Gamma \vdash v_b : \text{Int}(i_b) \quad \Gamma \vdash v_o : \text{Int}(i_o) \quad \Psi; \phi \vdash i_b \mapsto \langle \tau_1, \cdots, \tau_n \rangle \\ \text{for some } 1 \leq m \leq n, \ \tau_m \equiv \text{Array}(\tau_e, i) \quad \phi \vdash \mathtt{sizeof}(\tau_e) = k \\ \phi \vdash \mathtt{ValidAccess}((\tau_1, \cdots, \tau_n), m, i_o, k) \quad \Delta; \Gamma[r \mapsto \tau_e]; \Psi; \phi \vdash I \end{array}}{\Delta; \Gamma; \Psi; \phi \vdash \mathtt{load}\texttt{<}k\texttt{>}\ r, v_o(v_b); I}$$

$$\frac{\begin{array}{c} \Gamma \vdash v_b : \mathrm{Int}(i_b) \quad \Gamma \vdash v_o : \mathrm{Int}(i_o) \quad \Psi; \phi \vdash i_b \mapsto \langle \tau_1, \cdots, \tau_n \rangle \\ \text{for some } 1 \leq m \leq n, \ \tau_m \equiv \mathrm{Array}(i) \quad 1 \leq k \leq 4 \quad x \notin \Delta \\ \phi \vdash \mathrm{ValidAccess}((\tau_1, \cdots, \tau_n), m, i_o, k) \quad \Delta \cup \{x\}; \Gamma[r \mapsto \mathrm{Int}(x)]; \Psi; \phi \vdash I \end{array}}{\Delta; \Gamma; \Psi; \phi \vdash \mathrm{load}\texttt{<}k\texttt{>} \ r, v_o(v_b); I}$$

Here, the judgment $\Gamma \vdash v : \tau$ indicates the operand v has type τ. $\Psi; \phi \vdash i \mapsto \tau$ indicates that Ψ contains a mapping $i' \mapsto \tau$ and ϕ implies $i = i'$ (written $\phi \models i = i'$). $\phi \vdash \mathrm{sizeof}(\tau) = i$ states the size of type τ is determined to be i, provided that ϕ is valid. $\mathrm{ValidAccess}$ expresses bounds and alignment checks:

$$\frac{\begin{array}{c} \phi \vdash \mathrm{sizeof}(\tau_1) = i_1 \quad \cdots \quad \phi \vdash \mathrm{sizeof}(\tau_m) = i_m \\ \phi \models (i_1 + \cdots + i_{m-1}) \leq i \quad \phi \models i \leq (i_1 + \cdots + i_m) - k \\ \phi \models (i - (i_1 + \cdots + i_{m-1})) \bmod k = 0 \end{array}}{\phi \vdash \mathrm{ValidAccess}((\tau_1, \cdots, \tau_n), m, i, k)}$$

Branch. The following is the typing rule for the conditional branch instruction beq. First, it ensures that all of its operands have Int types, and an instruction sequence (which has code type $\forall(\emptyset; \emptyset). \mathrm{code}(\Gamma'; \Psi'; \phi'))$ exists at the destination address v_d. Then, it checks the current state extended with "$v_1 = v_2$" entails the requirement of the code type (expressed by the judgment at the third line); this check is for those times when the branch is taken. Finally, the typing rule checks the rest of the instruction sequence after extending the current state with "$v_1 \neq v_2$"; this is for times when the branch is not taken.

$$\frac{\begin{array}{c} \Gamma \vdash v_1 : \mathrm{Int}(i_1) \quad \Gamma \vdash v_2 : \mathrm{Int}(i_2) \quad \Gamma \vdash v_d : \mathrm{Int}(i_d) \\ \Psi; \phi \vdash i_d \mapsto \forall(\emptyset; \emptyset). \mathrm{code}(\Gamma'; \Psi'; \phi') \\ \Gamma; \Psi; \phi \wedge (i_1 = i_2) \models \Gamma'; \Psi'; \phi' \\ \Delta; \Gamma; \Psi; \phi \wedge \neg(i_1 = i_2) \vdash I \end{array}}{\Delta; \Gamma; \Psi; \phi \vdash \mathrm{beq} \ v_1, v_2, v_d; I}$$

Coercion. The instructions pack_h and pack_r create existential types. The suffix h (or r) means that the instruction works on heap-value (or word-value) types. Below is the typing rule for pack_r. Roughly speaking, it ensures that the constructed existential type $\exists(\vec{x}' \mid \Psi'; \phi'). \tau'$ is indeed a proper abstraction which hides concrete values $\vec{i}$ in abstract variables $\vec{x}'$.

$$\frac{\begin{array}{c} \Gamma \vdash r : \tau \quad \tau^w \equiv \exists(\vec{x}' \mid \Psi'; \phi'). \tau' \quad |\vec{i}| = |\vec{x}'| \quad \mathrm{FV}(\tau^w) \cup \mathrm{FV}(\vec{i}) \subseteq \Delta \\ \Psi; \phi \models \Psi'[\vec{i}/\vec{x}'] \quad \phi \models \phi'[\vec{i}/\vec{x}'] \quad \phi \vdash \tau = \tau'[\vec{i}/\vec{x}'] \quad \Delta; \Gamma[r \mapsto \tau^w]; \Psi; \phi \vdash I \end{array}}{\Delta; \Gamma; \Psi; \phi \vdash \mathrm{pack}_r \ r \text{ as } \tau^w \text{ using } \vec{i}; I}$$

Conversely, the instructions unpack_h and unpack_r destruct (or *open*) existential types, introducing new variables $\vec{x}$ into the scope. The following is the typing rule for unpack_r.

$$\frac{\begin{array}{c} \Gamma \vdash r : \exists(\vec{x}' \mid \Psi'; \phi'). \tau' \quad |\vec{x}| = |\vec{x}'| \quad \vec{x} \cap \Delta = \emptyset \\ \Delta \cup \vec{x}; \Gamma[r \mapsto \tau'[\vec{x}/\vec{x}']]; \Psi \cup \Psi'[\vec{x}/\vec{x}']; \phi \wedge (\phi'[\vec{x}/\vec{x}']) \vdash I \end{array}}{\Delta; \Gamma; \Psi; \phi \vdash \mathrm{unpack}_r \ r \text{ as } \vec{x}; I}$$

For guarded types ϕ' ? τ_1' : τ_2', the typing rules involve checking the truth or falsehood of the condition ϕ' under the current constraint ϕ, that is, $\phi \models \phi'$ or $\phi \models \neg\phi'$. The typing rules for $\mathbf{guard}_r$ and $\mathbf{unguard}_r$ are shown below.

$$\frac{\Gamma \vdash r : \tau \quad \tau^w \equiv \phi' \text{ ? } \tau_1' : \tau_2' \quad \mathrm{FV}(\tau^w) \subseteq \Delta \quad \begin{array}{c} (\phi \models \phi' \text{ and } \phi \vdash \tau = \tau_1') \text{ or } (\phi \models \neg\phi' \text{ and } \phi \vdash \tau = \tau_2') \\ \Delta; \Gamma[r \mapsto \tau^w]; \Psi; \phi \vdash I \end{array}}{\Delta; \Gamma; \Psi; \phi \vdash \mathbf{guard}_r \; r \; \mathbf{as} \; \tau^w; I}$$

$$\frac{\Gamma \vdash r : \phi' \text{ ? } \tau_1' : \tau_2' \quad \left(\phi \models \phi' \text{ and } \Delta; \Gamma[r \mapsto \tau_1']; \Psi; \phi \vdash I\right) \text{ or } \left(\phi \models \neg\phi' \text{ and } \Delta; \Gamma[r \mapsto \tau_2']; \Psi; \phi \vdash I\right)}{\Delta; \Gamma; \Psi; \phi \vdash \mathbf{unguard}_r \; r; I}$$

4 Implementations

We have implemented a type-checker for CTAL_0, a simple translator from CTAL_0 to IA-32 [10] assembly, and an experimental C compiler that produces CTAL_0 assembly code. The implementations are available from our web site [12].

4.1 Type-Checker and Translator

Our implementation of the type-checker supports several additional features that are not formalized, including a few IA-32 instructions (such as `call` and `ret`) which are automatically replaced by certain combinations of CTAL_0 instructions. In order to check the validity of entailment relations $\phi \models \phi'$, our implementation uses the CVC Lite theorem prover [13]. Currently we assume all arithmetic operations are done in infinite precision, but arithmetic modulo 2^{32} could also be employed.

Additionally, we have implemented a translator that translates well-typed CTAL_0 assembly programs into IA-32 assembly programs, enabling us to run them on real-world machines. As the instructions of CTAL_0 resemble those of IA-32, the translation is fairly straightforward.

4.2 Experimental C Compiler

Because C is not a safe language, it is impossible to directly translate C programs into CTAL_0 assembly code. Therefore, along with compilation, our compiler performs several transformations on the source program and guarantees its safety. The transformation strategy we adopted roughly follows that proposed by Fail-Safe C [4]. The main key to the transformations is the *fat* representation of integers and pointers, which we describe in the following.

Fat Integers. CTAL_0 requires clear distinction between pointers and arbitrary integers, though they are occasionally intermixed in C programs. To fill the gap, our compiler regards all integers appearing in C as non-pointers and separately manages *meta-data* which contain only definite pointers. More specifically, every

Fat Integer

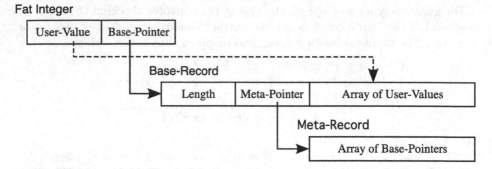

Fig. 4. Structure of fat integers

integer or pointer is represented by two words, with one word containing a *user-value* which is what programmers see and the other a *base-pointer* which is automatically controlled by the compiler. We call integers and pointers in this format *fat integers*, after Fail-Safe C [4].

If a fat integer represents a non-pointer integer, its base-pointer part will contain a null pointer (i.e., zero). Otherwise it will contain a valid pointer to a *base-record* which represents a memory block allocated by programmers. As shown in Fig. 4, a base-record consists of three parts. The first part contains the length of the whole record, and the last part, which is an array, stores the data manipulated by programmers. Moreover, because all integers and pointers are now represented by two words, in order to preserve the original semantics of C programs we also have to double the size of all allocated memory blocks. This is done by attaching to a base-record a new block, called a *meta-record*, consisting of an array that is equal in length to the base-record's array part. When a fat integer is stored into the base-record, its user-value is written into the base-record itself and its base-pointer is written into the attached meta-record.

The fat integer mechanism makes it possible to freely intermix integers and pointers as they both have exactly the same representation, yet preserving the memory safety. For instance, if a variable p of type int * possesses a valid pointer, then (int *)(int)p can also be used as a valid pointer.

Figure 5 presents the $CTAL_0$ type for base-records. Although it looks a bit complicated, it indeed expresses the structure of base-records described so far. Because the array part of a base-record is expressed by an untyped array type, we can store any value into there; this means that, at the level of C, a pointer to one type can be freely casted to a pointer to another type. Base-pointers can be null if they are associated with non-pointer fat integers, thus τ_{Ptr}, the type for base-pointers, utilizes a guarded type to express a maybe-null pointer.

Example. Figure 6 shows a well-typed $CTAL_0$ program corresponding to a pointer dereference (i.e., memory load) operation "*p" in the C language, where p is declared as int * (this program is essentially the same as the one our compiler

$\mu(\alpha_{\mathrm{Rec}}^{h}).\exists(x_{\ell},x_{m}\mid\Psi_{m};\top).\langle\mathrm{Array}(\mathrm{Int}(x_{\ell}),4),\mathrm{Array}(\mathrm{Int}(x_{m}),4),\mathrm{Array}(x_{\ell}-8)\rangle$
where
$\quad\Psi_{m}\equiv\{x_{m}\mapsto\langle\mathrm{Array}(\tau_{\mathrm{Ptr}},x_{\ell}-8)\rangle\}$
$\quad\tau_{\mathrm{Ptr}}\equiv\exists(x_{p}\mid\{x_{p}\mapsto(x_{p}=0)\ ?\ \langle\rangle:\alpha_{\mathrm{Rec}}^{h}\};\top).\mathrm{Int}(x_{p})$

Fig. 5. CTAL_0 type for base-records

emits for the expression *p). The pointer p is actually represented by a fat integer, so let us denote its user-value by p_{u} and its base-pointer by p_{b}, and assume that the registers r1 and r2 initially contain p_{u} and p_{b} respectively. Then, the program in Fig. 6 could be summarized as the following 5 steps.

1. Perform a null check (at line 3 in the program), that is, ensure that p_{b} is not null.
2. Perform a bounds check in two steps. First, ensure that p_{u} is not less than $p_{b}+8$, which is the address of the array part of the base-record pointed by p_{b} (line 10). Next, ensure that $p_{u}+4$ is not greater than the address of the end of the base-record (line 14). Here, 4 is the size of the value to be loaded.
3. Perform an alignment check (line 18), that is, ensure that the offset of p_{u} relative to the array part of the base-record is a multiple of 4.
4. Load the user-value of *p from the base-record (line 19).
5. Load the base-pointer of *p from the meta-record associated with the base-record (line 22). Notice that, since the meta-record lacks the first two parts of the base-record (see Fig. 4), the offset should be properly adjusted in advance (line 21).

Supported Features. As described so far, our compiler supports arbitrary casts between integers and pointers by employing the fat integer mechanism. It also supports arrays, structures and unions by simply treating them as untyped memory blocks, and variable argument functions by replacing the variable parts of their arguments with arrays (for instance, void f(int x, ...) is transformed into void f(int x, char *args)).

In our framework, the appropriate CTAL_0 type for every variable and function can be determined by its C type. Therefore our compiler requires no type annotations on source programs, while generating explicitly typed CTAL_0 code.

5   Extension for Function Pointers

The structure of fat integers explained in Sect. 4 cannot hold function pointers, i.e., pointers to instruction sequences which are not expressible by array types.

One approach to handle them is to enlarge each fat integer to three words, and let the third word keep a maybe-null pointer to an instruction sequence. This simple approach, however, would produce a lot of garbage words, because few function pointers are used in practice. Therefore we have adopted another approach, which is to keep function pointers in the second meta-pointer parts of

```
        # r1 contains the user-value pᵤ and r2 contains the base-pointer p_b
 1:  unpack_r r2 as x_b          # unpack p_b so that it has type Int(x_b)
 2:  apply abort, ···
 3:  beq r2, 0, abort            # abort if p_b is null
 4:  unguard_h x_b               # obtain x_b ↦ μ(α_Rec^h). ···
 5:  unroll_h x_b                # obtain x_b ↦ ∃(x_ℓ, x_m | Ψ_m; ⊤). ···
 6:  unpack_h x_b as (x_ℓ, x_m)  # obtain x_b ↦ ⟨···⟩ and x_m ↦ ⟨···⟩
 7:  mov r4, r1                  # set r4 to the offset pᵤ − p_b
 8:  sub r4, r2
 9:  apply abort, ···
10:  blt r4, 8, abort            # abort if the offset is below the array part
11:  load<4> r3, 0 (r2)          # set r3 to the length of the base-record minus 4
12:  sub r3, 4
13:  apply abort, ···
14:  blt r3, r4, abort           # abort if the offset exceeds the length
15:  mov r3, r4                  # set r3 to the offset mod 4
16:  mod r3, 4
17:  apply abort, ···
18:  blt 0, r3, abort            # abort if the offset is not divisible by 4
19:  load<4> r3, r4 (r2)         # set r3 to the user-value of the result (i.e., *p)
20:  load<4> r5, 4 (r2)          # set r5 point to the meta-record
21:  sub r4, 8                   # adjust the offset by subtracting 8
22:  load<4> r4, r4 (r5)         # set r4 to the base-pointer of the result
        # r3 and r4 now contain the user-value and the base-pointer of the result
```

Fig. 6. A CTAL_0 program corresponding to a pointer dereference operation in C (the second operands for `apply` instructions are omitted for brevity).

base-records (recall Fig. 4): a meta-pointer now points to either a meta-record (as before), or an instruction sequence. In the latter case, we put up a flag by setting the length field of the base-record to -1. This relation between the length and the meta-pointer fields can be established by using a guarded type.

Here, one more problem has to be solved: in order to invoke the pointed functions, we must know certain characteristics of them, in particular the number of arguments they take and the types of their return values. To solve this problem, we assume that all functions pointed by function pointers take exactly one pointer argument and return a pointer value. In other words, we assume the functions uniformly have declarations like "`char *f(char *arg);`". The compiler automatically prepares for each function a wrapper function called a *generic entry function* which has the above form. When a generic entry function is called, it extracts arguments from the array it received, calls the original function giving those arguments, wraps the result value in an array, and returns it. For example, the generic entry function corresponding to a function

```
int add(int x, int y) { /* ... */ }
```

will look like the following.

```
char *generic_add(char *args) {
    char *result = malloc(4);
    *(int *)result = add(*(int *)args, *(int *)(args + 4));
    return result;
}
```

6 Related Work

6.1 Source-Level Certification for C

For the certification of safety properties (particularly the memory safety) of C programs, a number of source-level instrumentation tools have been proposed. These tools produce C source code as their direct output, and then optionally invoke conventional compilers such as GCC [14] in order to generate assembly code. Compared to the tools, our approach of assembly-level certification has two main advantages. First, it does not require the source code of the programs to be checked, enabling end users to check closed-source product software. Second, it makes the trusted computing base much smaller, because we need not trust compilers and other source-level tools, which tend to be rather big systems.

Fail-Safe C [4] is a system which guarantees the memory safety of C programs by performing program transformations. Fail-Safe C provides the full feature of the ANSI C with its original semantics, except that erroneous programs may abort. The transformation strategy used in our compiler implementation is largely inspired by Fail-Safe C. In particular, we borrowed the notions of fat integers and generic entry functions (originally called *generic entry points*). Compared to ours, Fail-Safe C incorporates more complex and efficient transformations. However, they make the invariant managed by the system much bigger and thus hardly expressible at the level of assembly languages.

CCured [3] is also a transformation system which can ensure primarily the memory safety of C programs. CCured performs a sophisticated static analysis on programs and classifies pointers into several kinds, including SAFE pointers on which no unsafe cast operations are performed, and WILD pointers whose properties cannot be predicted. Because SAFE pointers involve less run-time checks than WILD ones, a lot of run-time overheads can be eliminated by the analysis. However, pointers sometimes need to be classified manually. Our compiler, on the other hand, accepts unmodified C programs, though it produces less efficient code. Since something like a SAFE pointer is expressible in CTAL_0, we expect similar static analyses could also be incorporated into our compiler.

Deputy [15,16] enriches the type system of C by allowing several kinds of annotations on types. For example, a pointer type can be annotated with the length of the memory block it points. Annotations can depend on certain run-time values such as the values of local variables, and Deputy will insert run-time check code into the original program if it cannot statically determine the validity of annotations. Deputy employs an inference algorithm that can discover annotations which are not explicitly written in the program. However, programmers must supply more or less annotations in order to enable Deputy to work well.

Cyclone [17] is a memory-safe dialect of C. Cyclone does not modify data representations by default, but programmers can instruct it to, for example, use a fat representation for a pointer. In addition, Cyclone supports a limited form of explicit memory deallocation. These features give programmers a finer control over low-level data structures. However, they make Cyclone slightly different from C, requiring more work in porting existing C programs to Cyclone. In contrast, our approach is to deal with the C language itself, therefore no porting task is imposed though advanced language features are not available.

6.2 Strongly Typed Assembly Languages

Typed Assembly Language (TAL) [5] is the basis of our language $CTAL_0$. While $CTAL_0$ is aimed at C, an unsafe language, TAL is mainly intended to be used with ML-like type-safe languages. Dependently Typed Assembly Language [6], an extension of TAL for dependent types, is focusing on safe languages, too.

TALx86 [18] is also an extension of TAL which provides a fragment of the Intel IA-32 architecture [10]. It targets programs written in an imperative language called Popcorn. Although Popcorn programs look similar to those of C, Popcorn and TALx86 do not support several unsafe features such as pointer arithmetics and arbitrary casts, while our compiler utilizes the untyped fragment of $CTAL_0$ to deal with such unsafe features of the C language.

Harren et al. [19] proposed an assembly-level framework to certify the safety of C programs processed by CCured. Compared to $CTAL_0$, their framework includes richer dependent type mechanisms, in particular dependently typed records in which the type of each field can depend on values of other fields. Furthermore, it supports mutations of such record values. According to [19], they had implemented a verifier that can handle several high-level features of CCured including run-time type information. However, their framework heavily relies on externally supplied components called Type Policies, which must be trusted. For example, the examination of run-time type information is totally dealt with by Type Policies in an undocumented manner. In contrast, our $CTAL_0$ is closed in itself and requires no such external trusted components. In addition, as with TAL, their framework seems not to be capable of handling data that are not statically typable.

7   Conclusion

We have presented $CTAL_0$, an extension of Typed Assembly Language. Its main design goal is to be capable of expressing most features of the C language, and in order to achieve the goal, its type system supports untyped array types and guarded types. In addition, we have implemented a type-checker and an experimental C compiler for $CTAL_0$. By performing several program transformations, our compiler supports free mixing of integers and pointers, structures, unions, variable-argument functions and function pointers.

One direction of future work is to enrich the type system of $CTAL_0$, possibly including the support for stack pointers and linking of separately type-checked object files. Another direction is to improve our compiler, in particular to provide currently missing features such as interoperability with existing libraries, and to produce more efficient code by employing static analyses and optimizations. We also plan to conduct an experiment to measure the performance of the compiler.

References

1. Kernighan, B.W., Ritchie, D.M.: The C Programming Language, 2nd edn. Prentice-Hall, Englewood Cliffs (1988)
2. SecurityFocus: SecurityFocus vulnerability database, http://www.securityfocus.com/vulnerabilities
3. Necula, G.C., Condit, J., Harren, M., McPeak, S., Weimer, W.: CCured: Type-safe retrofitting of legacy software. ACM Transactions on Programming Languages and Systems 27(3), 477–526 (2005)
4. Oiwa, Y., Sekiguchi, T., Sumii, E., Yonezawa, A.: Fail-safe ANSI-C compiler: An approach to making C programs secure (progress report). In: Okada, M., Pierce, B.C., Scedrov, A., Tokuda, H., Yonezawa, A. (eds.) ISSS 2002. LNCS, vol. 2609, pp. 133–153. Springer, Heidelberg (2002)
5. Morrisett, G., Walker, D., Crary, K., Glew, N.: From system F to typed assembly language. In: Proc. of POPL, pp. 85–97 (1998)
6. Xi, H., Harper, R.: A dependently typed assembly language. In: Proc. of ICFP, pp. 169–180 (2001)
7. Morrisett, G., Crary, K., Glew, N., Walker, D.: Stack-based typed assembly language. In: Leroy, X., Ohori, A. (eds.) TIC 1998. LNCS, vol. 1473, pp. 28–52. Springer, Heidelberg (1998)
8. Walker, D., Morrisett, G.: Alias types for recursive data structures. In: Harper, R. (ed.) TIC 2000. LNCS, vol. 2071, pp. 177–206. Springer, Heidelberg (2000)
9. Maeda, T., Yonezawa, A.: Writing practical memory management code with a strictly typed assembly language. In: Proc. of SPACE (2006)
10. Intel Corporation: Intel 64 and IA-32 architectures software developer's manual (2006)
11. Turner, D.N., Wadler, P., Mossin, C.: Once upon a type. In: Proc. of FPCA, pp. 1–11 (1995)
12. Kosakai, T.: $CTAL_0$ implementations distribution site, http://www.yl.is.s.u-tokyo.ac.jp/~kosakai/ctalz/
13. Barrett, C., Berezin, S.: CVC Lite: A new implementation of the cooperating validity checker. In: Alur, R., Peled, D.A. (eds.) CAV 2004. LNCS, vol. 3114, pp. 515–518. Springer, Heidelberg (2004)
14. Free Software Foundation: The GNU compiler collection, http://gcc.gnu.org/
15. Zhou, F., Condit, J., Anderson, Z., Bagrak, I., Ennals, R., Harren, M., Necula, G., Brewer, E.: SafeDrive: Safe and recoverable extensions using language-based techniques. In: Proc. of OSDI, pp. 45–60 (2006)
16. Condit, J., Harren, M., Anderson, Z., Gay, D., Necula, G.C.: Dependent types for low-level programming. In: Proc. of ESOP (2007)

17. Jim, T., Morrisett, G., Grossman, D., Hicks, M., Cheney, J., Wang, Y.: Cyclone: A safe dialect of C. In: Proc. of USENIX ATC, pp. 275–288 (2002)
18. Morrisett, G., Crary, K., Glew, N., Grossman, D., Samuels, R., Smith, F., Walker, D., Weirich, S., Zdancewic, S.: TALx86: A realistic typed assembly language. In: Proc. of WCSSS, Atlanta, GA, USA, May 1999, pp. 25–35 (1999)
19. Harren, M., Necula, G.C.: Using dependent types to certify the safety of assembly code. In: Hankin, C., Siveroni, I. (eds.) SAS 2005. LNCS, vol. 3672, pp. 155–170. Springer, Heidelberg (2005)

Information Flow Testing
The Third Path Towards Confidentiality Guarantee

Gurvan Le Guernic[1,2,*]

[1] Kansas State University - Manhattan, KS 66506 - USA
[2] IRISA - Campus universitaire de Beaulieu, 35042 Rennes - France
http://www.irisa.fr/lande/gleguern
Gurvan.Le_Guernic@irisa.fr

Abstract. Noninterference, which is an information flow property, is typically used as a baseline security policy to formalize confidentiality of secret information manipulated by a program. Noninterference verification mechanisms are usually based on static analyses and, to a lesser extent, on dynamic analyses. In contrast to those works, this paper proposes an information flow testing mechanism. This mechanism is sound from the point of view of noninterference. It is based on standard testing techniques and on a combination of dynamic and static analyses. Concretely, a semantics integrating a dynamic information flow analysis is proposed. This analysis makes use of static analyses results. This special semantics is built such that, once a path coverage property has been achieved on a program, a sound conclusion regarding the noninterfering behavior of the program can be established.

1 Introduction

With the intensification of communication in information systems, interest in security has increased. This paper deals with the problem of confidentiality, more precisely with *noninterference* in sequential programs. This notion is based on ideas from classical information theory [1] and has first been introduced by Goguen and Meseguer [2] as the absence of *strong dependency* [3].

> "information is transmitted from a source to a destination only when *variety* in the source can be conveyed to the destination" Cohen [3, Sect.1].

A sequential program, P, is said to be *noninterfering* if the values of its public (or low) outputs do not depend on the values of its secret (or high) inputs. Formally, noninterference is expressed as follows: a program P is noninterferent if and only if, given any two initial input states σ_1 and σ_2 that are indistinguishable with respect to low inputs, the executions of P started in states σ_1 and σ_2 are *low-indistinguishable*. *Low-indistinguishable* means that there is no observable

---

* The author was partially supported by National Science Foundation grants CCR-0296182, ITR-0326577 and CNS-0627748.

I. Cervesato (Ed.): ASIAN 2007, LNCS 4846, pp. 33–47, 2007.

difference between the public outputs of both executions. In the simplest form of the *low-indistinguishable* definition, public outputs include only the final values of low variables. In a more general setting, the definition may additionally involve intentional aspects such as power consumption, computation times, etc.

Static analyses for noninterference have been studied extensively and are well surveyed by Sabelfeld and Myers [4]. Recently, and to a lesser extent, dynamic analyses for noninterference have been proposed [5–7]. However, to be useful, those dynamic analyses must be combined with an information flow correction mechanism in order to enforce noninterference at run-time. As shown by Le Guernic and Jensen [8], in order to prevent the correction mechanism to become a new covert channel, additional constraints are put on the dynamic analysis. Those constraints limit the precision achievable by a monitor enforcing noninterference. A dynamic information flow analysis which is not used at run-time to *enforce* noninterference could therefore be more precise than its equivalent noninterference monitor.

This paper develops an information flow testing mechanism based on such a dynamic information flow analysis which is not aimed at enforcing noninterference at run-time. It is presented as a special semantics integrating a dynamic information flow analysis combined with results of a static analysis. A distinguishing feature of the dynamic information flow analysis proposed, compared to other standard run-time mechanisms, lies in the property overseen. Dynamically analyzing information flow is more complicated than, *e.g.*, monitoring divisions by zero, since it must take into account not only the current state of the program but also the execution paths *not taken* during execution. For example, executions of the following programs (a) **if** h **then** $x :=1$ **else** **skip** and (b) **if** h **then** **skip** **else** **skip** in an initial state where h is `false` are equivalent concerning executed commands. In contrast, (b)'s executions are noninterfering, while (a)'s executions are not. Executions of (a), where x is not equal to 1, do not give the same final value to x if h is `true` or `false`.

The next section starts by giving an overview of the dynamic information flow analysis at the basis of the approach. It then describes the testing technique used and, finally, presents the language studied. Before characterizing in Sect. 3.2 and 3.3 the static analyses used by the dynamic analysis and stating some properties of the proposed analysis, Section 3 presents the semantics which incorporates this dynamic analysis. Finally, Sect. 4 concludes.

2   Presentation of the Approach

With regard to noninterference, a dynamic analysis suited only for the detection of information flows, and not their correction, can be used only for noninterference testing. The idea behind noninterference testing is to run enough executions of a program in order to cover a "high enough percentage" of all possible executions of the program. In cases where the dynamic analysis results enable to conclude that all the executions evaluated are safe, users gain a confidence in the "safe" behavior of the program which is *proportional to the coverage percentage*.

When dealing with the confidentiality of secret data, a percentage lower than 100% does not seem acceptable. The aim of noninterference testing is then to cover all possible executions. It is not possible to run an execution for every possible input set (as there are frequently infinitely many input values). However, the results of a dynamic information flow analysis may be the same for many executions with different inputs. Therefore, it may be possible to conclude about the noninterference behavior of any execution of a program by testing a limited, hopefully finite, number of executions. Before presenting the testing approach proposed in this paper, this section introduces some terminology, formally defines what is meant by "noninterfering execution" and gives an overview of the dynamic information flow analysis proposed in Section 3.

2.1   Overview of the Noninterference Analysis

A *direct flow* is a flow from the right side of an assignment to the left side. Executing "$x := y$" creates a direct flow from y to x. An *explicit indirect flow* is a flow from the test of a conditional to the left side of an assignment in the branch executed. Executing "**if** c **then** $x := y$ **else skip end**" when c is **true** creates an explicit indirect flow from y to x. An *implicit indirect flow* is a flow from the test of a conditional to the left side of an assignment in the branch which is not executed. Executing "**if** c **then** $x := y$ **else skip end**" when c is **false** creates an implicit indirect flow from y to x.

A *"safe" execution is a noninterfering execution.* In this article, as commonly done, noninterference is defined as the absence of strong dependencies between the secret inputs of an execution and the final values of some variables which are considered to be publicly observable at the end of the execution.

For every program P, two sets of variable identifiers are defined. The set of variables corresponding to the secret inputs of the program is designated by $\mathcal{S}(\mathrm{P})$. The set of variables whose final value are publicly observable at the end of the execution is designated by $\mathcal{O}(\mathrm{P})$. No requirements are put on $\mathcal{S}(\mathrm{P})$ and $\mathcal{O}(\mathrm{P})$ other than requiring them to be subsets of $\mathbb{X}$. A variable x is even allowed to belong to both sets. In such a case, in order to be noninterfering, the program P would be required to, at least, reset the value of x.

In the following definitions, we consider that a program state may contain more than just a value store. This is the reason why a distinction is done between program states (ζ) and value stores (σ). Following Definition 1, two program states ζ_1, respectively ζ_2, containing the value stores σ_1, respectively σ_2, are said to be *low equivalent* with regards to a set of variables V, written $\zeta_1 \overset{V}{=} \zeta_2$, if and only if the value of any variable belonging to V is the same in σ_1 and σ_2.

Definition 1 (Low Equivalent States).
Two states ζ_1, respectively ζ_2, containing the value stores σ_1, respectively σ_2, are low equivalent with regards to a set of variables V, written $\zeta_1 \overset{V}{=} \zeta_2$, if and only if the value of any variable belonging to V is the same in σ_1 and σ_2:

$$\zeta_1 \overset{V}{=} \zeta_2 \iff \forall x \in V : \sigma_1(x) = \sigma_2(x)$$

Definition 2 (Noninterfering Execution).
Let $\Downarrow_s$ denote a big-step semantics. Let $\overline{\mathcal{S}(P)}$ be the complement of $\mathcal{S}(P)$ in the set X. For all programs P, program states ζ_1 and ζ_1', an execution with the semantics $\Downarrow_s$ of the program P in the initial state ζ_1 and yielding the final state ζ_1' is noninterfering, if and only if, for every program states ζ_2 and ζ_2' such that the execution with the semantics $\Downarrow_s$ of the program P in the initial state ζ_2 yields the final state ζ_2':

$$\zeta_1 \overset{\overline{\mathcal{S}(P)}}{=} \zeta_2 \;\Rightarrow\; \zeta_1' \overset{\mathcal{O}(P)}{=} \zeta_2'$$

The dynamic information flow analysis uses results of static analyses. The semantics integrating the dynamic analysis, now on called *analyzing semantics*, treats directly the direct and explicit indirect flows. For implicit indirect flows, a static analysis is run on the unexecuted branch of every conditional whose test carries variety — i.e. is influenced by the secret inputs of the program.

A program state for this semantics is composed of a value store, σ, mapping variables to values, and a tag store, ρ, mapping variables to a tag. This tag reflects the level of *variety* of a variable. At any point of the execution, a variable whose tag is $\bot$ would have the exact same value for any execution started with the same public inputs. A variable whose tag is $\top$ may have a different value for an execution started with the same public inputs. In other words, the variety in the secret inputs may be carried to the variables which are tagged $\top$, and only those variables.

2.2   Noninterference Testing

The main idea behind noninterference testing has been exposed above. Figure 1 sketches this idea. Let P be a program whose secret inputs are represented by h, public inputs by l, and public outputs by a color (or level of gray). $P(l_i, h_j)$, where (l_i, h_j) are input values, is the public output, represented by a color, of the execution of P with the inputs (l_i, h_j). In the representations of Fig. 1, public input values are represented on the x-axis and secret input values are represented on the y-axis. Each point of the different graphs corresponds to the execution of P with, as inputs, the coordinates of this point. Whenever a point in the graph is colored, the color corresponds to the public output value of the execution of P with, as inputs, the coordinates of the colored point. Figure 1(a) represents the execution of P with inputs (l_0, h_0). Its public output value is represented by the color (or level of gray) displayed and its tag — result of the dynamic information flow analysis — is $\bot$ (the public output does not carry variety). Figure 1(b) shows the meaning of this tag. As the public output tag of $P(l_0, h_0)$ is $\bot$, it means that for any secret inputs h_j the public output value of $P(l_0, h_j)$ is the same as for $P(l_0, h_0)$. Even if there exist secret inputs h_1 for which the public output tag of $P(l_0, h_1)$ is $\top$, any execution of P with public inputs l_0 is noninterfering. It only means that the dynamic analysis is not precise enough to directly detect that the execution of P with inputs (l_0, h_1) is noninterfering. However, this result can be indirectly deduced from the result of the dynamic analysis of the execution of P with inputs (l_0, h_0).

The main challenge of noninterference testing is to develop a dynamic analysis for which it is possible to characterize a set of executions which associate the same tag to the public output as an execution which as already been tested. For example, assume that it has been proved that all executions in the dashed area in Fig. 1(c) associate the same tag to the public output as the execution of P with inputs (l_0, h_0). As this tag is $\perp$, it is possible to conclude from the single execution of P with inputs (l_0, h_0) that all colored (or grayed) executions in Fig. 1(d) are noninterfering. Therefore, with only a limited number of executions, as in Fig. 1(e), it is possible to deduce that the program is noninterfering for a wide range of inputs which can be characterized.

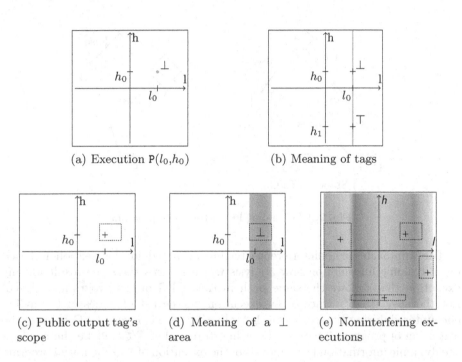

(a) Execution $P(l_0,h_0)$ (b) Meaning of tags

(c) Public output tag's scope

(d) Meaning of a $\perp$ area

(e) Noninterfering executions

Fig. 1. Sketch of the main idea of noninterference testing

Which executions need to be tested? As exposed above, in order to be able to conclude on the interference behavior of a program by testing it, it is necessary to be able to characterize a finite number of executions which are sufficient to conclude about all executions of this program. It is then necessary to develop a dynamic analysis which has the right balance between the number of executions covered by one test and the precision of the analysis.

The solution approached here assumes there is no recursive calls and is based on "acyclic Control Flow Graphs" (aCFG). As its name suggests an aCFG is a Control Flow Graph (CFG) without cycles. In an aCFG, there is no edge from the last nodes of the body of a loop statement to the node corresponding to the test of this loop statement. Instead, there is an edge from every last node of the body of the loop to the node corresponding to the block following the loop statement. Figure 2(a) shows the standard CFG of the following code: "**if** c_1 **then while** c_2 **do** P_1 **done else** P_2 **end**". Figure 2(b) shows its aCFG. In an acyclic CFG, there is a finite number of paths. The maximum number of paths is equal to 2^b, where b is the number of branching statements (**if** and **while** statements) in the program.

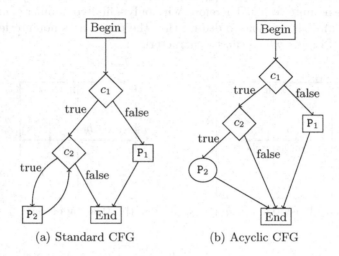

(a) Standard CFG   (b) Acyclic CFG

Fig. 2. CFG and aCFG of the same program

The approach to noninterference testing proposed in this section is based on a dynamic information flow analysis which returns the same result for any execution that follows the same path in the aCFG of the program analyzed. Let the acyclic CFG trace of an execution be the list of nodes of the aCFG encountered during the execution. Let $\tau[\![\sigma \vdash P]\!]$ be the acyclic CFG trace of the execution of program P with initial value store σ. Let $\mathbb{T}[\![\zeta \vdash P]\!]$ be the result of the dynamic information flow analysis of the execution of P in the initial program state ζ (its formal definition is given on page 40). The constraint imposed on the dynamic information flow analysis for the noninterference testing approach proposed is formalized in Hypothesis 1.

Hypothesis 1 (Usable for noninterference testing)
For all programs P, value stores σ_1 and σ_2, and tag stores ρ:

$$\tau[\![\sigma_1 \vdash P]\!] = \tau[\![\sigma_2 \vdash P]\!] \quad \Rightarrow \quad \mathbb{T}[\![(\sigma_1, \rho) \vdash P]\!] = \mathbb{T}[\![(\sigma_2, \rho) \vdash P]\!]$$

With such a dynamic analysis, the problem of verifying the noninterference behavior of any execution is reduced to the well known testing problem of achieving 100% feasible paths coverage [9–13]. For path whose branch conditions are linear functions of inputs, Gupta et al. [14] propose a technique which finds a solution in one iteration or guarantees that the path is infeasible.

2.3   The Language: Syntax and Standard Semantics

The language used to describe programs studied in this article is an imperative language for sequential programs. Expressions in this language are deterministic — their evaluation in a given program state always results in the same value — and are free of side effects — their evaluation has no influence on the program state. The standard semantics of the language is given in Fig. 3. The evaluation symbol ($\Downarrow$) is given a subscript letter in order to distinguish between the standard semantics ($\mathcal{S}$) and the analyzing one ($\mathcal{A}$). The standard semantics is based on rules written in the format: $\sigma \vdash P \Downarrow_{\mathcal{S}} \sigma'$. Those rules means that, with the initial program state σ, the evaluation of the program P yields the final program state σ'. Let $\mathbb{X}$ be the domain of variable identifiers and $\mathbb{D}$ be the semantics domain of values. A program state is a value store σ ($\mathbb{X} \rightarrow \mathbb{D}$) mapping variable identifiers to their respective value. The definition of value stores is extended to expressions, so that $\sigma(e)$ is the value of the expression e in the program state σ.

$$\frac{}{\sigma \vdash \mathbf{skip} \Downarrow_{\mathcal{S}} \sigma} \qquad \frac{\sigma(e) = \mathbf{true} \quad \sigma \vdash P^l \; ; \mathbf{while}\ e\ \mathbf{do}\ P^l\ \mathbf{done} \Downarrow_{\mathcal{S}} \sigma'}{\sigma \vdash \mathbf{while}\ e\ \mathbf{do}\ P^l\ \mathbf{done} \Downarrow_{\mathcal{S}} \sigma'}$$

$$\frac{}{\sigma \vdash x := e \Downarrow_{\mathcal{S}} \sigma[x \mapsto \sigma(e)]} \qquad \frac{\sigma(e) = v \quad \sigma \vdash P^v \Downarrow_{\mathcal{S}} \sigma'}{\sigma \vdash \mathbf{if}\ e\ \mathbf{then}\ P^{\mathbf{true}}\ \mathbf{else}\ P^{\mathbf{false}}\ \mathbf{end} \Downarrow_{\mathcal{S}} \sigma'}$$

$$\frac{\sigma \vdash P^h \Downarrow_{\mathcal{S}} \sigma^h \quad \sigma^h \vdash P^t \Downarrow_{\mathcal{S}} \sigma^t}{\sigma \vdash P^h \; ; P^t \Downarrow_{\mathcal{S}} \sigma^t} \qquad \frac{\sigma(e) = \mathbf{false}}{\sigma \vdash \mathbf{while}\ e\ \mathbf{do}\ P^l\ \mathbf{done} \Downarrow_{\mathcal{S}} \sigma}$$

Fig. 3. Rules of the standard semantics

3   The Analyzing Semantics

The dynamic information flow analysis and the analyzing semantics are defined together in Fig. 4. Information flows are tracked using tags. At any execution step, every variable has a tag which reflects the fact that this variable may carry variety or not.

3.1   A Semantics Making Use of Static Analysis Results

Let $\mathbb{X}$ be the domain of variable identifiers, $\mathbb{D}$ be the semantics domain of values, and $\mathbb{T}$ be the domain of tags. In the remainder of this article, $\mathbb{T}$ is equal to $\{\top, \bot\}$. Those tags form a lattice such that $\bot \sqsubseteq \top$. $\top$ is the tag associated to variables that *may* carry variety — i.e. whose value may be influenced by the secret inputs.

The analyzing semantics described in Fig. 4 is based on rules written in the format:

$$\zeta \vdash P \Downarrow_{\mathcal{A}} \zeta' : X$$

This reads as follows: in the analyzing execution state ζ, program P yields the analyzing execution state ζ' and a set of variables X. An analyzing execution state ζ is a pair (σ, ρ) composed of a value store σ and a tag store ρ. A value store $(\mathbb{X} \to \mathbb{D})$ maps variable identifiers to values. A tag store $(\mathbb{X} \to \mathbb{T})$ maps variable identifiers to tags. The definitions of value store and tag store are extended to expressions. $\sigma(e)$ is the value of the expression e in a program state whose value store is σ. Similarly, $\rho(e)$ is the tag of the expression e in a program state whose tag store is ρ. $\rho(e)$ is formally defined as follows, with $\mathcal{V}(e)$ being the set of free variables appearing in the expression e:

$$\rho(e) = \bigsqcup_{x \in \mathcal{V}(e)} \rho(x)$$

Definition 3 ($\mathbb{T}[\![\zeta \vdash P]\!]$).
$\mathbb{T}[\![\zeta \vdash P]\!]$ *is defined to be the final tag store of the execution of P with the initial state ζ. Therefore, for all programs P, value stores σ and tag stores ρ, if the evaluation of P in the initial state (σ, ρ) terminates then there exists a value stores σ' and a set of variables X' such that:*

$$\zeta \vdash P \Downarrow_A (\sigma', \mathbb{T}[\![\zeta \vdash P]\!]) : X'$$

The set of variables X contains all the variables whose value may be modified by an execution of P having the same trace than the current execution — i.e. all executions whose trace is $\tau[\![\sigma \vdash P]\!]$.

The semantics rules make use of static analyses results. In Fig. 4, application of a static information flow analysis to the piece of code P is written: $[\![\rho \vdash P]\!]^{\sharp_G}$. The analysis of a program P must return a pair $(\mathfrak{D}, \mathfrak{X})$. $\mathfrak{D}$, which is a subset of $(\mathbb{X} \times \mathbb{X})$, is an over-approximation of the dependencies between the initial and final values of the variables created by any execution of P. $\mathfrak{D}(x)$, which is equal to $\{y \mid (x, y) \in \mathfrak{D}\}$, is the set of variables whose initial value may influence the final value of x after an execution of P. $\mathfrak{X}$, which is a subset of $\mathbb{X}$, is an over-approximation of the set of variables which are potentially defined — i.e. whose value may be modified — by an execution of P. This static analysis can be any such analysis that satisfies a set of formal constraints which are stated below.

The analyzing semantics rules are straightforward. As can be expected, the execution of a **skip** statement with the semantics given in Fig. 4 yields a final state equal to the initial state. The execution of the assignment of the value of the expression e to the variable x yields an execution state (σ', ρ'). The final value store (σ') is equal to the initial value store (σ) except for the variable x. The final value store maps the variable x to the value of the expression e evaluated with the initial value store $(\sigma(e))$. Similarly, the final tag store (ρ') is equal to the initial tag store (ρ) except for the variable x. The tag of x after the execution of the assignment is equal to the tag of the expression computed using the initial tag store $(\rho(e))$. $\rho(e)$ represents the level of the information flowing into x through direct flows.

For an **if** statement, the branch (P^v) designated by the value of e is executed and the other one $(P^{\neg v})$ is analyzed. The final value store is the one returned

$$\frac{}{\zeta \vdash \mathbf{skip} \; \Downarrow_{\mathcal{A}} \; \zeta : \emptyset} \qquad\qquad (\mathrm{E}_{\mathcal{A}}\text{-SKIP})$$

$$\frac{}{(\sigma,\, \rho) \vdash x := e \; \Downarrow_{\mathcal{A}} \; (\sigma[x \mapsto \sigma(e)],\; \rho[x \mapsto \rho(e)]) : \{x\}} \qquad (\mathrm{E}_{\mathcal{A}}\text{-ASSIGN})$$

$$\frac{\zeta \vdash P^{\mathrm{h}} \; \Downarrow_{\mathcal{A}} \; \zeta^{\mathrm{h}} : X^{\mathrm{h}} \qquad \zeta^{\mathrm{h}} \vdash P^{\mathrm{t}} \; \Downarrow_{\mathcal{A}} \; \zeta^{\mathrm{t}} : X^{\mathrm{t}}}{\zeta \vdash P^{\mathrm{h}} \; ; \; P^{\mathrm{t}} \; \Downarrow_{\mathcal{A}} \; \zeta^{\mathrm{t}} : X^{\mathrm{h}} \cup X^{\mathrm{t}}} \qquad (\mathrm{E}_{\mathcal{A}}\text{-SEQUENCE})$$

$$\frac{\sigma(e) = v \qquad (\sigma,\, \rho) \vdash P^v \; \Downarrow_{\mathcal{A}} \; (\sigma^v,\, \rho^v) : X^v \qquad [\![\rho \vdash P^{\neg v}]\!]^{\sharp \mathcal{G}} = (\mathfrak{D}, \mathfrak{X})}{X^e = X^v \cup \mathfrak{X} \qquad \rho' = \rho^v \sqcup \big((X^e \times \{\rho(e)\}) \cup (\overline{X^e} \times \{\bot\}) \big)}{(\sigma,\, \rho) \vdash \mathbf{if}\ e\ \mathbf{then}\ P^{\mathtt{true}}\ \mathbf{else}\ P^{\mathtt{false}}\ \mathbf{end} \; \Downarrow_{\mathcal{A}} \; (\sigma^v,\, \rho') : X^v} \qquad (\mathrm{E}_{\mathcal{A}}\text{-IF})$$

$$\frac{\sigma(e) = \mathtt{false} \qquad [\![\rho \vdash P^l \; ; \; \mathbf{while}\ e\ \mathbf{do}\ P^l\ \mathbf{done}]\!]^{\sharp \mathcal{G}} = (\mathfrak{D}, \mathfrak{X})}{\rho' = \rho \sqcup \big((\mathfrak{X} \times \{\rho(e)\}) \cup (\overline{\mathfrak{X}} \times \{\bot\}) \big)}{(\sigma,\, \rho) \vdash \mathbf{while}\ e\ \mathbf{do}\ P^l\ \mathbf{done} \; \Downarrow_{\mathcal{A}} \; (\sigma,\, \rho') : \emptyset} \qquad (\mathrm{E}_{\mathcal{A}}\text{-WHILE}_{\mathtt{false}})$$

$$\frac{\sigma(e) = \mathtt{true} \qquad \sigma \vdash P^l \; ; \; \mathbf{while}\ e\ \mathbf{do}\ P^l\ \mathbf{done} \; \Downarrow_{\mathcal{S}} \; \sigma^v}{[\![\rho \vdash P^l \; ; \; \mathbf{while}\ e\ \mathbf{do}\ P^l\ \mathbf{done}]\!]^{\sharp \mathcal{G}} = (\mathfrak{D}, \mathfrak{X})}{\rho^{\mathfrak{D}} = \big\{ (x\, ,\, \bigsqcup_{y \in \mathfrak{D}(x)} \rho(y)) \mid x \in \mathbb{X} \big\}}{\rho^{\mathfrak{R}} = \rho^{\mathfrak{D}} \sqcup \big((\mathfrak{X} \times \{\rho(e)\}) \cup (\overline{\mathfrak{X}} \times \{\bot\}) \big)}{(\sigma,\, \rho) \vdash \mathbf{while}\ e\ \mathbf{do}\ P^l\ \mathbf{done} \; \Downarrow_{\mathcal{A}} \; (\sigma^v,\, \rho^{\mathfrak{R}}) : \mathfrak{X}} \qquad (\mathrm{E}_{\mathcal{A}}\text{-WHILE}_{\mathtt{true}})$$

Fig. 4. Rules of the analyzing semantics

by the execution of P^v. The final tag store (ρ') is the least upper bound of the tag store returned by the execution of P^v and a tag store reflecting indirect flows. This latter tag store associates the tag of the branching condition to variables potentially defined by an execution having the same trace or an execution of the other branch. If the tag of the branching condition is $\bot$, the final tag store is therefore equal to the tag store returned by the execution of P^v.

The execution of while statements is similar to the execution of if statements. However, in order to be able to apply the testing technique exposed in Section 2.2, it is required to have the same tag store for every execution following the same path in the acyclic CFG. Therefore, the final tag store is computed from the result of a static analysis of the branch executed (skip if the branching condition is false) and not from the tag store obtained by the execution of the branch designated by the branching condition. For the same reason, the set of variables returned by the execution of a while statement is obtained by static analysis of the branch executed.

3.2 Hypotheses on the Static Analysis Used

The static analysis used on unexecuted branches is not formally defined. In fact, the dynamic analysis can use any static analysis which complies with the three following hypotheses and returns a pair, whose first element is a relation between variables — i.e. a set of pairs of variables — and second element is a set of variables.

The first two hypotheses require a sound static analysis. Hypothesis 2 simply requires the static analysis used to be a *sound* analysis of defined variables. More precisely, it requires that the second element of the static analysis result ($\mathfrak{X}$) contains all the variables which may be defined by an execution of the analyzed program. This is a straightforward requirement as the result of the static analysis is used to take into account implicit indirect flows. Hypothesis 3 requires the static analysis used to be a *sound* analysis of dependencies between the final values of variables and their initial values. The last hypothesis requires only the static analysis to be deterministic.

Hypothesis 2 (Sound detection of modified variables.)
For all tag stores ρ_i, analysis results $(\mathfrak{D}, \mathfrak{X})$, testing execution states (σ_i, ρ_i) and (σ_f, ρ_f), programs P and sets of variables X such that:

1. $[\![\rho_i \vdash P]\!]^{\sharp g} = (\mathfrak{D}, \mathfrak{X})$
2. $(\sigma_i, \rho_i) \vdash P \Downarrow_{\mathcal{A}} (\sigma_f, \rho_f) : X$,

the following holds: $\forall x \notin \mathfrak{X} \,.\, \sigma_f(x) = \sigma_i(x)$.

Hypothesis 3 (Sound detection of dependencies.)
For all analysis results $(\mathfrak{D}, \mathfrak{X})$, tag stores ρ_1, testing execution states (σ_1, ρ_1), (σ_1', ρ_1'), (σ_2, ρ_2) and (σ_2', ρ_2'), programs P, and sets of variables X_1 and X_2 such that:

1. $[\![\rho_1 \vdash P]\!]^{\sharp g} = (\mathfrak{D}, \mathfrak{X})$
2. $(\sigma_1, \rho_1) \vdash P \Downarrow_{\mathcal{A}} (\sigma_1', \rho_1') : X_1$,
3. $(\sigma_2, \rho_2) \vdash P \Downarrow_{\mathcal{A}} (\sigma_2', \rho_2') : X_2$,

for all x in $\mathfrak{X}$: $\big(\forall y \in \mathfrak{D}(x) \,.\, \sigma_1(y) = \sigma_2(y)\big) \quad \Rightarrow \quad \sigma_1'(x) = \sigma_2'(x)$.

Hypothesis 4 (Deterministic static analysis)
The static analysis used is a deterministic analysis. For all tag stores ρ and programs P, the following holds: $\mid range([\![\rho \vdash P]\!]^{\sharp g}) \mid = 1$.

What is the reason for having a tag store in parameter of the static analysis? In fact, there is no need for the tag store which is given to the static analysis. This additional parameter to the static analysis has been added in order to be able to use existing noninterference type systems in a straightforward way.

   Using this tag store, it is easy to construct an analysis satisfying the hypotheses presented above from a type inference mechanism for a sound noninterference type system. Let $\mathbb{X}\uparrow^\rho$ be the set of variables whose tag in ρ is $\top$. Let Γ_ρ be a typing environment in which variables belonging to $\mathbb{X}\uparrow^\rho$ are typed secret, other variables can be typed secret or public. Let $\mathbb{X}\downarrow_\Gamma$ be the set of variables typed public in Γ and $\mathbb{X}\uparrow^\Gamma$ the set of variables typed secret in Γ. Let $\mathfrak{D}_\Gamma$ be a relation among variables which associates every variable of $\mathbb{X}\uparrow^\Gamma$ to every variable $(\mathbb{X})$, and associates every variable of $\mathbb{X}\downarrow_\Gamma$ to every variable of $\mathbb{X}\downarrow_\Gamma$. If P is well-typed under Γ_ρ and the program "**if** h **then** P **else skip end**" is well-typed under Γ'_ρ with h typed secret in Γ'_ρ, then $(\mathfrak{D}_\Gamma, \mathbb{X}\uparrow^{\Gamma'})$ is a result satisfying the Hypotheses 2 and 3 if any variable tagged $\bot$ in ρ has the same value in σ_1 and σ_2.

3.3   Another Characterization of *Usable* Static Analyses

The above hypotheses define which static information flow analyses are *usable*, i.e. which static analyses can be used with the special semantics given in Fig. 4. However, Hypotheses 2 and 3 are stated using the special semantics itself. This makes it more difficult to prove that a given static analysis satisfies those hypotheses.

Figure 5 defines a set of *acceptability* rules. The result $(\mathfrak{D}, \mathfrak{X})$ of a static information flow analysis of a given program (P) is *acceptable* for the analyzing semantics only if the result satisfies those rules. This is written: $(\mathfrak{D}, \mathfrak{X}) \models$ P. In the definitions of those rules, $\mathcal{I}d$ denotes the identity relation. $\circ$ is the operation of composition of relations.

$$(S \circ R) = \bigcup_{(a,b)\in R} \{(a,c) \mid (b,c) \in S\}$$

Using the acceptability rules of Fig. 5, it is possible to characterize some static information flow analyses which are *usable* with the analyzing semantics without referring to the analyzing semantics itself. It is also possible to generate a *usable* static information flow analysis by fix-point computation on the acceptability rules; in fact, only on the rule for loop statements. However, those acceptability rules do not define a most precise usable static analysis.

As stated by Theorem 1, any *acceptable* static analysis result satisfies Hypothesis 2. Theorem 2 states that any *acceptable* static analysis result satisfies Hypothesis 3.

Theorem 1 (Acceptable imply sound detection of defined variables)
For all programs P, and analysis result $(\mathfrak{D}, \mathfrak{X})$ such that $(\mathfrak{D}, \mathfrak{X}) \models$ P, the Hypothesis 2 holds.

Proof As $\mathfrak{X}$ contains an over-approximation of variables on the left side of every assignments in P, a variable which is not in this set can not be assigned to. And therefore, its value remains unchanged.

Theorem 2 (Acceptable imply sound detection of dependencies)
For all programs P, and analysis result $(\mathfrak{D}, \mathfrak{X})$ if $(\mathfrak{D}, \mathfrak{X}) \models$ P then the Hypothesis 3 holds.

$$(\mathfrak{D}, \mathfrak{X}) \models \mathbf{skip} \quad \text{iff} \quad \mathfrak{D} \supseteq \mathcal{I}d$$

$$(\mathfrak{D}, \mathfrak{X}) \models x := e \quad \text{iff} \quad \mathfrak{D} \supseteq \mathcal{I}d[x \mapsto \mathcal{V}(e)] \quad \wedge \quad \mathfrak{X} \supseteq \{x\}$$

$(\mathfrak{D}, \mathfrak{X}) \models \mathbf{P}^h \; ; \; \mathbf{P}^t$
iff there exist $(\mathfrak{D}^h, \mathfrak{X}^h)$ and $(\mathfrak{D}^t, \mathfrak{X}^t)$ such that:
$$(\mathfrak{D}^h, \mathfrak{X}^h) \models \mathbf{P}^h \quad \wedge \quad (\mathfrak{D}^t, \mathfrak{X}^t) \models \mathbf{P}^t$$
$$\mathfrak{D} \supseteq (\mathfrak{D}^h \circ \mathfrak{D}^t) \quad \wedge \quad \mathfrak{X} \supseteq (\mathfrak{X}^h \cup \mathfrak{X}^t)$$

$(\mathfrak{D}, \mathfrak{X}) \models \mathbf{if} \; e \; \mathbf{then} \; \mathbf{P}^{\mathrm{true}} \; \mathbf{else} \; \mathbf{P}^{\mathrm{false}} \; \mathbf{end}$
iff there exist $(\mathfrak{D}^{\mathrm{true}}, \mathfrak{X}^{\mathrm{true}})$ and $(\mathfrak{D}^{\mathrm{false}}, \mathfrak{X}^{\mathrm{false}})$ such that:
$$(\mathfrak{D}^{\mathrm{true}}, \mathfrak{X}^{\mathrm{true}}) \models \mathbf{P}^{\mathrm{true}} \quad \wedge \quad (\mathfrak{D}^{\mathrm{false}}, \mathfrak{X}^{\mathrm{false}}) \models \mathbf{P}^{\mathrm{false}}$$
$$\mathfrak{X} \supseteq (\mathfrak{X}^{\mathrm{true}} \cup \mathfrak{X}^{\mathrm{false}}) \quad \wedge \quad \mathfrak{D} \supseteq (\mathfrak{D}^{\mathrm{true}} \cup \mathfrak{D}^{\mathrm{false}} \cup (\mathfrak{X} \times \mathcal{V}(e)))$$

$(\mathfrak{D}, \mathfrak{X}) \models \mathbf{while} \; e \; \mathbf{do} \; \mathbf{P}^l \; \mathbf{done}$
iff there exists $(\mathfrak{D}^l, \mathfrak{X}^l)$ such that: $(\mathfrak{D}^l, \mathfrak{X}^l) \models \mathbf{P}^l$ and
$$\mathfrak{D} \supseteq ((\mathfrak{D}^l \circ \mathfrak{D}) \cup \mathcal{I}d \cup (\mathfrak{X} \times \mathcal{V}(e))) \quad \wedge \quad \mathfrak{X} \supseteq \mathfrak{X}^l$$

Fig. 5. Acceptability rules for *usable* analysis results

Proof The proof follows directly from the acceptability rules. The value of every assigned variables depends on the values of the variables appearing in the expression on the right side of the assignment. The rule for sequences links the dependencies created by both statements. Variables whose value can be modified in a conditional are accurately stated to depend on the values of variables appearing in the branching condition. And finally, in the rule for `while` statements, $\mathfrak{D}^l \circ \mathfrak{D} \subseteq \mathfrak{D}$ ensures that the dependencies created by one or more iterations of the loop are contained in $\mathfrak{D}$. While $\mathcal{I}d \subseteq \mathfrak{D}$ ensures that dependencies existing in case of no iteration at all are also contained in $\mathfrak{D}$.

Therefore, a static information flow analysis, which satisfies Hypothesis 4 and whose results are acceptable ($[\![\rho \vdash \mathbf{P}]\!]^{\sharp g} \models \mathbf{P}$), is *usable* by the analyzing semantics — i.e. it satisfies Hypotheses 2, 3 and 4.

3.4   Properties of the Analyzing Semantics

Section 3.1 formally defined the dynamic information flow analysis proposed in this article. The soundness of this analysis with regard to the notion of noninterfering execution (Definition 2) is proved by Theorem 3. This means that, at the end of any two executions of a given program P started with the same public inputs (variables which do not belong to $\mathcal{S}(\mathbf{P})$), any variables whose final tag is $\perp$

has the same final value for both executions. Theorem 4 states that the dynamic analysis results for two executions following the same path in the acyclic CFG are identical. Therefore, the dynamic information flow analysis proposed can be used with the testing technique presented in Section 2.2.

Theorem 3 (Sound Detection of Information flows)

Assume that the analyzing semantics $\Downarrow_{\mathcal{A}}$ uses a static analysis $(\llbracket \rrbracket^{\sharp_g})$ for which Hypotheses 2, 3 and 4 hold. For all programs P, sets of variables X_1 and X_2, and execution states (σ_1, ρ_1), (σ_1', ρ_1'), (σ_2, ρ_2) and (σ_2', ρ_2') such that:

1. *$\forall x \in \mathcal{S}(P).\ \rho_1(x) = \top$,*
2. *$\forall x \notin \mathcal{S}(P).\ \sigma_1(x) = \sigma_2(x)$,*
3. *$(\sigma_1, \rho_1) \vdash P \Downarrow_{\mathcal{A}} (\sigma_1', \rho_1') : X_1$,*
4. *$(\sigma_2, \rho_2) \vdash P \Downarrow_{\mathcal{A}} (\sigma_2', \rho_2') : X_2$,*

the following holds: $\forall x \in \mathbb{X}.\ (\rho_1'(x) = \bot) \Rightarrow (\sigma_1'(x) = \sigma_2'(x))$.

*Proof The proof goes by induction on the derivation tree of the third local hypothesis and by cases on the last evaluation rule used. For inductions, the set $\mathcal{S}(P)$ is replaced by the set of variables whose tag is $\top$, and the second local hypothesis (with $\mathcal{S}(P)$ replaced) is proved to be an invariant. The proof is straightforward for **skip** and assignments, and goes by simple induction for sequences. For conditionals, if both executions execute the same branch then the conclusion follows from a simple induction. Otherwise, it means that the expression tested (e) does not have the same value for both execution; and therefore that $\rho_1(e)$ is $\top$. Hence, as any variables which are modified in the branch executed (X) or potentially modified by an execution of the other branch (𝔛) receive the tag of e in the final tag store (ρ_1'), the desired conclusion is vacuously true for variables assigned by any of the two executions and follows directly from the second local hypothesis for the other variables.*

Theorem 4 (Identical Same Path Analysis Results)

If the analyzing semantics $\Downarrow_{\mathcal{A}}$ uses a static analysis $(\llbracket \rrbracket^{\sharp_g})$ for which Hypotheses 2, 3 and 4 hold then Hypothesis 1 holds.

*Proof Once again, the proof goes by induction and cases on the derivation tree. The proof is direct for **skip**, assignments and sequences. For if statements, as the trace is the same then the branch executed is the same and the proof follows by induction. For while statements, the final tag store is constructed from the result of the static analysis of the statement. Therefore, the conclusion follows directly from Hypothesis 4.*

4   Conclusion

To the best of the author knowledge, this article proposes the first information flow testing mechanism which enjoys the property of being sound with regard to noninterference. It is based on a special semantics integrating a dynamic information flow analysis which is sound from the point of view of noninterference for the tested execution, and returns the same sound result for any execution following the same path in the acyclic Control Flow Graph (aCFG) of the program. After testing once every path in the aCFG, a sound conclusion with regard to noninterference can be stated for the program under test. The dynamic analysis combines information obtained from executed statements with static analysis results of some unexecuted pieces of code. No particular static analysis is required to be used. Instead, three hypotheses on the results of the static analysis used are defined. It is proved that any static analysis respecting those hypotheses can be soundly used. A construction mechanism to obtain such a static analysis from existing noninterference type systems is given. Additionally, a set of constraints relating statements and the result of their static analysis is defined independently from anything else. This set of constraints is proved to subsume the three hypotheses stated before.

Given test cases covering all the feasible paths in the aCFG, the testing mechanism proposed returns a conclusion as strong as the conclusion returned by the static analysis used by the testing semantics. Moreover, this result is at least as precise as the result returned by the static analysis alone. The increase in precision is proportional to the number of if statements whose condition is not influenced by a secret.

To the author knowledge, there is no similar work. The vast majority of research on noninterference concerns static analyses and involves type systems [4]. Some "real size" languages together with security type system have been developed (for example, JFlow/JIF [15] and FlowCaml [16]). A few dynamic information flow analyses have been proposed [5, 7, 17]. However, those analyses are applied on final users executions and are therefore required to correct "bad" flows. In order to prevent this correction mechanism to become a new covert channel, additional constraints are applied on the dynamic analysis [8]. Those additional constraints limit the precision achievable by such dynamic analyses. While testing, there is no need for a correction mechanism and therefore a higher precision can be achieved.

Noninterference testing is an interesting field of study having its own specific challenges. It may be hard, so not impossible [14], to come out with a valid set of executions in order to cover all feasible paths in the aCFG. However, in many cases, the noninterference mechanism proposed in this article is more precise than the static analyses which can be used by the testing technique proposed. Thus, noninterference testing may allow to validate some specific programs whose validation is out of reach of static analyses, or at least help find information flow bugs.

References

1. Ashby, W.R.: An Introduction to Cybernetics. Chapman & Hall, Sydney, Australia (1956)
2. Goguen, J.A., Meseguer, J.: Security policies and security models. In: Proc. Symp. on Security and Privacy, pp. 11–20. IEEE Computer Society Press, Los Alamitos (1982)

3. Cohen, E.S.: Information transmission in computational systems. ACM SIGOPS Operating Systems Review 11(5), 133–139 (1977)

4. Sabelfeld, A., Myers, A.C.: Language-based information-flow security. IEEE J. on Selected Areas in Communications 21(1), 5–19 (2003)

5. Vachharajani, N., Bridges, M.J., Chang, J., Rangan, R., Ottoni, G., Blome, J.A., Reis, G.A., Vachharajani, M., August, D.I.: Rifle: An architectural framework for user-centric information-flow security. In: Proceedings of the International Symposium on Microarchitecture (2004)

6. Le Guernic, G., Banerjee, A., Jensen, T., Schmidt, D.: Automata-based Confidentiality Monitoring. In: Proc. Asian Computing Science Conference. LNCS, Springer, Heidelberg (2006)

7. Shroff, P., Smith, S.F., Thober, M.: Dynamic dependency monitoring to secure information flow. In: Proc. Computer Security Foundations Symposium, IEEE Computer Society, Los Alamitos (2007)

8. Le Guernic, G., Jensen, T.: Monitoring Information Flow. In: Proc. Workshop on Foundations of Computer Security, DePaul University, pp. 19–30 (2005)

9. Ntafos, S.C.: A comparison of some structural testing strategies. IEEE Transactions on Software Engineering 14(6), 868–874 (1988)

10. Beizer, B.: Software Testing Techniques. International Thomson Computer Press (1990)

11. Williams, N., Marre, B., Mouy, P., Muriel, R.: Pathcrawler: Automatic generation of path tests by combining static and dynamic analysis. In: Dal Cin, M., Kaâniche, M., Pataricza, A. (eds.) EDCC 2005. LNCS, vol. 3463, pp. 281–292. Springer, Heidelberg (2005)

12. Godefroid, P., Klarlund, N., Sen, K.: DART: Directed Automated Random Testing. In: Proc. Programming Language Design and Implementation. ACM SIGPLAN Notices, vol. 40, pp. 213–223 (2005)

13. Sen, K., Agha, G.: Cute and JCute: Concolic unit testing and explicit path model-checking tools. In: Ball, T., Jones, R.B. (eds.) CAV 2006. LNCS, vol. 4144, pp. 419–423. Springer, Heidelberg (2006)

14. Gupta, N., Mathur, A.P., Soffa, M.L.: Automated Test Data Generation Using an Iterative Relaxation Method. In: Proc. Symposium on Foundations of Software Engineering, pp. 231–244. ACM Press, New York (1998)

15. Myers, A.C.: JFlow: Practical mostly-static information flow control. In: Proc. Symp. on Principles of Programming Languages, pp. 228–241 (1999)

16. Pottier, F., Simonet, V.: Information flow inference for ML. ACM Trans. on Programming Languages and Systems 25(1), 117–158 (2003)

17. Le Guernic, G.: Automaton-based Confidentiality Monitoring of Concurrent Programs. In: Proc. Computer Security Foundations Symposium (2007)

Large Scale Simulation of Tor:
Modelling a Global Passive Adversary

Gavin O' Gorman and Stephen Blott

Dublin City University
Glasnevin, D9, Dublin, Ireland
{gogorman,sblott}@computing.dcu.ie

Abstract. Implementing global passive adversary attacks on currently
deployed low latency anonymous networks is not feasible. This paper
describes the implementation of a large scale, discrete event based simulation of Tor, using the SSFNet simulator. Several global passive adversary attacks are implemented on a simulated Tor network comprised
of approximately 6000 nodes. The attacks prove to be highly accurate
(80 percent stream correlation rate) for low traffic conditions but significantly less effective on denser, multiplexed links (18 percent success
rate).

1   Introduction

The Internet, specifically TCP/IP, was not designed to provide anonymity. One
solution to this problem is to create an overlay network, that is, a network which
runs on top of an existing TCP/IP network. By abstracting away from IP addresses of hosts, the overlay network allows for the explicit control of the routing
of its messages. This control enables the obfuscation of sender and receiver addresses, and thus offers a degree of anonymity.

An accurate, scalable testbed for implementing new features and measuring
anonymity is required to test theorized attacks against these overlay networks.
Establishing test networks in a lab is a limited option, such a test network could
not scale to current and future deployment sizes. Creating a comprehensive analytical model is difficult given the level of complexity in current overlay networks.

One solution is to use discrete event-based simulation. This is the approach
described in this paper.

- We describe a discrete event-based simulation of a popular low latency
  anonymising network, Tor, using the SSFNet simulator. Our simulation models the Tor routing of HTTP data with circuits, stream multiplexing, proxies,
  routers and exit routers.
- We have implemented several preliminary global passive adversary attacks
  using approximately 4500 HTTP clients, 100 HTTP servers and over 950
  Tor routers.

I. Cervesato (Ed.): ASIAN 2007, LNCS 4846, pp. 48–54, 2007.

Tor. Several anonymous network designs have been developed which attempt to apply mixes to low latency traffic. The most widely-used of these tools is Tor [1], the second generation onion router. The current Tor network contains approximately 900 router nodes with hundreds of thousands of streams transiting the network [2].

The Tor network consists of proxies, onion routers and exit routers. A user runs a Tor proxy on their local machine which offers a SOCKS interface to TCP applications. This Tor proxy begins the process of establishing a circuit through the Tor network of onion routers, to a suitable exit router and finally to the target TCP server. Circuits are established in a telescoping manner. On circuit establishment, the incoming TCP stream is routed over the circuit.

SSFNet. Discrete event-based simulation is used to create an abstract representation of the important elements of a system. Event based simulation allows one to build models of systems and investigate how the system might work under different conditions.

The Scalable Simulation Framework (SSF) [3], has been designed to model large scale simulations. The framework describes an interface for a simulation kernel. This generic kernel can then be built upon to implement varying simulators, of which network simulators are one type.

2 Our Implementation

Apart from some simulation specific techniques for ensuring a linear time execution of events, the simulation code itself is very similar to that of a real application. Three distinct network elements were created, on top of those already provided by the simulation libraries. These network elements are a proxy, a router and an exit router.

2.1 Protocol

The circuit establishment protocol described in the Tor design document [1] is simulated exactly. Encryption is not simulated; for our purposes, there is no need.

Traffic routed through the modeled Tor network is provided by a HTTP traffic generator, SSF.OS.WWW distributed with the SSFNet protocols. Further details of the traffic generator can be found in the appendix of [4].

Data received from the HTTP client is broken into 512-byte cells, labelled with the correct stream ID and sent to the router associated with that stream. Each router passes the data on, until the exit router receives it, recreates the original data, and sends this to the target server.

Several traffic streams may be multiplexed over circuit connections. For example, if the proxy receives a new incoming client connection and chooses as the first router on its path one to which a connection is already available, then that socket is reused. A new stream ID is allocated to the stream, the circuit establishment procedure is followed, and the stream is correctly routed.

2.2   Topology

The network topology used is taken from the SSFNet website. It is an simplification of a US ISP. The topology consists of 24 interconnected autonomous systems (AS), where each AS is composed of a number of sub networks. One proxy, two onion routers and one exit router were added to each of the subnetworks, evenly distributing the nodes throughout the network. This results in 325 proxies, 650 router nodes and 325 exit router nodes in the whole network, approximating the number of onion routers in the currently deployed Tor network. The number of clients per LAN was then set to 5, resulting in a total of 5760 clients.

3   Attacks and Results

We have implemented a number of attacks as discussed in detail below. The results from these attacks allow us to demonstrate the correctness of the Tor simulation, in that the results we observe are very similar to those previously published.

The attacks are performed with an increasing number of clients to model an increase in density of traffic across multiplexed connections. Also, with more traffic, there will be greater delay across the network.

The simulation is run for 1120 seconds. The initial 1000 seconds is to allow for the BGP and OSPF routing to settle. After this 1000 seconds, the HTTP clients begin connecting to the Tor network and to their target server. After 60 seconds, at time 1060, tcpdump output is recorded for another 60 seconds until time 1120, at which point the simulation terminates. The initial 60 seconds is to allow the Tor routers to settle into equilibrium.

3.1   Connection Start Tracking Attack

Connection start tracking was described by Serjantov et. al[5]. It works by tracking the initialization time of a connection as it spans the network. If a stream is seen to enter and then emerge from the network in a certain timeframe, it is possible to associate the two events. As demonstrated by Serjantov et al., the attack requires lone connections to successfully link streams. However, on a busy multiplexed network, connection start and end tracking serves as an effective filter to reduce the number of potential streams.

In our implementation of this attack, we take the time of the first HTTP response packet, add a variable delay (d) to it and compare this time with all recorded Tor streams. As the traffic is multiplexed, it is not possible to determine exactly when traffic streams start and end. Also with the extra delay introduced by more traffic, there is the need for a variable delay value. We perform the attack using values of d ranging from .1 to 2 seconds, increasing in increments of .1s, and with increasing numbers of clients as described above.

As seen in Fig. 1(a), the initial start and end tracking filter eliminates a high percentage of streams, up to 98% on the sparse traffic network and 96% on the densest network.

3.2   Packet Counting Attack

A packet counting attack introduced in [6] and further expounded in [5] consists
of counting the number of packets entering a node and subsequently leaving
a node for a given time interval. By comparing the number of packets for a
particular stream entering a node with the number of packets leaving the node
it can be possible to determine to which node/link the packets from that stream
are being sent.

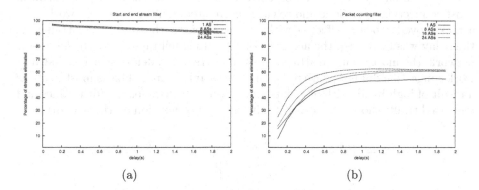

(a)   (b)

Fig. 1. Start connection tracking and packet counting filters

The same method of varying the d value is used as above, but the streams
being analyzed are those that have previously been filtered by the start and end
time attack. Figure 1(b) shows that the 2% to 4% of streams left by the start
and end time attack are further reduced by approximately 5% to 15% with the
packet counting attack.

3.3   Stream Correlation Attack

Fixed Time Window. Traffic correlation attacks were proposed and implemented in [7]. The technique is to set a windows size W and count the number
of packets received, beginning at time t, during that window size. This process is
repeated for the duration of the stream. The sequence of packet counts can then
be compared with the sequences from other streams in the network. The cross
correlation coefficient function used to compare these sequences is below [7]:

$$r(d) = \frac{\sum_i((x_i - \mu)(x'_{i+d} - \mu'))}{\sqrt{\sum_i(x_i - \mu)^2}\sqrt{\sum_i(x'_{i+d} - \mu')^2}}$$

The two streams being compared are x and x' with d being the delay value. x_i
is the ith packet count of stream x and x'_i is the ith packet count of stream x'. μ
is the average of packet counts in stream x and μ' is the average of packet counts
in stream x'. The more the result tends towards 1, the greater the similarity of

the streams. This same correlation function was also used in [8,9] for end to end traffic confirmation.

Some minor modifications to the attack are needed. The first is that the Tor protocol breaks the HTTP data into 512 byte cells. As such, the number of packets being sent from the HTTP server is not the same as the number of packets received at the Tor proxy. Allowing for this is straightforward.

For the fixed interval attack, a time window of 1s is used, as recommended by Shmatikov & Wang [8]. The fixed time interval attack is highly effective, Fig, 2, with approximately 80% of streams correctly identified on the low traffic network. Most connections were lone and so easily correlated. On the denser networks, the attack proved to be less effective with the extra noise of the multiplexed traffic. As the delay was increased, the accuracy of the attack fell rapidly. With the denser network, the most accurate attacks are still at .1s delay, demonstrating that network congestion did not prove to be an issue as anticipated. This is most likely as a result of high bandwidth of clients and servers. Realistic bandwidth values and increased traffic should demonstrate the effect of congestion on the network.

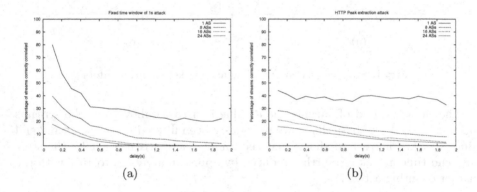

(a)   (b)

Fig. 2. Success rate of correlation attacks

Peak Extraction. An alternative to using a fixed time interval is to break each stream into fixed fractions, count the number of packets observed in these fractions and correlate them with the function above. The values for these fractions can be determined by examining the HTTP stream. HTTP traffic is bursty. A certain web page will contain a number of objects, each of which is downloaded individually and can be observed as a burst of traffic, or a peak, across the connection. We obtain ratios for each peak termination. These ratios can then be applied to the Tor stream. Allowing for the delay d the corresponding packet counts should be equal.

The results of the peak extraction attack are presented in Fig. 2(b). The attack is not as effective as the fixed window of 1s attack, however it is slightly more robust when inaccurate delay values are used. The percentage of streams successfully identified decreases at a lower rate than the fixed interval attack. The success rate surpasses the fixed interval attack for larger delay values.

4   Related Work

Initial analytical work [10], using traffic matrices, provided metrics for measuring the effort required to thwart stream correlation attacks. This work was extended, using entropy to measure anonymity [11]. Real traffic measurements are taken from a campus network, however no attacks are described.

Later work by Levine et al. [7] describes global passive adversary attacks for stream correlation. The technique used is described in the results section. The Levine et al. attacks do not account for the multiplexing of traffic streams. The cross correlation coefficient was later utilized by Bissias et al. [9] to correlate encrypted HTTP streams.

Shmatikov & Wang [8] extend the original attack of Levine et al. by proposing and testing a new defense. This defense, adaptive padding, involves applying padding to ensure that streams are indistinguishable from each other. As with Levine et al. the attacks are performed on links with non-multiplexed streams. Also, as is pointed out in the paper, stream times are also not taken into account, whereas in our attacks, we filter results by checking start and end time.

Zhu et al. [12] use mutual information and frequency analysis (wavelets/FFT) to correlate TCP traffic streams. In ongoing experimental work, we have applied frequency analysis to HTTP streams generated by the simulation. As yet, the accuracy of the method appears quite low as the bursty nature of HTTP traffic does not lend itself to frequency analysis.

In terms of scale, Bauer et al. [13] have implemented perhaps the most ambitious attacks to date, using approximately 60 Tor nodes distributed across the globe in a test network. Our simulation in contrast utilise approximately 6000 nodes.

5   Future Work

Our initial work on TCP stream analysis, using wavelets and Fourier transforms shows promise. We intend developing these attacks in conjunction with more realistic topologies. Additional work to verify the fidelity of the simulation to the real Tor client will consist of packet count and timing analysis on small scale networks.

Beyond that, we intend measuring the average delay for streams crossing the network and introducing delay to the Tor nodes. We can measure the impact this has on the network in terms of Quality of Service and effectiveness against stream correlation. The overall goal is to determine the optimal compromise between latency and anonymity for anonymous networks.

6   Conclusion

We have developed an initial Tor simulation. We have begun verification the simulation with the implementation of previously discussed attacks and obtained expected results. The simulation needs to be extended to replicate the traffic control techniques Tor utilises. Given that, we will be able to reliably measure quality of service across the network. This, in combination with the attacks presented will allow us to quantify the compromise between latency and annonymity for a given network configuration.

The ability to test and implement new features on the Tor simulation will, we believe, prove to be invaluable for the Tor developers and future researchers.

References

1. Dingledine, R., Mathewson, N., Syverson, P.: Tor: The second-generation onion router. In: Proceedings of the 13th USENIX Security Symposium (August 2004)
2. Developers, T.: Tor website (June 2007), http://tor.eff.org
3. Cowie, J., Liu, H.: Towards realistic million-node internet simulations. In: Proceedings of the 1999 International Conference on Parallel and Distributed Processing Techniques and Applications (1999)
4. Feldmann, A., Gilbert, A., Huang, P., Willinger, W.: Dynamics of IP traffic: A study of the role of variability and the impact of control. In: Proceedings of ACM SIGCOMM 1999, pp. 301–313. ACM Press, New York (1999)
5. Serjantov, A., Sewell, P.: Passive attack analysis for connection-based anonymity systems. In: Snekkenes, E., Gollmann, D. (eds.) ESORICS 2003. LNCS, vol. 2808, Springer, Heidelberg (2003)
6. Back, A., Möller, U., Stiglic, A.: Traffic analysis attacks and trade-offs in anonymity providing systems. In: Moskowitz, I.S. (ed.) Proceedings of Information Hiding Workshop (IH 2001). LNCS, vol. 2137, pp. 245–257. Springer, Heidelberg (2001)
7. Levine, B.N., Reiter, M.K., Wang, C., Wright, M.K.: Timing attacks in low-latency mix-based systems. In: Juels, A. (ed.) FC 2004. LNCS, vol. 3110, Springer, Heidelberg (2004)
8. Shmatikov, V., Wang, M.-H.: Timing analysis in low-latency mix networks: Attacks and defenses. In: Gollmann, D., Meier, J., Sabelfeld, A. (eds.) ESORICS 2006. LNCS, vol. 4189, Springer, Heidelberg (2006)
9. Bissias, G.D., Liberatore, M., Levine, B.N.: Privacy vulnerabilities in encrypted http streams. In: Danezis, G., Martin, D. (eds.) PET 2005. LNCS, vol. 3856, Springer, Heidelberg (2006)
10. Venkatraman, B., Newman-Wolfe, R.: Performance analysis of a method for high level prevention of traffic analysis using measurements from a campus network. Computer Security Applications Conference, Proceedings, 10th Annual (1994) 288–297 (1994)
11. Newman, R.E., Moskowitz, I.S., Syverson, P., Serjantov, A.: Metrics for traffic analysis prevention. In: Dingledine, R. (ed.) PET 2003. LNCS, vol. 2760, Springer, Heidelberg (2003)
12. Zhu, Y., Fu, X., Graham, B., Bettati, R., Zhao, W.: On flow correlation attacks and countermeasures in mix networks. In: Martin, D., Serjantov, A. (eds.) PET 2004. LNCS, vol. 3424, Springer, Heidelberg (2005)
13. Bauer, K., McCoy, D., Grunwald, D., Kohno, T., Sicker, D.: Low-Resource Routing Attacks Against Anonymous Systems. Technical Report CU-CS-1025-07, University of Colorado at Boulder (2007)

Privacy Enhancing Credentials

Junji Nakazato, Lihua Wang, and Akihiro Yamamura

National Institute of Information and Communications Technology
4-2-1, Nukui-Kitamachi, Koganei, Tokyo 184-8795, Japan
{nakazato, wlh, aki}@nict.go.jp

Abstract. Using pairing techniques, we propose an anonymous authenticated key exchange scheme based on credentials issued by a trusted third party. The protocol satisfies several security properties related to user privacy such as unforgeability, limitability, non-transferability, and unlinkability.

1 Introduction

Privacy issues have arisen because many users are becoming increasingly more concerned about how their sensitive information will be used. Current technology in electronic services such as e-commerce, e-business, and e-government allows service providers to easily track individual's actions, behaviors, and habits. The information (or data) obtained in the transactions may be sold for business purposes even though the users may not want this to be done. Therefore, they would like to conceal personal information related to their identity as much as possible. In this paper, we propose a new technique to solve privacy issues arising from open-network transactions. Such a scheme could have many applications. For example, potential applications could be for users to secure video rentals on demand or use single sign-on tickets. Video-on-demand systems allow them to select and watch videos over a network possibly as part of an interactive television system. For users to use such a systems, an access control should be implemented by service providers to verify their eligibility to watch these videos or request services. Thus, their identity may be exposed when a request reaches the service provider. Also, videos that users choose reflect taste and characteristics, matters that they want to keep confidential. Likewise, tickets to request service providers to provide services using a single sign-on scheme could leak user histories of what services they have requested. In either cases, users are exposed to threats where their sensitive information may be disclosed to undesirable entities.

There are two possible solutions. The first is to use oblivious transfer or private information retrieval to conceal which video a user has asked to watch. He/She can covertly ask the service provider to provide his/her request; however, this method does not address privacy issues in single sign-on schemes. The second is anonymize the request made by the user to the service provider. In this scenario, as the request received by the service provider is anonymous, the service provider may not necessarily have the means to determine whether the request is valid because the user cannot be traced back using the transmitted

I. Cervesato (Ed.): ASIAN 2007, LNCS 4846, pp. 55–61, 2007.

Table 1. Functions and requirements

		previous [4]	proposed
Functions	Credential Systems	Yes	Yes
	Flexibility of content[1]	Yes	No
	Authenticated key exchange	No	Yes
Requirements	Unforgeability	Yes	Yes
	Limitability	Yes	Yes
	Non-transferability[2]	No	Yes
	Anonymity	No	Yes
	Unlinkability	No	Yes

[1] Ng, Susilo, and Mu's scheme [4] can include any data in the credential, but our proposed protocol only contains data to share the key.

[2] Non-transferability means no party can transfer valid data to another. Consequently, it is different from Ng, Susilo, and Mu's [4].

request. This can be accomplished if a trusted third party issues a valid credential that enables the user to obtain the service from the provider anonymously without disclosing his/her identity. An anonymous credential system is an effective solution that can satisfy these properties. Organizations issue credentials to users for different organizations. Each organization knows user only by different pseudonyms respectively. Users can convince different organizations of only the fact that they have such credentials without revealing any information of the users (*anonymity*). Moreover, even if a user uses such a credential of multiple times, it cannot be linked to each other (*unlinkability*).

We report our current study of a scheme where a user and a service provider can establish an authenticated and secure channel after the protocol using a privacy enhanced credential in such a way that the scheme attains anonymity, unlinkability, unforgeability, limitability, and non-transferability.

The efficient anonymous credential proposed by J. Camenisch and A. Lysyanskaya is based on strong RSA assumption and Decision Diffie-Hellman (DDH) assumptions [2]. Our proposed scheme is similar to the one introduced by Ng, Susilo, and Mu [4]. Our proposed scheme achieves non-transferable anonymous credentials using a pairing technique on the elliptic curves over finite fields. Table 1 compares the functionalities and the security properties of their scheme with ours. We found that Ng, Susilo, and Mu's scheme could be tailored to fit such security requirements using different methods.

2   Proposed Scheme

2.1   Description of Proposed Scheme

We define participants in the proposed scheme as: an *authority*, a *user*, a *server* (or a *signer*), and *verifiers* (or *services*) satisfying the following properties:

Authority (A): provides system parameters and public/private key pairs. It distributes these securely to all participants in the protocol. After that, A will not take part in the protocol.

User (U): wants to receive services from two or more specific V_j's. First, U sends a request to S, and receives a credential through a secure channel. When U wants to obtain a service, she/he sends a ticket that is generated from the valid credential designated to V_j by S.

Server (S): issues a credential to U for her/him to use the service provided by the designated V_j. S is a trusted third party.

Verifiers (V_j ($j = 1, \ldots, n$)): check whether or not the ticket is valid. If so, V_j performs the protocol to exchange keys with U to establish an authenticated and secure channel, otherwise V_j does not.

We assumed the protocol flow between U and A would be carried out through secure channels and no adversaries could obtain any information. However, the protocol is carried out using an insecure channel when U sends a ticket to any V_j because the user is anonymous to V_j and therefore an authenticated channel cannot be employed for this purpose. Thus, any adversary can obtain information at this stage of the protocol.

2.2 Security Requirements

A malicious user may try to access to V_j, i.e., gain access that is not allowed. V_j should be able to detect these invalid attempts at access. At the same time, the protocol must protect the privacy of the user, even if V_j colludes with other V_i's. Therefore, our proposed scheme must at least satisfy *unforgeability, limitability, non-transferability*, and *unlinkability*.

Unforgeability: Nobody can forge a valid credential to generate a valid ticket with V_j without collaboration with S.

Limitability: U who was issued a valid credential by S can generate a ticket to V_j that is designated by S in the credential; U cannot forge a valid credential to generate a ticket to V_i that is not designated by S, even if he/she has been given some legitimate credential for V_j.

Non-transferability: There are two cases that should be considered:
1. V_j who received the ticket from U cannot forge it a ticket to a ticket to any other V_i.
2. U who was issued a valid credential by S cannot transfer it to any other U' to generate a valid ticket without leaking U's secret keys.

Unlinkability: U may use a credential issued by S to generate tickets to several verifier V_j's. No one can determine whether two tickets σ_1 and σ_2 have been generated by U. Even if V_1 colludes with V_2, no efficient algorithm exists to find the correlation between tickets sent to V_1 and V_2.

2.3 Bilinear Pairings and Complexity Assumption

The proposed scheme is based on *pairings*. A pairing is derived from either a modified Weil or Tate pairing on a supersingular elliptic curve or an abelian variety over a finite field (see [1,3] for further details). Let us briefly review the terminology and symbols that are used in the proposed scheme.

Let $\mathbb{G}_1$ denote an additive group of some large prime order q and $\mathbb{G}_2$ denote a multiplicative group also of order q. Let P denote a generator of $\mathbb{G}_1$. A map, $\hat{e} : \mathbb{G}_1 \times \mathbb{G}_1 \rightarrow \mathbb{G}_2$, is said to be an admissible bilinear pairing if the following properties hold:

1. Bilinear: Given any $Q, R \in \mathbb{G}_1$ and $a, b \in \mathbb{Z}_q$, we have $\hat{e}(aQ, bR) = \hat{e}(Q, R)^{ab}$.
2. Non-degenerate: $\hat{e}(P, P) \neq 1_{\mathbb{G}_2}$.
3. Computable: There is an efficient algorithm to compute $\hat{e}(Q, R)$ for any $Q, R \in \mathbb{G}_1$.

The following three problems have been assumed to be intractable for any polynomial time algorithm.

Discrete Logarithm Problem: Given $P, aP \in \mathbb{G}_1$, find $a \in \mathbb{Z}_q^*$.

Computational Diffie-Hellman (CDH) Problem [1]: Given $P, aP, bP \in \mathbb{G}_1$, find $abP \in \mathbb{G}_1$.

Bilinear Diffie-Hellman (BDH) Problem [1]: Given $P, aP, bP, cP \in \mathbb{G}_1$, find $\hat{e}(P, P)^{abc} \in \mathbb{G}_2$.

2.4   Privacy Enhancing Designated Credentials

System parameters $params = (\mathbb{G}_1, \mathbb{G}_2, q, \hat{e}, P, Q, F, \mathsf{H}(\cdot))$. P, Q, and F are non-trivial elements of $\mathbb{G}_1$ and let $\mathsf{H}(\cdot)$ be a hash function of $\{0,1\}^* \rightarrow \mathbb{G}_1$.

Key generation. The public/secret key pairs of S, U, and V_j are defined to be $(x_\mathsf{S}, R_\mathsf{S})$, $(x_\mathsf{U}, R_\mathsf{U})$, and (x_j, R_j) $(j = 1, \ldots, n)$, respectively, where $R_\mathsf{S} = x_\mathsf{S}P, R_\mathsf{U} = x_\mathsf{U}P, R_j = x_jP$. The secret keys x_S, x_U, and x_j $(j = 1, \ldots, n)$ are selected randomly from $\mathbb{Z}_q^*$, and the public keys are elements of group $\mathbb{G}_1$.

2.5   Basic Protocol

Verifiers in the basic protocol are designated by S. S knows all the verifier V_i's that U can access. In addition, the data have no time restrictions. They can be used as many times as wishes. Because this paper reports work in progress, we will only discuss the basic protocol. There are other schemes where U can specify verifier V_i's and schemes with time restrictions, i.e., the credential becomes invalid after a certain period. We should note that authentication between U and S is done by some other means not provided by the proposed scheme.

Request credential: Assume that user U would like to access V_i $(i \in I$, where $I \subseteq \{1, \ldots, n\})$. User U computes $X = x_\mathsf{U}Q$ and sends it together with U's identity as a request to S.

Receiving the request, S checks whether the secret information, x_U, is included in the request, $\hat{e}(X, P) \stackrel{?}{=} \hat{e}(Q, R_\mathsf{U})$. If no attempt at fraud is found, then S proceeds to issue a credential. It chooses b uniformly and randomly from $\mathbb{Z}_q^*$, and computes $Y_1 = b^{-1}x_\mathsf{S}(X + F)$ and $Y_2 = bP$. Then, S designates verifier list $I \subseteq \{1, \ldots, n\}$, and computes $W_i = bR_i$ $(i \in I)$. Finally, S sets $S = (Y_1, Y_2, W_i)$ and sends the credential (S, I) to U.

$$\begin{array}{ll} \text{U} & \text{S} \end{array}$$

U		S

$X = x_\mathsf{U} Q$
$$\xrightarrow{\quad (X, \mathsf{U}) \quad}$$

$\hat{e}(X, P) \overset{?}{=} \hat{e}(Q, R_\mathsf{U})$
$I \subseteq \{1, \ldots, n\}$
$b \in_R \mathbb{Z}_q^*$
$Y_1 = b^{-1} x_\mathsf{S} (X + F)$
$Y_2 = bP, W_i = bR_i \ (i \in I)$
$S = (Y_1, Y_2, W_i)$

$$\xleftarrow{\quad (S, I) \quad}$$

$\hat{e}(Y_1, Y_2) \overset{?}{=} \hat{e}(X + F, R_\mathsf{S})$
$\hat{e}(W_i, P) \overset{?}{=} \hat{e}(R_i, Y_2) \ (i \in I)$

$\quad\quad\quad\quad\quad\quad\quad\quad V_i$

$c_1, c_2 \in_R \mathbb{Z}_q^*$
$\sigma_i = \hat{e}(Y_1, W_i)^{c_1 c_2}$
$M = c_1 c_2 X$
$A_1 = c_1 F$
$A_2 = c_2 R_\mathsf{S}$
$B_1 = c_1 \mathsf{H}(seed)$
$B_2 = c_2 \mathsf{H}(seed)$

$$\xrightarrow{\quad (\sigma_i, M, A_1, A_2, \; B_1, B_2, seed) \quad}$$

$(\hat{e}(M, R_\mathsf{S}) \hat{e}(A_1, A_2))^{x_i} \overset{?}{=} \sigma_i$
$\hat{e}(A_1, \mathsf{H}(seed)) \overset{?}{=} \hat{e}(F, B_1)$
$\hat{e}(A_2, \mathsf{H}(seed)) \overset{?}{=} \hat{e}(R_\mathsf{S}, B_2)$
$d \in_R \mathbb{Z}_q^*$
$T_1 = (x_i + d)^{-1} Q, \; T_2 = dP$

$$\xleftarrow{\quad (T_1, T_2) \quad}$$

$\hat{e}(T_1, T_2 + R_i) \overset{?}{=} \hat{e}(Q, P)$
$K' = KDF(c_1 c_2 x_\mathsf{U} T_1)$
$\quad\quad\quad\quad\quad\quad\quad\quad\quad K = KDF((x_i + d)^{-1} M)$

Fig. 1. Proposed protocol

User U verifies the received credential as $\hat{e}(Y_1, Y_2) \overset{?}{=} \hat{e}(X + F, R_\mathsf{S})$, $\hat{e}(W_i, P) \overset{?}{=} \hat{e}(R_i, Y_2)$.

Request for service: Assume that U would like to ask for service V_i, where i belongs to I. Then U chooses c_1, c_2 uniformly and randomly from $\mathbb{Z}_q^*$, and computes $\sigma_i = \hat{e}(Y_1, W_i)^{c_1 c_2}$, $M = c_1 c_2 X$, $A_1 = c_1 F$, $A_2 = c_2 R_\mathsf{S}$, $B_1 = c_1 \mathsf{H}(seed)$, and $B_2 = c_2 \mathsf{H}(seed)$. Whenever asking for a service, $\mathsf{H}(seed)$ makes a fresh generator from a random value to satisfy the non-transferability by U.

The validated ticket $(\sigma_i, M, A_1, A_2, B_1, B_2, seed)$ is sent to verifier V_i which checks whether the ticket has been correctly generated using a credential issued by S.

$$(\hat{e}(M, R_\mathsf{S}) \hat{e}(A_1, A_2))^{x_i} \overset{?}{=} \sigma_i \tag{2.1}$$

$$\hat{e}(A_1, \mathsf{H}(seed)) \overset{?}{=} \hat{e}(F, B_1) \tag{2.2}$$

$$\hat{e}(A_2, \mathsf{H}(seed)) \overset{?}{=} \hat{e}(R_\mathsf{S}, B_2). \tag{2.3}$$

If no frauds are found, V_i then computes a session key.

Key exchange: V_i chooses d uniformly and randomly from $\mathbb{Z}_q^*$, and computes $T_1 = (x_i + d)^{-1}Q$, $T_2 = dP$, and $K = KDF((x_i + d)^{-1}M)$, where KDF is a key derivation function such as the KDF1 defined in IEEE Standard 1363-2000.

Then, data T_1 and T_2 are sent to U, and U checks the validity, $\hat{e}(T_1, T_2 + R_i) \overset{?}{=} \hat{e}(Q, P))$. If no frauds are found, U then computes session key $K' = KDF(c_1 c_2 x_U T_1)$. If the protocol is carried out correctly, we have $K = K'$ and this will be used as the secret key between U and V_i. The flow for the protocol is shown in Fig. 1.

3   Security

Unforgeability. Forging a valid ticket may be attempted by many entities other than the targeted verifier (say V_1). Here, we will discuss unforgeability of the scheme by a legitimate user (say U).

If V_1 accepts the data $(\sigma_1, M, A_1, A_2, B_1, B_2, seed)$ and U can generate the same session key with V_1, the forging attack succeeds. If there are no polynomial time algorithms forging a valid ticket succeeding with non-negligible probability, then the scheme is secure.

Clearly, under the CDH assumption, to obtain session key $K' = K = (x_1 + d)^{-1}M$ using the given $T_1 = (x_1 + d)^{-1}Q$, data M must have the form $M = yQ$ for some known $y \in \mathbb{Z}_q^*$. However, note that to pass verification equations (2.2) and (2.3), data (A_1, A_2) must have the form $A_1 = c_1 F$ and $A_2 = c_2 R_S$, for some known $c_1, c_2 \in \mathbb{Z}_q^*$. Now substitute $M = yQ$, $A_1 = c_1 F$, $A_2 = c_2 R_S$ into verification equation (2.1), then the left-hand side is $(\hat{e}(M, R_S)\hat{e}(A_1, A_2))^{x_i} = (\hat{e}(yQ + c_1 c_2 F, R_s))^{x_i}$. Note that $yQ + c_1 c_2 F = zP$ for some $z \in \mathbb{Z}_q^*$ because $yQ + c_1 c_2 F$ is an element of $\mathbb{G}_1$. However, finding parameter z is a discrete logarithm problem to U. Accordingly, to forge a valid σ_1, U has to solve the BDH problem, i.e., given $\langle P, zP, R_1 = x_1 P, R_S = x_S P \rangle$, to compute $\hat{e}(P, P)^{zx_S x_1}$. According to the complexity assumption, there are no polynomial time algorithms to solve the BDH problem. Therefore our scheme satisfies the Unforgeability.

Limitability. User U may request and obtain a credential from S. Then, U may want to forge the valid credential issued by S. Here, we are assuming that V_1 has not been designated in the credential issued by S.
U has the information, $R_S, R_j (j \in \{1, \ldots, n\})$; x_U ; $Y_1, Y_2, W_i (i \in I, i \neq 1)$, apart from public parameters $P, Q, F \in \mathbb{G}_1$. Then, U would like to forge $(\sigma_1, M, A_1, A_2, B_1, B_2, seed)$. In detail, using the data $\langle Y_1, W_i (i \in I, i \neq 1) \rangle$ issued by S, U can compute $\sigma_i^0 = \hat{e}(Y_1, W_i) = \hat{e}(x_U Q, R_S)^{x_i} \hat{e}(F, R_S)^{x_i}$.

Both $\hat{e}(x_U Q, R_S)^{x_i}$ and $\hat{e}(F, R_S)^{x_i}$ are BDH problems for user U. Therefore, σ_i^0 cannot be split. In fact, $\sigma_i^0 = \hat{e}(x_U Q + F, R_S)^{x_i} = (\hat{e}(P, P)^{wx_S})^{x_i}$ for some unknown $w \in \mathbb{Z}_q^*$. Let $g = \hat{e}(P, P)^{wx_S} = \hat{e}(X + F, R_S) \in \mathbb{G}_2$; this then implies that U has found g^{x_1} using the given g^{x_i} where $i \in I, i \neq 1$, which is a discrete logarithm problem in $\mathbb{G}_2$. Our scheme satisfies limitability according to the complexity assumption described in Section 2.3.

Non-transferability. The proof has been omitted due to limited space. The main point (e.g., case 2) is that, to successfully transfer the credential to another party (say, Tom) the transferred data must have passed verification and Tom can generate the same session key with V_i. According to the analysis of unforgeability, as Tom must know the value of $x_U c_1 c_2$, where he has selected c_1 and c_2 himself, U has to reveal his/her secret key x_U to Tom.

Unlinkability. Unlinkability will be proved under the decisional bilinear Diffie-Hellman (DBDH) assumption [5] in the full version of this paper. Note that unlinkability implies anonymity. That is to say, our scheme also satisfies anonymity.

4   Discussion

The contribution of our anonymous authenticated key exchange scheme can be summarized as follows. The basic protocol achieves **anonymous authenticated key exchange**, i.e., S issues the credential for U to share the key with V anonymously, i.e., U can share a secret key with V anonymously and securely; U does not necessarily leak any of her/his identity information to V but V can authenticate U.

We did not discuss additional properties of **hidden verifiers** or **time restrictions** and these properties will be fully discussed in the full version of the paper. The first implies that the proposed protocol can convert an open verifier to a hidden verifier for S; when U requests a credential of V, U chooses some services, and sends these to S with a random value to hide service. The second implies that the proposed protocol can attach time restrictions function easily; it only need changes generator F of the protocol into $H(t)$, where t is the time information.

References

1. Boneh, D., Franklin, M.: Identity-based Encryption from the Weil Pairing. In: Kilian, J. (ed.) CRYPTO 2001. LNCS, vol. 2139, pp. 213–229. Springer, Heidelberg (2001)
2. Camenisch, J., Lysyanskaya, A.: An Efficient System for Non-transferable Anonymous Credentials with Optional Anonymity Revocation. In: Pfitzmann, B. (ed.) EUROCRYPT 2001. LNCS, vol. 2045, pp. 93–118. Springer, Heidelberg (2001)
3. Joux, A.: The Weil and Tate Pairings as Building Blocks for Public Key Cryptosystems. In: Fieker, C., Kohel, D.R. (eds.) Algorithmic Number Theory. LNCS, vol. 2369, pp. 20–32. Springer, Heidelberg (2002)
4. Ng, C.Y., Susilo, W., Mu, Y.: Designated Group Credentials. In: Proc. of ASIACCS 2006, pp. 59–65 (2006)
5. Waters, B.: Efficient Identity-Based Encryption Without Random Oracles. In: Cramer, R.J.F. (ed.) EUROCRYPT 2005. LNCS, vol. 3494, pp. 114–127. Springer, Heidelberg (2005)

Browser Based Agile E-Voting System

Sriperumbuduru Kandala Simhalu and Keiji Takeda

Carnegie Mellon Cylab, Japan
{eskay,tkeiji}@cmu.edu

Abstract. In the recent past, in spite of several real world implementations available for Internet [browser-based] e-voting, there seems to be a pattern emerging, one of apathy towards improving voter convenience / participation. The goal of the proposed system evolves from the premise that, there should be a priority shift towards addressing the needs of the Voter, hence, most of the other requirements of this system, such as Security, Anonymity, Universal Verifiability, Individual Verifiability, Receipt-Freeness and Fairness are a direct by-product of this goal. In order to secure a higher voter participation, the proposed system considers the trade-offs between strict adherence to essential properties and practicality / user-convenience. To further secure the voter confidence/trust, a practical approach to Individual Verifiability has been implemented, without compromising the Receipt-Freeness property. So, with such flexibility and consumer-oriented approach, it is but evident that Agility is the hallmark of this project.

Keywords: E-Voting; Anonymity, Individual Verifiability, Agile Voting.

1 Introduction

Internet-based E-Voting has been a topic of intense discussion worldwide in the recent past [1,2,3]. There have been efforts made, both in the academia and the industry to research ways of implementing secure, practical and scalable e-voting systems.

This paper is yet another effort to provide a practical, voter-friendly e-voting system. The motivation behind this paper is to provide self-organized groups, along the lines of the Agile team model[5], with the ability to conduct frequent and practical browser-based polling on myriad topics. In order to meet the requirements of such a practical system, a browser-based system would seem appropriate, given the potential of such an application, in terms of its reach and ubiquity. Practicality forms the foundation stone for formulation of the requirements and subsequently the implementation of this system. One of the reasons for taking up this approach is to increase the voter participation. It has been found that the voter turnout over the last 40 years has been declining[6], which is definitely not desirable for the free world.

2 Browser-Based E-Voting System

There are currently a considerable number of implementations of Internet based e-voting systems[2,3,4,7,8,9,10,11,12,15,16,17,18]. However, only browser based,

I. Cervesato (Ed.): ASIAN 2007, LNCS 4846, pp. 62–69, 2007.

open-source e-voting systems would be considered in this paper. As this paper's primary focus is voter convenience/participation, so, a browser-based system would be appropriate, as it increases the reach. As for open-source systems, the voters can get them evaluated by an expert. A comprehensive study on e-voting schemes is beyond the scope of this paper, however one can find an informative study on electronic voting schemes done by Poovendran et al.[13].

2.1 Existing Browser-Based Open-Source E-Voting Systems

This section deals with the existing browser-based open-source systems. The respective systems are described briefly in terms of features they exhibit. The below mentioned systems were the high-profile ones, as most of them are products coming out of well-acclaimed universities or governments.

2.1.1 Adder
Adder is an homomorphic-based remote Internet voting system[4]. As per[4], it adheres, "to the following design goals:Transparency, Universal Verifiability, Privacy, Distributed Trust. Each procedure is "supervised" by multiple authorities, and the final sum cannot be revealed without the cooperation of a given number of authorities. Any attempt to undermine the procedure will require the corruption of a large number of authorities. Authorities and voters may overlap arbitrarily. Thus, it is possible for the voters themselves to ensure trustworthiness (or have an active role in it)."

2.1.2 Condorcet Internet Voting Service (CIVS)
As per [14], "CIVS is a web-based free Internet voting service that makes it easy to conduct elections and polls on the Web. Each voter ranks a set of possible choices. Combined, these rankings are used to construct an overall ranking that anonymously summarizes the opinions of all voters. "

2.1.3 KOA
As per [8,19,20],"KOA stands for *Kiezen Op Afstand* and denotes an experiment in voting over the Internet conducted by the Dutch government. The experiment was specifically conducted for the European elections in June 2004."

"The KOA system may well be the first Free Software Internet voting system developed for, used by, and subsequently released by a government in the world."

2.2 An Overview of the Proposed System

The system has two distinct roles, the Poll Initiator and the Poll Invitee. The Poll Initiator is responsible for most of the administrative work that goes into the making of a poll, such as creating groups, creating polls and sending ballots to Poll Invitees via e-mail. The Poll Invitee has to click on the link provided to him/her through e-mail in order to vote / authenticate and verify results. Figure(s) 1 and 2, depict the interactions between the Poll Initiator/Poll Invitee and the various system components. The proposed system has two major focus areas, voter participation and Individual Verifiability. The previous related work [27,28,29] which involves the selection of

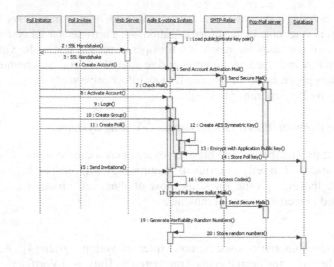

Fig. 1. Poll Initiator Interactions

random numbers apart from the core candidate selection process, either do not provide Individual Verifiability, or they do provide but without maintaining the Receipt-Freeness property. Another related work at MIT[30], has been shown to have serious privacy and security issues[31].

3 *Agile* E-Voting

Below are the properties of the proposed system, and the description of how each of them satisfies the primary requirements of voter participation/convenience.

Security: There are several measures taken to ensure security of the proposed system. First of all, the communication channel between the voter's browser and the server is secured using Secure Socket Layer/Transport Layer Security(SSL/TLS)[21]. Hence, the HTTP traffic from/to the voter to/from the server is now secured. This helps to gain the voters' confidence in the system, as eavesdropping, and to an extent man-in-the middle attack[22,23] can be ruled out. Secondly, the system uses a combination of symmetric key[24] and public key infrastructure[25], to make sure that the vote cast, cannot be tampered with, by adversaries. For each Poll created, an AES[26] key is generated, and the votes cast for that poll are encrypted using the AES key and stored against that poll. This AES key is itself encrypted using the application/owner's public key, and again stored against the poll. So, the vote data stored is secured, as it is now in encrypted form.

Anonymity: In order to overcome the privacy issues, the voter is provided with a unique randomized token for a particular poll that s/he is part of. So, this offers a first level of anonymity, as the voter now is not bound to his/her identity. So, his/her eligibility to vote is only recognized by the random token provided to him/her.

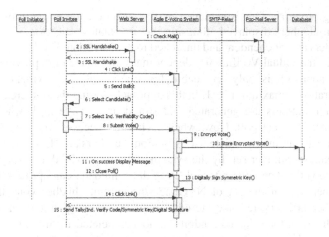

Fig. 2. Poll Invitee Interactions

A Second level of Anonymity is created when the voter uses this token to vote. The final vote is encrypted and stored against the poll, and not against the random token. This provides another layer of anonymity, as now, the encrypted vote cannot be traced back to any particular voter, even if the random token from the e-mail sent to the voter, gets compromised. The design created to implement this requirement would not only allow Anonymity as discussed above, but also would provide the voter with convenient ways to help his/her participation. The token distribution is done using email. The Poll Initiator would send a mail to the voter with a link that would have the token embedded within that link. So, all that the voter has to do, is click that link in order to cast vote. As the vote is cast, it is encrypted and stored against the Poll.

Universal Verifiability: As all of the voters have to check if only valid votes were cast, and no invalid voters were counted, so, during the tally phase, the poll invitee list and the votes cast have to be displayed for verification. Now, this needs to be done while keeping the anonymity property intact. The system design separates the random voter-token storage, and the storage of the vote cast by the voter. Additionally, during the tally phase, the system displays all the encrypted votes, along with the AES symmetric key for that particular Poll with which the votes were encrypted. Also, the digital signature of the symmetric key, signed by the public key of the application/owner is displayed along with the public key itself. Apart from this, the random tokens eligible for the particular poll along with the vote cast status is also displayed. So, this helps the voters to completely verify the polling process for that particular poll.

Individual Verifiability: This property has been the most controversial and difficult one to implement. None of the existing browser-based open-source systems implement this property successfully. However, others such as, Sensus[18] provide Individual Verifiability but at the cost of Receipt-Freeness. Compromising the property of Receipt-freeness would lead to vote buying, as now the voter has a receipt that would identify his/her vote. The proposed system is perhaps the only known browser-based open-source system that provides Individual Verifiability without compromising any other e-voting property. This is achieved by the system using an additional(optional) set of random numbers displayed alongside the candidates' selection area. The set of random numbers are independent and unrelated to the candidate list. Here, we have two approaches for Individual Verifiability depending on the scale of deployment.

The First approach is only applicable for small scale deployment, say with a voter-to-poll ratio of maximum 20:1. In this approach, during the poll creation, $(2 * N)$ unique random numbers are generated and stored against the poll, where N is the number of voters for that poll. Now, when each voter accesses the system using the token, then along with the candidate list, N random numbers are chosen randomly from the $(2 * N)$ random number set, by the system, and are provided as a single selection input set to the voter. The voter after selecting the candidate, can opt for choosing one random number, out of the set of N. Once s/he submits his/her vote, the selected random number is encrypted and stored alongside the encrypted vote, against that particular poll. Also, the selected random number is deleted from the $(2 * N)$ set, for that particular poll. Hence, for the next voter to poll, the set of N random numbers would come from[$(2 * N) - 1$], the subsequent voter would get his/her N random numbers from $[(2 * N) - 2]$, and the last voter, would get it from the set of $[(2 * N) - N]$ = N random numbers. This procedure ensures that each of the $(2 * N)$ unique random numbers would appear at least once on any of the voter's N random number list, during the poll.

So, why are we taking such a lot of pain in innovating conditions in this procedure? The reasons are obvious, first, to make sure it is Receipt-Free, so that the voter cannot prove to a candidate at the tally stage, that the random number against the vote is what s/he had chosen. Secondly, to be able to uniquely identify his/her vote during the tally stage.

Now, as it is a remote Internet voting, so the voter has complete control over the machine, hence, the voter has the option of taking a screen shot and using it as a receipt/proof of his/her candidate selection. But, even if the voter selects a random number and takes a screen shot before clicking the submit button, still s/he would not be able to prove to others that the random number chosen was indeed his/her selection.

The reasons being:

1) The voter can change the selection value anytime before voting.
2) As for every voter, a new set of N random values show up on the screen, every time s/he accesses the voting link, before actually submitting the vote.
3) As there is a possibility of the same random number [which was not chosen by previous voters who had cast the vote] appearing on different voter screens, so the screen shot of the random selection loses its authenticity, as a proof of candidate selection.

Hence, the voter cannot prove to others convincingly, about his/her candidate selection, but s/he is completely sure that the random number against the vote displayed during the tally phase is what s/he selected, because, after his/her submission of the vote, that particular random number gets deleted from the $(2 * N)$ list, and would never appear on any subsequent voter's N random number list.

So, now lets move on to the second approach of Individual Verifiability. This approach is applicable for small as well as large scale deployment.

Here, instead of (2 * N) random numbers generated and N random number list provided to the voter, which does not seem to be scalable, as well as user-friendly, now we have N +(P -1) random numbers generated, where N is the number of voters participating for a particular poll, and P is the size of the set of random numbers provided to the voter. The rest of the procedures/reasons/benefits are the same as that of the first approach. The value of N need not be equal to that of the number of voters, we chose N+(P-1), just to make sure with a probability of 1, that any random number shown once on the N-random number list of the voter [which was not selected by any previous/current user], would at least appear once in the list of N-random numbers displayed to the subsequent voters. One can always lower the probability value, and set the value of N and P accordingly in order to make sure that there are not many similar random numbers showing up at the same time on the screen of voters, who might simultaneous access and vote. However, the system takes care of the issue of simultaneous access by voters. First of all, the screen gets refreshed after a certain short time interval, hence a new set of random numbers would get displayed after every refresh. Any random numbers shown on the previous list, if used up by other voters during this time interval, would never show up as part of the N-random number set for this voter as well as subsequent voters.

Secondly, even if two or more users get the same random number and select it as part of their Individual Verifiability, the system would only allow the first request of vote submission to succeed, the subsequent request(s)/voter(s) would be appropriately notified and a new set of random numbers would be displayed for re-submission. Thus, Individual Verifiability with Receipt-Freeness would lead to increased voter participation.

Receipt-Freeness: This property relieves the user from the burden of managing obscure data, thus being more user-friendly. The Individual Verifiability property itself would bring in the necessary confidence/trust needed from the user towards the proposed system. Additionally, the possibility of vote buying is nullified, due to receipt-freeness, as the candidates/adversaries would not be able to convincingly verify the voters' selection. The implementation of this property perhaps needed the least effort.

Fairness: As the poll is underway, no-one should be able to calculate the partial tally. The voter gets to view/verify the result only after the poll is closed by the Poll Initiator. The Poll Initiator never gets to view the results, unless s/he is part of the electorate him/herself, and in the later case, s/he can only view the result after the poll is closed, thus maintaining fairness.

4 Comparison Matrix

The previous section addressed the properties of the proposed system, and did an evaluation of the system based on those properties. Below is a quick comparison between the existing systems and the proposed *agile e-voting* system on various properties.

S.No.	Application	Anonymity	Security	Universal Verifiability	Individual Verifiability	Fairness	Receipt-freeness	Login-free
1	Adder	Yes	Yes	Yes	No	Yes	Yes	No
2	CIVS	No	Yes	No	No	Yes	No	Yes
3	KOA	Yes	Yes	Yes	No	Yes	No	No
4	*Agile e-voting*	Yes	Yes	Yes	Yes	Yes	Yes	Yes

Fig. 3. Comparison Matrix - Between various browser-based open-source e-voting systems

5 Conclusion

An innovative voter-friendly browser-based agile system was proposed in this paper. The e-voting properties such as, Security, Anonymity, Verifiability, Receipt-Freeness and Fairness were implemented by the system. The essential value addition that the proposed system brings to the industry, is the attempt to put the focus back onto the voter, and derive/relate other requirements based on the voter convenience. It was shown that the proposed Agile e-voting system addressed most of the issues in the existing browser-based e-voting systems. Most importantly, a new approach to Individual Verifiability was crafted, which would allow the voter to cross verify his/her vote during the tally phase. The evaluation of the system as per the properties mentioned earlier was detailed out. The tricky In-coercibility property implementation would be the logical next first step towards future enhancements. Thus, with such user-friendly features implemented, the agile e-voting system hopefully would aid in increasing the voter participation.

References

1. Brace Kimball, W.: Overview of Voting Equipment Usage in United States, Direct Recording Electronic(DRE) Voting. Kimball Brace's Statement to United States Election Assistance Commission (May 5, 2004)
2. Kevin, C.: CRS Report for Congress, Internet Voting. Order Code RS20639 (January 31, 2003)
3. California Internet Voting Task Force: A Report on the Feasibility of Internet Voting (January 2000)
4. Kiayias, A., Michael, K., David, W.: An Internet Voting System Supporting User Privacy. In: Jesshope, C., Egan, C. (eds.) ACSAC 2006. LNCS, vol. 4186, Springer, Heidelberg (2006)
5. Rising, L., Janoff, N.S.: (2000) The Scrum Software Development Process for Small Teams. IEEE Software (July/August, 2000)
6. Niemi, R.G., Weisberg, H.F.: Controversies in Voting Behavior. CQ Press, Washington, D.C (2001)
7. VoteHere VHTi: Frequently Asked Questions, http://www.votehere.com/faq_toc.php
8. Cochran, D.: Secure internet voting in Ireland using the Open Source: Kiezen op Afstand (KOA) remote voting system. Master's thesis, University College Dublin (2006)
9. Kim, K.: Killer Application of PKI to Internet Voting. In: IWAP 2002. LNCS, vol. 1233, Springer, Heidelberg (2002)

10. GNU.FREE: Heavy-Duty Internet Voting,
    http://www.j-dom.org/users/re.html
11. An Untraceable, Universally Verifiable Voting Scheme, Professor Philip Klein, Seminar in
    Cryptology (December 12, 1995)
12. http://www.e-poll-project.net/
13. Krishna, S., Sampigethaya, S.K., Poovendran, R.: A Framework and Taxonomy for
    Comparison of Electronic Voting Schemes. Elsevier Journal of Computers and
    Security 25(2), 137–153 (2006)
14. Condorcet Internet Voting Service,
    http://www.cs.cornell.edu/andru/civs.html
15. PollPub, http://www.pollpub.com/
16. BuzzVote, http://www.buzzvote.com/
17. VoteHereVHTi: Frequently Asked Questions,
    http://www.votehere.com/faq_toc.php
18. Sensus, http://lorrie.cranor.org/voting/sensus/
19. Kiniry, J., Morkan, A., Cochran, D., Fairmichael, F., Chalin, P., Oostdijk, M., Hubbers, E.:
    The KOA remote voting system: A summary of work to date. In: Proceedings of
    Trustworthy Global Computing (2006)
20. Nijmeegs instituut voor informatica en informatiekunde. Security of Systems,
    http://www.sos.cs.ru.nl/research/koa/ ; KiezenopAfstand 2004
21. IETF RFC 4346: The Transport Layer Security (TLS) Protocol, Version 1.1. URL,
    http://www.ietf.org/rfc/rfc4346.txt
22. Alberto, O., Marco, V.: Man-In-The-Middle Attacks,
    http://www.blackhat.com/presentations/bh-usa-03/
    bh-us-03-ornaghi-valleri.pdf
23. Diffie, W., Hellman, M.E.: Exhaustive Cryptanalysis of the NBS Data Encryption Standard.
    Computer 10(6), 74–84 (1977)
24. Menezes, A., van Oorschot, P., Van stone, S.: Handbook of Applied Cryptography. CRC
    Press, Boca Raton, USA
25. Hellman, M.E.: An Overview of Public Key Cryptography. IEEE Communications
    Magazine, 42–49 (May 2002)
26. Advanced Encryption Standard(AES), Federal Information Processing Standards
    Publication 197 (November 26, 2001)
27. Neff, C.A.: Practical high certainty intent verification for encrypted votes. Draft(2004),
    http://www.votehere.net/vhti/documentation/vsv2.0.3638.pdf
28. Reynolds, D.J.: A method for electronic voting with coercionfree receipt. FEE 2005 (2005),
    Presentation, http://www.win.tue.nl/ berry/fee2005/ presentations/reynolds.ppt
29. Moran, T., Naor, M.: Receipt Free Universally Verifiable Voting With Everlasting Privacy.
    In: Dwork, C. (ed.) CRYPTO 2006. LNCS, vol. 4117, pp. 373–392. Springer, Heidelberg
    (2006)
30. Ronald, L.: Rivest.: The ThreeBallot Voting System (October 2006),
    http://theory.lcs.mit.edu/rivest/
    Rivest-TheThreeBallotVotingSystem.pdf
31. Jones, H., Juang, J., Belote, G.: ThreeBallot in the Field (December 2006),
    http://courses.csail.mit.edu/6.857/projects/
    threeBallotPaper.pdf

Risk Balance in Exchange Protocols

Mohammad Torabi Dashti and Yanjing Wang

CWI, Amsterdam
{dashti,y.wang}@cwi.nl

Abstract. We study the behaviour of rational agents in exchange protocols which rely on trustees. We allow malicious parties to compromise the trustee by paying a cost and, thereby, present a game analysis that advocates exchange protocols which induce balanced risks on the participants. We also present a risk-balanced protocol for fair confidential secret comparison.

1 Introduction

Exchange protocols aim to establish successful exchanges of electronic goods between two parties who possibly have conflicting interests. Fairness, stipulating that either both or none of the parties achieve their goals, is recognised as a crucial requirement for exchange protocols (e.g. see [1]). Achieving fairness in deterministic asynchronous exchange protocols with no trusted parties is however impossible [6]. The existing methods, therefore, either are based on gradual release of information or gradual increase of privilege to approximate fairness, or rely on trusted third parties (TTPs).

This paper focuses on exchange protocols which rely on a TTP, while malicious participants are allowed to, by paying a cost, compromise the TTP.[1] We thereby present a game analysis that advocates protocols which induce (nearly) the same amount of risk on the participants. Our main result states that in such risk-balanced protocols, the difference between participants' utilities is limited to a factor independent of the TTP's trustworthiness. Hence, none of the participants would hugely suffer compared to the other one, in case the trustee is compromised by the opponent.

Existing game analyses of exchange protocol assume non-compromisable trustees, e.g. [2,3,5,9]. This is in contrast to the premise of our analysis that TTPs, by paying a cost, can be compromised. In a similar study, the authors of [10] assume that participants may have limited trust in TTPs and propose algorithms to determine whether a rational agent would engage in an exchange using cascades of TTPs or not. They however do not consider that participants may have the choice to compromise TTPs.

Studying the ways a compromised TTP may affect fair exchange protocols and methods to limit its damages are not well studied. As a notable exception to this, Asokan explores the concept of verifiable TTPs [1] in optimistic protocols, where the TTP's incentive for cheating is lowered, as its malicious behaviour can be detected.

As an example of a risk-balanced protocol, we present a fair protocol for confidentially comparing secrets. Existing protocols for this purpose either do not aim at fairness [7], or do not involve TTPs [13,14], thus only achieve probabilistic fairness, or are universal multi-party computing protocols [4] that are not optimised for this task.

---

[1] Note that a *trusted* entity, in general, may not be *trustworthy*, cf. [8].

I. Cervesato (Ed.): ASIAN 2007, LNCS 4846, pp. 70–77, 2007.

2 Game Abstraction of Exchange Protocols

From a game theoretical point of view, a two-party exchange protocol with a compromisable TTP can be seen as a two-party strategic game, in which the agents can either follow the protocol faithfully or compromise the TTP. If both parties play faithfully, then they normally "earn" the goods from the opponent and "lose" their own goods. However, when engaging in the exchange, each agent has to take some risk due to the fact that the opponent may manage to compromise the TTP. In such cases, the agent who compromises the TTP can earn the amount that the other (honest) party risks, and lose only the cost of compromising the TTP.

Formally, we have the following game abstraction [2]:

Definition 1. *(Protocol game) Given a two-party exchange protocol* Prot *with a TTP, the strategic game* $G(\mathsf{Prot})$ *is defined as follows:*

$A\backslash B$	$\mathcal{H}_B$	$\mathcal{DH}_B$
$\mathcal{H}_A$	$g_B^A - g_A^A, g_A^B - g_B^B$	$-r_A^A, r_A^B - c_B$
$\mathcal{DH}_A$	$r_B^A - c_A, -r_B^B$	$r_B^A - r_A^A - c_A, r_A^B - r_B^B - c_B$

where $\mathcal{H}_x$ *is the strategy of* x *that is according to the protocol;* $\mathcal{DH}_x$ *is the strategy of* x *in which* x *compromises the TTP and may stop following the normal course of the protocol when she has to release its goods;* g_x^y *is* y*'s evaluation of the goods that* x *wants to exchange;* r_x^y *is* y*'s evaluation of the risk that* x *has, if the TTP is compromised by the opponent of* x*; and* c_x *is the cost* x *pays to compromise the TTP.* [3]

In the following we assume:

- Agents have incentives to exchange goods: $g_x^y > g_x^x$ if $x \neq y$. For simplicity, we assume that there is a fixed exchange rate $\rho > 1$ such that $g_x^y = \rho g_x^x, x \neq y$.
- The risks of the agents comply with the same exchange rate: $r_x^y = \rho r_x^x, x \neq y$.
- The subjective values of the goods are the same: $g_A^A = g_B^B = g > 0$.
- The costs of compromising the TTP are the same for both agents: $c_A = c_B = c$.

With these assumptions, $G(\mathsf{Prot})$ can be simplified to $SG(\mathsf{Prot})$:

$A\backslash B$	$\mathcal{H}_B$	$\mathcal{DH}_B$
$\mathcal{H}_A$	$(\rho-1)g, (\rho-1)g$	$-a, \rho a - c$
$\mathcal{DH}_A$	$\rho b - c, -b$	$\rho b - a - c, \rho a - b - c$

Where $a = r_A^A$ and $b = r_B^B$.

To apply game theoretical analysis, we assume that the agents are rational utility-maximisers. A strategy profile is a joint strategy that determines a unique utility pair; for example $(\mathcal{H}_A, \mathcal{H}_B)$ is a strategy profile while $((\rho-1)g, (\rho-1)g)$ is the corresponding utility pair. A strategy profile (S_A, S_B) is called a Nash equilibrium if no agent gets higher utility by switching to another strategy, given the strategy of the other agent

---

[2] Due to space constraints we omit introducing basics of game theory, and instead refer to [11].
[3] We assume that both parties can compromise the TTP at the same time. For example, they both may exploit vulnerabilities in the TTP's software to read certain information off its storage.

according to the profile. In this paper, we consider the Nash equilibria of a simplified protocol game as the expected executions of the corresponding protocol by rational agents. We write $\text{Utility}_x(S_A, S_B)$ as the utility of x if the agents select the strategy profile (S_A, S_B).

3   Risk Balance

We define a requirement on exchange protocols, which we call Δ-*condition*, that puts an upper bound on the difference between the risks that a protocol induces on its participants. We show that this condition in turn puts a limit on the difference between participants' expected utilities. The limit on utility differences turns out to be independent of c. This is a desirable property since it ensures that no matter how trustworthy the TTP might be in an execution, the difference between participants' utilities is limited to a value independent of c, hence none of the participants would hugely suffer (or benefit) compared to the other one. This can be interpreted as fairness in a meta level.

In the following, when the context of the simplified protocol game is clear, let $\Delta = |a - b|$ and $\Delta_U(S_A, S_B) = |\text{Utility}_A(S_A, S_B) - \text{Utility}_B(S_A, S_B)|$.

Definition 2. *An exchange protocol* Prot *satisfies* Δ-*condition iff* $\Delta < (1 - \frac{1}{\rho})g$ *in* $SG(\text{Prot})$. *Such a protocol* Prot *is called* risk-balanced.

Now we are ready to state the main theoretical result of the paper:

Theorem 1. *For any risk-balanced protocol* Prot, *there are Nash equilibria in* $SG(\text{Prot})$, *and for each such Nash equilibrium* (S_A, S_B) *the following holds:*

$$\Delta_U(S_A, S_B) < (\rho - \frac{1}{\rho})g.$$

Proof.   Suppose Prot satisfies Δ-condition, then we have:

$$\Delta_U(\mathcal{DH}_A, \mathcal{DH}_B) = |\rho b - a - c - (\rho a - b - c)| = (\rho + 1)\Delta < (\rho - \frac{1}{\rho})g$$

Now, since $\Delta_U(\mathcal{H}_A, \mathcal{H}_B) = |(\rho - 1)g - (\rho - 1)g| = 0$, we only need to prove the following two claims to prove the theorem:

1. Under the Δ−condition, $(\mathcal{H}_A, \mathcal{DH}_B)$ and $(\mathcal{DH}_A, \mathcal{H}_B)$ are not the Nash equilibria of $SG(\text{Prot})$.
2. Either $(\mathcal{H}_A, \mathcal{H}_B)$ or $(\mathcal{DH}_A, \mathcal{DH}_B)$ is a Nash equilibrium of $SG(\text{Prot})$.

Proof of (1): Suppose $(\mathcal{H}_A, \mathcal{DH}_B)$ is a Nash equilibrium of $SG(\text{Prot})$, then according to the definition of Nash equilibrium we have:

$$\begin{cases} \text{Utility}_A(\mathcal{H}_A, \mathcal{DH}_B) \geq \text{Utility}_A(\mathcal{DH}_A, \mathcal{DH}_B) \\ \text{Utility}_B(\mathcal{H}_A, \mathcal{DH}_B) \geq \text{Utility}_B(\mathcal{H}_A, \mathcal{H}_B) \end{cases}$$

namely,

$$\begin{cases} -a \geq \rho b - a - c \\ \rho a - c \geq (\rho - 1)g \end{cases} \Rightarrow \rho a - \rho b \geq (\rho - 1)g$$

It follows that $\Delta \geq (1-\frac{1}{\rho})g$, contradicting the Δ-condition. For the case of $(\mathcal{DH}_A, \mathcal{H}_B)$, proof goes likewise.

Proof of (2): Suppose $(\mathcal{H}_A, \mathcal{H}_B)$ is not a Nash equilibrium, then either A or B can be better off by switching to a dishonest strategy, given that the opponent sticks to the honest strategy. Without loss of generality, we assume A can get higher utility by switching from $\mathcal{H}_A$ to $\mathcal{DH}_A$, namely, $\rho b - c > (\rho - 1)g$. Since $(\rho - 1)g > 0$ then $\rho b - c - a > -a$. It follows that $\mathcal{DH}_A$ is the strictly dominant strategy for A. Given that A chooses $\mathcal{DH}_A$, we argue that B will also choose $\mathcal{DH}_B$ as follows: Utility$_B(\mathcal{DH}_A, \mathcal{DH}_B)$ − Utility$_B(\mathcal{DH}_A, \mathcal{H}_B) = \rho a - b - c - (-b) = \rho a - c \geq \rho(b - \Delta) - c = \rho b - c - \rho\Delta > (\rho - 1)g - (\rho - 1)g = 0$. It follows that $(\mathcal{DH}_A, \mathcal{DH}_B)$ is a Nash equilibrium.

Suppose $(\mathcal{DH}_A, \mathcal{DH}_B)$ is not a Nash equilibrium, then either A or B can be better off by switching to a honest strategy. Without loss of generality, we assume that A can get higher utility by switching from $\mathcal{DH}_A$ to $\mathcal{H}_A$. Therefore $-a > \rho b - a - c$, namely $0 > \rho b - c$. It follows that $\mathcal{H}_A$ is the strictly dominant strategy for A. Given that A chooses $\mathcal{H}_A$, B will also choose $\mathcal{H}_B$ since Utility$_B(\mathcal{H}_A, \mathcal{H}_B)$−Utility$_B(\mathcal{H}_A, \mathcal{DH}_B) = (\rho - 1)g - (\rho a - c) \geq (\rho - 1)g - (\rho(b + \Delta) - c) = (\rho - 1)g - (\rho b - c + \rho\Delta) > (\rho - 1)g - (\rho - 1)g = 0$. Therefore, $(\mathcal{H}_A, \mathcal{H}_B)$ is a Nash equilibrium. $\square$

Remark 1. According to theorem 1, under the Δ−condition, Δ_U is either 0 or $(\rho+1)\Delta$. A robust protocol would minimise Δ_U independent of ρ and g, by guaranteeing $\Delta = 0$, namely $a = b$, which implies $\Delta_U = 0$.

4   A Fair Risk-Balanced Exchange Protocol

In this section, inspired by the confidential secret comparison protocol of [13], we design two exchange protocols that rely on TTPs. The first one, undesirably, violates the Δ-condition, serving as a concrete example for motivating risk-balanced protocols. Then, we propose a protocol which, under certain conditions, is risk-balanced.

Notations. We assume that each two parties X and Y share a secret symmetric key $\mathcal{K}(XY)$. [4] We write $[M]_\mathcal{K}$ for the encryption of M with key $\mathcal{K}$. It is assumed that the participants have access to a secure encryption algorithm, and a one-way collision-resistant hash function h. Agents A and B are the players of our protocols, whom we assume share a secret nonce $\aleph$. The TTP is named Γ.

A fair confidential secret comparison protocol. Let $\mathcal{E}_P$, for $P \in \{A, B\}$, denote P's knowledge set. Suppose A wants to prove to B that she knows of a secret $\mathcal{I}$ (that is $\mathcal{I} \in \mathcal{E}_A$). However, if B does not already know of $\mathcal{I}$ (that is $\mathcal{I} \notin \mathcal{E}_B$), A does not want to reveal $\mathcal{I}$ to him. Moreover, A and B wish to exchange this epistemic statement "*I know $\mathcal{I}$.*" mutually, and, in a fair manner.

The goal is thus to design a protocol that achieves the following (cf. [13]): (G1) Only if both A and B know $\mathcal{I}$, then A learns that B knows $\mathcal{I}$, and likewise for B. (G2) By means of the protocol, only A and B, and no one else, may learn that A or B know $\mathcal{I}$.

---

[4] We could as well construct our protocols based on asymmetric encryption techniques.

(G3) By means of the protocol, no one learns $\mathcal{I}$. (G4) B learns that A knows $\mathcal{I}$, iff A learns that B knows $\mathcal{I}$ (which is fairness).

To achieve these goals, we follow the straightforward approach of using on-line TTPs, e.g. see [15] (considering off-line TTPs being left as future work). Below, $\Rightarrow$ denotes communicating over confidential authenticated channels, sending a message over insecure channels is denoted by $\rightarrow$, and FTP is a secure publicly accessible server operated by Γ. We write $\Gamma \downarrow$ FTP : a when Γ makes a available on FTP.

1. $A \Rightarrow \Gamma : (f_{\text{prov}}, A, B, \omega)$, where $\omega = h(\mathcal{I}, \aleph, A, B)$
2. $B \Rightarrow \Gamma : (f_{\text{verif}}, A, B, \Omega_B)$, where $\Omega_B = \{h(i, \aleph, A, B) \mid i \in \mathcal{E}_B\}$
3. Γ checks if $\omega \in \Omega_B$. If yes, then $\Gamma \downarrow$ FTP : ω, else $\Gamma \downarrow$ FTP : $\bot$.
4. A, B fetch the result from FTP.

Flags f_{prov} and f_{verif} merely indicate the purposes of the corresponding messages. It is easy to check that goals G1, G2 and G3 are achieved. In particular, Γ does not learn the content of the exchanged secret $\mathcal{I}$. Besides, using confidential channels is only to protect the content of A's message from B, and vice versa. An outsider would not benefit from observing these messages in plain, as she does not know $\aleph$. She may however observe whether an exchange is a successful comparison of *some* secret or not (cf. § 5).

The protocol is fair (G4) as B learns that A possesses $\mathcal{I}$ iff A learns that $\mathcal{I} \in \mathcal{E}_B$. Using public announcements on FTP ensures that benign communication failures cannot deprive the participants from achieving fairness. Using authenticated channels is needed to ensure the freshness of the requests. Without these, A could, e.g., compose $\omega' = h(\mathcal{I}', \aleph, A, B)$ with $\mathcal{I}' \neq \mathcal{I}$ and replay B's old message to Γ, and learn whether $\mathcal{I}' \in \mathcal{E}_B$ or not, while B not even being aware that this new comparison takes place. [5]

A severe defect of the protocol is nonetheless the uneven risk distribution that it induces. The security of this protocol obviously relies on Γ being correct. If Γ is compromised by A in the course of the protocol, then B will be seriously harmed since A (together with Γ), once getting access to Ω_B, can later on check any piece of information against $\mathcal{E}_B$ without contacting B. However, if B takes the control of Γ in his hands, then he can only check one single $\mathcal{I}$ against $\mathcal{E}_B$. This infringes on the protocol's fairness in a meta level: if A compromises Γ, the amount of harm to B is not proportional to the harm caused to A when Γ is compromised by B. Therefore, when engaging in the protocol, B takes more risk than A, hence causing $b \gg a$, if $|\mathcal{E}_B| \gg 1$ (see § 3).

A fair risk-balanced exchange protocol. Below, we propose an extension of the previous protocol that is risk-balanced. The idea is to force A to contact B for each $\mathcal{I}$ that she wants to compare against $\mathcal{E}_B$. For this purpose, we use a scheme similar to RSA encryption [12] and blind signatures. For each exchange, B randomly chooses two distinct large prime numbers p and q and computes $n = p \cdot q$ and $\phi = (p - 1) \cdot (q - 1)$. Then, B chooses a random number α, such that $1 < \alpha < \phi$ and $gcd(\alpha, \phi) = 1$, i.e. α and ϕ are relatively prime. B then calculates $\bar{\alpha}$ satisfying $\alpha.\bar{\alpha} \equiv 1 \bmod \phi$. Below, it is assumed that $\mathcal{E}_B$ is an ordered set, and, as before, $\mathcal{I}$ is the secret to be checked against

---

[5] B could learn the results of such comparisons via FTP, if he knew that he should fetch these results. Honest B must however not be forced to periodically poll the FTP server.

$\mathcal{E}_B$. We assume that $\mathcal{I}$ and elements of $\mathcal{E}_B$ can be encoded as integers smaller than n.

1. B generates n and $(\alpha, \bar{\alpha})$ as described above. B then computes $\pi = h(\omega_1, \cdots, \omega_\ell)$, where $\omega_j = h(i_j^{\bar{\alpha}} \bmod n)$, when $\mathcal{E}_B = \{i_1, \cdots, i_\ell\}$.
2. $B \rightarrow A : \alpha, n$
3. A generates a random number $\lambda < n$ such that $gcd(\lambda, n) = 1$.
4. $A \rightarrow B : (\mathcal{I} \cdot \lambda^\alpha) \bmod n$
5. $B \rightarrow A : (\mathcal{I} \cdot \lambda^\alpha)^{\bar{\alpha}} \bmod n, \pi$
6. A computes $((\mathcal{I} \cdot \lambda^\alpha)^{\bar{\alpha}} \lambda^{-1}) \bmod n = \mathcal{I}^{\bar{\alpha}} \bmod n$. Then A lets $\omega = h(\mathcal{I}^{\bar{\alpha}} \bmod n)$.
7. $A \rightarrow \Gamma : [f_{\text{prov}}, A, B, \omega, \pi]_{\mathcal{K}(A\Gamma)}$
8. $B \rightarrow \Gamma : [f_{\text{verif}}, A, B, \Omega_B]_{\mathcal{K}(B\Gamma)}$, where $\Omega_B = \{\omega_1, \cdots, \omega_\ell\}$
9. Γ checks whether π corresponds to Ω_B. If yes then

   Γ checks whether $\omega \in \Omega_B$. If yes, then

   $\quad \Gamma \downarrow$ FTP $: \omega$, and A, B fetch the result from FTP.

   else

   $\quad \Gamma \downarrow$ FTP $: \bot$, and A, B fetch the result from FTP.

It can be checked that this protocol satisfies G1, G2, G3 and G4. Note that authenticated channels are not used in this protocol. This is because, differently from the previous protocol, the freshness of the messages need not be checked by the TTP, since to replay A's message, B would need to construct another set $\mathcal{E}'_B$ with the same π value as of $\mathcal{E}_B$, which is infeasible as h is collision-resistant. Similarly, to replay B's message, A would need to contact B to compute $\mathcal{I}'^{\bar{\alpha}}$ for a new $\mathcal{I}'$, hence giving B the choice to use a new $\bar{\alpha}$ or decline the exchange altogether.

Concerning risk balance, if A compromises Γ, then she can cheat on B with computing $\omega \in \Omega_B$ without informing B of the result. However, to check another secret $\mathcal{I}' \neq \mathcal{I}$ against Ω_B she needs to contact B. Similarly, if B compromises Γ, he can only cheat on A by computing $\omega \in \Omega_B$ without informing A of the result. The risks induced on A and B are thus equal, given that losing one piece of information causes the same harm from both A's and B's points of view. In this case, we have $a = b$ (see § 3), implying $\Delta_U = 0$, hence the protocol being risk-balanced.

To summarise, if Γ is not compromised, then the protocol satisfies G1, G2, G3 and G4. In case Γ is compromised, the protocol may not achieve G4 anymore. Rational agents will however end up with equal utilities even when Γ is compromised. In other words, the amount of expected harm to a cheated B would be limited and proportional to the damage that B could cause to A if Γ was compromised by B, and vice versa.

5 Discussions

We motivate why the values of $\mathcal{I}^{\bar{\alpha}}$ and $i^{\bar{\alpha}}$, $i \in \mathcal{E}_B$ need to be hashed in our risk-balanced protocol. We assume that these values were not hashed and, thereby, demonstrate an attack on the protocol which undermines its risk balance.

Let us assume that $\omega = \mathcal{I}^{\bar{\alpha}}$ and $\omega_j = i_j^{\bar{\alpha}}$, all computed modulo n, thus removing the hash function from the protocol. The idea of the attack is that if A compromises Γ, then she gets access to the members of $\mathcal{E}_B$. This is because A knows α (message 2 above) and with compromising Γ, she gets access to $\{i_j^{\bar{\alpha}} \mid i_j \in \mathcal{E}_B\}$, from which she would be able to compute $\{(i_j^{\bar\alpha})^\alpha \bmod n \mid i_j \in \mathcal{E}_B\} = \mathcal{E}_B$. We conclude that in case hash functions were not used in the protocol, A, by compromising Γ, could cause more damage to B, compared to the damage B could cause to A by compromising Γ (compare with the first protocol of section 4). This can undermine the protocol's risk balance, and, thus has to be prevented.

Below, we mention two shortcomings of our risk-balanced protocol. Addressing these issues constitute our future work. (1) We note that in the protocol, Γ would always learn whether the exchange was successful or not (outsider parties can easily be prevented from seeing the result altogether, e.g. using encryption), although the shared information $\mathcal{I}$ is not revealed to Γ. Leaking this little information can in principle be harmful to the participants: An interrogator who knows that you share some secret with a comrade would be hard to thwart before you both reveal that very secret. Hiding this information from Γ remains to be studied. (2) A drawback of the protocol is its communication costs and the computation burden it imposes on Γ. The computation cost on B is also much heavier than A. Equivalent protocols with less, and evenly distributed, computation and communication costs are thus desirable.

Acknowledgements. We are grateful to Wouter Teepe for many helpful discussions, and to Srijith Nair for commenting on an earlier version of the paper.

References

1. Asokan, N.: Fairness in electronic commerce. PhD thesis, University of Waterloo (1998)
2. Buttyán, L., Hubaux, J.: Toward a formal model of fair exchange – a game theoretic approach. Technical Report SSC/1999/39, EPFL, Lausanne (1999)
3. Buttyán, L., Hubaux, J., Capkun, S.: A formal model of rational exchange and its application to the analysis of syverson's protocol. J. Computer Security 12(3-4), 551–587 (2004)
4. Cachin, C., Camenisch, J.: Optimistic fair secure computation. In: Bellare, M. (ed.) CRYPTO 2000. LNCS, vol. 1880, pp. 93–111. Springer, Heidelberg (2000)
5. Chadha, R., Mitchell, J., Scedrov, A., Shmatikov, V.: Contract signing, optimism, and advantage. In: Amadio, R.M., Lugiez, D. (eds.) CONCUR 2003. LNCS, vol. 2761, pp. 366–382. Springer, Heidelberg (2003)
6. Even, S., Yacobi, Y.: Relations among public key signature systems. Technical Report 175, Computer Science Dept., Technion, Haifa, March (1980)
7. Fagin, R., Naor, M., Winkler, P.: Comparing information without leaking it. Commun. ACM 39(5), 77–85 (1996)
8. Gollmann, D.: Why trust is bad for security. ENTCS 157(3), 3–9 (2006)
9. Imamoto, K., Zhou, J., Sakurai, K.: An evenhanded certified email system for contract signing. In: Qing, S., Mao, W., Lopez, J., Wang, G. (eds.) ICICS 2005. LNCS, vol. 3783, pp. 1–13. Springer, Heidelberg (2005)
10. Ito, C., Iwaihara, M., Kambayashi, Y.: Fair exchange under limited trust. In: Buchmann, A.P., Casati, F., Fiege, L., Hsu, M.-C., Shan, M.-C. (eds.) TES 2002. LNCS, vol. 2444, pp. 161–170. Springer, Heidelberg (2002)
11. Osborne, M., Rubinstein, A.: A Course in Game Theory. MIT Press, Redmond, Washington (1999)
12. Rivest, R., Shamir, A., Adleman, L.: A method for obtaining digital signatures and public-key cryptosystems. Commun. ACM 21(2), 120–126 (1978)

13. Teepe, W.: Reconciling Information Exchange and Confidentiality — A Formal Approach. PhD thesis, Rijksuniversiteit Groningen (2006)
14. Traore, J., Boudot, F., Schoenmakers, B.: A fair and efficient solution to the socialist millionaires' problem. Discrete Applied Mathematics 111, 23–36 (2001)
15. Zhou, J., Gollmann, D.: A fair non-repudiation protocol. In: Security and Privacy 1996, pp. 55–61. IEEE Computer Society Press, Los Alamitos (1996)

Scalable DRM System for Media Portability

Hyoungshick Kim

Samsung Electronics, Software Laboratory, Home S/W Platform Team
416, Maetan-3Dong, Yeongtong-Gu,
Suwon, Gyeonggi-Do, Korea 443-742
hyungsik.kim@samsung.com

Abstract. We present a new digital rights management (DRM) system for media portability using dynamic multimedia adaptation. For a user to share multimedia resources over home network, several DRM technologies based on the domain have been introduced. Domain-based approaches enable users to access contents on multiple devices within the same domain. However, most of current DRM systems were only designed for a homogeneous environment where common AV profiles are supported. It is a challenge to share the domain contents between domain members with diverse capabilities while ensuring the protection of the intellectual property rights for the legally obtained contents. In this paper, we propose an architecture that enables DRM contents to be securely shared between various home devices in a seamless manner.

Keywords: DRM, Home Network, Media Portability, Transcoding, Scalability.

1 Introduction

In order to take advantage of the online distribution while at the same time preventing illegal redistribution of the content, digital rights management (DRM) technologies are recently employed for restricting the use of the contents within usages granted by the content holder. Consumers, however, want to enjoy contents on any of their devices without limitation. In particular, the emerging standards and technologies for home entertainment networking are developed to enable all kinds of home devices to access the multimedia resources between the devices [3].

In order to satisfy both of the contents holders and the users over home network, the notion of authorized domain is introduced by identifying a set of devices which a home user owns [4][22]. In a DRM system supporting the domain concept, a user freely enjoys contents among devices within the authorized domain. Most commercial DRM technologies have already defined the authorized domain [7][8][11] which aims to meet the requirements for sharing between networked devices.

In order to share DRM contents effectively, however, the only domain management is not enough. In practice, transcoding for media portability is necessarily required to enable sharing contents among a multitude of playback devices with different device capabilities and dynamic channel capacities [1]. For example, a high-definition (HD) video content for home set-top box must be adapted to target displays of other devices such as a mobile phone that may not even support

I. Cervesato (Ed.): ASIAN 2007, LNCS 4846, pp. 78–85, 2007.
© Springer-Verlag Berlin Heidelberg 2007

standard-definition (SD) resolution because of its limited processing capability or small display. However, such content adaptation may introduce security implications. First of all, translation of DRM protected contents may pose serious threats to the security of the DRM system since the decrypted plaintext content is clearly revealed to the transcoder. In addition, the creation of the associated license should be also required when new DRM content has been created from the result of the translation.

For solving these problems, general DRM interoperability solutions may be considered. Several approaches are previously introduced in this challenging area [12][13][16][17][19]. In general, however, DRM interoperability solutions seem too heavy and complex. Conventional interoperability approaches require common trusted frameworks such as certificates management and keys management for secure communication between participating entities. The common trusted frameworks incur not only the cost of new mechanisms but also many business negotiations among participants in DRM value chains [8]. Furthermore, in the connected interoperability approach, the translation processes are handled by an online mediator on the outside of the home network through re-acquisition methods [12][19]. In general, it is difficult to guarantee continuous network connectivity to Internet.

In this paper, we focus on the challenges involved in scalability issues of both the DRM contents and the associated licenses. In order to enhance scalability of the DRM protected contents, we apply the scalable coding methods [20][21] directly to the generation of the scalable DRM protected contents. Also, we propose a method for compression of digital signatures which are appended to the license.

2 Problems

Our proposed system is intended for satisfying security requirements derived from both DRM protected contents and the associated license within an authorized domain. Both objects must be securely translated for one of supported AV profiles in a playback client device. Before addressing the detailed description of our system, we briefly review two main problems identified by previous approaches.

2.1 Secrecy of Protected Content

During a delivery of a DRM protected content from a media server to a playback client through AV operations such as copy, move or streaming, intermediary devices over home network may perform some transcoding operations such as bit rate reduction, changing resolution, spatial down sampling, or frame rate reduction to adapt to application capabilities. Transcoding often refers to the process of transforming audio and video from the original format in which the multimedia was encoded into a possibly different format or quality.

In the process of translation, the plaintext media stream of the protected content may be insecure in the view of end-to-end security from the media server to the client since decryption of the protected content is generally required at the transcoders. The transcoders decrypt the DRM protected content before transcoding it. For doing this, the transcoders must manage the content encryption key (*CEK*). In most DRM systems, *CEK* can be extracted from a DRM license by the only authorized entities (e.g. domain members). Consequently, we need to assume that the transcoder is also an authorized participant and the transcoding operation is allowed under the terms stated by the DRM system. It is shown in Figure 1.

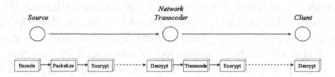

Fig. 1. Conventional system for transferring of a DRM content between a media server and a client

These approaches not only increase processing overhead for decryption and re-encryption but also require a strong security assumption on the transcoder. Transcoding method that requires the decryption of the protected content is not desirable in environment that transcoders may be not trust since it violates the end-to-end security guarantee of privacy [14].

2.2 Verifying License

Another important issue is to generate a valid license for a newly translated DRM content. Before installing a DRM license to render the associated DRM protected content, most DRM clients must check the validity of the license object for preventing against the modification of a DRM license or rogue content holder attack. For this purpose, the content holder's own secret information is required since a valid license can be generated by the only honest contents holder. The most intuitive solution is to use the content holder's signature or MAC (Message Authentication Code) [7].

Unlike conventional DRM systems, we cannot assume that the identical licenses are shared between domain members. As a result of the transcoding of DRM protected content, the creation of a new DRM license may be also required since hash value or content identifier of the associated DRM protected content are modified. By these modifications, new hash value or the changed content identifier must be included into the DRM license object. Therefore, the transcoder must also hold the content holder's unique secret information such as his sign key for generating the DRM license.

To exercise the localized licensing, the delegation of content holder's authority to transcoder using some advanced cryptographic primitives [15][18] such as proxy signature are previously introduced [2][13][24]. However, previous approaches have some limitations. First of all, assuming an authorized proxy of contents holder is not acceptable in conventional DRM world yet. To accept these as industrial technologies, contents holders need time to verify the security of the technologies since many cryptographers are still skeptical about the proof of the security for proxy signature or proxy re-encryption. Also, the existence of the delegated device may cause the single server failure problem. To access an interoperable service, the home devices must always contact the designated transcoder who holds the role of proxy. In

CE environment, it is difficult to assume that there is the specific device without cease since a device may be commonly turned off or broken down.

3   DRM System for Multiple AV Profiles

In this section, we focus on the distribution of the DRM protected content and the associated license. Our proposed system translates both objects in local home network without breaking end-to-end security between a content holder and a media player. In a practical environment, the content holder can be a combination of contents providers and service providers.

The multimedia adaptation problem for DRM contents deals with a media server, S and a media player, P. In general, given a DRM content c_n and a license l_n for an AV profile p_n, our goal is to translate them into the new DRM content c_m and the associated license l_m for the specific AV profile p_m in a secure and seamless manner. In general DRM systems, c_n consists the metadata of the content and the encrypted plaintext media stream s_n with a CEK, denoted as $E_{CEK}\{s_n\}$. At this time, we assume that the plaintext media stream s_n is encoded using a scalable video coding and a media stream s_i can be transcoded from s_n using dropping some enhancement layers if i is less than n. A scalable video coding provides a unique representation of one video signal allowing simultaneous access to the scene at different scales: spatial, temporal and quality.

Not all video coding technologies are suitable for scalability. AVC is expected to be basis of interoperability for home network. To guarantee interoperability and take advantage of these devices in home network technologies, scalable video coding shall support base layer compatibility with AVC standard. Recently, the Joint Video Team (JVT) is finalizing the standardization of MPEG-4 SVC: the scalable video coding extension of MPEG-4 AVC [6][9]. In this paper, we assume that home network and the related DRM standard technologies support AV profile which can be encoded by scalable coding such as MPEG-4 SVC.

Our proposed system consists of two parallel steps, 'content translation', and 'license translation' which are processed on the media server S and the media player P. Upon completing protocols successfully for content purchase, the media server S stores the purchased content. The media server S translates the encrypted media stream s_n and the digitally signed l_n with the contents holder's sign key then delivers them to the media player P when the player P requests to share the content. Upon successful receiving the translated DRM content and the associated license, the player P passes them to the DRM agent.

3.1   Content Translation

The contents holder H passes raw audio and video input through the specific encoder to produce scalable encoded streams. The content is encoded into multiple layers consisting of one base layer and multiple enhancement layers using layered coding. The base layer is encoded at the minimum rate necessary to decode the content stream, and its decoding results in the lowest quality version of the content. Each enhancement layer provides progressive refinement of the encoded content [10].

For protecting the secrecy of the plaintext media stream, the encoded streams must be encrypted with the *CEK*. The encrypted streams can be generated from scalable compressed bitstreams. The server S parses the scalable bitstreams, and groups the data into n layers $g_1, g_2, \dots , g_n$. After grouping the scalable coded data into layers, the contents holder H sequentially encrypts them using *CEK*. After completing the purchase, the encrypted group data $E_{CEK}\{g_j\}$ for $1 \leq j \leq n$ and additional metadata M as the DRM Protected content are stored to a media server S. Not only general DRM information such as content identifier but also the location information for transcoding must be included into metadata M. In general, these data can be directly represented common DRM file formats in Conventional DRM systems.

In the step of playback, a media player P can download only a difference between quality levels rather than downloading the entire multimedia stream for minimizing communication cost. When the media player P requests the media server S to download a DRM content c_m for a AV profile p_m where $1 \leq m \leq n$, the media server S transfers the data $E_{CEK}\{g_i\}$ for $1 \leq i \leq m$ and the metadata M to the player P. The server S achieves secure transcoding without operations such as decryption and re-encryption. The server S simply reads the metadata of the DRM protected content and then truncates a set of group data at the appropriate locations. It is not required that the specific compression, decoding, or encryption algorithms are implemented in the media server S. Therefore, we do not assume that the server S should implement DRM clients or be one of the authorized domain members.

For access the content, the media player P starts to decrypt the encrypted group data $E_{CEK}\{g_i\}$ for $1 \leq i \leq m$ using the content encryption key *CEK* if the player P already holds the key *CEK*. In general, the *CEK* is included to the associated license as encrypted form with the domain key. Therefore, the *CEK* can be obtained if the media player P is a member of the authorized domain. After successfully decrypting data, the resulting plain multimedia stream is passed to the DRM client.

3.2 License Translation

When the media server S translates the protected DRM content and then distributes on the fly them to the media player P, the associated DRM license may be also delivered to the player P. The associated DRM license must be newly generated due to the changed values such as the hash value of the translated DRM protected content or the associated content identifier.

The simplest solution is to download all associated licenses $l_1, l_2, \dots , l_n$ from the content holder H and to deliver one of them according to the requested AV profile p_m. However, downloading all associated license is not efficient solution since the associated licenses $l_1, l_2, \dots , l_n$ generally include redundant information.

Clearly, the most efficient method is to aggregate possible licenses into one which consists of common factors and uncommon factors.

In uncommon parts, the main overhead is to append the content holder H's signature and MAC value of the DRM license itself for all profiles. The number of the appended signatures and MAC values are linear in the number of AV profiles in home.

For minimizing the size of these data, one solution is to generate the associated license l_m in local network without regard to the contents holder H. In our system, we propose the following technique using a variant of aggregate signature schemes [5]. An aggregate signature scheme is useful for compressing the list of signatures on distinct messages. Our proposed scheme can be efficiently implemented compared with the general aggregate signature schemes since we only consider that the DRM licenses are issued by a unique content holder H.

Given a permutation description d, a permutation family is one-way if it is infeasible to invert the corresponding permutation. A permutation family is trapdoor if each description d has some corresponding trapdoor $t \in T$ such that it is easy to invert the permutation corresponding to s using t, but infeasible without t.

Our scheme generates the compressed signature using a trapdoor permutation $\pi: D \to D$ and a random oracle $h: \{0, 1\}^* \to D$ where D is a group with operation $\cdot$. The scheme comprises the following three algorithms:

- Key Generation: For the contents holder H, the trapdoor permutation π and the trapdoor information t are randomly selected. The selected values t and π are used as the signing key and verification key, respectively.
- Signing: Given the possible licenses $l_1, l_2, \ldots, l_n$, the compressed signature is computed by the contents holder H as the follows:
  The contents holder H then sequentially computes σ_i repeatedly applying the inverse of the permutation π^{-1} and the random oracle h where σ_0 is the unit element in the group D as the follows:

$$\sigma_i = \pi^{-1}(h(l_i) \cdot \sigma_{i-1}), \text{ for } 1 \leq i \leq n. \tag{1}$$

Each intermediate value σ_i means the signature of the DRM license l_i.

- Verification: For verifying the validity of the signature σ_k, the media player P computes the verification value v_k as follows:

$$v_k = h(l_k)^{-1} \cdot \pi(\sigma_k). \tag{2}$$

It is clearly true that there is a $h(l_k)^{-1}$ since D is a group. The media player P sequentially computes the verification values v_i repeatedly until computing v_1 as follows:

$$v_i = h(l_i)^{-1} \cdot \pi(v_{i+1}). \tag{3}$$

We can verify the validity of the signature by checking whether v_1 is the same as the unit element in the group D.

The advantage of the proposed scheme is to generate the valid signatures of the associated licenses without the key management or too heavy cryptographic operations. The media server S locally generates the signature σ_m of the license l_m from the stored σ_n without regard to the trust relationship with the contents holder H. In addition, for computing MAC value of the DRM license l_m, the media server needs to hold the MAC key of the DRM protected content. It can be solved by delivering the signed MAC key MK instead of MAC value of the DRM content. The media server S computes the MAC value of the license l_m using the signed MAC key. Figure 2 shows the protocol of the overall system.

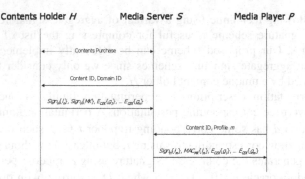

Fig. 2. The overview of the proposed system

In general, the delivered values can be easily adapted to the conventional file formats such as a license object or a DRM protected content without modifying them. Therefore, our approach does not require new standardized DRM file formats.

4 Conclusion

In this paper, we have presented a new DRM system for multiple AV profiles.

To share DRM contents between diverse home devices, the proposed system provides scalable DRM contents and the compression of the associated license. The proposed system which is based on a scalable coding and the aggregate signature scheme, encodes a content sequence such as audio/video frames into protected data that can be streamed or copied to heterogeneous clients.

It would be interesting to analysis the performance of the proposed system. In the future, we plan to investigate how our system can be efficiently implemented using a specific DRM technology such as OMA DRM. We will also investigate a formal security proof of the system.

References

1. Eskicioglu, A.M., Delp, E.J.: An integrated approach to encrypting scalable video. In: IEEE ICME, pp. 573–576. IEEE Computer Society Press, Los Alamitos (2002)
2. Taban, G., Cárdenas, A.A., Gligor, V.D.: Towards a secure and interoperable DRM architecture. In: Proceedings of the 6th ACM Workshop on Digital Rights Management, pp. 69–78 (2006)
3. DLNA. DLNA Overview and Vision, http://www.dlna.org/en/industry/about/dlna_white_paper_2006.pdf.
4. van den Heuval, S.A.F.A., Jonker, W., Kamperman, F.L.A.J., Lenoir, P.J.: Secure Content Management in Authorized Domains. In: Proceedings of IBC 2002, pp. 467–474 (2002)
5. Boneh, D., Gentry, C., Lynn, B., Shacham, H.: A survey of two signature aggregation techniques. RSA's CryptoBytes 6(2) (2003)
6. Reichel, J., Schwarz, H., Wien, M.: Joint Scalable Video Model JSVM-6, Doc. JVT-S202 (2006)

7. Open Mobile Alliance. DRM Specification 2.0, http://www.openmobilealliance.org/
8. Popescu, B.C., Crispo, B., Tanenbaum, A., Kamperman, F.: A DRM Security Architecture for Home Networks. In: Proceedings of the 4th ACM Workshop on Digital Rights Management, pp. 1–10 (2004)
9. Wiegand, T., Sullivan, G., Reichel, J., Schwarz, H., Wien, M.: Scalable Video Coding-Joint Draft 6, Doc. JVT-S201 (2006)
10. McCanne, S., Jacobson, V., Vetterli, M.: Receiver-driven layered multicast. In: Proceedings of ACM SIGCOMM, pp. 117–130 (1996)
11. Kamperman, F., Szostek, L., Wouter, B.: Marlin common domain: authorized domains in marlin technology. In: 4th IEEE Consumer Communications and Networking Conference, pp. 935–939 (2007)
12. Koenen, R.H., Lacy, J., Mackey, M., Mitchell, S.: The long march to interoperable digital rights management. Proceedings of the IEEE 92(6) (2004)
13. Kravitz, D.W., Messerges, T.S.: Achieving media portability through local content translation and end-to-end rights management. In: Proceedings of the Fifth ACM Workshop on Digital Rights Management (2005)
14. Wee, S.J., Apostolopoulos, J.G.: Secure Scalable streaming and secure transcoding with JPEG-2000, IEEE ICIP (2003)
15. Ateniese, G., Hohenberger, S.: Proxy Re-Signatures: New Definitions, Algorithms, and Applications. In: Proceedings of the ACM Conference on Computer and Communication Security (CCS), pp. 310–319 (2005)
16. Safavi-Niani, R., Sheppard, N., Uehara, T.: Import/Export in digital rights management. In: Proceedings of the 4th ACM Workshop on Digital Rights Management, pp. 99–110 (2004)
17. Senoh, T., Ueno, T., Kogure, T.: DRM renewability & interoperability. In: 1st IEEE Consumer Communications and Networking Conference, pp. 424–429. IEEE Computer Society Press, Los Alamitos (2004)
18. Ateniese, G., Fu, K., Green, M., Hohenberger, S.: Improved Proxy Re-Encryption Schemes with Applications to Secure Distributed Storage. In: Proceedings of the 12th Annual Network and Distributed System Security Symposium. Internet Society, pp. 29–44 (2005)
19. Kalker, T., Carey, K., Lacy, J., Rosner, M.: The Coral DRM interoperability framework. In: 4th IEEE Consumer Communications and Networking Conference, pp. 930–934 (2007)
20. Radha, H., Chen, M.: A framework for efficient progressive fine granularity scalablevideo coding. IEEE Transactions on Circuits and Systems for Video Technology 2(3), 332–344 (2001)
21. Radha, H., Chen, M.: The MPEG-4 fine-grained scalable video coding method for multimediastreaming over IP. IEEE Transactions on Multimedia 3(1), 53–68 (2001)
22. Sovio, S., Asokan, N., Nyberg, K.: Defining Authorization Domains Using Virtual Devices. In: SAINT Workshops 2003, pp. 331–336 (2003)
23. Kim, H., Lee, Y., Chung, B., Yoon, H., Lee, J., Jung, K.: Digital Rights Management with Right Delegation for Home Networks. In: Rhee, M.S., Lee, B. (eds.) ICISC 2006. LNCS, vol. 4296, pp. 233–245. Springer, Heidelberg (2006)

Computational Semantics for Basic Protocol Logic – A Stochastic Approach

Gergei Bana, Koji Hasebe, and Mitsuhiro Okada

[1] Dept of Mathematics, Tulane University, New Orleans, LA, USA
gbana@tulane.edu
[2] Research Center for Verification and Semantics, AIST, Osaka, Japan
k-hasebe@aist.go.jp
[3] Department of Philosophy, Keio University, Tokyo, Japan
mitsu@abelard.flet.keio.ac.jp

Abstract. This paper relates formal and computational models of cryptography in case of active adversaries when formal security analysis is done with first order logic. Instead of the way Datta et al. defined computational semantics to their Protocol Composition Logic, we introduce a new, fully probabilistic method to assign computational semantics to the syntax. We present this via considering a simple example of such a formal model, the Basic Protocol Logic by K. Hasebe and M. Okada [7] , but the technique is suitable for extensions to more complex situations such as PCL. We make use of the usual mathematical treatment of stochastic processes, hence are able to treat arbitrary probability distributions, non-negligible probability of collision, causal dependence or independence.

Keywords: cryptographic protocols, formal methods, first order logic, computational semantics.

1   Introduction

Linking the formal and computational models of cryptography has become of central interest. In this paper we consider the relationship of the two models when formal security analysis is done with first order logic, and a computational semantics (instead of formal) is assigned to the syntax. Proving that the axioms and inference rules of the syntax hold in the semantics implies that a property provable in the syntax must be true in the computational model.

Recently, Datta et al. in [5] gave a computational semantics to the syntax of their Protocol Composition Logic of [4]. In their treatment, every action by the honest participants is recorded on each execution trace (of identical probabilities), and bit strings emerging later are checked whether they were recorded earlier and to what action they corresponded (of the adversary, only send and receive actions are recorded). This way, they first define when a property is *satisfied on a particular trace*, and they say the property is *satisfied in the model* if it is satisfied on an overwhelming number of traces. As the comparisons are done on each trace separately it is not possible to track correlations, and problems arise from the possibility of wrongly identifying bit-strings, even when the probabilities of coincidences are negligible.

I. Cervesato (Ed.): ASIAN 2007, LNCS 4846, pp. 86–94, 2007.

Our approach puts more emphasis on probabilities. Instead of defining what is satisfied on each trace, we say that a property is satisfied in the model if a "cross-section" of traces provides the right probabilities for computational realizations of the property in question. An underlying stochastic structure ensures that we can detect if something depends on the past or does not. It is not coincidences on traces that we look for, but correlations of probability distributions. We introduce our method on a rather simple syntax, namely, a somewhat modified version of Basic Protocol Logic (or BPL, for short) by K. Hasebe and M. Okada [7] and leave extensions to more complex situations such as the PCL to future work. The reason for this is partly the limited space, partly to avoid distraction by an elaborate formal model from the main ideas, but also that a complete axiomatization of the syntax used by Datta et al. for their computational PCL has not yet been published anywhere, only fragments are available. We would like to emphasize though that our point is not to give a computational semantics to BPL but to provide a technique that works well in much more general situations as well.

There is an on-going debate about how the this approach is related to that of Datta et al., and our opinion about specific problems of their approach and why we think our approach solves those problems is in the long version of our paper [3].

Formal methods emerged from the seminal work of Dolev and Yao [6]. The first to link it to computational methods were Abadi and Rogaway in [1] "soundness" for passive adversaries. Active adversaries are considered by, among others, Backes et al. in [2] and Micciancio and Warinschi [8]. Using first order logic as opposed to other formal approaches has multiple advantages. The language of Backes et al. is complicated, includes probabilities, making it harder to work with. The soundness of Micciancio and Warinschi includes a very limiting condition, namely, that the computational interpretation of any secure formal trace must be computationally secure.

2 Basic Protocol Logic

In this section, we briefly describe the syntax of Basic Protocol Logic modified to be suitable for computational interpretation. For the original BPL, please consult [7].

Sorts and Terms. Our language is order-sorted:

- C_{name}, C_{nonce} : finite sets of constants of sort name and of constants of sort nonce;
- terms of sorts name and nonce are also terms of sort message;
- C_{coin_A} : finite set of constants of sort coin_A;
- $C_{\text{coin}} := \bigcup_{A \in C_{\text{name}}} C_{\text{coin}_A}$; terms of sort coin_A are also of sort coin

Compound terms of sort message are built by the grammar: $t ::= M \mid m \mid \langle t, t \rangle \mid \{t\}_P^\rho$, where $M \in C_{\text{name}} \cup C_{\text{nonce}}$, m is free variable of sort message, P is constant or free variable of sort name, and ρ is constant or free variable of sort coin. We write $\{n, A_2\}_Q^{r^A}$ instead of $\{\langle n, A_2 \rangle\}_Q^{r^A}$. We use the following notations:

- $A, B, A_1, A_2, ...$ ($Q, Q', Q_1, Q_2, ...$ resp.): constants (variables, resp.) of sort name;
- $N, N', N_1, N_2, ...$ ($n, n', n_1, n_2, ...$ resp.): constants (variables, resp.) of sort nonce;
- $r^A, r_1^A, r_2^A, ...$ ($s^A, s_1^A, s_2^A, ...$, or $s, s', s_1, s_2, ...$, resp.): constants of sort coin_A (variables of sort coin_A, or variables of sort coin, resp.)
- $M, M', M_1, M_2, ...$ ($m, m', m_1, m_2, ...$) : constants (variables) of sort message

Let $P, P', P_1, P_2, \ldots$ denote any term of sort name, and let $\rho, \rho', \rho_1, \rho_2, \ldots$ denote anything of sort coin. $t, t', t_1, t_2, \ldots$ denote terms, and $\nu, \nu', \ldots$ denote terms of sort nonce.

Formulas. We use five binary predicate symbols: $t = t'$, $t \sqsubseteq t'$, P generates ν, P receives t, and P sends t. The meta expression $acts$ is used to denote one of the action predicates: $generates, receives$ and $sends$. Atomic formulas are either of the form $P_1 \, acts_1 \, t_1; P_2 \, acts_2 \, t_2; \cdots ; P_k \, acts_k \, t_k$, or $t = t'$, or $t \sqsubseteq t'$. The first one is called *trace formula*. A trace formula is used to represent a sequence of the principals' actions. We also use $\alpha_1; \cdots ; \alpha_k$ (or α, for short) to denote $P_1 \, acts_1 \, t_1; \cdots ; P_k \, acts_k \, t_k$. For α ($\equiv \alpha_1; \cdots ; \alpha_m$) and β ($\equiv \beta_1; \cdots ; \beta_n$), we say β *includes* α (denoted by $\alpha \subseteq \beta$), if there is a one-to-one, increasing function $j : \{1, ..., m\} \to \{1, ..., n\}$ such that $\alpha_i \equiv \beta_{j(i)}$. Formulas are defined by

$$\varphi ::= \alpha \mid t_1 = t_2 \mid t_1 \sqsubseteq t_2 \mid \neg\varphi \mid \varphi \wedge \varphi \mid \varphi \vee \varphi \mid \varphi \to \varphi \mid \forall m\varphi' \mid \exists m\varphi'$$

where m is some bound variable, and φ' is obtained from φ by substituting m for every occurrence in φ of a free variable m' of the same sort as m.

Roles. A *protocol* is a set of *roles*, and each role for a principal (say, Q) is described as a trace formula of the form $\alpha^Q \equiv Q \, acts_1 \, t_1; \cdots ; Q \, acts_k \, t_k$.

The Axioms of Basic Protocol Logic. For the lack of space, we just indicate the nature of the axioms. A complete description of them is in [3]. They have three groups: **(I)**: *term axioms* list a set of axioms for equality and subterm relations that we can prove they are sound and that were sufficient to prove correctness of actual protocols we checked. Examples of such axioms are $\forall m(t_1 = t_2 \wedge t_2 = t_3 \to t_1 = t_3)$, or $\forall m Q s s^B (\{t_1\}_A^{s^B} = \{t_2\}_Q^s \to t_1 = t_2 \wedge Q = A \wedge s = s^B)$. Some of the original term axioms of BPL turned out not to be computationally sound, we therefore restricted them to a smaller set that was still enough to prove correctness for a number of protocols. **(II)**: straightforward axioms for trace formulas, such as $\beta \to \alpha$ when $\alpha \subseteq \beta$. **(III)**: this group is about relationships between properties, including an *ordering axiom* as $\forall Q_1 Q_2 n m (n \sqsubseteq m \to \neg(Q_2 \, sends/receives/generates \, m; Q_1 \, generates \, n))$, and two *nonce verification* axioms expressed by formulas with meanings such as: if A and B are constant names, and if A sent out a nonce n_1 encrypted with the public key of B that was not sent in any other way, and name Q received this nonce in some other form, then the encrypted nonce had to go through B.

3   Computational Semantics

Computational Asymmetric Encryption Schemes. The fundamental objects of the computational world are strings, strings $= \{0, 1\}^*$, and families of probability distributions over strings. These families are indexed by a *security parameter* $\eta \in \mathbb{N}$ (which can be roughly understood as key-lengths). Pairing is an injective *pairing function* $[\cdot, \cdot]$: strings $\times$ strings $\to$ strings. We assume that changing a bit string in any of the argument to another bit string of the same length does not influence the length of the output of the pairing. Let plaintexts, ciphertexts, publickey and secretkey be nonempty subsets of strings. The set coins is some probability field that stands for coin-tossing, *i.e.*, randomness. A *computational asymmetric encryption scheme* is a triple $\Pi = (\mathcal{K}, \mathcal{E}, \mathcal{D})$

where: $\mathcal{K}$: param × coins → publickey × secretkey is a key-generation algorithm with param = $\mathbb{N}$, $\mathcal{E}$: publickey × plaintexts × coins → ciphertexts is an encryption function, and $\mathcal{D}$: secretkey × strings → plaintexts is such that for all (e, d) output of $\mathcal{K}(\eta, \cdot)$ and $c \in$ coins, $\mathcal{D}(d, \mathcal{E}(e, m, c)) = m$ for all $m \in$ plaintexts. All these algorithms are computable in polynomial time with respect to the security parameter. We assume that the length of the output of the encryption depends only on the length of the plaintext.

Stochastic Model for the Computational Execution of BPL. We define a computational semantics, mention that the syntactic axioms hold if the encryption scheme is CCA-2 secure, and so, if a formula is provable in the syntax, it must be true in any computational model.

First, since probabilities and complexity are involved, we need a probability space for each value of the security parameter. Since time plays an important role in the execution, what we need is the probability space for a *stochastic process*. We assume that for each security parameter, there is a polynomially bounded maximum number of execution steps n^η. We will denote the finite probability space for an execution of a protocol with security parameter η by Ω^η, subsets of which are called events. Let $\mathcal{F}^\eta$ denote the set of all subsets of Ω^η (including the empty set). A subset containing only one element is called an *elementary event*. The set Ω^η is meant to include all randomness of an execution of the protocol. A *probability measure* p^η assigns a probability to each subset such that it is additive with respect to disjoint unions of sets (so it is enough to assign a probability to each element of Ω^η, then the probability of any subset can be computed). When it is clear which probability space we are talking about, we will just use the notation Pr.

In order to describe what randomness was carried out until step $i \in \{0, 1, ..., n^\eta\}$, we assign a subset $\mathcal{F}_i^\eta \subseteq \mathcal{F}^\eta$ to each i, such that $\mathcal{F}_i^\eta$ is closed under union and intersection, and includes $\emptyset$ and Ω^η, and $\mathcal{F}_i^\eta \subseteq \mathcal{F}_{i+1}^\eta$. The set $\{\mathcal{F}_i^\eta\}_{i=1}^{n^\eta}$ is called *filtration*. Since everything is finite, $\mathcal{F}_i^\eta$ is *atomistic*, that is, each element of it can be obtained as a union of disjoint, minimal (with respect to inclusion) nonempty elements. The minimal nonempty elements are called *atoms*. We introduce the notation

$$\mathbf{Pr} = \{(\Omega^\eta, \{\mathcal{F}_i^\eta\}_{i=0}^{n^\eta}, p^\eta)\}_{\eta \in \text{param}}.$$

We included $\mathcal{F}_0^\eta$ to allow some initial randomness such as key generation. A discrete *random variable* on Ω^η is a function on Ω^η taking some discrete value. Since $\mathcal{F}_i^\eta$ contains the events determined until step i, a random variable g^η depends only on the randomness until i exactly if g is constant on the atoms of $\mathcal{F}_i^\eta$; this is the same as saying that for any possible value c, the set $[g^\eta = c] := \{\omega \mid g^\eta(\omega) = c\}$ is an element of $\mathcal{F}_i^\eta$. In this case, we say that g^η is *measurable* with respect to $\mathcal{F}_i^\eta$. We will, however need a somewhat more complex dependence-notion. We will need to consider random variables that are determined by the randomness until step i_1 on certain random paths, but until step i_2 on other paths, and possibly something else on further paths. For this, we have to first consider a function $J^\eta : \Omega^\eta \to \{0, 1, ..., n^\eta\}$ that tells us which time step to consider on each ω. This function should only depend on the past, so for each $i \in \{0, 1, ..., n^\eta\}$, we require that the set $[J^\eta = i] \in \mathcal{F}_i^\eta$. We will call this function a *stopping time*. The events that have occurred until the stopping time J^η are contained in

$$\mathcal{F}_J^\eta := \{S \mid S \subseteq \Omega^\eta, \text{ and for all } i = 0, 1, ..., n^\eta, \ S \cap [J^\eta = i] \in \mathcal{F}_i^\eta\}.$$

Then, a random variable f^η depends only on the events until the stopping time J^η iff for each c in its range, $[f^\eta = c] \in \mathcal{F}_J^\eta$. Furthermore, a random variable h^η on Ω^η is said to be independent of what happened until J^η iff for any $S \in \mathcal{F}_J^\eta$ and a c possible value of h^η, $\Pr([h^\eta = c] \cap S) = \Pr([h^\eta = c])\Pr(S)$. Finally, it is easy to see that for each random variable f^η, there is a stopping time J_f^η such that f^η is measurable with respect to $\mathcal{F}_{J_f}^\eta$, and J_f^η is minimal in the sense that f^η is not measurable with respect to any other $\mathcal{F}_J^\eta$ if there is an ω such that $J^\eta(\omega) < J_f^\eta(\omega)$.

Example 1. Suppose coins are tossed three times. Then $\Omega = \{(a,b,c) \mid a,b,c = 0,1\}$. Let $(1,\cdot,\cdot) := \{(1,b,c) \mid b,c = 0,1\}$. $(0,\cdot,\cdot)$, etc. are defined analogously. At step $i = 1$, the outcome of the first coin-tossing becomes known, $\mathcal{F}_1 = \{\emptyset, (0,\cdot,\cdot), (1,\cdot,\cdot), \Omega\}$. At step $i = 2$, the outcome of the second coin becomes known too, therefore $\mathcal{F}_2$, besides $\emptyset$ and Ω, contains $(0,0,\cdot)$, $(0,1,\cdot)$, $(1,0,\cdot)$ and $(1,1,\cdot)$ as atoms, and all possible unions of these. $\mathcal{F}_3$ is all subsets. A function g that is measurable with respect to $\mathcal{F}_1$, is constant on $(0,\cdot,\cdot)$ and on $(1,\cdot,\cdot)$, that is, g only depends on the outcome of the first coin tossing, but not the rest. Similarly, an f measurable on $\mathcal{F}_2$, is constant on $(0,0,\cdot)$, on $(0,1,\cdot)$, on $(1,0,\cdot)$ and on $(1,1,\cdot)$. A stopping time is for example the J that equals the position of the first 1, or 3 if there is never 1: $J((a_1,a_2,a_3)) = i$ if $a_i = 1$ and $a_k = 0$ for $k < i$, and $J((a_1,a_2,a_3)) = 3$ if $a_k = 0$ for all $k = 1,2,3$. The atoms of $\mathcal{F}_J$ are $(1,\cdot,\cdot)$, $(0,1,\cdot)$, $\{(0,0,1)\}$ and $\{(0,0,0)\}$.

Principals, Nonces, Random Seeds. Let $\mathbf{Pr} = \{(\Omega^\eta, \{\mathcal{F}_i^\eta\}_{i=0}^{n^\eta}, p^\eta)\}_{\eta \in \mathsf{param}}$ be the stochastic space of the execution of the protocol. Below, we define how principals, nonces and random seeds for the encryptions are represented on this space.

Principals are essentially bit strings describing their names, along with their public and secret keys. So let $\mathcal{P} = P^\eta$ be a set of (polynomially bounded number of) elements of the form $(A^\eta, (e_A^\eta, d_A^\eta))$ where $A^\eta \in \{0,1\}^{n^\eta}$, and (e_A^η, d_A^η) is a pair of probability distributions on Ω^η measurable with respect to $\mathcal{F}_0^\eta$ such that $\Pr[\omega : (e_A^\eta(\omega), d_A^\eta(\omega)) \notin Range(\mathcal{K}(\eta, \cdot))]$ is a negligible function of η. We assume that if $A = B$, then $(e_A^\eta, d_A^\eta) = (e_B^\eta, d_B^\eta)$.

Nonces are bit-strings, for each security parameter, uniformly distributed over the bit-strings of some fixed length. Let $\mathcal{N}$ be a set of elements of the form $\{N^\eta\}_{\eta \in \mathsf{param}}$ where $N^\eta : \Omega^\eta \to \{0,1\}^{m^\eta} \cup \{\bot\}$ ($\bot$ means N^η has no bit-string value on that particular execution), such that over $\{0,1\}^{m^\eta}$, N^η is uniformly distributed. This set describes the nonces that were generated with overwhelming probability during the execution of the protocol. The nonces also have to be independent of what happened earlier when they are being generated, but we will require this later.

For the random seeds of encryptions, let $\mathcal{R}$ be a set of elements of the form $R = \{R^\eta\}_{\eta \in \mathsf{param}}$ where $R^\eta : \Omega^\eta \to \mathsf{coins} \cup \{\bot\}$. Let $\mathcal{R}_g$ be the subset of $\mathcal{R}$ which are properly randomized, that is, for which the values in coins have the distribution required for the encryption scheme (on the condition that the value is not $\bot$). Dishonest participants may encrypt with improperly randomization.

Messages. Messages are simply randomly distributed bit-strings. So let the set of messages be $\mathcal{M}$ elements of the form $M = \{M^\eta\}_{\eta \in \mathsf{param}}$, where $M^\eta : \Omega^\eta \to \{0,1\}^{n^\eta} \cup \{\bot\}$. We render two messages equivalent if they only differ on sets of negligible probability: for M_1, M_2, we write $M_1 \approx M_2$ iff $p^\eta[\omega : M_1(\omega) \neq M_2(\omega)]$ is a negligible function of η.

We factor everything out with respect to the above equivalence, as those distributions that are equivalent, cannot be computationally distinguished. Therefore, $D_M := \mathcal{M}/\approx$, let $D_N := \mathcal{N}/\approx \subset D_M$, and let

$$D_P := \{A \in \mathcal{M} : (A^\eta, (e_A^\eta, d_A^\eta)) \in \mathcal{P} \text{ for some } (e_A^\eta, d_A^\eta)\}/\approx \subset D_M$$

Pairing, Encryption, and Subterm Relation of Computational Messages. We first define what we mean by pairing and encryption of messages on our stochastic field. They are defined in the most straightforward way, by fixing the randomness ω for representatives of the equivalence-classes with respect to $\approx$: For any $X, X_1, X_2 \in D_M$, we write that $X =_C \langle X_1, X_2 \rangle$, if for some (hence for all) $M_1 = \{M_1^\eta\}_{\eta \in \mathsf{param}} \in X_1$ and $M_2 = \{M_2^\eta\}_{\eta \in \mathsf{param}} \in X_2$ (i.e. M_1 and M_2 are arbitrary elements of the equivalence-classes X_1 and X_2), the ensemble of random variables $\{\omega \mapsto [M_1^\eta(\omega), M_2^\eta(\omega)]\}_{\eta \in \mathsf{param}}$ is an element of X.

For encryption of messages, if $A \in \mathcal{P}$, and $R \in \mathcal{R}$, then we will write that $X =_C \{X_1\}_A^R$ if for any (hence for all) $M_1 = \{M_1^\eta\}_{\eta \in \mathsf{param}} \in X_1$, the ensemble of random variables $\{\omega \mapsto \mathcal{E}(e_A^\eta(\omega), M_1^\eta(\omega), R(\omega))\}_{\eta \in \mathsf{param}}$ is an element of X. If the value of any of the input distributions is $\perp$ then we take the output to be $\perp$ as well.

Now we can define subterm relation: With the previous definition of pairing and encryption, we can consider an element of the free term algebra $T(D_M)$ over D_M as an element of D_M. Let $\sqsubseteq_{T(D_M)}$ denote the subterm relation on $T(D_M)$. This generates a subterm relation $\sqsubseteq_C$ on D_M by defining $X_1 \sqsubseteq_C X_2$ to be true iff there is an element $X \in T(D_M)$ such that $X_1 \sqsubseteq_{T(D_M)} X$ and $X_2 =_C X$.

Execution Trace. Execution trace is defined as $Tr = \{Tr^\eta\}_{\eta \in \mathsf{param}}$, $Tr^\eta : \omega \mapsto Tr^\eta(\omega)$ with either $Tr^\eta(\omega) = P_1^\eta(\omega) \, acts_1^\eta(\omega) \, s_1^\eta(\omega); ...; P_{n^\eta(\omega)}^\eta(\omega) \, acts_{n^\eta(\omega)}^\eta(\omega) \, s_{n^\eta(\omega)}^\eta(\omega)$ where for each η security parameter, $\omega \in \Omega^\eta$, $n^\eta(\omega)$ is a natural number less than n^η, $P_i^\eta(\omega) \in D_P$, $acts_i^\eta(\omega)$ is one of *generates*, *sends*, *receives* and $s_i^\eta(\omega) \in \{0,1\}^*$; or $Tr^\eta(\omega) = \perp$ with $n^\eta(\omega) = 0$. For each η, ω, and $i \in \{1, ..., n^\eta\}$, let $Tr_i^\eta(\omega) = P_i^\eta(\omega) \, acts_i^\eta(\omega) \, s_i^\eta(\omega)$ if $i \in \{1, ..., n^\eta(\omega)\}$ and otherwise let $Tr_i^\eta(\omega) = \perp$. We require that Tr_i^η be measurable with respect to $\mathcal{F}_i^\eta$ for all i. We require that any of Tr is PPT computable from the earlier ones.

Domain of Interest. In our computational semantics, we want the syntactic formulas to have meanings such that if something happens on a certain subset of randomness (but not a single fixed randomness), then something else must also happen on that same set. But, as the security parameter is present, we can only claim such things about a sequence of sets that have non-negligile probability. So consider any set of subsets $\mathcal{D}^\eta \in \mathcal{F}^\eta$, $\mathcal{D} = \{\mathcal{D}^\eta\}_{\eta \in \mathsf{param}}$ with non-negligible $p^\eta(\mathcal{D}^\eta)$. We say that for $X_1, X_2 \in D_M$, $X_1 = X_2$ on $\mathcal{D}$ if there are $M_1 = \{M_1^\eta\}_{\eta \in \mathsf{param}} \in X_1$ and $M_2 = \{M_2^\eta\}_{\eta \in \mathsf{param}} \in X_2$ with $M_1^\eta(\omega) = M_2^\eta(\omega)$ for all $\omega \in \mathcal{D}^\eta$. We say that $X_1 \sqsubseteq_C X_2$ on $\mathcal{D}$ iff there is an element $X \in T(D_M)$ such that $X_1 \sqsubseteq_{T(D_M)} X$ and $X_2 =_C X$ on $\mathcal{D}$.

Computational Semantics. For a given security parameter, an *execution* is played by a number of participants. We assume that the principals corresponding to names in the syntax (that is, they correspond to elements in C_{name}) are *regular* (non-corrupted). We assume that these participants generate their keys and encrypt correctly with a CCA-2 encryption scheme, and never use their private keys in any computation except for decryption. For other participants (possibly corrupted), we do not assume this. We further assume that pairing of any two messages differs from any nonce and from any principal name on sets of non-negligible probability. The network is completely controlled by an adversary. The sent and received bit strings are recorded in a trace in the order they happen. Freshly generated bit-strings produced by the regular participants are also recorded. The combined algorithms of the participants and the adversary are assumed to be probabilistic polynomial time. Such a situation produces a *computational trace structure associated to the execution* of the form

$$\mathfrak{M} = (\Pi, [\cdot, \cdot], \mathbf{Pr}, \mathcal{P}, \mathcal{N}, \mathcal{R}_g, Tr, \Phi_C, \mathcal{D}),$$

where Φ_C gives the computational interpretation of constants of the syntax, that is, Φ_C is a one-to-one function on $C_{\text{name}} \cup C_{\text{nonce}} \cup C_{\text{coin}}$ such that (i) $\Phi_C(A) \in D_P$ for any $A \in C_{\text{name}}$ such that $(e^{\eta}_{\Phi_C(A)}, d^{\eta}_{\Phi_C(A)})$ is measurable with respect to $\mathcal{F}_0$ and has the correct key distribution, and for different constants are independent of each other; (ii) $\Phi_C(N) \in D_N$ for any $N \in C_{\text{nonce}}$; (iii) $\Phi_C(r) \in \mathcal{R}_g$ for any $r \in C_{\text{coin}}$; and $\mathcal{D} = \{\mathcal{D}^{\eta}\}_{\eta \in \eta}$, $\mathcal{D}^{\eta} \in \mathcal{F}^{\eta}$ a sequence of subsets where we focus our attention with $p^{\eta}(\mathcal{D}^{\eta})$ non-negligible.

An *extension* of Φ_C to evaluation of free variables is a function Φ that is the same on constants as Φ_C, and for variables Q, n, m, s^A, s of sort name, nonce, message, coin$_A$ and coin respectively, $\Phi(Q) \in D_P$, $\Phi(n) \in D_N$, $\Phi(m) \in D_M$, $\Phi(s^A) \in \mathcal{R}_g$ and $\Phi(s) \in \mathcal{R}$ hold. Then, for any t term, $\Phi(t) \in D_M$ is defined on terms as (i) $\Phi(\langle t_1, t_2 \rangle) = \langle \Phi(t_1), \Phi(t_2) \rangle$; (ii) $\Phi(\{t\}^r_P) = \{\Phi(t)\}^{\Phi(r)}_{\Phi(P)}$; where, as we mentioned earlier, elements of $T(D_M)$ are considered as elements of D_M.

Observe, that the interpretation of a symbolic object is an equivalence class of ensembles of random variables that are defined everywhere, not the ensembles themselves and not on a limited domain. Therefore, we say that an ensemble of random variables $M = \{M^{\eta}\}_{\eta \in \text{param}}$ such that M^{η} is defined on $\mathcal{D}^{\eta}$ is a *realization* of the term t through Φ on $\mathcal{D}$, which we denote $M \lll_{\Phi, \mathcal{D}} t$, if there is an $M_1 \in \Phi(t)$ with $M_1^{\eta}(\omega) = M^{\eta}(\omega) \neq \perp$ for all $\omega \in \mathcal{D}^{\eta}$; and if also $t = \{t'\}^{\rho^A_P}_P$, then we further require that there is an $M' \in \Phi(t')$ such that $M' \lll_{\Phi, \mathcal{D}} t'$ and $\Phi(\rho^A)^{\eta}$ on $\{0, 1\}^{m^{\eta}}$ is independent of $\mathcal{F}^{\eta}_{J_{M'}}$ on the condition that $\Phi(\rho^A)^{\eta} \neq \perp$ (where for $J^{\eta}_{M'}$ see the paragraph before Example 1). We now define when a formula φ is *satisfied* by Φ:

- For any terms t_1, t_2, $\varphi \equiv t_1 = t_2$ is satisfied by Φ, iff $\Phi(t_1) = \Phi(t_2)$ on $\mathcal{D}$, and $\varphi \equiv t_1 \sqsubseteq t_2$ is satisfied by Φ iff $\Phi(t_1) \sqsubseteq_C \Phi(t_2)$ on $\mathcal{D}$.
- For any term u and *acts=sends/receives*, $\varphi \equiv P$ *acts* u is satisfied by Φ iff there are stopping times J^{η} such that apart from sets of negligible probability, $Tr^{\eta}_{J^{\eta}(\omega)}(\omega)$ is of the form A^{η} *acts* $M^{\eta}(\omega)$ for $\omega \in \mathcal{D}^{\eta}$ where $M := \{M^{\eta}\}_{\eta \in \text{param}} \lll_{\Phi, \mathcal{D}} u$ and $A := \{A^{\eta}\}_{\eta \in \text{param}} \lll_{\Phi, \mathcal{D}} P$. We will denote this as $Tr_J \lll_{\Phi, \mathcal{D}} P$ *acts* u.
- If *acts=generates* then the u above is a nonce ν, and so $M := \{M^{\eta}\}_{\eta \in \text{param}} \lll_{\Phi, \mathcal{D}} u$ means there is an $N \in \Phi(\nu)$ such that $M^{\eta}|_{\mathcal{D}^{\eta}} = N^{\eta}|_{\mathcal{D}^{\eta}}$ in this case, and we further require that there is an $N' \approx N$ such that N'^{η} is independent of $\mathcal{F}^{\eta}_{J-1}$ on $[N' \neq \perp]$.

- $\varphi \equiv \beta_1; ...,; \beta_n$ is satisfied by Φ if each of β_k is satisfied by Φ, and if J_k is the stopping time belonging to β_k, then for each $\eta \in$ param and $\omega \in \mathcal{D}^\eta$, $J_k^\eta(\omega) < J_l^\eta(\omega)$ whenever $k < l$.
- Satisfaction of φ, $\neg\varphi$, $\varphi_1 \vee \varphi_2$, $\varphi_1 \wedge \varphi_2$, $,\exists m\varphi$, $\forall m\varphi$ are defined the usual way.

A formula φ is *true* in the structure $\mathfrak{M}$, iff φ is satisfied by every Φ extension of Φ_C.

Soundness. Since we can prove that the axioms are true in the structure $\mathfrak{M}$, by a standard argument of first order logic, the following theorem is true:

Theorem 1. *With our assumptions on the execution of the protocol, if the associated computational trace structure is $\mathfrak{M} = (\Pi, [\cdot, \cdot], \mathbf{Pr}, \mathcal{P}, \mathcal{N}, \mathcal{R}_g, Tr, \Phi_C, \mathcal{D})$, then, a formula that is provable in BPL, is true in $\mathfrak{M}$.*

The proof goes by showing the soundness of the BPL axioms as the axioms of first order logic are trivially satisfied. For proving soundness of group **(I)** of the axioms, we use our conditions on computational pairing, CCA-2 security (e.g. for $\forall m Q ss^B(\{t_1\}_A^{s^B} = \{t_2\}_Q^s \to t_1 = t_2 \wedge Q = A \wedge s = s^B)$), and that equal formulas have equal interpretations (for $\forall m(t_1 = t_2 \wedge t_2 = t_3 \to t_1 = t_3)$). Soundness of group **(II)** is trivial as the notion of subtrace is preserved by interpretation. In **(III)**, the ordering axiom is sound as for the interpretation of a trace formula we required that the order is preserved and because generated nonces have to be independent of the past. Nonce-verification axioms are true, because if they were not, then an algorithm could be constructed that breaks CCA-2 security. For more details we refer to [3] and they will published in a full version.

As a collorary, if an agreement property in the form of the query-form given in [7] is provable in BPL proof system, then the agreement property is true for any computational realization of the protocol where honest participants follow CCA-2 encryption.

4   Conclusions

We have given a computational semantics to Basic Protocol Logic that uses stochastic structures, and stated a soundness theorem. Next, we would like to apply our methods to the much more complex formal syntax of PCL.

References

1. Abadi, M., Rogaway, P.: Reconciling two views of cryptography. Journal of Cryptology 15(2), 103–127 (2002)
2. Backes, M., Pfitzmann, B., Waidner, M.: A composable cryptographic library with nested operations. In: Proceedings of CCS 2003, pp. 220–230. ACM Press, New York (2003)
3. Bana, G., Hasebe, K., Okada, M.: Computational semantics for bpl - a stochastic approach. Available at IACR ePrint Archive, Report 2007/156
4. Datta, A., Derek, A., Mitchell, J.C., Pavlovic, D.: A derivation system and compositional logic for security protocols. Journal of Computer Security 13, 423–482 (2005)
5. Datta, A., Derek, A., Mitchell, J.C., Shmatikov, V., Turuani, M.: Probabilistic polynomial-time semantics for a protocol security logic. In: Caires, L., Italiano, G.F., Monteiro, L., Palamidessi, C., Yung, M. (eds.) ICALP 2005. LNCS, vol. 3580, pp. 16–29. Springer, Heidelberg (2005)

6. Dolev, D., Yao, A.C.: On the security of public-key protocols. IEEE Transactions on Information Theory, 29(2), 198–208, March, Preliminary version presented at FOCS 1981 (1983)
7. Hasebe, K., Okada, M.: Completeness and counter-example generations of a basic protocol logic. In: Proceedings of RULE 2005, vol. 147(1), pp. 73–92. Elsevier, Amsterdam (2005), Available also at: http://dx.doi.org/10.1016/j.entcs.2005.06.038
8. Micciancio, D., Warinschi, B.: Soundness of formal encryption in the presence of active adversaries. In: Naor, M. (ed.) TCC 2004. LNCS, vol. 2951, pp. 133–151. Springer, Heidelberg (2004)

Management Advantages of Object Classification in Role-Based Access Control (RBAC)

Mohammad Jafari and Mohammad Fathian

Department of Information Technology, Faculty of Industrial Engineering, University of
Science and Technology (IUST), Narmak, Tehran, Iran
{m_jafari, fathian}@iust.ac.ir

Abstract. This paper investigates the advantages of enabling object classification
in role-based access control (RBAC). First, it is shown how the merits of the
RBAC models can be ascribed to its using of abstraction and state of
dependencies. Following same arguments, it is shown how inclusion of object
classification will ameliorate dependencies and abstractions in the model. The
discussion contains examining seven criteria to compare object-classification-
enabled RBAC with plain RBAC and trivial-permission-assignment models, in
order to show the advantages of object classification in a more formal manner.
The criteria are: number and complexity of decisions, change management cost,
risk of errors, policy portability and reuse, enforcement and compliance, support
for traditional information classification policies, and object grouping and
management support.

Keywords: Access Control, Role-Based Access Control (RBAC), Object
Classification.

1 Introduction

The family of RBAC models is very well studied in the literature; borders have been
clarified by introducing reference models [20], and finally, it has been codified in
form of a standard [1]. Many extensions have been proposed to RBAC in order to
increase its power and expressiveness. This paper will focus on object classification
as one of such extensions and argue how it can improve its management efficiency.

Many contributors have glimpsed the idea of object classification during their
discussion of RBAC. Sandhu mentions the concept of "object attributes" as a means of
grouping objects, the same way as roles categorize subjects; though he doubts whether
this idea fits in the scope of RBAC [19]. Later, he hints at the idea of "generic
permission" as a special form of permission applied only to one group of objects;
nonetheless, he neglects the concept as being a matter of implementation [20]. "Team-
based access control" is another scheme which limits access rights of users to their
team's resources [22]. It can be viewed as an effort for object classification. In this
model, objects are grouped into generic entities named "object types" and the
permissions of each role are expressed in form of rights to access these "object types"
rather than objects themselves. The notion of "role templates" proposed in [11] is an
effort to restrict the privileges of a role to certain kind of objects in order to make

I. Cervesato (Ed.): ASIAN 2007, LNCS 4846, pp. 95–110, 2007.

content-based access control possible. Roles templates, special "parameterized roles", are actually a means to classifying objects. Objects are classified into categories, which are then used as parameters to role templates, in order to limit the authority of the role to a single category of objects. This notion is used in [12] as a basis to introduce the concept of "object-specific role", a special kind of role the capabilities of which is restricted to a certain group of objects. In other words, this work suggests manipulating the meaning of role, in order to make object classification possible.

The most significant work on object classification however, seems to be done by Covington et al. in [3]. The notion of "object roles" in their "generalized RBAC" is the most evident effort to empower RBAC with object classification, and is similar to the approach of this paper from a conceptual point of view. Recently, Junghwa in [24] proposed a formalization of object classification together with support of object hierarchies and provided some reason in favor of adding this concept to RBAC.

Although rarely noticed in the mainstream of RBAC-related literature, many implementers of RBAC have realized the importance of object classification and include mechanisms to support it. Hence, the notion of object classification is no new idea in the world of implementation. There are often a large number of objects in real systems and defining access rights regarding every single object is impractical [16]. Classification of files in form of directories and applying access rights to the whole directory is one typical example. Using DTD schema as a categorizing mechanism for XML documents in [4, 5] can serve as another instance.

This paper starts with establishing a conceptual basis for measuring the management efficiency of an access control model by focusing on the notion of "dependencies". Three typical models are then considered as the center of discussions: "TPA model", "Plain RBAC", and "object-classification-enabled RBAC", coded as TPA, P-RBAC, and OC-RBAC respectively. On the basis of dependencies and abstractions, it is shown how object classification can bring about many management advantages compared with P-RBAC and TPA models. These insights are then formulated in form of Omicron notation (O(n)). Taken together, the main contribution of this paper is to provide arguments in favor of enabling object classification in RBAC and formulating them.

The remainder of this work proceeds as follows: In section 1.1 an overview of RBAC model is presented in which particular attentions is paid to the state of "dependencies" between the entities of the model. On this ground, some shortcomings believed to exist in the P-RBAC are discussed in section1.2. Section 2 outlines object classification in its simplest form which is then formalized in 2.1 by emulating the definitions of RBAC. Section 3 dwells upon the advantages of OC-RBAC through examination of the seven criteria. Section 4 is where the paper concludes with a summary and probable future works.

1.1 RBAC Review

From a managerial point of view, one of the main points underlying RBAC is separating subjects from their access permission, using an extra layer of abstraction, named "role". The keyword here is "abstraction" which is a well-known concept in

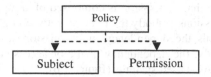

Fig. 1. Dependencies of the access control policy in TPA

system design. From this point of view, RBAC model contrasts TPA models (such as access matrix), in which subjects' permissions are directly assigned to them.

In TPA models, access control policy is stated in form of (subject, permission) pairs, and hence, each of its entries contains a reference to a subject and a permission. This dependency is the root of many problems, as will be discussed later. Access control lists are one of the most well-known examples of using such a model that suffer from many managerial deficiencies. One of the most important contributions of RBAC is believed to be improvement of their manageability [8].

RBAC eliminates the direct relationship between subjects and permissions by setting up the "role" entity which mediates between the two and removes the coupling of policy to permissions. In this model, access control policy can be divided into two components: one component decides the roles of each subject and the other component specifies the access rights of each role. The two components can be expressed in form of subject-role and role-permission pairs respectively. These two components are henceforth called "major" and "minor" components of the RBAC policy to accentuate their cost and importance which will be discussed in section 3.1. (figure 2.a).

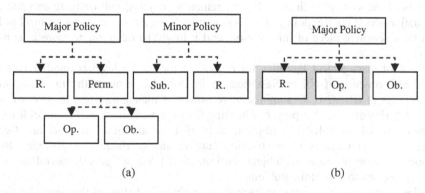

(a)   (b)

Fig. 2. a. Major and minor access control policies with their dependencies. b. Detailed dependencies of the major access control policy in RBAC model. The permission entity is replaced by its constituents, namely objects and operations. The shading denotes less-frequently changing entities.

1.2 Absence of Object Classification in P-RBAC

The "permission" entity deserves more elaboration as it is a key entity in any access control model. Permission is a general term that refers to the right of doing some unit of work in a system [10]. For the sake of simplicity, we will skip complex forms of permissions and assume that permission is composed of an operation exercised on an object. Therefore permissions embody the relation between the objects and operations (figure 2.a). This reveals the dependency of permissions to operations as well as objects, and consequently, the dependency of major access control policy to objects and operations in P-RBAC-based systems (figure 2.b).

Normally, the set of operations is constant across all similar systems, because the set of possible operations is related to the essence of a system [1]. A similar argument holds about roles. Roles are the same across similar systems, because they correspond to the nature of the system. It has also been argued that roles must be engineered in such a manner that they remain stable even against business restructuring [18]. For example, the set of operations (credit, debit, etc.) and roles (clerk, accountant, manager, etc.) are similar among all banking systems; contrary to the set of objects which is dependant to a particular instance of a system. Any banking system has its own set of objects (particular accounts, bills, etc.), even in different departments of a same company. This persistent nature of roles and operations is depicted by the shading in figure 2.b.

The dependency of major access control policy to objects implies that the role-permission decision is utterly an organization-dependent practice. Despite the abstract and system-independent nature of roles, permissions, and hence the whole policy, are dependent to objects. This means that the major access control policy is dependent to one particular system, and implies that the same process of role-permission assignment must be reiterated even for most similar organizations.

Moreover, in the implementation level, the major access control policy will experience a tough coupling to object names (as it is apparent in functional specifications of RBAC models in [9] and [1]). Therefore, any changes in the set of objects of the system, such as adding or renaming objects, will obligate an update to the major access control policy. This is not suitable, as the major access control policy is a very sensitive piece of information, and it might be desirable to store it as read-only.

Lack of management facilities for objects at the model level is another fact that highlights absence of object classification in P-RBAC. One of the most important advantages of RBAC is its administrative power of managing users in form of roles [6, 7, 9]. However, such a power is missing for objects, at least in the model level. In systems based on P-RBAC, objects, even if they are quite similar, are treated separately, and there is no abstraction support in the model for grouping them. Proposing concepts such as "object attributes" in [19], or "generic permissions" in [20] are efforts to solve this problem.

These problems can be traced back to the imbalanced state of the dependencies in the RBAC model. The following section will try to show how object classification can solve these problems, by enhancing the state of dependencies in the model.

2 Proposed Object Classification Scheme

Object classification is realized by declaring a new entity named "category". Other names such as "object role" or "object class" have been proposed for similar concepts elsewhere in the literature [3, 16]. The abstraction of "category" serves the same functionality to objects as the abstraction of "role" does to subjects. A many-to-many relation is defined between objects and categories by which objects can be grouped and classified from several different points of views. Access rights are granted to roles in by using categories in the major access control policy. A subject is authorized to access an object iff at least one of its roles is allowed to access one of the categories assigned to that object.

In this scheme, major access control policy would no more depend on the objects themselves, but rather on object categories. Permissions will now stay on a higher level and involve operations on categories rather than system-specific objects. Consequently, the dependencies of the major access control policy will be refined as shown in figure 3.b. As depicted in figure 3.b, major policy is no more depending upon any frequently-changing entities. Since the category of each object should be determined, an extra component will appear in the minor part of access control policy in order to decide categories of objects (figure 3.a).

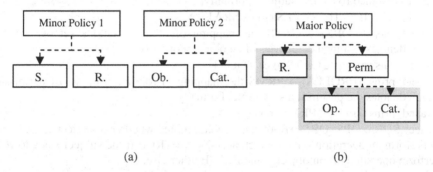

(a)   (b)

Fig. 3. a. Minor access control policies and their dependencies when object classification is involved. b. Major access control policy dependencies when object classification is involved.

From a managerial point of view, three steps are needed to be taken in order to establish the major access control policy in OC-RBAC: Role engineering, category engineering and policy decision. The role engineering and policy establishment processes are similar to P-RBAC. The category engineering may be associated with the process of "asset classification" which is a major domain in information security management standards [14, 15]. Actually the asset classification practice can be realized in form of category engineering.

2.1 Formal Definition

Here, a formal definition of OC-RBAC is presented. This definition obviously resembles the definitions of RBAC. Some details of the original RBAC model (e.g. role activation) are intentionally eliminated for the sake of brevity. Bringing those concepts back to the model is straightforward. SUBS, ROLES, OPS, CATS, and OBS are the sets of subjects, roles, operations, categories and objects respectively.

PRMS = (OPS×CATS) which denotes the set of all permissions. It is noteworthy that not all pairs in this set are semantically meaningful because not every operation is valid for all categories. Some operations might be meaningful only for some particular categories of objects. For example, in a file system, "read" and "write" operations are applicable to all kinds of files while the "execute" operation is applicable only to a specific file category, called executables. This observation opens the way to defining integrity constraints on the set of permissions.

SRA $\subseteq$ SUBS × ROLES, a many-to-many mapping between subjects and roles which denotes the assigned roles of each subject.

OCA $\subseteq$ OBS × CATS, a many-to-many mapping between objects and categories which denotes the assigned categories of each object.

PRA $\subseteq$ PRMS × ROLES, a many-to-many mapping between permissions and roles which denotes the assigned permissions of each role.

asnd_roles: (s:SUBS)$\to$ ROLES the mapping of subject s onto a set of roles which denotes assigned roles of a subject. Formally:

asnd_roles (s) = {r$\in$ ROLES|(s,r) $\in$ SRA}

asnd_cats: (o:OBS)$\to$ CATS the mapping of object o onto a set of categories which denotes assigned categories of an object. Formally:

asnd_cats (o) = {c$\in$ CATS|(o,c) $\in$ OCA}

asnd_prms: (r:ROLES)$\to$ PRMS the mapping of role r onto a set of permissions which denotes the permissions of a role. Formally:

asnd_prms (r) = {p$\in$ PRMS|(p,r) $\in$ PRA}

acc: SUBS×OPS×OBS$\to$Boolean, which denotes whether a subject is authorized to perform an operation on an object. acc(s,op,o)=TRUE if the subject s is allowed to perform operation op on object o and FALSE otherwise.

Modified object access authorization property: A subject s can perform an operation op on object o only if there exists a role r that is included in the subject's roles set and there exists a permission in r's assigned permissions set that authorizes performing operation op on one of the categories containing object o. Namely:

$$access (s,op,o) \Rightarrow$$
$$\exists r\in ROLES, \exists c\in CATS, \exists p\in PRMS$$
$$r \in asnd\_roles (s) \wedge p \in asnd\_perms (r) \wedge (op,c)\in p \wedge c\in asnd\_cats (o)$$

3 Discussion

Object classification is very similar to roles-subjects assignment and hence its advantages can be intuitively sensed through comparison. The concept of category improves the state of dependencies in the P-RBAC model, the same way the concept of role did to TPA model. This section will enumerate the advantages of OC-RBAC over the P-RBAC and TPA. Seven criteria are considered for the comparison of models and the results are summarized in Table 1. The criteria are: number and complexity of decisions, change management costs, policy portability and reuse, risk of errors, ease of enforcement and compliance, ease of applying information classification policies, and support from model for object grouping and management.

Table 1. Comparing management features of the three models for access control. M/m: manager-level/operator-level complexity; I/i: high/low impact (manager/operator); P/p: higher/lower probability.

	TPA	P-RBAC	OC-RBAC
Number and Complexity of Decisions	$M.O(n^2)$	$M.O(n) + m.O(n)$	$M.O(1) +$ $m.O(n)$
Change Management Cost (Detailed in table 2)	very poor	good	better
Risk of Errors (Error Likelihood × Impact)	$I.p.O(n^2)$	$I.p.O(n) +$ $i.P.O(n)$	$i.P.O(n) +$ $I.p.O(1)$
Policy Portability and Reuse	None	$M.O(n) + m.O(n)$	$m.O(n)$
Enforcement and Compliance	None	Manual	Automated
Support for Traditional Information Classification Policies	None	Complex	Trivial
Object Grouping and Management Support	Implementation-level	Implementation-level	Direct Support from Model

3.1 Number and Complexity of Decisions

Management complexity is an important criterion for evaluating the models in question. More complex models need more management resources and therefore lead to more management costs. Moreover, complexity is the root cause of many management errors and also complicates evaluation. Thus, reducing management complexity can be considered as an advantage. We will assume two indicators for the complexity of an access control model: the number of decisions to be made in order to establish the access control policy, and the complexity of each decision. The number of decisions to be made in the process of policy establishment is a good indicator of the management complexity of an access control system because larger number of decisions means utilizing more management resources and higher probability of unintentional mistakes [8]. But counting the number of decisions is not sufficient as different decisions involve different costs. Decisions may be so simple that can be made by an operator or so complicated that require involvement of the board of directors. Noticing the difference between major and minor components of the access control policy, it can be observed that different costs are burdened for decisions in each of the two components. The major access control policy wich involves role-permission decisions needs far more elaboration than the subject-role decisions of minor access control policy. Since roles are often correspond to organizational positions, deciding the role of a subject is a daily task that can be done by an ordinary operator. Even, there have been some efforts to automate such task by using rule-based mechanisms [23]. For instance, it is trivial to realize who the secretary or server administrator is, and therefore, assigning these roles to the corresponding subjects is straightforward. On the contrary, deciding about the access rights of a role in an organization is a complex job usually done by managers and security engineers, and may also need to be examined against higher-level security policies of a system. For instance, when a new employee enters in a company, say in clerk in a bank office, his/her organizational position is usually straightforward and an ordinary operator can enter this information in the system. But when a new position appears in the organization, such as a new "IT manager" position in a bank office, careful study should be undertaken to detail the permissions of this new role. Besides, new positions usually appear as a consequence of some organizational change which is supposed to happen very rarely; while leaving or joining an organization, or changes in organizational positions are regular events which may occur even daily in large systems. This distinction will play a major role in estimating management cost of the decisions in each of these two types of policies. Thus, different costs must be assumed for the sorts of decisions in the two components of the access control policy. We will use m for the cost of a minor policy decisions and M for a decision in major access control policy.

Multiplying total number of decisions of each type by their cost, the total cost imposed by each model can be calculated as an indicator of its complexity. The sets S, Op, O, R and C which are the set of all subjects, operations, objects, roles and categories respectively are important parameters in this calculation. T_i and d_i are the total cost and the total number of decisions of the each model respectively.

In the TPA model depicted in figure 1, the policy is determined by deciding whether to permit each of the triplets of the form (s, op, o) in which $s \in S$, $op \in Op$ and $o \in O$. So, the total number of decisions can be calculated as $d_1 = |S|.|Op|.|O|$ in which $|S|$, $|Op|$ and $|O|$ are the number of elements in the corresponding sets. As discussed in section 1.1, normally there are constant number of operations in a system. This claim is trivial and also confirmed by practical case studies [22]. So, $d_1 = |S|.|O|.const$. If n is assumed to be the maximum of $|S|$ and $|O|$, the total number of decisions in the TPA model follows:

$$d_1 = O(n).O(n).O(1) = O(n^2).$$

All of the decisions in TPA are major because they involve deciding the access rights of a subject. Therefore the total cost for the TPA is figured out as:

$$T_1 = M.O(n^2). \tag{1}$$

In the P-RBAC model there are two policy components. The minor policy is determined by deciding the roles of each subject. There are $|R|$ roles in the system and $|S|$ subjects, and it should be determined whether each subject is the member of each role. Therefore, for each pair (s,r) in which $s \in S$ and $r \in R$, there is a binary decision to determine whether the subject s is a member of role r. Thus, $d_{2\,(Minor)} = |S|.|R|$.

The major policy is determined by deciding whether to permit each of the triplets (r, op, o) in which $r \in R$, $op \in Op$ and $o \in O$. Consequently, $d_{2\,(Major)} = |R|.|Op|.|O|$ and the total number of decisions can be summed up as follows:

$$d_2 = d_{2\,(Major)} + d_{2\,(Minor)} = |S|.|R| + |R|.|Op|.|O|.$$

The number of operations is constant as discussed before. The number of roles in the system can also be assumed as constant because it is insignificant compared to the number of subjects and objects and it does not grow significantly as the system gets larger. This was discussed in section 1.1 and is also shown to be true in practical case studies as in [22] and [6]. Thus, $d_2 = |S|.const + |O|.const$. Multiplying each term by its cost, the total management cost of the P-RBAC model can be figured out as follows. Again n is assumed to be the maximum of $|S|$ and $|O|$:

$$T_2 = M.O(n) + m.O(n). \tag{2}$$

The access control policy in OC-RBAC model is composed of one major and two minor components. The first minor component of the policy pertains to determining each subject's roles and is similar to the one in the P-RBAC model; therefore $d_{3\,(Minor\,1)} = |S|.|R|$. Likewise, the other minor component of the policy involves assigning appropriate categories to each object; thus $d_{3\,(Minor\,2)} = |O|.|C|$.

The major policy is similar to that of P-RBAC with the set of objects replaced by the set of categories; therefore $d_{3\,(Major)} = |R|.|Opl|.|C|$. As argued before, the number of operations in a system is constant. The number of categories is also constant with similar reasons as given for roles. Accordingly, the total number of decisions is summed up as follows:

$d_3 = d_{3\,(Major)} + d_{3\,(Minor\,1)} + d_{3\,(Minor\,2)} = |S|.|R| + |O|.|C| + |R|.|Opl|.|C|$
$= |S|.const + |O|.const + const.$

By assuming $n=\max(|S|,|O|)$, and multiplying costs total cost of OC-RBAC is:

$$T_3 = m.O(n) + m.O(n) + M.const = m.O(n) + M.O(1) \tag{3}$$

Considering equations 1 through 3, one can vividly observe an improvement in the complexity of models. As the system grows, more objects and subjects enter the system and the value of n increases. The growth of complexity in the TPA model is of quadratic order while the complexity of P-RBAC grows linearly. In P-RBAC models, the growth function is composed of a term with the factor of M (administrative cost) as well as a term with factor of m (operator cost). This implies that the growth of complexity is endured by both managers and operators. However, when object classification is involved, the growth function has only a term with the factor of m (operator costs) and the complexity is shouldered only by operators. Accordingly, object classification can lead to significant reduction in the management complexity of the access control system.

3.2 Change Management Cost

Change can occur in many forms to an access control policy and ease of managing change is a major criterion for evaluating access control models. Here, some typical forms of change are discussed and the capabilities of each model in managing them are compared. A summary of this comparison is depicted in Table 2.

Table 2. Cost of managing five typical sorts of change in the models under discussion. (M: manager-level complexity; m: operator-level complexity).

Change Type	TPA	P-RBAC	OC-RBAC
subject access rights	$M.O(n)$	$m.O(1)$	$m.O(1)$
role access rights	$M.O(n^2)$	$M.O(n)$	$M.O(1)$
object access permissions	$M.O(n)$	$M.O(1)$	$m.O(1)$
category permissions	$M.O(n^2)$	$M.O(n)$	$M.O(1)$
total change	$M.O(n^2)$	$m.O(n)+M.O(n)$	$m.O(n) + M.O(1)$

Subject Access Rights: In the TPA model, changing the access rights of a subject usually involves reviewing all of its rights to access every single object in the system. Given that the number of objects is n, this involves $O(n)$ operations. All of these operations are administrative since they involve a decision in major access control policy; thus they are weighted with M and the total cost is $M.O(n)$.

In both plain and OC-RBAC, normal changes in a subject's access right mean a change in that subject's role and random changes in subjects' rights are not supposed to happen on a regular basis. Actually, if changes to subject's rights cannot be interpreted into changes in its role, then the role engineering in the system is flawed and "new" or "modified" roles need to be introduced. Consequently, we can safely presume that any changes to subject's access rights is in form of changes in its role which involve only $O(1)$ operation. These operations are related to the minor access control policy and cost m, thereby leading to the total cost of $m.O(1)$.

Role Access Rights: A major change in the access rights of a group of subjects may imply a change in the access rights of a role. In the TPA model, there is no support for roles; consequently this kind of change will lead to reviewing access rights of a number of subjects. As explained before, the cost of changing the access rights of a single subject is $M.O(n)$. Accordingly, changing the access rights of a group of subjects is $M.O(n^2)$, because this groups may contain as many as $O(n)$ subjects.

In P-RBAC, this kind of change can be handled by reviewing a role's rights to access each object in the system which takes $O(n)$ operations, since the number of objects is $O(n)$. Since these operations belong to major access control policy, they cost M and thus, the total cost is $M.O(n)$.

In the OC-RBAC model such changes can be handled by reviewing the particular role's rights to access each category of objects. As the number of categories is constant, this involves only $O(1)$ major operations which leads to a cost of $M.O(1)$ in total.

Object Access Permissions: This occurs when an object is at the focus of the change. For example, when the security label of a document is changed from "top secret" to "secret", an object-centric change takes place. In TPA model, handling such a change involves reviewing every subject's rights to access the object in question. This takes $O(n)$ operations as total number of subjects is $O(n)$. All of these operations are administrative the cost of which is M, thereby leading to total cost of $M.O(n)$.

In P-RBAC, there is no need to examine the access rights of every single subject since roles can be examined instead. Hence, this kind of change takes only $O(1)$ operations as the number of roles in the system is limited. However, these operations are all administrative and cost M because they involve a decision about the access rights of roles and belong to the major access control policy. This leads to total cost of $M.O(1)$.

If object classification is available, there are well-engineered categories that group objects together in a logical manner. For this reason, it can be assumed that permissions relating to an object do not change arbitrarily, but rather in form of a change in its set of assigned categories. Changing the categories of an object involves a single decision in the minor component of the access control policy, and hence costs m, which leads to total cost of $m.O(1)$.

Category Access Permission: Although rarely, there are times when altering access rights of a whole category of objects is necessary. An example of such change is when the roles that can access a confidential document need to be changed. In TPA model, this case resembles the case of changing a subject's access rights, which involves examining all subjects' rights to access each object in the system, leading to a cost of $M.O(n^2)$.

In P-RBAC model there is no support for categories; therefore in such a case, each role's rights to access corresponding objects must be reexamined. This involves $O(n)$ decisions for each of the roles in the system which leads to a total of $O(n).O(1)$ operations. Since these operations are administrative and cost M, the total cost of this kind of change for this model is $M.O(n)$.

If object classification is enabled, changing the permissions of a category involves reinspection of the each role's rights to access that particular category. This takes only $O(1)$ administrative operations leading to $M.O(1)$ total cost.

Total Change in Some Area: There may be times when a major revision of the access control policy is required which involves a number of object and subjects from different roles and categories. This kind of change is so severe that no role or categories can be preserved and a complete reengineering in needed in that area of the system. In such cases, that particular subset of the system can be assumed as a single system which needs policy establishment from scratch. The cost of this total reengineering is similar to the cost of complete policy establishment process that was calculated in section 3.1.

3.3   Risk of Errors

The total risk of errors involved in the management process is another criterion for comparing the three models under discussion. The risk of error is the product of error probability and error impact. Since major management decisions are made through more elaboration and by allocating more resources (such as committees, double checking, formal acceptance, etc.) the probability of making an error can be assumed to be lower than operator decisions; therefore different probabilities are assumed for administrative and operator errors which are denoted by p and P respectively. On the other hand, error in a management decision has a more profound impact than an error made by an operator; thus, different impact factors are assumed for these two kinds of decisions which are denoted by I and i respectively. Accordingly, each management decision involves a risk of $I.p$ (low-probability, but high-impact) while operator decisions have a risk of $i.P$ (low-impact, but high probability).

In the TPA model, there are $O(n^2)$ management decisions each of which incurs a risk of $I.p$, therefore the total risk of errors in this model is $I.p.O(n^2)$. In P-RBAC however, there are $O(n)$ management decisions as well as $O(n)$ operator decisions, leading to a total risk of $I.p.O(n) + i.P.O(n)$. In the OC-RBAC model, there are $O(n)$ operator decisions and $O(1)$ management decisions; therefore the total risk is $i.P.O(n) + I.p.O(1)$. Comparing the three figures, the advantage of P-RBAC over TPA, and similarly, the advantage of OC-RBAC over P-RBAC is obvious.

3.4 Policy Portability

Policy portability can be of value to many organizations. Porting the access control policy to branch offices and subsidiaries brings about management and financial advantages as well as policy consistency. Moreover, similar organizations that share same sets of roles, categories and operations can benefit from this capability by collaborating to develop a shared access control policy and thus economize in security costs.

The TPA model has no provisions for such a notion as the access control policy is tightly system-dependent. P-RBAC however, has facilitated policy portability to some extent by abstracting subjects in form of more general entities namely roles. Similar organization sharing a same set of roles can use the same major access control policy if they modify the permissions to include their own objects. Therefore policy portability is possible provided that some manual modifications are applied. These modifications comprise revising the major access control policy to take objects of the new system into account. There are $O(1)$ roles and $O(n)$ objects in the new system, and revising the major access control policy requires deciding the rights of each of the roles to access each object, which needs a sum of $O(n)$ management decisions costing M. In order to have a complete access control policy, the minor component must also be established. This requires $O(n)$ operator decisions for determining the members of each role. The total cost of porting a P-RBAC policy to a new system is thereby $M.O(n) + m.O(n)$.

When object classification is available, since the major access control policy does not rely on any system-specific entities (objects or subjects), it is general enough to be ported to similar systems automatically and without manual modifications. Roles, operations and categories stay nearly the same across all organizations of the same type because they are related to the essence of a system rather than a particular instance. Results from case studies do not oppose this presumption [21, 6]. Accordingly, since the major policy needs no change, it can be ported without modification and the adopting system only needs to develop its own minor access control policies in order to assign local subject and objects to existing roles and categories respectively. As discussed before, this incurs $O(n)$ decision of operator cost, leading to the total cost of $m.O(n)$.

As a very simplified example, a software development environment can be assumed in which there are some software managers (SM), a number of developers (D) and several quality managers (QM). Objects in this environment can be grouped into source code (SC), test case (TC), management document (MD), and developer documents (DD). Typical operations can be recounted as create, read, modify, and execute the latter of which is only applicable to "source code" and "test case". Setting all forms of inheritance aside, a very simple major access control policy can look like as shown in table 3.

The access control policy depicted in the foregoing example is general enough to be adopted by several software projects and can serve as a standard policy of a company. Each project only needs to specify the members of roles and categories (minor components of the policy) trivially in order to have a complete access control policy. In this manner, the major access control policy can be ported and reused many times across similar systems.

Table 3. A simplified instance of major access control policy for a software project; the policy is general enough to be adopted by several projects. (R:read; M:modify; C:create; E:execute).

	Source Code	Test Case	Management Documents	Developers Document
Project Manager	R	E	C/R/M	R
Quality Manager	R	C/E	R/M	R/M
Developer	C/R/M/E	E	-	C/R/M

3.5 Enforcement and Compliance

System-independence has a very significant advantage for policy establishment authorities like government agencies and national or international standard bodies. In the medical arena as an example, there can be a unified set of roles, operations and categories that holds for any health care organization. Therefore a regulatory body can establish a general policy for all of the similar organizations in one field and enforce it. Consequently, national or international access control policies serving as unifying standards are possible. Enforcement of such policies can be easily automated by requiring use of a particular major access control policy. The subordinate systems would be required to use a standard major access control policy and hence, make sure they comply with the standard. Automated policy enforcement and compliance checking result from the abstract nature of the major access control policy which is the direct outcome of using object classification. Such facility is neither present in the TPA model nor in P-RBAC. However, as P-RBAC policies contain some level of abstraction, enforcing an RBAC policy is possible in a manual manner and by human intervention. The policy portability and the ability to express global policies can be considered as being among the most important advantages of equipping RBAC with object classification. These features can be seen as a further realization of the original goals of RBAC for elevating the access control policy from a matter of implementation to a high-level organizational and even inter-organizational issue as noted in [19].

3.6 Support for Traditional Information Classification Policies

Information classification is one of the traditional origins of access control and is still needed by current security applications. This can be in form of vertical information

Table 4. Expressing Bell-LaPadula security policy by using object classification

Category Role	Top-Secret	Secret	Confidential	Unclassified ...
Top-Secret	read/write	read	read	read
Secret	write	read/write	read	read
Confidential	write	write	read/write	read
Unclassified	write	write	write	read/write
...				

classification of military systems or horizontal classification which is more commonly used by civilian organizations. These kinds of policies cannot be expressed in TPA model in a systematic manner due to lack of abstraction. In P-RBAC, expressing such policies is a complex job which involves complicated schemes [17]. However, using object classification, expressing such policies is straightforward. Table 4 depicts a simple major policy similar to the well-known Bell-LaPadula [2] policy.

3.7 Object Management and Grouping Support

One of the obvious advantages of categorizing objects is the ability to manage them more systematically through grouping. Beyond trivial management advantages that result from hierarchical grouping of objects, this can prevent inconsistency in access control policies caused by unintentional mistakes. Furthermore, it can be helpful in eliminating redundancy at the implementation level. These benefits have encouraged RBAC implementers to include some form of object classification in their product, although there is no direct support for such concepts in the model. Enabling object classification in the model-level acts as a unifying mechanism for all object classification implementations.

4 Conclusion

This paper showed how the merits of role-based access control model can be traced back to its state of dependencies and abstractions and by following this interpretation it formalized the benefits of object classification from a management point of view. The preliminary topics for future works will be straightforward if attention paid to the duality of role and category abstractions. Following this duality, the model can be further extended to include concepts such as "category hierarchies" (as in [24]) and "separation of categories" as emulations of "role hierarchies" and "separation of duties". Automated enforcement of major access control policies is another area which is worth further studies. Especially, methods for combining different policies in systems adopting more than one major access control policy, such as a military hospital that must comply with both health-care and military standards. This can be a ground for combining policies designed from different points of view which is believed to be one of the limitations of current RBAC [13] and can open the way for a divide-and-conquer approach in policy design.

References

1. American National Standards Institute: American National Standard for Information Technology, Role Based Access Control, ANSI/INCITS 359 (2004)
2. Bell, D.E., Lapadula, L.J.: Secure Computer Systems: Mathematical Foundations, Mitre Corp., Bedford, MA, Technical Report ESD-TR-73-278 (1973)
3. Covington, M.J., Moyer, M.J., Ahamad, M.: Generalized Role-Based Access Control for Securing Future Applications. In: Proceedings of 23rd National Information Systems Security Conference, Baltimore, MD, October 2000 (2000)

4. Damiani, Ernesto, Vimercati, De Capitani Di, S., Paraboschi, Stefano, Samarati, Pierangela.: Design and Implementation of an Access Control Processor for XML Documents. In: Proceedings of the 9th International World Wide Web Conference on Computer Networks: the International Journal of Computer and Telecommunications Networking, pp. 59–75 (2000)

5. Damiani, Ernesto, Vimercati, De Capitani Di, S., Paraboschi, Stefano, Samarati, Pierangela.: A Fine-Grained Access Control System For XML Documents. ACM Transactions on Information and System Security 5(2), 169–202 (2002)

6. Ferraiolo, D.F., Kuhn, R.: Role-Based Access Control. In: Proceedings of the 15th NIST-NSA National Computer Security Conference, Baltimore, Maryland, October 1992, pp. 554–563 (1992)

7. Ferraiolo, D.F., Cugini, J.A., Kuhn, D.R.: Role-Based Access Control: Features and Motivations. In: Proceedings of the 11th Annual Computer Security Applications, New Orleans, LA, December 1995, pp. 241–248 (1995)

8. Ferraiolo, D.F., Barkley, J.F., Kuhn, D.R.: A Role-Based Access Control Model and Reference Implementation within a Corporate Intranet. ACM Transactions on Information and System Security 2(1), 34–64 (1999)

9. Ferraiolo, D.F., Sandhu, Ravi, Gavrila, Serban, Kuhn, D.R., Chandrmouli, Ramaswamy.: Proposed NIST Standard for Role-Based Access Control. ACM Transactions on Information and System Security 4(3), 224–274 (2001)

10. Ferraiolo, D.F., Kuhn, D.R., Chandramouli, Ramaswamy.: Role-Based Access Control, Artech House London (2003)

11. Giuri, Luigi, Iglio, Pietro.: Role Templates For Content-Based Access Control. In: Proceedings of the Second ACM Workshop on Role-Based Access Control, pp. 153–159 (1997)

12. Goh, Cheh, Baldwin, Adrian.: Towards a More Complete Model of Role. In: Proceedings of the Third ACM Workshop on Role-Based Access Control, pp. 55–62 (1998)

13. Hu, Ferraiolo, V.C., Kuhn, D.F., Rick, D.: Assessment of Access Control Systems, National Institute of Standard Technology, Interagency Report 7316 (2006)

14. International Standard Organization: Information Technology-Security Techniques-Code of Practice for Information Security Management, ISO/IEC 17799:2005 (2005)

15. International Standard Organization: Information Technology-Security Techniques-Information Security Management Systems Requirements, ISO/IEC 27001:2005 (2005)

16. Kumar, Arun, Karnik, Neeran, Chafle, Girish.: Context Sensitivity in Role-Based Access Control. ACM SIGOPS Operating Systems Review 36(3), 53–66 (2002)

17. Osborn, Sylvia, Sandhu, Ravi, Munawer, Qamar.: Configuring Role-Based Access Control to Enforce Mandatory and Discretionary Access Control Policies. ACM Transactions on Information and System Security 3(2), 85–106 (2000)

18. Roeckle, Haio, Schimpf, Gerhard, Weidinger, Rupert.: Process-Oriented Approach for Role-Finding to Implement Role-Based Security Administration in a Large Industrial Organization. In: Proceedings of the Fifth ACM Workshop on Role-based Access Control, pp. 103-110 (2000)

19. Sandhu, Ravi, Coyne, Edward. J., Feinstein, Hal, L., Youman, Charles, E.: Role-Based Access Control: A Multi-Dimensional View. In: Proceedings of 10th Annual Computer Security Applications Conference, December 1994, Orlando, Florida, pp. 54–62 (1994)

20. Sandhu, Ravi, Coynek, Edward, J., Feinsteink, Hal, L., Youmank, C.E.: Role-Based Access Control Models. IEEE Computer 29(2), 38–47 (1996)

21. Schaad, Andreas, Moffett, Jonathan, Jacob, Jeremy.: The Role-Based Access Control System of a European Bank: a Case Study and Discussion. In: Proceedings of the Sixth ACM Symposium on Access Control Models and Technologies, pp. 3–9 (2001)
22. Thomas, R.K.: Team-Based Access Control (TMAC): A Primitive for Applying Role-Based Access Controls in Collaborative Environments. In: Proceedings of the Second ACM Workshop on Role-Based Access Control, pp. 13–19 (1997)
23. Al-Kahtani, M.A., Sandhu, R.: Induced Role Hierarchies with Attribute-Based RBAC. In: Proceedings of the Eighth ACM Symposium on Access Control Models and Technologies, pp. 142–148 (2003)
24. Chae, J.: Towards Modal Logic Formalization of the Role-based Access Control with Object Classes. In: FORTE 2007. LNCS, vol. 4574, pp. 97–111. Springer, Heidelberg (2007)

An Integrated Model for Access Control and Information Flow Requirements

Samiha Ayed, Nora Cuppens-Boulahia, and Frédéric Cuppens

ENST-Bretagne, Cesson Sevigne 35576, France

Abstract. Current information systems are more and more complex. They require more interactions between different components and users. So, ensuring system security must not be limited to using an access control model but also, it is primordial to deal with information flows in a system. Thus, an important function of a security policy is to enforce access to different system elements and supervise information flows simultaneously. Several works have been undertaken to join together models of access control and information flow. Unfortunately, beyond the fact that the reference model they use is BLP which is quite rigid, these research works suggest a non integrated models which do nothing but juxtapose access control and information flow controls or are based on a misuse of a mapping between MLS and RBAC models. In this paper, we suggest to formalize DTE model in order to use it as a solution for a flexible information flow control. Then, we integrate it into an unique access control model expressive enough to handle access and flow control security rules. The expressivity of the OrBAC model makes this integration possible and quite natural.

Keywords: DTE, OrBAC, MLS, RBAC, Security Policy.

1 Introduction

With diversity of possible attacks on an information system and with the different security properties that we try to ensure, maintaining and guaranteing system security is being more and more complex task. On the one hand, to protect a system, we must control all actions done from the beginning until the end of a user's sessions. So, a user must be authenticated and must be controlled when accessing objects. All actions that this user performs in the system have to be authorized. On the other hand, information systems present multiuser aspects and they manage interactions between different system parts. These interactions must be also supervised since they can lead to a misuse of system's objects or to a compromising of the system's integrity. To address these different issues, many models were proposed to satisfy different security requirements of a system [1]. Thus, there are models which are interested in integrity and confidentiality properties. Other models are interested in usage control and others in flow control. To secure a system, more than one model must be used since security requirements are as various as the diversity of these models. But there is no model that gathers these different security concerns. Workflow Management Systems are a very

I. Cervesato (Ed.): ASIAN 2007, LNCS 4846, pp. 111–125, 2007.
© Springer-Verlag Berlin Heidelberg 2007

eloquent example of systems which need more than one security control model. Indeed, they not only present a diversity of objects and users but also various dependencies between different tasks and so between users. Access to the same object can be needed simultaneously, also writing on documents and modifying them must conform to the execution order. Moreover, the information flow has to be checked. All these system constraints have to be managed with a global security policy. This policy must deal with access and flow control requirements. Many works were done in order to converge access and information flow control. Several authors have discussed the relationship between RBAC and MLS lattice based systems [2–8, 10–12]. All these works are treated in details later. The basic idea that we retain is that the majority of them are founded on a mapping of RBAC notions and MLS notions. In these models, subject clearances are used as security levels to be assigned to roles in a role-based system. Beyond the limitations of MLS models, we consider that a such correspondence is a misunderstanding of MLS notions. We go in further details in the following section. Thus, the contribution of this paper is twofold. First, we go beyond MLS models as an example of flow control models. For this purpose, we base our study of flow control on a more flexible model which is able to permit us defining a flow control policy far from MLS constraints, say DTE (Domain Type Enforcement) model [15–17], we take close interest in this model, we explain our proper vision of it and finally we formalize it in order to use the formalism in defining our integrated model. Second, using DTE, we are leaded to the obligation of using contextual rules to express a security policy which manages information flows and object accesses. So, we propose to base our model on OrBAC model [18, 19] In OrBAC model, security rules are contextual. This characteristic of OrBAC security rules is necessary and sufficient to take into account information flows control. Moreover, OrBAC is able to express confinement aspect, a key concept in security management of complex systems. The entity *organization* defined in OrBAC model allows us to handle this aspect. Combining OrBAC access rules and a formally stated DTE, we present a different model to integrate access control and information flow requirements.

The remainder of this paper is organized as follows. Section 2 details related works. Section 3 provides different motivations of this work. Section 4 clarifies DTE model and defines our formalism. Section 5 introduces an overview of the OrBAC model and its components. Our integrated model for access and information flow control is presented in section 6. Finally, section 7 concludes the paper and outlines future work.

2   Related Works

Many works have addressed the issue of converging access control and information flow requirements. Nyanchama and Osborn have initially addressed the issue of combining RBAC and Bell-Lapadula (BLP) models in [2]. They examined the application of information flow analysis to role-based systems. Thus, [2] defines a flow policy which describes the authorized flows in the system. It classifies flows in different categories. Then, during process execution we must derive the set of flows generated. The two sets are compared to deduce and ensure that a given role-based scheme is consistent with the specified policy defined with basic flow axioms. Also, to determine this consistency, [2] uses graph theory to deal with the issue. It considers the set of roles and the role-based protection scheme and it draws a graph G1 to represent actual potential flows. A second graph G2 represents relations between flows defined in relation to the flow policy. It defines categories as nodes and edges as permissible information flows between categories. A role-based scheme is consistent with the system security policy if and only if the former graph is a subgraph of the latter. After this first tentative, Nyanchama and Osborn have tackled the issue with a different approach in [3]. In fact they introduced the notion of context. A context is viewed as the set of information accessed via a role. Using this concept, [3] proposes a realization of mandatory access control in role-based protection. In their formulation, role contexts are treated as the equivalent of security levels. They consider two concerns. The first is an acyclic information flow among role contexts. The second is equivalent rules to the simple security property and *-property of traditional multilevel security. [3] proposes a number of access constraints that would realize the equivalent of BLP rules. Finally, it concludes that in MAC, information flows must be acyclic. So the approach proposed ensures that information flows, caused either by role execution or user-role assignment, will be acyclic. In [5] Osborn was based on Nyanchama model described in [3]. She considers details of a single role or node and a given edge. Then, the model determines under what conditions such structures violate MAC constraints. [5] defines a more detailed structure. The new graph contains assignable roles. So it is very restricted compared to general role graphs. In other words, it is more interesting to analyze every role and every edge in a general role graph to verify if roles are assignable, and at what levels they are assignable. Sandhu was also interested in the issue but he goes in the other direction [4]. His approach represents another vision of simulating MAC controls in RBAC models. It is based on configuring RBAC components. It considers similarities between MLS security levels and RBAC roles. So a role is identified to a level of a login session. Its basic idea is to suppose two hierarchies in RBAC model, one for read and another for write. Thus, to each user we associate two roles, one for read (RR) and one for write (RW). Consequently, permissions are divided into groups of read and write privileges and so they must be assigned separately to RR and RW. [4] examines different variations of lattice based access controls (LBAC) and translates each of them into a role hierarchy. It defines a construction using a single pair of roles to accommodate lattices with different variations of the *-property. An extension of this work is presented in [7] and [10] considering different DAC variations. [7] focus on the importance of the administrative aspect. An implementation of these ideas can be found in [8]. In [6], Kuhn uses a construction of a role hierarchy. He defines an assignment of object categories to privilege sets and an assignment of categories to roles. So, to each role it assigns the categories associated with its privilege set and categories associated with privilege sets of its ancestors.

The first limitation of this work is related to category mapping which must be regenerated if changes are made in the role structure. The second is that the hierarchy created by the algorithm must be a tree, rather than a lattice hierarchy. Atluri, huang and bertino have used a convergence between RBAC and MLS to apply it to WorkFlow Management Systems. They define in [11] and [12] models of WFMS based in petri nets and they define an RBAC security policy. They associate levels to different objects used in the system and so to tasks using these objects. Then, they apply the MLS approach to their model taking into account different task dependencies. But their approach is localized into a workflow execution fully secure and partially correct. In other words, the approach does not enforce all task dependencies. So it can affect functional workflow execution.

Most approaches aiming at integrating access control and information flow requirements actually combines the RBAC and BLP models. The RBAC model is used to specify access control requirements by assigning users to roles and permissions to roles. A user is permitted to perform an access if he has activated one role this user is assigned to and if this access is permitted by the role. BLP is the first and mostly used information flow control model. It is based on the Multilevel security (MLS) policy and is used to prevent a high malicious subject from creating information flow to lower security levels. For this purpose, BLP defines two requirements: the simple security property (a subject is only permitted to read lower classified objects) and the *-property (a subject is only permitted to modify higher classified objects).

3   Motivation

Various previous works are essentially based on the same idea. They defined similarities between RBAC and MLS systems. The choice of RBAC is done to handle access control. Then, an application of MLS levels is done on system roles. They investigate clearance notion present in MLS systems and they apply it to roles. Thus, using a mapping between RBAC roles and MLS clearances they associate a clearance to each role. There is actually nothing wrong with identifying a role with a clearance level and assigning users to these roles. What is wrong in these approaches is to apply the BLP principles to the role behavior, especially the *-property. To illustrate our claim, let us consider an MLS application that manages classified objects and provides means to declassify or encrypt these objects. In the RBAC policy, one may consider that users assigned to the role R_secret (corresponding to the secret security level) are permitted to declassify and encrypt secret objects. Now, let us consider three different scenarios:

1. A user logs in the application at the secret level and attempts to declassify a secret object.
2. A user logs in the application at the secret level, creates a digest of a secret object and attempts to declassify this digest.
3. A user logs in the application at the secret level, has an access to a secret object using a browser and attemps to declassify this object through this browser.

We can consider that the first scenario is secure if both the login and declassification functions are trusted (i.e. they do not contain a Trojan Horse) and the secret object to be declassified has high integrity (i.e. this object has not been previously manipulated by a malicious application which hid some secret data the user did not want to declassify). This scenario actually corresponds to a robust declassification as defined in [9]. Regarding the second scenario, it is also secure if the application used to create the digest is a trusted function. Finally, regarding the third scenario, it is not secure if we consider that a browser is not a trusted application since this browser may call the declassification function to illegally declassify other objects. Notice that the conclusion would be the same if we replace declassification by encryption in the third scenario because a malicious browser could use the fact that an object is encrypted to create an illegal covert channel. Now if we apply the BLP principles to the role R_secret, then these three scenarios will be considered insecure since they all violate the *-property principle. This is clearly unsatisfactory. This is why we claim that it is incorrect to identify roles with clearance levels and then apply the BLP principles to these roles. Actually, the BLP principles apply to processes acting on behalf of users to prevent these processes from creating illegal information flow when they contain a Trojan Horse. By contrast, roles should define permissions of user, not of processes. Therefore, all previous works are based on BLP model to ensure flow control. This model present some weaknesses. Although it is able to protect a system from trojan horse used to access a document, BLP is unable to prevent a Trojan horse from altering or destroying data as it permits processes to write into files they can not read. BLP can not detect covert channels and remove them. As an MLS model, it is unable to be used to define policies outside multilevel security, which is not very used in practise because of it restrictions. To go away from these different constraints and drawbacks, we propose in this paper to use another model more flexible to control information flows, say DTE. DTE is presented in the following section. On another side, information flow are generally conditioned by program executions or generated after a process execution. For this reason, flow control must be contextual and not exclusively role dependent. Thus, to specify our integrated model, we choose using OrBAC model instead of RBAC model since it permits us defining contextual and dynamic rules. All the same, OrBAC allows us to express the confinement aspect as it defines explicitly the authority (organization) who defines and manages the security policy. So, our security policy is expressed using OrBAC contextual security rules and integrated DTE concepts. In this way, with the integrated model we propose, we ensure a fine grained access control and manage a more flexible information flow which is constrained by strictness of security levels.

4   DTE: Domain Type Enforcement

4.1   DTE Principles

In a system execution, processes dependencies and users interactions include data exchange. Information flows can be either explicit (as in assignment statements) or implicit (as in conditional statements) [13]. It can be due to functional dependency (e.g. x depends on y, hence there is a flow from y to x), or deductive (if knowing the value of x implies knowing the value of y, hence there is a flow from y to x) [14]. These data may have different sensitivity levels. So, if no security mechanism is applied on such exchange, the data transfer between processes may lead to a leak of confidential information and to a misuse of some documents or information. To limit the damage that it can be caused, confinement mechanisms have been developed [22, 23]. They are based on the idea of restraining the privilege access of subjects on objects. So, confinement is to restrict actions of programs in execution. BLP was the first model which was developed to address this issue and to deal with flow control. But it has some weaknesses we had already explained. Away from multilevel security domain, DTE model has been developed to satisfy security requirements of a system. Since there is no works which detail all DTE functionalities as they were specified, we propose in this section to clarify this technique and give our proper vision concerning its concepts. Domain and Type Enforcement (DTE) [15–17] is a technique originally proposed to protect the integrity of military computer systems and was intended to be used in conjunction with other access control techniques. As with many access control schemes, DTE views a system as a collection of active entities (subjects) and a collection of passive entities (objects) and groups them into domains and types. This classification not only reduces the size of the access control matrix but also simplifies the management. DTE defines two tables to base its access control definition. The first table is a global table called Domain Definition Table (DDT). It governs the access of domains to types (domain-type controls). Each row of the DDT represents a domain and each column represents a type. When a subject attempts to access an object, we must verify the entry corresponding to the domain of the subject and the type of the object in the DDT. If the access needed is defined in the matrix then the access is allowed, if not, the access is denied. The second table is called Domain Interaction Table (DIT). It governs the interaction between domains (Inter-domain controls). Each row and each column of the DIT represents a domain. The intersection cell denotes the access privilege that the domain corresponding to column possesses on the domain corresponding to row. To be stronger, DTE has defined the manner to be used to pass from a domain to another. So, if a subject S belongs to a domain D_1 then it wants to pass to a domain D_2, it must refer the DIT. The intersection of D_1 and D_2 in DIT should contain an entry indicating the activity or the program that S must perform to access to D_2. This entry is called the entry point. Thus, each domain has one or many entry points which consist in programs or activities to invoke by a subject in order to enter this domain. Any subject belonging to another domain must execute an entry point of the destination domain to be able to access this domain. When passing from a domain to another, a subject looses all its privileges of the source domain and gets a privileges set of destination domain. This notion of entry point makes the inter-domain communication more strict and precise. Although DTE model seems simple and enough strong it was not very used as a flow control model.

[16] presents a DTE integration into a μ-kernel. It suggests to centralize all access control decisions in user mode. The μ-kernel uses just a domain abstraction. Later, a work done in [17] extends the integration of DTE introducing both domains and types into kernel. [24–26] are concerned in using DTE in Unix and they present examples of DTE policies expressed in DTEL (DTE Language).

To more explain a DTE policy let us consider figure 1. It presents a DTE policy defined for Unix system. In this specification, *Types* declares one or more object types to be available to other parts of a DTEL specification. *Domains* declares different domains. Then, a domain specification is expressed as a list of tuples. It defines a restricted execution environment composed of four parts:

(1) "entry point" programs, identified by pathname, that a process must execute in order to enter the domain (e.g., (/bin/bash)), (2) access rights to types of objects (e.g., (rwxcd → root_t)), (3) access rights to subjects in other domains (e.g., (exec → root_d)). A DTEL domain controls a process's access to files, a process's access via signals to processes running in other domains, and a process's ability to create processes in other domains by executing their entry point programs. If a domain A has auto access rights to another domain B, a subject in A automatically creates a subject in B when it executes, via exec(), an entry point program of B, and (4) signals exchange between processes of source and destination domains. *Assign* associates a type with one or more files.

Policy of figure 1 shows how to protect a system from the wu-ftpd vulnerability to prevent an attacker from obtaining a root shell. This policy example will be reused in section 6 to clarify our integrated model.

All Works done around DTE use DTEL to specify the security policy. No reflection has been undertaken until now to formally define and use DTE model. A such formalism can be powerful enough to provide expressive security policies. In this paper, we propose to define a formalism allowing us to define merely a security policy which takes into account the flow control between system entities. Afterwards, this formalism must be blended with an access control model in order to deal with flow and access control simultaneously. This twofold control could make our security policy more useful and increases assurance that it is correctly specified. The premise of this formalism is that access control is based on domains and types. It provides facilities to express relationships between system entities. Thus we do not define a new model but an integrated one.

4.2 Our DTE Formalism

DTE has not been very much used since it has just inspired the design of some OS like SELinux. To use DTE as an approach to flow control, we propose to formalize the model. For this purpose let us introduce the following formal definitions.

Definition 1: *(domain) S is a set of all system subjects (active entities). S is divided into equivalence classes. Each class represents a domain D including a set of subjects having the same role in the system.*

Definition 2: *(type) O is a set of all system objects (passive entities). O is divided into equivalence classes. Each class represents a type T including a set of objects having the same integrity properties in the system.*

Definition 3: *(Entry Point) An entry point is a program or an activity which must be executed to pass from a domain D_1 to a domain D_2, denoted $EP(D_1, D_2)$ or $EP_{1,2}$. An entry point implies two rules:*

- *subjects passing from D_1 to D_2 obtain a set of privileges depending on the entry point they execute,*
- *subjects passing from D_1 to D_2 loose all their D_1 privileges.*

The first rule means that the execution of an entry point defines the set of privileges that subjects will obtain when transiting from a domain D_1 to a domain D_2. These privileges are included into or equal to the set of privileges that D_2 subjects have. Each domain can have more than one entry point. The execution of these different entry points implies different privilege sets. The second rule means that if a subject leaves a domain it can not return to it only by executing one of its entry points.

```
 1  ♯ ftpd protection policy
 2  types root_t login_t user_t spool_t binary_t lib_t passwd_t shadow_t dev_t config_t ftpd_t ftpd_xt w_t
 3  domains root_d login_d user_d ftpd_d
 4  default_d root_d
 5  default_et root_t
 6  default_ut root_t
 7  default_rt root_t
 8  spec_domain root_d (/bin/bash sbin/init /bin/su) (rwxcd→root_t rwxcd→spool_t rwcdx→user_t rwdc→ftpd_t
    rxd→lib_t rxd→binary_t rwxcd→passwd_t rxwcd→shadow_t rwxcd→dev_t rwxcd→config_t rwxcd→w_t)
    (auto→login_d auto→ftpd_d) (0→0)
 9  spec_domain login_d (/bin/login /bin/login.dte) (rxd→root_t rwxcd→spool_t rxd→lib_t rxd→binary_t
    rwxcd→passwd_t rxwcd→shadow_t rwxcd→dev_t rxwd→config_t rwxcd→w_t) (exec→root_t exec→user_d)
    (14→0 17→0)
10  spec_domain user_d (/bin/bash /bin/tcsh) (rwxcd→user_t rwxcd→root_t rwxcd→spool_t rxd→lib_t
    rxd→binary_t rwxcd→passwd_t rxwcd→shadow_t rwxcd→dev_t rxd→config_t rwxcd→w_t) (exec→root_d)
    (14→0 17→0)
11  spec_domain ftpd_d (/usr/sbin/in.ftpd) (rwcd→ftpd_t rd→user_t rd→root_t rxd→lib_t r→passwd_t
    r→shadow_t rwcd→dev_t rd→config_t rdx→ftpd_xt rwcd→w_t d→sppol_t) () (14→root_d 17→root_d)
12  assign -u /home user_t
13  assign -u /tmp spool_t
14  assign -u /var spool_t
15  assign -u /dev dev_t
16  assign -u /scratch user_t
17  assign -r /usr/src/linux user_t
18  assign -u /usr/sbin binary_t
19  assign -e /usr/sbin/in.ftpd ftpd_xt
20  assign -r /home/ftp/bin ftpd_xt
21  assign -e /var/run/ftp.pids-all ftpd_t
```

Fig. 1. Sample DTE policy file

If we suppose the following DDT and DIT:

	T_1	T_2	T_3
D_1	true	false	true
D_2	false	false	true
D_3	false	true	false

	D_1	D_2	D_3
D_1	–	$EP_{1,2}$	–
D_2	$EP_{2,1}$	–	$EP_{2,3}$
D_3	–	–	–

DDT entries, true and false, indicate if the domain has an access to different types or not. DIT entries define the entry points must be executed to transit from a domain to another. If we consider that a subject s belonging to the domain D_1 want to accede an object o belonging to T_2, it will refer to the DDT. s has no access to T_2, but consulting DDT and DIT it can find a manner to accede

T_2. In fact, D_3 has access to T_2 and s has an entry point allowing it to accede D_2. Also, the DIT present an entry point from D_2 to D_3. So, to accede o, s must execute $EP_{1,2}$ to pass to D2 then it must execute $EP_{2,3}$ to pass to D_3. Being in D_3, s obtain privileges allowing it acceding o since DDT contains an entry from D_3 to T_2. This path that s construct to accede o is called "confidence path". The following definition gives a formal definition of "confidence path".

Definition 4: *(confidence path) is a set of entry points $< EP_{i,k}, EP_{k,l}, \ldots, EP_{m,j} >$ which must be executed by a subject s to pass from D_i to D_j in order to obtain access to object to which it has not initially the access. Privileges granted through this confidence path are restricted to minimum privileges required to perform the access needed.*

The DTE formalism is based on two kinds of rules expressing and substituting DDT and DIT. These two rules are formally defined in the following.

Definition 5: *(SR_DDT) is a security rule substituting a DDT entry. It is defined as a 4-uplet : SR_DDT = (rule_type, domain, type, privilege) where Rule_type belongs to {permission, prohibition}.*

An instance of this rule can be: SR_DDT = (Permission, professor, exam, change) meaning that only professors have privileges to change exams.

So, we express a DDT as a set of rules defined according to definition 5.

Definition 6: *(SR_DIT) is a security rule substituting a DIT entry. It is defined as a 4-uplet: SR_DIT = (rule_type, domain1, domain2, entry point) where Rule_type belongs to {permission, prohibition}.*

An instance of this rule can be: SR_DIT = (Permission, engineering, http_d, /usr/bin/httpd) meaning that engineers have permission to pass from engineering domain to http_d domain by executing the program /usr/bin/httpd. When transiting to http_d, engineers obtain a set of http_d privileges defined by the execution of the entry point and they loose all privileges of source domain.

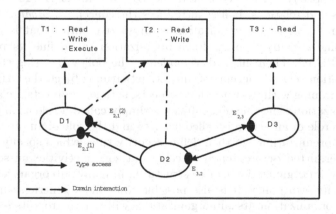

Fig. 2. Sample of a graphic system topology

As an example of a DTE policy, let us consider the figure 2. It presents a system consisting of three domains D_1, D_2 and D_3. These domains have different accesses to three object types T1, T2 and T3. Also, they have interactions between them defined through different entry points. We remark that D_1 has two entry points. In the system specification we can suppose that $EP_{2,1}(1)$ grants read and execute privileges to D_2 subjects and $EP_{2,1}(2)$ grants write privilege to D_2 subjects. Table 1 summarizes the DTE policy corresponding to figure 2.

Thus, we define our DTE control flow policy as a set of SR_DDT and SR_DIT rules. Such policy satisfies information flow requirements. Our integrated model uses this policy to deal with information flow control. We choose to base our model on OrBAC model as it is enough expressive and it allows us to integrate our flow control policy using access control rules. OrBAC offers *context* notion which permits us to define dynamic rules and to express our control flow policy using these rules. The sequel gives an overview of OrBAC and how we use it.

Table 1. DTE policy corresponding to figure 2

SR_DDT	SR_DIT
(Permission, D_1, T_1, Read)	(Permission, D_2, D_1, $E_{2,1}(1)$)
(Permission, D_1, T_1, Write)	(Permission, D_2, D_1, $E_{2,1}(2)$)
(Permission, D_1, T_1, Execute)	(Permission, D_2, D_3, $E_{2,3}$)
(Permission, D_1, T_2, Read)	(Permission, D_3, D_2, $E_{3,2}$)
(Permission, D_1, T_2, Write)	
(Permission, D_2, T_2, Read)	
(Permission, D_2, T_2, Write)	
(Permission, D_3, T_3, Read)	

5   OrBAC in Brief

In order to specify a security policy, the OrBAC model [18, 19] defines several entities and relations. It first introduces the concept of *organization* which is central in OrBAC. An organization is any active entity that is responsible for managing a security policy. Each organization can define its proper policy using OrBAC. Then, instead of modeling the policy by using the concrete implementation-related concepts of subject, action and object, the OrBAC model suggests reasoning with the roles that subjects, actions or objects are assigned to in an organization. The role of a subject is simply called a role as in the RBAC model. The role of an action is called activity and the role of an object is called view. Each organization can then define security rules which specify that some roles are permitted or prohibited to carry out some activities on some views. Particularly, an organization can be structured in many sub organizations, each one having its own policy. It is also possible to define a generic security policy in the root organization. Its sub organizations will inherit from its security policy. Also, they can add or delete some rules and so, define their proper policy.

The definition of an organization and the hierarchy of its sub organizations facilitate the administration [20]. The security rules do not apply statically but their activation may depend on contextual conditions [21]. For this purpose, the concept of *context* is explicitly included in OrBAC. Contexts are used to express different types of extra conditions or constraints that control activation of rules expressed in the access control policy. So, using formalism based on first order logic, security rules are modeled using a 6-places predicate.

Definition 7: *an OrBAC security rule is defined as: security_rule (type, organization, role, activity, view, context) where type* ∈ {*permission, prohibition, obligation*}. An example of this security rule can be: security_rule (permission, a_hosp, nurse, consult, medical_record, urgency) meaning that, in organization a_hosp, a nurse is permitted to consult a medical record in the context of urgency.

6   Access and Information Flow Control Convergence

In this section, we present our integrated model for access control and information flow requirements. The model is based on OrBAC to express access control and it is enriched with a DTE approach to express information flow control. This convergence let us considering only one model (our proposed model) to specify security policy of a system. Finally, we exemplify the model.

6.1   Access Control Policy

OrBAC defines contextual rules which can depend on different contexts. These contexts can be related to conditions or circumstances under which a rule is valid or an activity is performed. If we observe SR_DDT and OrBAC rules we can deduce that the former are expressed by the latter using a default context. The default context is expressed in OrBAC as a context which is always true. So rules with such context are always valid. In fact, role, activity and view significance in OrBAC match respectively domain, privilege and type significance in DTE. So, an SR_DDT rule can be easily expressed using an OrBAC rule. This is a quite natural result as SR_DDT rules are specific access control rules. Further, OrBAC gives the possibility to define more fine access control rules than DDT in DTE can do since it presents different types of contexts. Indeed, with different OrBAC contexts we can express diverse conditions and temporal constraints. Thus, we can formulate dynamic and expressive rules which can not be expressed just by using DTE. That is why we have not choose DTE formalism to express both access an flow controls, otherwise we get a static integrated model with respect to access control aspects.

6.2   Information Flow Control Policy

As we have presented, OrBAC is an efficient model to express access control rules. So, it will be very useful if we succeed to express access and flow control using the same model. Our DTE formalism offers SR_DIT rules to define information flow control policy. But as we aforementioned, DTE is not very efficient in expressing access control, whereas OrBAC is. In the sequel, we present our approach to define our integrated model based on OrBAC and using a DTE approach. We suppose, due to space limitation, that this policy is closed meaning that all which is not permitted is denied and we do not deal with *obligations*.

Based on an OrBAC rule, SR_DIT [*SR_DIT = (rule_type, domain1, domain2, entry point)*] can be seen as a particular OrBAC rule. This rule must express the transition between different domains and must introduce entry point notion in order to preserve a secure information flows and to keep DTE aspects. Therefore, to consider this particular rule we suppose the following hypotheses: (1) the source domain is considered as the role in the OrBAC rule (we have already said that the two notions have equivalent significances), (2) the destination domain is considered as the view in OrBAC rule, (3) the transition between two domains can be expressed as an OrBAC activity since the basic role of this specific rule is to handle interactions between domains. So, we define the OrBAC activity as an Enter activity, (4) the entry point defines the manner to enter a domain. Thus, we can consider it as a condition of rule validation. Therefore, an entry point can be defined as a specific context in an OrBAC rule denoted through($E_{i,j}$). This context specifies that the rule is valid only through $E_{i,j}$ execution.

Thus, such a rule is expressed, in a specific organization org and handling transition between D_1 and D_2, as follows: *SR (permission, org, D_1, Enter, D_2, through($E_{1,2}$))*. These flow control rules can be enriched with other OrBAC contexts. Indeed, through($E_{i,j}$) context can be used in conjunction with different OrBAC contexts, for example temporal contexts, to express more restrictive or conditioned flow control. Also, We recall that a transition from a domain D_1 to a domain D_2 is possible only if there is the corresponding rule in the policy. In other words, handling domains interactions does not contain prohibitions. This interaction is allowed only if there is a corresponding permission. Such transitions between domains correspond, in our integrated formalism "access control/flow control", to a context change. Since transiting to another domain corresponds to the activation of a new context, new rules will be activated. These rules are those for which this context is valid. This dynamic management of the security policy and the closed policy hypothesis guarantee the loose of source domain privileges during transition. New granted privileges are defined according to the entry point executed. The entity *organization* is useful to control the flow in the inter-organizational environment. This will be developed in a forthcoming paper.

6.3   Example

To exemplify our proposed model, let us reconsider figure 1. Using our integrated model, line 9 is expressed as the following rules set. We suppose that we are in Unix system organization.

1. (permission, Unix, login_d, rxd, root_t ,*default*)
2. (permission, Unix, login_d, rwxcd, spool_t ,*default*)
3. (permission, Unix, login_d, rxd, lib_t ,*default*)

4. (permission, Unix, login_d, rxd, binary_t ,*default*)
5. (permission, Unix, login_d, rwxcd, passwd_t ,*default*)
6. (permission, Unix, login_d, rxwcd, shadow_t ,*default*)
7. (permission, Unix, login_d, rwxcd, dev_t ,*default*)
8. (permission, Unix, login_d, rxwd, config_t ,*default*)
9. (permission, Unix, login_d, rwxcd, w_t ,*default*)
10. (permission, Unix, login_d, *Enter*, root_d, *through(exec())*)
11. (permission, Unix, login_d, *Enter*, user_d, *through(exec())*)

The rules 1-9 express the access control policy. Rules 10 and 11 handle inter-actions between login_d and root_d, user_d. The whole set of these rules presents the security policy corresponding to line 9 of the first example in figure 1 of the section 4.1. This policy is based on OrBAC rules enriched with DTE approach. It is expressed using only one form of rules. If we consider for instance the first rule, "rxd" indicates the activity allowed by this rule. We use this notation just to simplify and reduce the list of security rules. In fact, "rxd" corresponds to three privilege activities: read (r), execute (x) and destroy (d). Thus, this rule corresponds to three rules in the policy. For the two last rules, the activity field contains *"Enter"* which specifies permitted transitions between domains since they are flow control rules. In this example we use the *"default"* context when expressing access control rules. This context implies no conditions on the activity performance. Such choice is done to simplify the example. Other contexts, such temporal contexts, can be used in conjunction to *"default"* context or to *"through"* context. *"through"* context is used in flow control rules to express the manner to enter corresponding domains. Transiting into root_d and user_d domains is released when executing exec() which activates one of the entry points defined for root_d and user_d respectively: (/bin/bash, /sbin/init, /bin/su) or (/bin/bash, /bin/tcsh). These entry points define privileges granted to login_d subjects migrating to root_d or user_d. Different domains used here are specified corresponding to our specification done in definition 1 of section 4.2. We remark that in this example login_d is used as a role in access control rules and root_d and user_d are used as views in information flow control rules. But, they can be used as domains in other access control rules. According to this policy, login_d has no access to the type user_t. If a login_d's subject requires an access to objects of this type, he must transit to root_d or user_d which have access to this type (see figure 1, lines 8 and 10). So, our integrated model ensure the aspect of *"confidence path"* defined in DTE formalism (see definition 4 of section 4.2).

7   Conclusion

In this paper, we have presented an integrated security model that is capable of taking into account information flow and access control. The security policy is based on OrBAC rules which integrate flow control using a DTE approach. OrBAC is an adequate choice since it permits us to define contextual and dynamic rules. Also, it is enough expressive to be able to integrate information flow control. The organization notion present in OrBAC allows to express confinement. Our approach remedies to weaknesses present in previous approaches based on MLS and RBAC models. In this paper, we have considered information flow control into the same organization. As part of future work, we will consider a more complex case where we supervise inter-organization flows. Indeed, organizations must exchange flows to have knowledge of what is happening globally in the system. These flows have to be managed in order to keep a secure execution environment of processes. Also, we intend to apply our integrated model to Workflow Management Systems (WFMS). This is a critical issue since such systems present a very important need of security. In fact, they present multi users aspects, inter-dependent execution and dynamic progression. The confinement aspect that the organization entity express will be very useful to define the inter-organization policy.

Acknowledgment

This work is partially supported by the RNRT project Polux.

References

1. Sandhu, R.S.: Lattice-Based Access Control Models. IEEE Computer 26(11), 9–19 (1993)
2. Nyanchama, M., Osborn, S.: Information Flow Analysis in Role-Based Security Systems. In: Proc. ICCI 1994. International Conference on Computing and Information, pp. 1368–1384 (1994)
3. Nyanchama, M., Osborn, S.: Modeling Mandatory Access Control in Role-Based Security Systems. In: IFIP Workshop on Database Security (1996)
4. Sandhu, R.: Role Hierarchies and Constraints for Lattice-Based Access Controls. In: Proc. Fourth European Symposium on Research in Computer Security, Rome, Italy (1996)
5. Osborn, S.: Mandatory Access Control and Role-Based Access Control Revisited. In: Proceedings of the second ACM workshop on Role-based access control, Fairfax, Virginia, United States, pp. 31–40 (1997)
6. Kuhn, D.R.: Role Based Access control on MLS Systems without Kernel changes. In: Proceedings of the third ACM Workshop on Role-Based Access Control, Fairfax, Virginia, United States, pp. 25–32 (1998)
7. Osborn, S., Sandhu, R., Munawer, Q.: Configuring Role-Based Access Control to Enforce Mandatory and Discretionary Access control Policies. ACM Transactions on Information and System Security 3(2), 85–106 (2000)
8. Demurjian, S.: Implementation of Mandatory Access control in Role-Based Security System. CSE367 Final Project report (2001)
9. Myers, A.C., Sabelfeld, A., Zdancewic, S.: Enforcing robust declassification. In: Proc. IEEE Computer Security Foundations Workshop, pp. 172–186 (June 2004)
10. Sandhu, R., Munawer, Q.: How to do discretionary access control using roles. In: Proc. of the 3rd ACM Workshop on Role Based Access Control (RBAC 1998), Fairfax, VA, USA (1998)

11. Atluri, V., Huang, W.-K.: Enforcing Mandatory and Discretionary security in Workflow Management Systems. Journal of Computer Security 5(4), 303–339 (1997)
12. Atluri, V., Huang, W.-K., Bertino, E.: A semantic Based Execution Model for Multilevel Secure Workflows. Journal of Computer Security 8(1) (2000)
13. Liu, L.: On secure Flow Analysis in Computer systems. In: Proc. IEEE Symposium on Research in Security and Privacy, pp. 22–33 (1980)
14. Millen, J.K.: Information Flow Analysis of Formal Specifications. In: Proc. IEEE Symposium on Research in Security and Privacy, pp. 3–8 (1981)
15. Badger, L., Sterne, D.F., Sherman, D.L., Walker, K.M., Haghighat, S.A.: Practical Domain and Type Enforcement for Unix. In: IEEE Symposium on Security and Privacy, Oakland, CA, USA (1995)
16. Tidswell, J., Potter, J.: Domain and Type Enforcement in a μ-Kemel. In: Proceedings of the 20th Australasian Computer Science Conference, Sydney, Australia (1997)
17. Kiszka, J., Wagner, B.: Domain and Type Enforcement for Real-Time Operating Systems. In: Proceedings ETFA 2003, Emerging Technologies and Factory Automation (2003)
18. Abou El Kalam, A., El Baida, R., Balbiani, P., Benferhat, S., Cuppens, F., Deswarte, Y., Miége, A., Saurel, C., Trouessin, G.: Organization Based Access Control. In: IEEE 4th International Workshop on Policies for Distributed Systems and Networks, Lake Come, Italy (2003)
19. Cuppens, F., Cuppens-Boulahia, N., Sans, T., Miége, A.: A formal approach to specify and deploy a network security policy. In: Second Workshop on Formal Aspects in Security and Trust (FAST), Toulouse, France (2004)
20. Cuppens, F., Cuppens-Boulahia, N., Miége, A.: Inheritance hierarchies in the Or-BAC model and application in a network environment. In: Second Foundations of Computer Security Workshop (FCS 2004), Turku, Finlande (2004)
21. Cuppens, F., Miége, A.: Modelling contexts in the Or-BAC model. In: 19th Annual Computer Security Applications Conference, Las Vegas (2003)
22. Boebert, W.E., Kain, R.Y.: A further Note on the Confinment Problem. In: Proceedings of the IEEE 1996 International Carnahan Conference on Security Technology, IEEE Computer Society, New York (1996)
23. Boebert, W.E., Kain, R.Y., Young, W.D.: The extended Access Matrix Model of Computer Security. ACM Sigsoft Software Engineering Notes 10(4) (1985)
24. Hallyn, S., Kearns, P.: Tools to Administer Domain and Type Enforcement. LISA XV. San Diego, CA (2001)
25. Oostendorp, K.A., Badger, L., Vance, C.D., Morrison, W.G., Petkac, M.J., Sherman, D.L., Sterne, D.F.: Domain and Type Enforcement Firewalls. In: Proceedings of the Thirteenth Annual Computer Security Applications Conference, San Diego, California, pp. 122–132 (1997)
26. Walker, K.M., Sterne, D.F., Lee Badger, M., Petkac, M.J., Shermann, D.L., Oostendorp, K.A.: Confining Root Programs with Domain and Type Enforcement (DTE). In: Proceedings of the 6th conference on USENIX Security Symposium, Focusing on Applications of Cryptography, San Jose, California, vol. 6 (1996)

Digital Rights Management Using a Master Control Device

Imad M. Abbadi

Information Security Group, Royal Holloway, University of London
Egham, Surrey, TW20 0EX, UK
I.Abbadi@rhul.ac.uk

Abstract. This paper focuses on the problem of preventing the illegal copying of digital content whilst allowing content mobility within a single user domain. This paper proposes a novel solution for binding a domain to a single owner. Domain owners are authenticated using two-factor authentication, which involves "something the domain owner has", i.e. a Master Control device that controls and manages consumers domains, and binds devices joining a domain to itself, and "something the domain owner is or knows", i.e. a biometric or password/PIN authentication mechanism that is implemented by the Master Control device. These measures establish a one-to-many relationship between the Master Control device and domain devices, and a one-to-one relationship between domain owners and their Master Control Devices, ensuring that a single consumer owns each domain. This stops illicit content proliferation. Finally, the pros and cons of two possible approaches to user authentication, i.e. the use of a password/PIN and biometric authentication mechanisms, and possible countermeasures to the identified vulnerabilities are discussed.

1 Introduction

Unauthorised reproduction of digital assets is not a new issue. Concerns about protecting digital assets are raised every time reproduction tools such as tape recorders or photocopiers become available to consumers. In the past, however, content piracy was limited to distribution via physical media. The recent digitisation of information, the development of telecommunication technologies such as broadband and mobile networks, and the spread of the Internet have led to a huge rise in digital content piracy, as content can be shared and transferred instantly with no loss of quality.

1.1 Authorised Domain

Most current DRM systems recognise that consumers have more than one device, which they would like to use to access their content without requiring multiple licences. Many DRM system providers (see, for example, section 1.3) have incorporated the concept of an *authorised domain* into their content protection

I. Cervesato (Ed.): ASIAN 2007, LNCS 4846, pp. 126–141, 2007.

solutions. Such a domain is a collection of devices belonging to a single owner, within which digital assets can be freely moved.

Devices in a domain can be divided into two categories as proposed in [1]: *roots* and *leaves*. The domain root (unique per domain) represents a licensed content holder. The leaves in a domain receive content (and means to access the content) from the domain root. The content piracy problem can then be divided into two sub-problems. The first is *Root Distribution*, where the root of the domain illegally distributes content and any associated passwords to an unlimited number of users. For example, the content holder could illegally distribute content and its associated password to devices outside the domain, i.e. devices which are not leaves in this domain. The second is *Leaf Distribution*, where an individual leaf in a domain illegally redistributes content to devices outside the domain, as if it is the licensed content holder. For example, after receiving content and any associated passwords/keys, a leaf device could illegally re-distribute the content and passwords/keys to $user_1$, which in turn re-distributes them to $user_2$, and so on (where $user_1$ and $user_2$ are not leaves in this domain).

A fundamental authorised domain requirement for DRM is to restrict Root Distribution to legitimate devices owned by the domain owner, and to completely prevent Leaf Distribution. In addition, an authorised domain system for DRM should satisfy other requirements as discussed in [1], such as: Ease of Use, Content Mobility, Performance, Content Backup and Recovery, Privacy and Robust Content Protection. As discussed below, the proposed scheme satisfies all these requirements.

Other Authorised Domains management solutions (see, for example, section 1.3) typically attempt to address these problems by using a counter to control the number of devices that can simultaneously access domain content. However such counter-based mechanisms have significant security and usability limitations. For example, in many schemes (see, for example, section 1.3) devices can abuse the system by joining and then leaving multiple domains to illegally use their content. Moreover, in many schemes, increasing the domain size limit requires re-initialising and reconfiguring the domain, and, in some schemes, domains cannot be expanded. In addition, there is no binding between the domain key (content protection key) and the domain owner; i.e. the Leaf Distribution problem arises. Also, all these solutions have additional problems in addressing other fundamental authorised domain requirements for DRM, such as: content backup and recovery, ease of use, performance, etc. These issues are discussed in section 1.3. The proposed scheme addresses all these points, as discussed in system analysis (see section 4).

1.2   The Novel Solution

Our system works by binding all devices in a domain to a single Master Control device (MC), which is bound to a single owner. Each domain has a unique key that is securely generated and stored inside the Master Control device. This key is not available in the clear even to the domain owner, is shared by all devices in the domain, cannot be copied between devices, and is used to encrypt content encryption keys. The domain key is transferred from the Master Control device to a device joining a domain after the Master Control device has authenticated the domain owner using either biometric or password/PIN authentication techniques. The domain key is then securely stored by the joining device. Only the domain-specific Master Control device can release the domain key to other devices after authenticating the domain owner. This binds the domain key, which protects domain content, to the domain owner, i.e. this binds all devices in the domain to the domain owner. The proposed scheme does not stop legitimate controlled content sharing or the downloading of digital content from a remote location, as outlined in section 4.1.

In addition, each domain has two associated limits, one to control the number of devices that can simultaneously access domain content, and the other to control the total number of devices that can join a domain. The latter limit is designed to stop domain owners abusing the system by allowing multiple devices to join and then leave their domains.

The Root Distribution problem is addressed by using the two counters as described above (increasing the counters is controlled by a third party trusted authority, and does not require re-initialising and reconfiguring the domain). The Leaf Distribution problem is addressed by binding the domain key to the domain owner as described above. In addition, our solution can be implemented irrespective of device type. The scheme only requires that user platforms on which content is to be stored and used have functionality that can be trusted to perform the proposed DRM scheme correctly.

1.3   Related Work

We now briefly review some of the more widely discussed schemes for managing an *authorised domain* for DRM (note that in the analyses below we mainly focus on the authorised domain implementation proposed by each scheme). More detailed analysis of these schemes can be found in [1]. There are other DRM schemes; however, many such schemes do not address the authorised domain concept, and only focus on binding a licence to a single device. Such schemes are not considered here, as they do not address the core theme of this paper. Nevertheless, such schemes (including some of the schemes discussed in this section, e.g. OMA[1] DRM [16]) could be integrated with the proposed scheme for downloading content from content distributors to an authorised domain, as outlined in section 3.4.

In the **OMA DRM** system [16], each device can join more than one domain, each of which is controlled by a Rights Issuer. Also, each device must securely store the domain keys, domain identifiers, and domain expiry times, provided by each Rights Issuer. Devices require secure storage to store these keys. In addition, each Rights Issuer must create and manage all domains for consumers who have bought content from this Rights Issuer, and control which and how many devices are included or excluded from each domain. In order for a device to use the

---

[1] http://www.openmobilealliance.org

content in a domain, it must set up an association with all the Rights Issuers from which the domain owner has downloaded content. This is because, as above, each Rights Issuer protects its content within a domain using a domain-specific protection key provided by the Rights Issuer. This is not user friendly, as it imposes a significant administrative overhead. Moreover, there is no mechanism to control whose device is assigned to a domain (there is no binding between the domain key and the domain owner). For example, a set of devices belonging to different users might join domain A, and the same devices could also join domain B. This means a device can access copyrighted content illegally by joining domains owned by different owners.

Apple Fairplay[2] protects and plays only digital music and video files. Content must be bought from Apple's iTunes music store, and only iPod devices and platforms running Mac OS X and Microsoft Windows can access such content, limiting interoperability. As stated by Rowell [19], *"Apple Fairplay is allowing Apple to lock iPod owners into its proprietary store"*. In addition, the domain size is restricted to five computers and unlimited number of iPods; it is potentially very inconvenient for a consumer who already has the maximum number of devices in his/her domain, if he/she is required to remove a device from the domain before a new device can be added. A user is authenticated using a username and password that can be shared with others (there is no binding between the domain key and the domain owner). Moreover, devices can abuse the system by joining and then leaving multiple domains. The domain key is protected using only software techniques, unlike the other discussed schemes that use hardware measures, and the software protection has been hacked many times; see, for example, the Hymn project[3]. Moreover, content can be backed up to a standard CD in unencrypted format, or transported elsewhere via email or FTP, enabling content proliferation, as described by Carden [2].

The **Digital Rights Management in a 3G Mobile Phone and Beyond** scheme [4], has the following main problems. The domain key is an asymmetric key pair that changes every time a device joins or leaves the domain, or when a device is revoked; this step requires the domain owner to connect all devices to the Internet to retrieve the new key. In addition, each time the domain key is changed it requires all licence files to be re-encrypted, each of which holds a content encryption key. Each domain device must therefore keep track of all these licence files. This requires extra administration, in addition to requiring greater storage and processing costs. This could result in a significant overhead if the number of items of content is large. There is also no binding between the domain asymmetric key and the domain owner.

The **DRM Security Architecture for Home Networks** [18] uses secret keys shared between pairs of devices for authentication, and a master key shared between each device and the domain manager. Each device is required to store the list of shared secret keys and the device master key, which increases the hardware costs. Extending the domain depends on the ability of all domain

---

[2] http://www.apple.com/lu/support/itunes/authorization.html
[3] http://hymn-project.org

devices to increase their storage; it also requires the domain to be re-initialised and all domain content to be re-encrypted. In addition, the system requires each downloaded digital asset to be associated with a global device revocation list. This list will grow with time, and potentially results in a large increase in download time and size. Moreover, this scheme does not address content and domain key backup and recovery.

The *xCP Cluster Protocol* [9] encrypts content encryption keys using a master key, which is changed every time a device joins or leaves the home network. This step requires all devices to be online, which is inconvenient for some devices such as car CD players, MP3 players, etc. In addition, every time a device is hacked, a new media key block is released. This is a large data structure that imposes a significant overhead when moving it between devices and generating the master key, especially on devices that have limited capabilities. Moreover, every time the domain membership changes the domain master key must be changed. Consequently, the content encryption key, which is encrypted with the domain master key, will need to be re-encrypted with the new master key. This means that all content and its associated encryption keys must be tracked. This requires extra administration, in addition to requiring greater storage and processing costs. This could result in a significant overhead if the number of items of content is large. There is also no binding between the domain master key and the domain owner. Finally, this scheme does not address content and domain key backup and recovery.

The *SmartRight* system [20] requires the presence of smart card readers on all devices, and at least two smart cards per device: one for content access and the other for presentation functionality. This increases the total cost, especially for smart card maintenance. In addition, in order to increase the domain size, the system has to be re-initialised with a new domain key. Moreover, if all Terminal cards are lost or fail, then all existing content will be unusable, and if the Terminal card that most recently joined the domain is lost or stolen, then no other devices can be added. Also, if the end user forgets which Terminal card most recently joined the domain, then he/she must try all Terminal cards. This would pose a serious usability issue in networks with a large number of Terminal cards. This scheme does not address content and domain key backup and recovery. In addition, there is no binding between the network key and the domain owner.

1.4 Organisation of the Paper

This paper is organised as follows. Sections 2 and 3 describe the proposed solution and the process workflow. Section 4 discusses and analyses how the proposed approach controls content sharing, how it binds devices to a single owner, and how domain membership is managed. Section 5 discusses user authentication methods, and section 6 provides conclusions.

2 Proposed Model

In this section we describe the main entities constituting the proposed model.

2.1 Domain Devices

Software-only techniques cannot provide a high degree of protection for secret keys stored in a device; for example, Apple FairPlay, which uses software-only techniques, has been hacked multiple times, as discussed in section 1.3. This and other problems raise the need for a trusted computing technology that can enforce policy-neutral access control mechanisms. This is not a new requirement for DRM schemes; for example, other schemes discussed in section 1.3, apart from Apple Fairplay, require hardware components trusted to securely store domain credentials and/or to enforce content usage rules; e.g. OMA-DRM [16] requires each device to possess a trusted secure storage to store domain credentials, a public/private key pair certified by a certification authority (CA), and requires devices to be trusted to enforce content usage rules. So it is clear that current hardware designs do not satisfy DRM main requirements and any solution would need to propose updating hardware components. However, a DRM system must be designed in such a way that it imposes minimum costs. In addition, hardware components should be easy and convenient to integrate in consumer devices without resulting in increasing consumer device size, and they should not introduce new vulnerabilities into end user computing equipment.

Therefore, we require that domain devices, including the Master Control Device (MC), are trusted platforms (TPs). These are computing platforms with the property that their state can be remotely tested, and which can be trusted to store security-sensitive data in ways testable by a remote party. A domain device could be a PC, laptop, PDA, mobile device, etc. We assume that each domain device possesses a DRM agent, which must be trusted to perform the DRM scheme correctly. In addition, each TP can verify that the DRM agent is running correctly in another device. Each domain device is assumed to possess an asymmetric encryption key pair. The corresponding private decryption key is bound to a particular environment configuration state. We assume that the DRM software agents that are authorised to read data encrypted using this key will not release the data outside the TP; even the domain owner should not be able to retrieve these data in clear. The TP must provide a protected execution environment, in which applications run in isolation, free from being observed or compromised by other processes running in the same protected partition, or by software running in any insecure partition [5].

A TCG compliant platform meets all the requirements of this scheme; see, for example, [5]. TCG compliant platforms are not expensive, and are currently available from a range of PC manufacturers, including Dell, Fujitsu, HP, Intel and Toshiba [6]. In addition, since early 2006, all Intel-based Apple computers are TCG compliant [26].

2.2 Master Control Device

The MC is responsible for: securely storing a domain owner Authentication Credential (a password/PIN or a biometric reference template) that is used to authenticate the domain owner before a device joins the domain (see section 5);

securely generating and protecting a secret domain key (K_D) that is used to encrypt content encryption keys; and authorising devices to join its domain by ensuring their processing environment is trusted. Only the MC has the privilege to transfer the domain key K_D to other devices joining its domain, and this key cannot be copied between domain devices. The MC is not required to be a dedicated device; it could, for example, be part of a domain device.

Each MC securely stores the Authentication Credential (the exact nature of which could vary — see section 5) alongside K_D and two sequentially incremented numbers initialised to zero, referred to as the Total Counter (c_T) and Current Counter (c_C). c_T represents the total number of devices that have joined the domain, while c_C represents the number of devices currently present within the domain. The main role of the MC and both counters is to control domain membership, as described in section 4.2. In addition, each MC is assumed to have an asymmetric signing key pair, certified by the CA. The private part of the key is held inside the MC trusted storage, and is used for entity authentication. This certificate is called a **domain certificate**, and such a certificate needs to include the following information: the fact that it is a domain certificate, a general description of the MC and its security properties, the maximum number of devices that can be in the domain at any one time (i.e. the maximum permitted value of c_C), the maximum number of devices that can join the domain (i.e. the maximum permitted value of c_T).

3   Process Workflow

The workflow of the proposed system is divided into five main phases: the first involves the MC and the domain owner; the second involves the MC and a joining device; the third involves the MC and a leaving device; the fourth involves exchanging content between domain devices and Content Distributors/Rights Issuers, between devices in the same domain, and between devices in different domains; and the last involves content backup and recovery.

3.1   Domain Establishment

This phase covers the communication process between the domain owner and the MC. The first time a consumer uses the MC, or on resetting the MC, the following initialisation procedure must be performed. The DRM agent in the MC executes, and instructs the domain owner to provide his/her Authentication Credential (a password/PIN or a biometric reference template — see section 5). The domain owner then provides the requested Authentication Credential. The DRM agent securely generates a secret key K_D, and binds it to the Authentication Credential. The DRM agent securely associates two counters, i.e. c_T and c_C, initialised to zero, with the stored Authentication Credential and the key K_D.

The domain key K_D is generated inside the secure environment of the MC, and is then securely stored by the MC. Given the assumptions in section 2.1, this means that it is not available in the clear even to the domain owner, and it cannot be copied between domain devices. In addition, it is unique per-domain, shared amongst all domain devices, and does not change during the life of the domain.

3.2 Adding a Device to a Domain

This phase covers the case when a device joins a domain. Adding a new device J to a user domain involves the following steps. J first sends a Join_Domain request to the MC. The request includes the execution status of the DRM agent on J (S_J, its exact nature is implementation dependent, see, for example, [22,23,24,25]), the public encryption key of J, and J's certificate.

Next, the MC checks that J is in physical proximity to itself, e.g. by using the Near Field Communication (NFC) protocol or measuring the Round-Trip Time (RTT) between the MC and J, see, for example, [7,8,10]. The MC verifies the certificate of J, extracts the signature verification key of J from the certificate, and checks that it has not been revoked, e.g. by querying an Online Certificate Status Protocol (OCSP) service, [15]. The MC then verifies that the DRM agent is running correctly in J by checking the value of S_J. How this verification occurs is implementation-dependent; see, for example, [22,23,24,25]). The MC then authenticates the domain owner using the stored Authentication Credential.

If authentication succeeds, the MC checks whether the public key of J is already a member of the domain (a device might need to rejoin a domain, for example, in case of hardware/software failure, as discussed in section 3.5). If the public key of J is not in the domain, the MC temporarily increments the values of both c_T and c_C (it does not store the incremented values at this stage). If the new value of c_T or c_C is greater than the maximum permitted value given in the domain certificate held by the MC, then the agent running on the MC exits with an appropriate error message. The maximum c_T and c_C values can be increased by updating the domain certificate, which requires an explicit authorisation from the CA; specifically, the CA must provide the MC with an appropriate new domain certificate. Domain owners could be charged more for higher maximum c_T and c_C values.

Next, the MC sends its certificate and the execution status of its DRM agent S_{MC} to J. J then verifies the certificate, extracts the signature verification key of the MC from the certificate, verifies that it has not been revoked, e.g. by querying an OCSP service, and then checks that this certificate was issued for an MC device, as discussed in section 2.2. J then verifies that the DRM agent is running correctly in the MC by checking the value of S_{MC}. As above, how this verification occurs is implementation-dependent.

The MC securely stores the public key of J, the updated c_T and c_C values. Subsequently, the MC encrypts K_D using J public encryption key, signs the encrypted message using the MCs signature key, and then releases the domain credentials to J. When J receives this message, it verifies the MCs signature and then decrypts the message. The key K_D is securely stored by J, as described in section 3.1.

3.3   Removing a Device from a Domain

This phase covers the case where a domain owner wishes to remove a device from the domain. In order for an existing domain device J to leave a domain, the domain owner follows a similar process described in section 3.2, except that the c_T value does not change, and the c_C value is decremented and the public key of leaving device is removed from the MC's trusted storage. Before a domain device leaves a domain, the MC authenticates and attests to the state of the leaving domain device in the same way as described in section 3.2. This is to ensure that the leaving domain device can be trusted to delete both K_D and its protection key from its protected storage. If a domain device is hacked, the domain owner must inform the CA, which will then include the hacked domain device public key in its revocation list. The MC checks whether the domain device public key has been revoked, e.g. by querying an OCSP service, before decrementing c_C and removing the public key of this device from the MC's trusted storage.

As described in the next section, hacked devices cannot receive new content, and c_T value does not decrement with leaving or hacked devices. These ensure that the domain owner cannot abuse the system by adding devices and then claiming they are hacked.

3.4   Exchanging Content

A variety of methods could be integrated into the proposed scheme for downloading digital content and associated Rights Objects from a Content Distributor/Right Issuer to an existing domain device J; see, for example, [16]. This typically involves the following. J downloading content C and an associated Rights Object R from a remote Content Distributor (or Rights Issuer), where C is encrypted using a content-specific secret key K_T (as $E_{K_T}(C)$). The key K_T is generated by the Content Distributor, encrypted using J public encryption key, and is stored inside R, which is signed by the Rights Issuer. Once content has been downloaded to J, the content encryption key K_T is decrypted by J using its private key, and then re-encrypted using the domain-specific key K_D (as $E_{K_D}(K_T)$).

Encrypted content $E_{K_T}(C)$ can be freely exchanged between devices. However, before transferring R between devices in the same domain the source device must ensure that the destination device public key has not been revoked, and then R and the encrypted K_T (i.e. $E_{K_D}(K_T)$) are encrypted using the destination device public encryption key. The encrypted value are then decrypted on the destination device and stored in the same way as described above. Thus only devices which hold K_D can decrypt $E_{K_D}(K_T)$ to obtain K_T, and thereby decrypt $E_{K_T}(C)$ to access C. The domain device that renders protected digital content enforces the rules inside R. This scheme does not require a real-time communications link between devices; messages can be exchanged using a portable storage medium, e.g. a USB memory stick. The proposed scheme does not stop legitimate controlled content sharing or the downloading of digital content from a remote location, as outlined in section 4.1.

3.5   Backup and Recovery Procedure

A DRM solution must be capable of recovering digital content in the event of system failure. For backup purposes, digital content encrypted using K_D can be stored in an offline medium, for example, a tape or CD-ROM. If the domain key K_D is lost and cannot be recovered, it follows that the domain content on the backup cannot be decrypted. Thus, backup provisions for K_D are needed.

Our backup strategy is based on the assumption that the MC has a trusted backup agent, and that a domain device has a trusted restore agent that can backup and recover K_D, Authentication Credential, the current values of both c_T and c_C, and the public key of each device member of the domain. We also assume that only a single domain device is used for Backup. The first device joins the domain is considered as the default backup device. However, the domain owner could assign a different backup device that must be a member of the domain. In this case, the MC authenticates and attests to the state of the leaving backup device in the same way as described in section 3.2. This is to ensure that the leaving backup device can be trusted to delete the existing backup from its protected storage.

A backup agent for an MC M_1 should validate the domain device public key and associated software execution environment before accepting it for backup. If it has been accepted, M_1 securely stores the domain device public key in its trusted storage, and then the backup agent produces a backup copy encrypted using the domain device public key, which should be bound to a trusted execution environment. The backup copy also includes the public key certificate for M_1. Every time a device joins or leaves a domain a successful backup needs to be produced, otherwise the join/leave request should fail.

The procedure for recovering a copy of K_D to a new MC M_2 is as follows. If M_1 has had a hardware failure and cannot be recovered, the trusted device restore agent first checks that the public key certificate for M_1 has been revoked, e.g. by querying an OCSP service. The trusted device restore agent then checks that the public key certificate for M_2 has not been revoked, e.g. by querying an OCSP service, and checks whether M_2 is authorised to hold K_D. As described in section 2.2, we assume that M_2's certificate contains a field to show that it corresponds to an MC device that is trusted to hold K_D. If M_2 is trusted and the certificate type is a domain certificate, then the trusted device releases to M_2 the string (Authentication Credential$||K_D||c_T||c_C$) and the public keys of all devices member of the domain, encrypted with M_2's public key. The domain owner must then use M_2 to rejoin domain devices that have failed to recover K_D (before M_2 increments the values of both counters it checks whether the joining device public key is already a member of the domain; if so it does not increment the domain counters). In this scenario, the MC acts as a central point in backup and recovery; the MC decides whether or not to accept a particular device for backup purposes. Moreover, restoration of the key K_D can only be implemented via an MC-certified device.

4   Discussion and Analysis

In this section we discusses and analyses how the proposed approach controls content sharing and binds devices to a single owner, and how domain membership is managed.

4.1   Controlling Content Sharing

The main goal of our scheme is to stop content decryption keys that are stored inside Rights Objects from being transferred unprotected to devices in different domains. This is achieved, as described earlier, by encrypting each content-specific key K_T with the domain-specific key K_D that is only available inside domain devices, and which is transferred to a device after authenticating the domain owner, and after incrementing and verifying the values of the domain counters, and verifying the device is trusted and is in physical proximity to the MC. Therefor only devices that possess the domain-specific K_D, i.e. devices in the same domain, could use domain protected content. **This is how we achieve binding domain owners to devices in their domains**.

As explained in section 3.3, K_D and its protection key are removed from a device when it leaves a domain, which prevents protected Rights Objects from being used by devices in multiple domains. However, this does not stop legitimate controlled content sharing; protected content can move between devices belonging to different domains. A consumer could, for example, obtain a protected content from anywhere; however, he/she can only use protected content by contacting the corresponding Rights Issuer, and downloading a trial Rights Object enabling him/her to temporarily use the protected content. If the consumer is interested, he/she could then buy a full usage licence, as explained in section 3.4. This concept is known as *super-distribution*, and has been proposed by OMA [16] as a means of allowing consumers to obtain digitally protected content from anywhere, and to use a restricted licence. This allows consumers to use content for a limited period, with lower quality, and/or limited features. When the consumer is happy with the protected content and decides to get a full licence, only then will he/she need to download the Rights Object, which is much smaller than the encrypted content.

4.2   Controlling Domain Membership

The proposed scheme enables the binding of a consumer domain to a single owner, helping to solve the two sub-problems of content piracy: Root Distribution and Leaf Distribution. The MC controls domain membership in the following ways.

1. It limits the number of devices that can be in a domain, hence limiting the number of devices that can simultaneously access domain content.

2. It limits the total number of devices that can join a domain, which stops domain owners abusing the system by allowing multiple devices to join and then leave a domain.

3. It stops piracy using digital media such as the Internet, because, as described in section 2.2, the content protection key K_D is securely stored inside the MC, is not available in the clear, and can only be transferred from the MC to other devices after their physical proximity has been checked; i.e. the physical location check, in conjunction with the use of counters, addresses the Root Distribution problem.

4. It imposes stringent restrictions on piracy using physical media. As the content protection key K_D is not available in the clear even to the domain owner, this prevents the domain owner from transferring this key to other users. In addition, as described earlier, the MC must be used to transfer this key to other devices, which can only occur after the MC's domain owner has been authenticated; i.e. the scheme prevents Leaf Distribution.

Most other schemes focus primarily on point (1). Our solution stops illicit content proliferation; the only way a domain owner could transfer the content protection key to another user's device is by transferring the domain content, the domain-specific MC, and the domain owner Authentication Credential. Whilst possible in principle, such a procedure is unlikely to be attractive to the domain owner, as it means that the other user's device would become part of the domain controlled by the MC, which would mean that fewer of the domain owner's devices could be added to the domain. Most importantly, devices which have joined the domain would not be able to re-transfer the domain key, as only the MC can re-transfer the domain key after authenticating the domain owner. Section 5 describes possible options for the means to be used to authenticate the domain owner, some of which could increase the restrictions on content piracy.

Most authorised domain implementation for DRM require the existence of a trusted hardware to protect domain credentials and to enforce content associated usage rules (see, for example, section 1.3). Our proposed scheme is designed in such a way that it imposes minimum costs; all requirements of this scheme are met using TCG compliant platforms (as discussed in section 2.1), which are not expensive, and currently available from a range of PC manufacturers, including Dell, Fujitsu, HP, Intel and Toshiba [6]. In addition, the Trusted Platform Module (TPM), which is the core component for TCG compliant platform, is currently produced by a range of microelectronics manufacturers, including Atmel[4], ST-Microelectronics[5] and Winbond[6]. Moreover, the TPM is convenient to integrate in consumer devices as it is not expensive, does not result in increasing consumer device size, and does not introduce new vulnerabilities into end user computing equipment [23,24,25]. The extra costs in implementing the solution could be covered from the expected reduction in piracy.

---

[4] www.atmel.com/dyn/resources/prod_documents/doc5010.pdf
[5] www.st.com/stonline/products/literature/bd/10926.pdf
[6] www.winbondusa.com/

5 Methods of Authentication and Possible Countermeasures

Users are subject to two-factor authentication that involves "Something the user has", i.e. the MC, that binds devices joining the domain to itself using the domain key K_D, as described in section 2.2, and either "something the user is", i.e. biometric verification, or "something the user knows", i.e. a password or PIN. The Authentication Credential, which is kept in the protected storage of the MC and is associated with the domain key, will thus be either a biometric reference template or a password/PIN. The Authentication Credential binds the MC and its domain to a single owner. In the remainder of this section we present the pros and cons of the two approaches to user authentication, and possible countermeasures.

Using biometric authentication ensures that joining a device to a domain requires the physical presence of the domain owner, which imposes more stringent restrictions on content piracy than use of a password/PIN. Using biometric authentication has the following advantages: biometric features are bound to a person, they cannot be shared, and there is no password to lose or forget. However, the following possible problems (and possible countermeasures specific to the proposed scheme) are associated with biometric technology.

- Biometric authentication requires biometric samples captured from a live user to be matched against a stored biometric reference template. The processing required to perform this matching might slow down the authentication process; however, in the proposed scheme, biometric authentication is required only when creating a domain and when a device joins or leaves the domain. These are likely to be relatively infrequent events, and hence the use of biometrics will not affect the overall system performance.
- Biometric characteristics are not secret, and can be copied and used to create fake artifacts to gain access to the system. Biometric characteristics can be copied from a variety of sources, such as detached real fingers, collecting fingerprints from surfaces, iris pictures, face pictures, masks, videos, voice recorders, etc. In addition, biometric samples could be copied whilst being transferred from a biometric sensor to a processing device [14,21]. Two measures need to be implemented to reduce the effect of these problems:
  1. Biometric liveness detection, which cannot be achieved using cryptographic mechanisms, can be achieved using one of the following three techniques: the intrinsic properties of a living body, e.g. physical properties, electrical properties, visual properties, etc; involuntary signs of a living body, e.g. blood pressure, perspiration, brain wave signals, etc; and bodily responses to external stimuli, e.g. blinking, smiling, pupil dilation, etc. For more information about these techniques, see, for example, [21].
  2. Protecting captured biometric samples whilst being transferred from the biometric sensor to the signal processing subsystem (in the proposed scheme the latter is part of the MC). This can be implemented using cryptographic techniques; see, for example, [3].

- The extracted biometric samples will vary, even for the same user, so an exact match between extracted features and a stored biometric template cannot be expected. This means that a feature-matching algorithm has associated tolerance settings, so that a sample is considered valid if the difference between the sample and the template is within the tolerance bounds. More relaxed tolerance settings will result in a higher False Acceptance Rate (FAR), and a lower False Rejection Rate (FRR), while stricter tolerance settings will result in a lower FAR and a higher FRR. Moreover, some biometric schemes possess a degree of uncertainty. For example, fingerprint biometric accuracy depends on the position of the finger on the reader, changes in external finger conditions, etc. Very high accuracy in biometric identification typically requires expensive biometric readers such as retina or iris biometric measurement systems; more information can be found in [12,13].

   In our scheme, having more relaxed tolerance settings reduces the effect of FRR problems without raising serious problems because of the higher FAR. This is because the MC is associated with a single owner and a single domain, and the domain key cannot be replicated on multiple MCs. These factors reduce the risk that an MC will be exposed to multiple users, and hence reduce the risks associated with a relatively high FAR.

Using a password/PIN as a method of authentication has the following advantages: it is used directly for user authentication, its verification is a simple process, it does not require excessive storage, and it is the most widely used user authentication method. However, the following possible problems (and possible countermeasures specific to the proposed scheme) are associated with the use of passwords/PINs.

- It can be shared with others. This does not affect our scheme because each password/PIN is bound to a single MC, within which the domain key is stored. Consequently, sharing the password/PIN is not useful without also sharing the associated MC. This is relatively hard to accomplish, and an MC owner is not likely to wish to hand over his/her MC.
- It is not bound to a person. In our scheme, the password/PIN is bound to a single MC that reduces the effect of this problem.
- It can be forgotten. A password needs to be long and complex to protect against dictionary analysis or brute force attacks, which makes it hard to remember [27]. There are approaches that help to solve this problem, such as implementing a password reminder, implementing a graphical password system [27,28], implementing a challenge-response scheme, etc. In addition, a challenge-response scheme can be used to help protect against the shoulder surfing problem [28].
- It is subject to both offline and online attacks, as described by Pinkas and Sander [17]. These can be counteracted by: preventing access to the password file, implementing delayed responses, and account locking that locks a user account for a fixed period after a limited number of unsuccessful login attempts. These measures prevent an attacker from checking a large number of passwords in a reasonable time.

6 Conclusion

This paper proposes a solution for the protection of proprietary digital content against illegitimate use. The basis of the solution is a means for identifying the ownership of domain devices. In addition, the general approach could also be useful in various other applications requiring strong authentication, because it strongly binds a domain to its owner. Moreover, the pros and cons of two possible approaches to user authentication, i.e. the use of a password/PIN and biometric authentication mechanisms, and possible countermeasures to the identified vulnerabilities are discussed.

Acknowledgment

The author would like to thank Chris Mitchell for his help and support, which have improved the paper.

References

1. Abbadi, I.: Digital asset protection in personal private networks. In: 8th International Symposium on Systems and Information Security (SSI 2006), Sao Jose dos Campos, Sao Paulo, Brazil (November 2006)
2. Carden, N.: iTunes and iPod in the enterprise. The Journal of the International Systems Security Association, 22–25 (May 2007)
3. Chen, L., Pearson, S., Vamvakas, A.: On enhancing biometric authentication with data protection. In: Proceedings of the Fourth International Conference on Knowledge-Based Intelligent Engineering Systems and Allied Technologies, vol. 1, pp. 249–252. IEEE, Los Alamitos (2000)
4. Dabbish, E.A., Messerges, T.S.: Digital rights management in a 3G mobile phone and beyond. In: Feigenbaum, J., Sander, T., Yung, M. (eds.) Proceedings of the 3rd ACM workshop on Digital Rights Management, pp. 27–38. ACM Press, New York (2003)
5. Gallery, E., Tomlinson, A.: Secure delivery of conditional access applications to mobile receivers. In: Mitchell, C.J. (ed.) Trusted Computing, ch. 7, pp. 195–237. IEEE, Los Alamitos (2005)
6. Trusted Computing Group.: Trusted platform module FAQ
7. Günther, A., Hoene, C.: Measuring round trip times to determine the distance between WLAN nodes. In: Boutaba, R., Almeroth, K.C., Puigjaner, R., Shen, S., Black, J.P. (eds.) NETWORKING 2005. LNCS, vol. 3462, pp. 768–779. Springer, Heidelberg (2005)
8. Huffaker, B., Fomenkov, M., Plummer, D.J., Moore, D., Claffy, K.: Distance metrics in the Internet. In: IEEE International Telecommunications Symposium (2002), http://www.caida.org/publications/papers/2002/Distance/distance.pdf
9. IBM Research Division Almaden Research Center.: xCP cluster protocol (2003), http://www-03.ibm.com/solutions/digitalmedia/doc/content/bin/xCPWhitepaper_final_1.pdf
10. International Organization for Standardization.: ISO/IEC 21481: Information technology — Telecommunications and information exchange between systems — Near Field Communication Interface and Protocol -2 (NFCIP-2) (2005)

11. International Organization for Standardization.: ISO/IEC 18033-2, Information technology — Security techniques — Encryption algorithms — Part 2: Asymmetric ciphers (2006)
12. Liu, S., Silverman, M.: A practical guide to biometric security technology. IT Professional 3(1), 27–32 (2001)
13. Maltoni, D., Maio, D., Jain, A.K., Prabahakar, S.: Handbook of Fingerprint Recognition. Springer, Berlin (2003)
14. Matsumoto, T., Matsumoto, H., Yamada, K., Hoshino, S.: Impact of artificial 'gummy' fingers on fingerprint systems. In: Proceedings of SPIE, vol. 4677, pp. 275–289 (2002)
15. Myers, M., Ankney, R., Malpani, A., Galperin, S., Adams, C.: X.509 Internet Public Key Infrastructure Online Certificate Status Protocol — OCSP. RFC 2560, Internet Engineering Task Force (June 1999)
16. Open Mobile Alliance.: DRM Specification — Version 2.0 (2006)
17. Pinkas, B., Sander, T.: Securing passwords against dictionary attacks. In: Proceedings of the 9th ACM conference on Computer and communications security, pp. 161–170. ACM Press, New York (2002)
18. Popescu, B.C., Kamperman, F.L.A.J., Crispo, B., Tanenbaum, A.S.: A DRM security architecture for home networks. In: Feigenbaum, J., Sander, T., Yung, M. (eds.) Proceedings of the 4th ACM workshop on Digital Rights Management, pp. 1–10. ACM Press, New York (2004)
19. Rowell, L.F.: The ballad of DVD JON. netWorker 10(4), 28–34 (2006)
20. Thomson.: SmartRight technical white paper (2003), http://www.smartright.org/images/SMR/content/SmartRight_tech_whitepaper_jan28.pdf
21. Toth, B.: Biometric liveness detection. The International Journal For Information Assurance Professionals 10(8), 291–298 (2005)
22. Trusted Computing Group.: Infrastructure Working Group Architecture, Part II, Integrity Management. Specification version 1.0 Revision 1.0 (2006)
23. Trusted Computing Group.: TPM Main, Part 1, Design Principles. Specification version 1.2 Revision 94 (2006)
24. Trusted Computing Group.: TPM Main, Part 2, TPM Structures. Specification version 1.2 Revision 94 (2006)
25. Trusted Computing Group.: TPM Main, Part 3, Design Principles. Specification version 1.2 Revision 94 (2006)
26. Weiss, A.: Will the open, unrestricted PC soon become a thing of the past? Journal of Trusted Computing 10(3), 18–25 (2006)
27. Wiedenbeck, S., Birget, J.-C., Brodskiy, A., Waters, J., Memon, N.: Authentication using graphical passwords: Effects of tolerance and image choice. In: Proceedings of the 2005 symposium on Usable privacy and security, pp. 1–12. ACM Press, New York (2005)
28. Wiedenbeck, S., Waters, J., Sobrado, L., Birget, J.-C.: Design and evaluation of a shoulder-surfing resistant graphical password scheme. In: Proceedings of the working conference on Advanced visual interfaces, pp. 177–184. ACM Press, New York (2006)

How to do Things
with Cryptographic Protocols*

Joshua D. Guttman

The MITRE Corporation

When a distributed system may need to operate in the presence of an adversary, when it must support the activities of parties that do not trust one another fully, then cryptographic protocols will play a fundamental role in its design. One example of their importance is their ability to allow principals to agree on keys that will be shared for a session with an authenticated peer. But more fundamentally, a cryptographic protocol is a mechanism to achieve agreement among specific sets of peers, whether on keys or other values. Thus, they can play a fundamental role in organizing transactions in distributed systems, and coordinating interactions among principals.

1 Goal of This Talk

There are three essential layers of coordination that protocols allow, and the goal of this talk is to explain them and their relationships. Two of these layers were considered in [6]. The third is new in this talk.

The Layer of Protocol Mechanics. First, each protocol uses cryptography to ensure that the actions of the participants mesh together in specific ways. When the secrets of a principals are uncompromised, its cryptographic use of these secrets demonstrates to its peers that it is participating in a transaction, and that it has completed certain steps. This layer explains the mechanics of protocols, the operational patterns of interaction that are possible for a number of participants. Strand spaces is one theory that allows us to understand the mechanics of protocols [5,2,1]. Several other approaches can also be used at this layer, e.g. [12,7,3]

The Trust Management Layer. The second layer concerns the decision-making process in which each participant engages during a protocol session. Sending a message in a session may commit the participant to certain consequences. For instance, in a contract signing protocol, a participant will be committed to the content of the contract after sending the last message. If the proposed contract was received previously in the same session, then the decision whether to make this commitment must be made as a part of executing the protocol. A protocol must provide a definition of the commitment each principal undertakes by sending each message, as a function of the values it has received earlier in the session. When a participant receives a message the protocol must provide a

---

* Supported by the MITRE-Sponsored Research Program.

I. Cervesato (Ed.): ASIAN 2007, LNCS 4846, pp. 142–149, 2007.
© Springer-Verlag Berlin Heidelberg 2007

definition of what is learnt by receiving it. What is learnt is normally the fact that other participants have made commitments before sending this message (or previous ones). What a recipient learns is a function of the values in the message, and other values in the same session. A principal's decision whether to transmit a particular message will typically depend on what it has learnt from messages received earlier in the session.

Although the protocol defines what one has committed oneself to by sending a message and what is learnt when receiving it, only the principal itself—not the protocol designer—can choose a policy on when to commit itself. We regard this policy as a theory T, e.g. in Datalog or some stronger logic. The idea of representing these policies in logical theories, and of using the commitments of other participants as additional premises, is frequently called *trust management* [8,9].

In our variant of trust management, a participant makes a commitment γ only when it follows from T together with the formulas $\rho_1, \ldots, \rho_i$ learnt previously in the current session. This same notion makes an appealing control structure for branching protocols: One a protocol allows the participant to send one of several alternative messages in the next step, the designer can guard each of them with a suitable commitment. A participant who can discharge some of these guards may choose non-deterministically among the corresponding messages to send. A participant who can discharge none of them must halt the session.

The State Layer. The third layer concerns the effects of executing a session of a protocol. These are changes to the states of the participants. For instance, after an electronic purchase protocol, a bank may have transferred money from the account of the purchaser to the account of the merchant, while the merchant has executed a transaction to ship the item from the warehouse. The new content of the current talk—beyond the ideas described in [6]—is to provide an account of how these changes of state of the principals may be isolated from the logical reasoning needed in protocol runs.

2   An Example: EPMO

In this talk, we will illustrate this claim using a single protocol and its variants, the protocol [6] for Electronic Purchase using a Money Order (EPMO).

This protocol allows principals in three roles—representing a client, a merchant, and a bank—to agree on a transaction. As a consequence of a successful transaction, the merchant incurs an obligation to ship some goods to the client, while the bank incurs an obligation to transfer the agreed purchase price from the client's account to the merchant's account.

The protocol EPMO (Figure 1) borrows ideas from Needham, Schroeder, and Lowe [11,10], using the authentication tests as a design principle [4]. Variables N_p range over nonces; $[\![t]\!]_P$ is the message t signed by P; $\{\!|t|\!\}_P$ is t encrypted using P's public key; and $\mathsf{hash}(t)$ is a cryptographic hash of t.

A customer and a merchant want to agree on a purchase, transferring payment with the aid of a bank. Here goods is a description of the items requested; price is the proposed price. N_m serves as a transaction number. After obtaining a quote

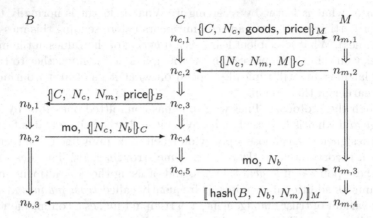

Fig. 1. EPMO with Money Order $\mathsf{mo} = [\![\mathsf{hash}(C,\ N_c,\ N_b,\ N_m,\ \mathsf{price})]\!]_B$

from the merchant, the customer obtains a "money order" containing N_b from the bank to cover the purchase, and delivers it to the merchant. The merchant "endorses" it by combining N_b with N_m, and delivers the endorsement to the bank. At the end of the protocol, the bank transfers the funds, and the merchant ships the goods.

B does not learn goods, and learns M only if the transaction completes. Although B does not transfer funds until M cashes the money order, B may put a "hold" on money in C's account. If the money order is not redeemed within an implementation-defined timeout period, then it expires and B releases the hold on C's account. EPMO is designed not to disclose which principals are interacting, nor the goods or price.

It does not protect against denial of service. An adversary can encrypt messages, using B's public key, to cause holds on all the money in C's account. Although a more complex protocol would prevent this attack, EPMO illustrates an interesting interplay between protocols and trust. Some resilient channel—such as the postal service—will periodically be used to issue a statement, allowing a reconciliation protocol to be run.

3   Protocol Mechanics of EPMO

The mechanics of EPMO are determined by the *authentication tests* [2,1], which are patterns for appraising what is achieved by protocol challenges and responses. For instance, C issues a challenge containing the nonce N_c in the first message, and receives N_c back in the next message; this effectively ensures that M (if M's private key is uncompromised) has received C's first message and has responded affirmatively to it. C reuses the same nonce in an authentication test with the bank; reception of $\mathsf{mo},\ \{\![N_c,\ N_b]\!\}_C$ ensures that B has received C's request for funds and accepted it.

Likewise, M and B use their nonces for authentication test interactions with their peers; each is transformed twice before being received back, thus authenticating the participation of each of the peers.

By contrast, a weakened version of EPMO is akin to the original Needham-Schroeder protocol. It omits M's identity from the second message, yielding $\{\!|N_c, N_m|\!\}_C$. The weakened protocol (see Figure 2) would have fundamentally

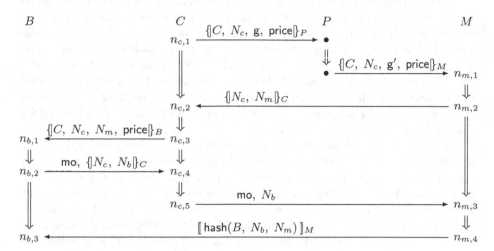

Fig. 2. EPMO Weakened as in Needham-Schroeder, with an attack

different mechanics: The merchant M would be unable to authenticate that C had intended to initiate a transaction with M, rather than with some dishonest merchant P. P could abuse the weakened protocol as a vehicle for money laundering, offsetting an unauditable transaction with M by causing a transaction between C and P to appear to be a transaction between C and M. Auditing—presumably done at the bank B—discloses no involvement of P.

4   Trust Management in EPMO

The participants in an electronic commerce protocol are certainly making commitments, such as to ship some goods, to transfer funds into an account, and to authorize funds to be transferred out of one's own account. Moreover, a participant's willingness to make these commitments depends on its understanding of the commitments that other participants have made. For instance, the client's willingness to authorize the transfer probably depends on his understanding that the merchant has committed itself to shipping the goods if paid. It also depends on the client's appraisal of whether the merchant will honor this commitment. Typically, this requires the client to believe that the merchant depends on its reputation, and that the business strategy of the merchant is to preserve this reputation so that the public will continue to do business with it. A swindler would instead have a different business strategy. A client believing that M is a swindler would have no reason to infer "M will ship goods" from the assertion "M says M will ship goods".

In fact, in our framework, this is the primary sense of trust. A principal A *trusts* B on subject matter ϕ means that in A's theory T_A, we have $T_1 \vdash (A \text{ says } \phi) \supset \phi$.

We thus equip each protocol with a set of commitments to be made on the various nodes. We use the symbol γ to associate transmission nodes with commitment a principal undertakes by sending the message. Thus, for instance, the client in EPMO makes its commitment to allowing the transfer of funds on its last node, $n_{c,4}$, so that $\gamma(n_{c,4})$ is the assertion that "price is authorized for transfer from C's account to M's account." The bank will accept this assertion if stated by the owner himself, i.e. the bank's theory derives "C says price is authorized for transfer from C's account to M's account implies that price is authorized for transfer from C's account to M's account."

The bank makes an assertion when it prepares the money order, on node $n_{b,4}$. It asserts that it will transfer price from C's account to the account of any principal A such that price is authorized for transfer from C's account to A's account. An essential ingredient is that the parameters to the assertion get their values from the protocol run within which they occur. Thus, B has not yet acquired information about which merchant C is interacting with. Thus, it must prepare a money order with the force of a bearer instrument. C may endorse it for any recipient A.

Indeed, we may connect the mechanics of the protocol with its trust interpretation at this point. In the weakened form of the EPMO protocol, C authorizes payment, but in the run shown in Fig. 2, something has gone wrong with this authorization. Namely, C has in fact authorized payment to P, since P is the merchant parameter of C's local run. The bank, however, delivers payment to M. A protocol is strong enough to bear its trust interpretation when this can never happen.

5   State: Effects of EPMO

The framework we have described so far raises a puzzle. The participants use a standard, monotonic logic to reason from their theories and from the assertions of others, as recorded in the rely formulas $\rho(n)$. These assertions are made by others on the basis of their mutable state. For instance, the bank issues the money order because the client's account has sufficient funds, and the state of the account will change over time. How can it be logically consistent to reason using these state-dependent assertions, without some mechanism to remove rely formulas when they may have become stale? The bank's assertion that it will pay price to the bearer of the money order would mislead a later receiver of the money order. The assertions contain no timestamps or other references to a period of validity. How can we prevent this?

On the other hand, there are also assertions that have an unlimited extent into the future, and these are associated with digital signatures.

Our answer, essentially, is that whenever an assertion is of limited extent, then protocols must prevent its escape from the session in which it was created.

In the strand space theory, we regard the history of a distributed system as a partially ordered structure. One event precedes another if there is a sequence of arrows leading from the former to the latter. The arrows in the sequence may include message transmission arrows $\rightarrow$ and strand succession arrows $\Rightarrow$. Thus, we may borrow some terms from special relativity. Given an event n, we regard its *forward light cone* as the set of events accessible from n using arrows, and its *backward* light cone as the set of events from which it is accessible. The forward and backward light cones define those events that n can causally affect, and those events that can have causally affected n, respectively. We write $n_0 \prec n_1$ to mean that n_0 strictly precedes n_1 in this causal ordering.

A *simultaneity* set or a space-like plane is a set of events no two of which are comparable in the causal ordering. Two events may be regarded as occurring at the same time if they both belong to one simultaneity set S. A *time* is a maximal simultaneity set S, i.e. one such that every $n \notin S$, there exists an $n' \in S$ such that either $n_0 \prec n_1$ or $n_1 \prec n_0$. Any family of disjoint times is linearly ordered by $\prec$. We also write $n \prec S_0$ if $n \prec n_0$ for some $n_0 \in S_0$; $n \preceq S_0$ means either $n \prec S_0$ or $n \in S_0$.

Two times S_0, S_1 (i.e. two maximal simultaneity sets) may be regarded as defining an interval $[S_0, S_1]$, namely that containing all n such that there exist $n_0 \in S_0$ and $n_1 \in S_1$ such that $n_0 \preceq n \preceq n_1$.

One can also distinguish long intervals from short intervals, in a loose way. This depends on the fact that all regular strands are relatively short, because cryptographic protocol implementors cause sessions to time out after a limited period. Clearly, the adversary is under no obligation to time out, and thus only the regular, protocol-abiding strands can serve to measure the passage of time. Indeed, we can use regular strands as yardsticks to bound the length of some intervals.

Let us say that an interval $[S_0, S_1]$ *is of length* ≤ 1 if there is a regular strand $m_0 \Rightarrow^+ m_j$ such that $m_0 \preceq S_0$ and $S_1 \preceq m_j$. In this case, one regular strand measures the whole interval. $[S_0, S_1]$ *is of length* $\leq k + 1$ if there is a sequence of strands $\langle m_{0,0} \Rightarrow^+ m_{0,j}, m_{0,0} \Rightarrow^+ m_{k,j'} \rangle$ where $m_{0,0} \preceq S_0$, $S_1 \preceq m_{k,j'}$, and $m_{i+1,0} \prec m_{i,j}$ for each i from 0 to k. In this case, the sequence of $k + 1$ strands form overlapping yardsticks that stretch from time S_0 to time S_1.

An interval $[S_0, S_1]$ may not be of any finite length, since there may be no sequence of regular strands that span it. Even if it is connected, it may be connected only using adversary strands. If $[S_0, S_1]$ is not of finite length, we call it *non-archimedean*.

The mechanics of protocols give designers a tool to use to control the lengths of protocol executions. For instance, the use of the merchant's nonce N_b in EPMO ensures that the interval $[S_0, S_1]$ is of length ≤ 2 if for some run of EPMO,

$n_{c,1} \in S_0$ and $n_{m,4} \in S_1$. This property is still true of the weakened EPMO of Fig. 2. Similarly, if $n_{c,1} \in S_0$ and $n_{m,4} \in S_1$, then the interval is of length ≤ 1.

In this way, the protocol designer can arrange that a volatile assertion, such as B's assertion that C's account has sufficient funds, cannot escape any interval bounding the current run. Thus, so long as a state change cannot take effect until a later interval, these state changes are necessarily invisible to the participants in the protocol. All of their logical reasoning will be based on compatible mutable facts.

Conclusion. In this talk, we have tried to explain how to do things with protocols at three layers. The layer of protocol mechanics determines what *agreement* participants must have achieved by the end of a protocol: Agreement on parameters to the session, agreement on who is excluded from sharing certain parameters (confidentiality), and agreement on the order in which events occurred (loose synchronization). The layer of trust management concerns the decision making of the participants: The *commitments* they must make to proceed in a session, their reliance on the commitments others have made in making their own decisions, and the theory or "business logic" that controls their run-time choices. The layer of state concerns *persistent mutable resources*—such as money in accounts and data in repositories—that is consumed or produced by transactions. In particular, we have emphasized the constraint that change of state should never invalidate the logical premises used in the trust management layer, and indicated how the causal structure of protocols can prevent mutable state from undermining logical trust management.

References

1. Doghmi, S.F., Guttman, J.D., Thayer, F.J.: Completeness of the authentication tests. In: Biskup, J., Lopez, J. (eds.) ESORICS. European Symposium on Research in Computer Security. LNCS, vol. 4734, pp. 106–121. Springer, Heidelberg (2007)
2. Doghmi, S.F., Guttman, J.D., Thayer, F.J.: Searching for shapes in cryptographic protocols. In: Tools and Algorithms for Construction and Analysis of Systems (TACAS). LNCS, vol. 4424, pp. 523–538. Springer, Heidelberg (2007), http://eprint.iacr.org/2006/435
3. Gordon, A.D., Jeffrey, A.: Types and effects for asymmetric cryptographic protocols. Journal of Computer Security 12(3/4), 435–484 (2003)
4. Guttman, J.D.: Authentication tests and disjoint encryption: a design method for security protocols. Journal of Computer Security 12(3/4), 409–433 (2004)
5. Guttman, J.D., Thayer, F.J.: Authentication tests and the structure of bundles. Theoretical Computer Science. Conference version appeared in IEEE Symposium on Security and Privacy, June 2002, 283(2), pp. 333–380 (May 2002)
6. Guttman, J.D., Thayer, F.J., Carlson, J.A., Herzog, J.C., Ramsdell, J.D., Sniffen, B.T.: Trust management in strand spaces: A rely-guarantee method. In: Schmidt, D. (ed.) ESOP 2004. LNCS, vol. 2986, pp. 325–339. Springer, Heidelberg (2004)
7. Heather, J., Schneider, S.: Toward automatic verification of authentication protocols on an unbounded network. In: Proceedings, 13th Computer Security Foundations Workshop, IEEE Computer Society Press, Los Alamitos (2000)

8. Lampson, B., Abadi, M., Burrows, M., Wobber, E.: Authentication in distributed systems: Theory and practice. ACM Transactions on Computer Systems 10(4), 265–310 (1992)
9. Li, N., Mitchell, J.C., Winsborough, W.H.: Design of a role-based trust management framework. In: Proceedings, 2002 IEEE Symposium on Security and Privacy, pp. 114–130. IEEE Computer Society Press, Los Alamitos (2002)
10. Lowe, G.: Breaking and fixing the Needham-Schroeder public-key protocol using FDR. In: Margaria, T., Steffen, B. (eds.) TACAS 1996. LNCS, vol. 1055, pp. 147–166. Springer, Heidelberg (1996)
11. Needham, R., Schroeder, M.: Using encryption for authentication in large networks of computers. Communications of the ACM 21(12) (1978)
12. Paulson, L.C.: The inductive approach to verifying cryptographic protocols. In: Journal of Computer Security (1998) (Also Report 443, Cambridge University Computer Lab)

A Formal Analysis for Capturing Replay Attacks in Cryptographic Protocols*

Han Gao[1], Chiara Bodei[2], Pierpaolo Degano[2], and Hanne Riis Nielson[1]

[1] Informatics and Mathematical Modelling, Technical University of Denmark,
Richard Petersens Plads bldg 322, DK-2800 Kongens Lyngby, Denmark
{hg,riis}@imm.dtu.dk
[2] Dipartimento di Informatica, Università di Pisa,
Largo B. Pontecorvo, 3, I-56127, Pisa, Italy
{chiara,degano}@di.unipi.it

Abstract. We present a reduction semantics for the LYSA calculus extended with session information, for modelling cryptographic protocols, and a static analysis for it. If a protocol passes the analysis then it is free of replay attacks and thus preserves freshness. The analysis has been implemented and applied to a number of protocols, including both original and corrected version of Needham-Schroeder protocol. The experiment results show that the analysis is able to capture potential replay attacks.

1 Introduction

Since the 80's, formal analyses of cryptographic protocols have been widely studied. Many formal methods have been put forward. Particular significant is the one built by Dolev and Yao. Indeed, most of the formal analysis tools were built upon it, e.g. Meadows and Syverson NRL [18], Millen Interrogator [19], Paulson inductive method [23], based on Isabelle [24], Blanchet's Prolog protocol verifier[2] and BAN logic [7], a logic of authentication used to analyse protocols, etc. Each tool is equipped to detect a certain amount of attacks, including replay attacks.

Replay attacks are classified by Syverson in [25] at the highest level as run-external and run-internal attacks, depending on the origin of messages. In this paper, we restrict our attention to *run-external attacks*. This type of attacks allows the attacker to achieve messages from one run of a protocol, often referred to as a *session*, and to send them to a principal participating in another run of the protocol. A *fresh* message means that it is not replayed from another session (old session or parallel session). In BAN logic, reasoning about the freshness of an entire message amounts to reasoning about the freshness of its fields, i.e. "if one part of a formula is known to be fresh, then the entire formula must also be fresh". We take advantage of the fact that the attacker can manipulate any message in clear, but it has no direct control on the encrypted messages. Indeed, in out framework, after each successful decryption, we check whether the

---

* This work has been partially supported by the project SENSORIA.

I. Cervesato (Ed.): ASIAN 2007, LNCS 4846, pp. 150–165, 2007.
© Springer-Verlag Berlin Heidelberg 2007

decrypted message is a replayed one from another session, which is a violation of freshness property.

Here we extend the LySa calculus [3,4] with annotations about sessions and we extend the control flow analysis in [3,4] as well. As expected, the new control flow analysis soundly over-approximates the behavior of protocols, by tracking the set of messages that are communicated over the network, and recording the potential values of variables. Since our analysis is sound, we capture malicious activities, if any, expressed in terms of annotation violations. Our static analysis is fully automatic and termination is always guaranteed. The proposed analysis has been implemented. The resulting tool was applied to some cryptographic protocols, such as Otway-Rees [22] and Needham-Schroeder [21].

As far as the security properties are concerned, replay attacks on security protocols can cause authentication and/or confidentiality violations. Besides the other security properties, e.g. authentication and confidentiality, checked with the CFA in [3,4] we here are able to address an orthogonal property like freshness. We analyse the Wide Mouthed Frog protocol and the Needham-Schroeder protocol, both of which do not achieve freshness property in the presence of a replay attacker.

The paper is organized as follows. In Section 2, we present the LySa calculus annotated with session information. We introduce the control flow analysis in Section 3. In Section 4 we describe a Dolev-Yao attacker extended to fit into our particular setting. In section 5, we make some experiments in analysing two versions of the Needham-Schoreder symmetric key protocol. Section 6 concludes the paper.

2   A Reduction Semantics for the LySa Calculus

LySa [3,4] is a process algebra, in the tradition of the π- [20] and Spi- [1] calculi. Among its peculiar features, there are: (1) the absence of channels: in LySa all processes have only access to a single global communication channel, the ether and (2) tests associated with input and decryption are expressed using pattern matching.

2.1   Syntax

LySa consists of terms and processes. The syntax of terms E and processes P is given below. Here $\mathcal{N}$ and $\mathcal{X}$ denote sets of names and variables, respectively. For the sake of simplicity, we only consider here some basic terms and encryptions. The name n is used to represent keys, challenges and names of principals. Encryptions are tuples of terms $E_1, \ldots, E_k$ encrypted under a shared key represented by the term E_0. We assume perfect cryptography in this paper.

$$E ::= n \mid x \mid \{E_1, \ldots, E_k\}_{E_0}$$
$$P ::= \langle E_1, \ldots, E_k \rangle.P \mid (E_1, \ldots, E_j; x_{j+1}, \ldots, x_k).P \mid$$
$$\text{decrypt } E \text{ as } \{E_1, \ldots, E_j; x_{j+1}, \ldots, x_k\}^l_{E_0} \text{ in } P \mid$$
$$(\nu\, n)P \mid P_1 | P_2 \mid !P \mid 0$$

In addition to the classical constructs for composing processes, LySa also contains an input construct with matching and a decryption operation with matching. The idea behind the matching is as follows: we allow a prefix of the received tuple to match a selection of values. If the test is passed, the remaining values are bound to the relevant variables. The label l in the decryption construct uniquely identifies each decryption point, which is from a numerable set Lab ($l \in Lab$), and is mechanically attached to processes.

Extended LySa. We change the syntax of standard LySa so that each term and process now carries an identifier of the session it belongs to. In what follows, we assume that SID is a fixed enumerable set of session identifiers s, and we denote $\mathcal{E}_1, \mathcal{E}_2, \ldots$ the extended terms and $\mathcal{P}, \mathcal{Q}, \ldots$ the extended processes defined below. Note that variables carry no annotation and therefore we shall consider $[x]_s$ and x to be the same (see below). Furthermore, there is no need for the nil process (0) to carry session information and hence $[0]_s$ and 0 are identical.

$$\mathcal{E} ::= [n]_s \mid x \mid [\{\mathcal{E}_1, \ldots, \mathcal{E}_k\}_{\mathcal{E}_0}]_s$$
$$\mathcal{P} ::= \langle \mathcal{E}_1, \ldots, \mathcal{E}_k \rangle.\mathcal{P} \mid (\mathcal{E}_1, \ldots, \mathcal{E}_j; x_{j+1}, \ldots, x_k).\mathcal{P} \mid$$
$$\text{decrypt } \mathcal{E} \text{ as } \{\mathcal{E}_1, \ldots, \mathcal{E}_j; x_{j+1}, \ldots, x_k\}^l_{\mathcal{E}_0} \text{ in } \mathcal{P} \mid$$
$$(\nu\,[n]_s)\mathcal{P} \mid \mathcal{P}_1 | \mathcal{P}_2 \mid [!\mathcal{P}]_s \mid 0$$

We define a function $\mathcal{F}$ and a function $\mathcal{T}$, in the style of [9], that map standard terms and processes into the extended ones, by attaching the session identifiers inductively. Note that $\mathcal{F}$ unwinds the syntactic structure of an extended term until reaching a basic term (a name or a variable), while $\mathcal{T}$ unwinds the structure of an extended process until reaching a nil (which is untagged) or a replication.

Definition 1. *Distributing Session Identifiers*

$$\mathcal{F} : E \times SID \to \mathcal{E}$$

$$-\mathcal{F}(n, s) = [n]_s \qquad\qquad -\mathcal{F}(x, s) = x$$
$$-\mathcal{F}(\{E_1, \ldots, E_k\}_{E_0}, s) = [\{\mathcal{F}(E_1, s), \ldots, \mathcal{F}(E_k, s)\}_{\mathcal{F}(E_0, s)}]_s$$

$$\mathcal{T} : P \times SID \to \mathcal{P}$$

$$-\mathcal{T}(\langle E_1, \ldots, E_k \rangle.P, s) = \langle \mathcal{F}(E_1, s), \ldots, \mathcal{F}(E_k, s) \rangle.\mathcal{T}(P, s)$$
$$-\mathcal{T}((E_1, \ldots, E_j; x_{j+1}, \ldots, x_k).P, s) =$$
$$(\mathcal{F}(E_1, s), \ldots, \mathcal{F}(E_j, s); x_{j+1}, \ldots, x_k).\mathcal{T}(P, s)$$

$$-\mathcal{T}(\text{decrypt } E \text{ as } \{E_1, \ldots, E_j; x_{j+1}, \ldots, x_k\}^l_{E_0} \text{ in } P, s) =$$
$$\text{decrypt } \mathcal{F}(E, s) \text{ as } \{\mathcal{F}(E_1, s), \ldots, \mathcal{F}(E_j, s); x_{j+1}, \ldots, x_k\}^l_{\mathcal{F}(E_0, s)} \text{ in } \mathcal{T}(P, s)$$

$$-\mathcal{T}(P \mid Q, s) = \mathcal{T}(P, s) \mid \mathcal{T}(Q, s) \qquad -\mathcal{T}((\nu\, n)P, s) = (\nu\,[n]_s)\mathcal{T}(P, s)$$
$$-\mathcal{T}(!P, s) = [!P]_s \qquad\qquad\qquad -\mathcal{T}(0, s) = 0$$

2.2   Operational Semantics

Below we assume the standard *structural congruence* $\equiv$ on LySA processes, as the least congruence satisfying the following clauses (as usual $fn(P)$ is the set of the free names of P):

$$P \mid 0 \equiv P \qquad\qquad (\nu x)0 \equiv 0$$
$$P \mid Q \equiv Q \mid P \qquad\qquad (\nu x)(\nu y)P \equiv (\nu y)(\nu x)P$$
$$(P \mid Q) \mid R \equiv P \mid (Q \mid R) \qquad (\nu x)(P \mid Q) \equiv P \mid (\nu x)Q \text{ if } x \notin fn(P)$$
$$P \equiv Q \text{ if } P \text{ and } Q \text{ are } \alpha\text{-equivalent}$$

Technically, the addition of session identifiers to the syntax of LySA means that it is necessary to carry on the session identifiers to the semantics of values, i.e. terms without variables. The extended value domain will be referred to as Val, ranged over by V built from the grammar $V \ ::= \ [n]_s \mid [\{V_1, \ldots, V_k\}_{V_0}]_s$ The equivalence relation $V_1 \overset{f}{=} V_2$ is defined to be the least equivalence over Val that (inductively) ignores the session identifers. For example, $[n]_s \overset{f}{=} [n]_{s'}$ for any s and s' and $[\{[n_1]_{s_1}, [n_2]_{s_2}\}_{[n_0]_{s_0}}]_s \overset{f}{=} [\{[n_1]_{s'_1}, [n_2]_{s'_2}\}_{[n_0]_{s'_0}}]_{s'}$ for any s, s', s_1, s_2, s'_1 and s_2. For the subsequent treatment, it is convenient introducing an auxiliary operator, $\mathcal{I}$, which extracts the (outermost) session identifier of an extended value V.

Definition 2. *Extracting Session Identifers* $\mathcal{I}: Val \rightarrow SID$

$$- \ \mathcal{I}([n]_s) = s \qquad - \ \mathcal{I}([\{v_1, \ldots, v_k\}_{v_0}]_s) = s$$

In BAN logic [7], the freshness property is described as "if one part of a formula is known to be fresh, then the entire formula must also be fresh", formally

$$\frac{P \mid\equiv \sharp(X)}{P \mid\equiv \sharp(X, Y)}$$

Because of the presence of the network attacker, who can manipulate any message in clear, we shall here only focus on the encrypted messages, which is not directly under the control of the attacker. Namely, after each successful decryption, we check whether there is any field of the encrypted tuple such that its session identifier is the same as expected. This point is made clearer in the semantics shown below.

Following the tradition of the π-calculus, we shall give the extended LySA a reduction semantics. The *reduction relation* $\rightarrow_\mathcal{R}$ is the least relation on closed processes that satisfies the rules in Table below and uses the standard notion of substitution, $P[V/x]$ and structural congruence, as defined above.

As far as the semantics is concerned, we consider two variants of *reduction relation* $\rightarrow_\mathcal{R}$, identified by a different instantiation of the relation $\mathcal{R}$, which decorates the transition relation. One variant ($\rightarrow_{RM}$) takes advantage of annotations, the other one ($\rightarrow$) discards them: essentially, the first semantics checks freshness of messages, while the other one does not (see below):

- the *reference monitor semantics* $\mathcal{P} \to_{RM} \mathcal{Q}$ takes $RM(s, s') = (s = s')$
- the *standard semantics* $\mathcal{P} \to \mathcal{Q}$ takes, by construction, $\mathcal{R}$ to be universally true.

More specifically, after each successful decryption the reference monitor checks whether *at least one* field of the encrypted message is coming from the expected session, i.e. it is *fresh*, which makes the entire encryption such.

(Com)	$\dfrac{\wedge_{i=1}^{j} V_i \overset{f}{=} V_i'}{\langle V_1, \ldots, V_k \rangle.\mathcal{P} \mid (V_1', \ldots, V_j'; x_{j+1}, \ldots, x_k).\mathcal{P}' \to_{\mathcal{R}} \mathcal{P} \mid \mathcal{P}'[V_{j+1}'/x_{j+1}, \ldots, V_k'/x_k]}$
(Dec)	$\dfrac{\wedge_{i=0}^{j} V_i \overset{f}{=} V_i' \wedge \vee_{i=1}^{j} \mathcal{R}(\mathcal{I}(V_i), \mathcal{I}(V_i'))}{\mathsf{decrypt}\ \{V_1, \ldots, V_k\}_{V_0}\ \mathsf{as}\ \{V_1', \ldots, V_j'; x_{j+1}, \ldots, x_k\}_{V_0'}^{l}\ \mathsf{in}\ \mathcal{P} \to_{\mathcal{R}} \mathcal{P}[V_{j+1}'/x_{j+1}, \ldots, V_k'/x_k]}$
(Res)	$\dfrac{\mathcal{P} \to_{\mathcal{R}} \mathcal{P}'}{(\nu\,[n]_s)\mathcal{P} \to_{\mathcal{R}} (\nu\,[n]_s)\mathcal{P}'}$ (Repl) $[!P]_s \to_{\mathcal{R}} \mathcal{T}(P, s) \mid [!P]_{s'}$ (s' is fresh)
(Par)	$\dfrac{\mathcal{P}_1 \to_{\mathcal{R}} \mathcal{P}_1'}{\mathcal{P}_1 \mid \mathcal{P}_2 \to_{\mathcal{R}} \mathcal{P}_1' \mid \mathcal{P}_2}$ (Congr) $\dfrac{P \equiv P' \wedge \mathcal{T}(P', s) \to_{\mathcal{R}} \mathcal{T}(P'', s)}{\mathcal{T}(P, s) \to_{\mathcal{R}} \mathcal{T}(P'', s)}$

The rule (Com) expresses that an output $\langle V_1, \ldots, V_j, V_{j+1}, \ldots, V_k \rangle.\mathcal{P}$ matches an input $(V_1', \ldots, V_j'; x_{j+1}, \ldots, x_k)$ in case the first j values are pairwise equal (under the equivalence $\overset{f}{=}$) when all the annotations are recursively removed. When the matching is successful each V_i is bound to the corresponding x_i. Note that the equivalence relation $\overset{f}{=}$ is defined over the extended value domain Val.

Similarly, the rule (Dec) expresses the result of matching an encryption $[\{V_1, \ldots, V_k\}_{V_0}]_s$ with $\mathsf{decrypt}\ V\ \mathsf{as}\ \{V_1', \ldots, V_j'; x_{j+1}, \ldots, x_k\}_{V_0'}$ in $\mathcal{P}$. As it was the case for communication, the first j values V_i and V_i' must be equal, and additionally the keys must be equal, i.e. $V_0 \overset{f}{=} V_0'$. When the matching is successful, each V_i is bound to the corresponding x_i. In the *reference monitor semantics* we ensure that the decrypted message comes from the current session by checking whether any of the first j values V_i and V_i' have the same session identifiers. In the *standard semantics* the disjunction $\vee_{i=j+1}^{k} \mathcal{R}(\mathcal{I}(V_i), \mathcal{I}(V_i'))$ is universally true and thus can be ignored.

In case of (Repl), the process is unfolded once. Note that the new session identifier, s', in this case, has to be unique, i.e. not occurring anywhere else along the evolution of the process $\mathcal{P}$. This makes sure that each copy of a protocol process has a unique session identifer such that different copies will not be mixed up.

The rule (Congr) makes use of the function $\mathcal{T}$, which bridges the gap between the semantics defined on the extended processes $\mathcal{P}$ and the structural congruence defined on the standard processes P.

The rules (Res) and (Par) are standard.

Following the line of BAN logic, the freshness of a LySA process is defined as follows:

Definition 3 (Freshness). *A process $\mathcal{P}$ ensures freshness property if for all the possible executions $\mathcal{P} \to_{\mathcal{R}}^* \mathcal{P}' \to \mathcal{P}''$ when $\mathcal{P}' \to \mathcal{P}''$ is derived using (Dec) on*

$$decrypt\ [\{V_1, \ldots, V_k\}_{V_0}]_s\ as\ \{V_1', \ldots, V_j'; x_{j+1}, \ldots, x_k\}_{V_0}^l\ in\ \mathcal{P}$$

there exists at least one i $(1 \leq i \leq j)$ such that $\mathcal{I}(V_i) = \mathcal{I}(V_i')$

It says that an extended process $\mathcal{P}$ ensures freshness property if there is no violation of the annotations in any of its executions.

2.3 Example

We shall use the simplified version (without timestamps) of the Wide Mouthed Frog protocol [7] (WMF) for illustrating how to encode protocols in our calculus. WMF is a symmetric key management protocol aiming at establishing a secret session key K_{ab} between the two principals A and B sharing secret master keys K_A and K_B, respectively, with a trusted server S. The protocol is specified by the following informal narration:

$$1.\ A \to S : \{B, K_{ab}\}_{K_A}$$
$$2.\ S \to B : \{A, K_{ab}\}_{K_B}$$
$$3.\ B \to A : \{Msg\}_{K_{ab}}$$

The extended LySA specification of the WMF protocol is $[!P]_0$ where $P = (\nu\ K_A)(\nu\ K_B)(A|B|S)$ contains three processes A, B and S, running in parallel, each of them models one principal's activity, and is as follows:

1.	A		$(\nu\ K_{ab})$
	$A \to$		$\langle A, S, \{B, K_{ab}\}_{K_A}\rangle.$
3'.		$\to A$	$(B, A; z).$
3''.		A	decrypt z as $\{; z_m\}_{K_{ab}}^{l1}$ in 0
2'.		$\to B$	$\mid (S, B; y).$
2''.		B	decrypt y as $\{A; k\}_{K_B}^{l2}$ in
3.	B		$(\nu\ Msg)$
	$B \to$		$\langle B, A, \{Msg\}_k\rangle.0$
1'.		$\to S$	$\mid (A, S; p).$
1''.		S	decrypt p as $\{B; k'\}_{K_A}^{l3}$ in
2.	$S \to$		$\langle S, B, \{A, k'\}_{K_B}\rangle.0$

3   Static Analysis

The LySA calculus is especially designed to model security protocols involving a number of principals, where each of them execute a sequence of actions, synchronised by communications. Because of interactions, in most of the cases, it is impossible to predict the exact behaviour of each principal. In this section, we present a control flow analysis aiming at collecting the central aspect of the information of a protocol of interest. This is done by over-approximating at static time the protocol behaviour along all the execution paths.

3.1 Domain of the Analysis

The control flow analysis describes a protocol behaviour by collecting all the communications that a process may participate in. This information, i.e. the tuples of values that maybe communicated over the network, is recorded in an analysis component κ, i.e. $\kappa \subseteq \wp(Val^*)$ is the *abstract network environment* that includes all the tuples forming a message that may flow on the network. As said before, successful communications involve pattern matching and variable binding, i.e. binding values to variables. To collect this information, we introduce another analysis component $\rho : \mathcal{X} \to \wp(Val)$ that maps the variables to the sets of values that they may be bound to.

Name Space. Both the analysis components κ and ρ have to do with recording values $V \in Val$ in some format. However, a LySa process may generate infinitely many values during an execution because of the restriction and replication constructs, e.g. $!(\nu\ n)\langle n \rangle$, which means that the analysis components have to be able to record infinitely many names.

For keeping the analysis component finite, we partition all the names used by a process into finitely many equivalence classes and we use the names of the equivalence classes instead of the actual names. This partition works in a way that names from the same equivalence class are assigned a common *canonical name* and consequently there are only finitely many canonical names in any execution of a given process. This is enforced by assigning the same canonical name to every name generated by the same restriction. The canonical name $\lfloor n \rfloor$ is for a name n; similarly $\lfloor x \rfloor$ is for a variable x. For example, a process, that may generate infinitely many names, is $!(\nu\ n)P$, as shown in the following chain of equivalences: $!(\nu\ n)P \equiv (\nu\ n')P' \mid !(\nu\ n)P \equiv (\nu\ n')P' \mid (\nu\ n'')P'' \mid !(\nu\ n)P \equiv \ldots$ Furthermore, the names n, n' and n'' are generated by the same restriction and hence have the same canonical name, i.e. $\lfloor n \rfloor = \lfloor n' \rfloor = \lfloor n'' \rfloor$. Hereafter, when unambiguous, we shall simply write n (resp. x) for $\lfloor n \rfloor$ (resp. $\lfloor x \rfloor$).

3.2 Analysis of Terms and Processes

For each term $\mathcal{E}$, the analysis will determine a superset of the possible values it may evaluate to. The judgement for terms takes the form $\rho \models \mathcal{E} : \vartheta$ where $\vartheta \subseteq Val$ is an acceptable *estimate* (i.e. a sound over-approximation) of the set of values that $\mathcal{E}$ may evaluate to in the environment ρ. The judgement is defined by the axioms and rules in the upper part of Table below. Basically, the rules demand that ϑ contains all the values associated with the components of a term. In the sequel we shall use two kinds of membership tests: the usual $V \in \vartheta$ that simply tests whether V is in the set ϑ and the *faithful* test $V \propto \vartheta$ that holds if there is a value V' in ϑ that equals V, when the annotations are inductively ignored.

The judgement for processes has the form: $\rho, \kappa \models_{RM} \mathcal{P} : \psi$ expressing that ρ, κ and ψ are valid analysis estimates of process $\mathcal{P}$. The additional component $\psi \subseteq \wp(Lab)$ is the possibly empty set of error-component which collects an over-approximation of the freshness violations: a label $l \in \psi$ means that the value binding after a successful decryption, marked with label l, violates the freshness annotations and therefore is not allowed. We prove in Theorem 2 (in Section 3.1) that when $\psi = \emptyset$ we may do without the reference monitor. The judgement is defined by the axioms and rules in the lower part of Table below (where $A \Rightarrow B$ means that B is analysed only when A is *true*) and are explained below. Note that we only check whether a proposed triple, (ρ, κ, ψ), is indeed valid; the algorithm to build solutions is sketched in Section 5.1.

$$\text{(Name)} \quad \frac{[n]_s \in \vartheta}{\rho \models [n]_s : \vartheta} \qquad\qquad \text{(Var)} \quad \frac{\rho(x) \subseteq \vartheta}{\rho \models x : \vartheta}$$

$$\text{(Enc)} \quad \frac{\wedge_{i=0}^{k} \rho \models \mathcal{E}_i : \vartheta_i \ \wedge \ \forall V_0, \ldots, V_k : \wedge_{i=0}^{k} V_i \in \vartheta_i \Rightarrow [\{V_1, \ldots, V_k\}_{V_0}]_s \in \vartheta}{\rho \models [\{\mathcal{E}_1, \ldots, \mathcal{E}_k\}_{\mathcal{E}_0}]_s : \vartheta}$$

$$\text{(Out)} \quad \frac{\wedge_{i=1}^{k} \rho \models \mathcal{E}_i : \vartheta_i \ \wedge \ \forall V_1, \ldots, V_k \wedge_{i=1}^{k} V_i \in \vartheta_i \Rightarrow \langle V_1, \ldots, V_k \rangle \in \kappa \ \wedge \rho, \kappa \models_{RM} \mathcal{P} : \psi}{\rho, \kappa \models_{RM} \langle \mathcal{E}_1, \ldots, \mathcal{E}_k \rangle.\mathcal{P} : \psi}$$

$$\text{(Inp)} \quad \frac{\wedge_{i=1}^{j} \rho \models \mathcal{E}_i : \vartheta_i \ \wedge \ \forall \langle V_1, \ldots, V_k \rangle \in \kappa : \wedge_{i=1}^{j} V_i \propto \vartheta_i \Rightarrow \wedge_{i=j+1}^{k} V_i \in \rho(x_i) \ \wedge \rho, \kappa \models_{RM} \mathcal{P} : \psi}{\rho, \kappa \models_{RM} (\mathcal{E}_1, \ldots, \mathcal{E}_j; x_{j+1}, \ldots, x_k).\mathcal{P} : \psi}$$

$$\text{(Dec)} \quad \frac{\begin{array}{c} \rho \models \mathcal{E} : \vartheta \ \wedge \ \wedge_{i=0}^{j} \rho \models \mathcal{E}_i : \vartheta_i \wedge \\ \forall [\{V_1, \ldots, V_k\}_{V_0}]_s \in \vartheta : \wedge_{i=0}^{j} V_i \propto \vartheta_i \Rightarrow \\ (\wedge_{i=j+1}^{k} V_i \in \rho(x_i) \ \wedge \rho, \kappa \models_{RM} \mathcal{P} : \psi \ \wedge \\ (\nexists i : 1 \leq i \leq k : (\mathcal{I}(V_i) = \mathcal{I}(\mathcal{E}_i)) \Rightarrow l \in \psi)) \end{array}}{\rho, \kappa \models_{RM} \text{ decrypt } \mathcal{E} \text{ as } \{\mathcal{E}_1, \ldots, \mathcal{E}_j; x_{j+1}, \ldots, x_k\}_{\mathcal{E}_0}^{l} \text{ in } \mathcal{P} : \psi}$$

$$\text{(Rep)} \quad \frac{\rho, \kappa \models_{RM} \mathcal{T}([P]_s) : \psi \ \wedge \ \rho, \kappa \models_{RM} \mathcal{T}([P]_{s'}) : \psi}{\rho, \kappa \models_{RM} [!P]_s : \psi} \qquad \text{(Nil)} \quad \rho, \kappa \models_{RM} 0 : \psi$$

$$\text{(Par)} \quad \frac{\rho, \kappa \models_{RM} \mathcal{P} : \psi \ \wedge \ \rho, \kappa \models_{RM} \mathcal{Q} : \psi}{\rho, \kappa \models_{RM} \mathcal{P} \mid \mathcal{Q} : \psi} \qquad \text{(Res)} \quad \frac{\rho, \kappa \models_{RM} \mathcal{P} : \psi}{\rho, \kappa \models_{RM} (\nu[n]_s)\mathcal{P} : \psi}$$

The rule for *output* does two things: first, all the expressions are abstractly evaluated and then it is required that all the combinations of the values found by this evaluation are recorded in κ. Finally, the continuation process must be analysed, which is also the case for *input* and *decryption* rules.

The rule for *input* incorporates pattern matching, which is dealt with by first abstractly evaluating all the of first j expressions in the input to be the sets ϑ_i for $i = 1, \ldots, j$. Next, if any of the sequences of length k in κ are such that the first j values component-wise are included in ϑ_i then the match is considered to be successful. In this case, the remaining values of the k-tuple must be recorded in ρ as possible bindings of the variables.

The rule for *decryption* handles the matching similarly to the rule for *input*. The only difference is that here the matching is performed also on the key. We use the faithful test for matching because the semantics ignores the annotations. After the successful matching, values are bound to the corresponding variables and, more importantly, the session identifiers of the key and of the first j components have to be checked equivalent. In case for some i, $\mathcal{I}(v_i) \neq \mathcal{I}(\mathcal{E}_i)$, meaning that not all the values are from the current session, the label of the decryption l is recorded in the error component ψ.

The rule for *replication* attaches two different session identifiers to two copies of the process before analysing both of them. Again the newly generated session identifier has to be unique in order not to mix processes up. We prove in Theorem 2 that it is enough to only analyse two copies of the process. For an informal argument: a replay attack is about replaying messages from a sessions to a principal not participating in the session and the control flow analysis treats sequential sessions and parallel session in the same way, analysing more than two sessions are not giving more information about attacks.

The rules for the inactive process, parallel composition and restriction are straightforward.

3.3   Semantic Properties

In this section, we shall show a list of lemmas and theorems concerning the semantics correctness. The detail proofs are omitted due to space limitations.

Our analysis respects the operational semantics of extended LySA. More precisely, we prove a subject reduction result for both the standard and the reference monitor semantics: if $\rho, \kappa \models \mathcal{P} : \psi$, then the same triple (ρ, κ, ψ) is a valid estimate for all the states passed through in a computation of $\mathcal{P}$. Additionally, we show that when the ψ component is empty, then the reference monitor is useless.

It is convenient to prove the following lemmata. The first states that estimates are resistant to substitution of closed terms for variables, and it holds for both extended terms and processes. The second lemma says that an estimate for an extended processes $\mathcal{P}$ is valid for every process congruent to $\mathcal{P}$, as well.

Lemma 1. *(Substitution)*

1. $\rho \models \mathcal{E} : \vartheta$ and $\mathcal{E}' \in \rho(x)$ imply $\rho \models \mathcal{E}[\mathcal{E}'/x] : \vartheta$
2. $\rho, \kappa \models P : \psi$ and $\mathcal{E} \in \rho(x)$ imply $\rho, \kappa \models P[\mathcal{E}/x] : \psi$

Proof. The proofs proceed by structural induction over terms.

Lemma 2. *(Congruence)*
If $P \equiv Q$ and $\rho, \kappa \models \mathcal{T}([P]_s) : \psi$ then $\rho, \kappa \models \mathcal{T}([Q]_s) : \psi$

Proof. By a straightforward inspection of each of the clauses defining $P \equiv Q$.

Subject reduction result holds for both the standard and the reference monitor semantics: if $\rho, \kappa \models_{RM} P : \psi$, then the same triple (ρ, κ, ψ) is a valid estimate for all the derivatives of P.

Theorem 1. *(Subject reduction)*

1. *If $P \rightarrow_{\mathcal{R}} Q$ and $\rho, \kappa \models P : \psi$ then also $\rho, \kappa \models Q : \psi$;*
2. *Furthermore, if $\psi = \emptyset$ then $P \rightarrow_{RM} Q$*

Proof. The proof is done by induction of the inference of $P \rightarrow_{\mathcal{R}} Q$.

The next result shows that our analysis correctly predicts when we can safely dispense with the reference monitor. We shall say that the reference monitor RM *cannot abort* a process P when there exist no Q, Q' such that $P \rightarrow_{\mathcal{R}}^* Q \rightarrow_{RM} Q'$ and $P \rightarrow_{RM}^* Q \nrightarrow_{RM}$. As usual, * stands for the transitive and reflexive closure of the relation in question, and $Q \nrightarrow_{RM}$ stands for $\nexists Q' : Q \rightarrow_{RM} Q'$.

Theorem 2. *(Static check for reference monitor)*

If $\rho, \kappa \models P : \emptyset$ then RM cannot abort P.

Proof Suppose *per absurdum* that such Q and Q' exist. A straightforward induction extends the subject reduction result to $P \rightarrow^* Q$ giving $\rho, \kappa \models_{RM} Q : \emptyset$. Theorem 1 part 2 of applied to $Q \rightarrow Q'$ gives $Q \rightarrow_{RM} Q'$ which is a contradiction.

3.4   Example

The least solution of the analysis of the WMF protocol and has a non-empty ψ-component, i.e.

$$\rho, \kappa \models_{RM} WMF : \psi$$

where ρ, κ and ψ have the following entries

$\rho : y \mapsto \{\{[A]_0, [K_{ab}]_0\}_{[K_B]_0}, \{[A]_1, [K_{ab}]_1\}_{[K_B]_1}\}$

$\quad z \mapsto \{\{[Msg]_0\}_{[K_{ab}]_0}, \{[Msg]_1\}_{[K_{ab}]_1}\}$

$\quad p \mapsto \{\{[B]_0, [K_{ab}]_0\}_{[K_A]_0}, \{[B]_1, [K_{ab}]_1\}_{[K_A]_1}\}$

$\quad k \mapsto \{[K_{ab}]_0, [K_{ab}]_1\}$

$\quad k' \mapsto \{[K_{ab}]_0, [K_{ab}]_1\}$

$\quad z_m \mapsto \{[Msg]_0, [Msg]_1\}$

$\kappa : \{\langle [A]_0, [S]_0, [\{[B]_0, [K_{ab}]_0\}_{[K_A]_0}]_0 \rangle, \langle [A]_1, [S]_1, [\{[B]_1, [K_{ab}]_1\}_{[K_A]_1}]_1 \rangle\} \cup$

$\quad \{\langle [B]_0, [A]_0, [\{[Msg]_0\}_{[K_{ab}]_0}]_0 \rangle, \langle [B]_1, [A]_1, [\{[Msg]_1\}_{[K_{ab}]_1}]_1 \rangle\} \cup$

$\quad \{\langle [S]_0, [B]_0, [\{[A]_0, [K_{ab}]_0\}_{[K_B]_0}]_0 \rangle, \langle [S]_1, [B]_1, [\{[A]_1, [K_{ab}]_1\}_{[K_B]_1}]_1 \rangle\}$

$\psi : \{l1, l2, l3\}$

According the rule for $[!P]_s$ in Table shown before, the analysis makes two copies of P with different session identifiers (0 and 1 in our case), which models two sessions running together.

The messages from both sessions are sent over the network, which the attacker has the total control of. Therefore, the attacher can fool a principal to accept a message actually coming from another session. This is suggested by the non-empty ψ: the three variables in ψ indicate that messages in step 1″, 2″ and 3″ may not be fresh. This is highly dangerous because the principal may be forced to use an old session to encrypt the security data and in case of an old session key is revealed, confidentiality is not preserved any longer. A possible attack derivable from the solution above is shown below, where M represents the attacker:

$$1.\ [A]_1 \to [S]_1 : \{[B]_1, [K_{ab}]_1\}_{[K_A]_1}$$
$$2.\ [S]_1 \to\ M : \{[A]_1, [K_{ab}]_1\}_{[K_B]_1}$$
$$M \to [B]_1 : \{[A]_0, [K_{ab}]_0\}_{[K_B]_0}$$
$$3.\ [B]_1 \to [A]_1 : \{[Msg]_1\}_{[K_{ab}]_0}$$

4   Modelling the Attackers

In a protocol execution, several principals exchange messages over an open network, which is accessible to the attackers and therefore vulnerable to malicious behaviour. We assume an active Dolev-Yao attacker [11]. It is active in the sense that it is not only able to eavesdrop, but also to replay, encrypt, decrypt or generate messages providing that the necessary information is within his knowledge.

This scenario can be modelled in extended LYSA as an attacker process running in parallel with the protocol process. Formally, we shall have $\mathcal{P}_{sys} \mid \mathcal{Q}$, where $\mathcal{P}_{sys}$ represents the protocol process and $\mathcal{Q}$ is some arbitrary attacker. The attacker acquires its knowledge by interacting with $\mathcal{P}_{sys}$, starting from the public knowledge. Note that the secret messages and keys, e.g. K_{ab}, are restricted to their scope in $\mathcal{P}_{sys}$ and thus they are not immediately accessible to the attacker.

4.1   Constructing Attacker Process

Our aim consists in finding a general way of constructing the attacker process, which is able to characterise all the attackers. The idea here is to define a formula, inspired by the work [3,4], and then to prove its correctness.

In order for the attacker process to interact with the protocol process, some basic information of the protocol process has to be known in advance. We shall say that a process $\mathcal{P}_{sys}$ has the type $(\mathcal{N}_f, \mathcal{A}_\kappa, \mathcal{A}_{Enc})$ whenever: (1) it is close, (2) all the free names of $\mathcal{P}_{sys}$ are in $\mathcal{N}_f$, (3) all the arities used for sending or receiving are in $\mathcal{A}_\kappa$ and (4) all the arities used for encryption or decryption are in $\mathcal{A}_{Enc}$. Obviously, $\mathcal{N}_f$, $\mathcal{A}_\kappa$ and $\mathcal{A}_{Enc}$ are all finite and can be computed by inspecting the process $\mathcal{P}_{sys}$.

One concern regarding the attacker process is about the names and variables it uses, which have to be apart from the ones used by $\mathcal{P}_{sys}$. Let all the names used by $\mathcal{P}_{sys}$ to be in a finite set $\mathcal{N}_c$, all the variables in a finite set $\mathcal{X}_c$ and all the session identifiers in a finite set $\mathcal{S}_c$; we can then postulate a new extended name $[n_\bullet]_{s_\bullet}$, where $n_\bullet$ is not in $\mathcal{N}_c$, a new variable $z_\bullet$ not in $\mathcal{X}_c$, and a new session identifier $s_\bullet$ not in $\mathcal{S}_c$.

In order to control the number of names and variables used by the attacker, we construct a semantically equivalent process $\overline{\mathcal{Q}'}$, for a process $\mathcal{Q}$ of type $(\mathcal{N}_f, \mathcal{A}_\kappa, \mathcal{A}_{Enc})$, as follows: 1) all restrictions $(\nu[n]_s)\mathcal{P}$ are α-converted into restrictions $(\nu[n']_{s_\bullet})\mathcal{P}$ where n' has the canonical representative $n_\bullet$, 2) all the occurrences of variables x_i in $(\mathcal{E}_1, \ldots, \mathcal{E}_j; x_{j+1}, \ldots, x_k).\mathcal{P}$ and of variables x_i in decrypt $\mathcal{E}$ as $\{\mathcal{E}_1, \ldots, \mathcal{E}_j; x_{j+1}, \ldots, x_k\}$ in $\mathcal{P}$ are α-converted to use variables x'_i with canonical representative $z_\bullet$. Therefore $\overline{\mathcal{Q}'}$ only has finitely many canonical names and variables.

---

(1) $\bigwedge_{k \in \mathcal{A}_\kappa} \forall \langle v_1, \ldots, v_k \rangle \in \kappa : \bigwedge_{i=1}^k v_i \in \rho(z_\bullet)$
the attacker may learn by eavesdropping

(2) $\bigwedge_{k \in \mathcal{A}_{Enc}} \forall [\{v_1, \ldots, v_k\}_{v_0}]_s \in \rho(z_\bullet) :$
$\quad\quad v_0 \propto \rho(z_\bullet) \Rightarrow \bigwedge_{i=1}^k v_i \in \rho(z_\bullet)$
the attacker may learn by decrypting messages with keys already known

(3) $\bigwedge_{k \in \mathcal{A}_{Enc}} \forall v_0, \ldots, v_k : \bigwedge_{i=0}^k v_i \in \rho(z_\bullet) \Rightarrow [\{v_1, \ldots, v_k\}_{v_0}]_{s_\bullet} \in \rho(z_\bullet)$
the attacker may construct new encryptions using the keys known

(4) $\bigwedge_{k \in \mathcal{A}_\kappa} \forall v_1, \ldots, v_k : \bigwedge_{i=1}^k v_i \in \rho(z_\bullet) \Rightarrow \langle v_1, \ldots, v_k \rangle \in \kappa$
the attacker may actively forge new communications

(5) $\{[n_\bullet]_{s_\bullet}\} \cup \mathcal{N}_f \subseteq \rho(z_\bullet)$
the attacker initially has some knowledge

We now have sufficient control over the capabilities of the attacker. Now, we extend the standard Dolev-Yao threat model with session identifiers. We express the extended Dolev-Yao condition for our LySA calculus and define a formula $\mathcal{F}_{RM}^{DY}$ of type $(\mathcal{N}_f, \mathcal{A}_\kappa, \mathcal{A}_{Enc})$ as the conjunction of the five components in Table shown above, where each line describes an ability of the attacker. Furthermore, we claim that the formula $\mathcal{F}_{RM}^{DY}$ is capable of characterising the potential effect of all attackers $\overline{\mathcal{Q}}$ of type $(\mathcal{N}_f, \mathcal{A}_\kappa, \mathcal{A}_{Enc})$.

The soundness of our Dolev-Yao condition is established by the following Theorem.

Theorem 3. (*Correctness of the extended Dolev-Yao condition*)

If (ρ, κ) satisfies $\mathcal{F}_{RM}^{DY}$ of type $(\mathcal{N}_f, \mathcal{A}_\kappa, \mathcal{A}_{Enc})$ then there exists ψ such that for all attackers $\mathcal{Q}$ of type $(\mathcal{N}_f, \mathcal{A}_\kappa, \mathcal{A}_{Enc})$ $\rho, \kappa \models_{RM} \overline{\mathcal{Q}} : \psi$

Proof. The proof is done by structural induction on $\overline{\mathcal{Q}}$.

5   Main Results

The session identifiers in the extended LySA are designed to make the capture of replay attacks easier, thus ensuring that the receiving messages are fresh. For the dynamic property, we say that $\mathcal{P}_{sys}$ guarantees *dynamic freshness* with respect to the annotations in $\mathcal{P}_{sys}$ if the reference monitor RM cannot abort $\mathcal{P}_{sys} \mid \overline{\mathcal{Q}}$ regardless of the choice of the attacker $\mathcal{Q}$.

Similarly, for static property we say that $\mathcal{P}_{sys}$ guarantees *static freshness* with respect to the annotations in $\mathcal{P}_{sys}$ if there exists ρ and κ such that $\rho, \kappa \models_{\mathsf{RM}} \mathcal{P} : \emptyset$ and (ρ, κ) satisfies $\mathcal{F}_{\mathsf{RM}}^{\mathsf{DY}}$.

Theorem 4. *If $\mathcal{P}$ guarantees static freshness then $\mathcal{P}$ guarantees dynamic freshness.*

Proof. If $\rho, \kappa \models_{\mathsf{RM}} \mathcal{P}_{sys} : \emptyset$ and (ρ, κ) satisfies $\mathcal{F}_{\mathsf{RM}}^{\mathsf{DY}}$ then, by Theorems 2 and 3, RM does not abort $\mathcal{P}_{sys} \mid \overline{\mathcal{Q}}$ regardless of the choice of attacker $\mathcal{Q}$.

5.1   Implementation and Complexity

To obtain an implementation we transform the analysis into a logically equivalent formation written in Alternation-free Least Fixed Point logic (ALFP) [12], and use the Succinct Solver [12], which computes the least interpretation of the predicate symbols in a given ALFP formula. The time complexity of solving a formula in the Succinct Solver is polynomial in the size of the universe, over which the formula is interpreted. For our implementation the universe is linear in the size of the process and a simple worst-case estimate of the degree of the complexity polynomial is given as one plus the maximal nesting depth of quantifiers in the formula. For our current implementation the nesting depth is governed by the maximal length of the sequences used in the communication and encryption. In practice, the implementation runs in sub-cubic time and we obtain running times well in few seconds for all of our experiments.

5.2   Validation of Needham-Schroeder Symmetric Key Protocol

Needham-Schroeder Symmetric Key Protocol is a classical protocol and has been used widely as an example for protocol verification. The protocol has 6 steps: in the first steps, a fresh session key K is generated by the trusted server S and sent to both parties, A and B; in the following two steps, B sends out a challenge to make sure A is in possession of the new session key. After a protocol run, A and B share a secret session key for secure communication. The protocol narration is listed below in the left,

1. $A \rightarrow S : A, B, N_a$	1. $A \rightarrow S :$ A, B, N_a
2. $S \rightarrow A : \{N_a, B, K, \{K, A\}_{K_b}\}_{K_a}$	2. $S \rightarrow A :$ $\{N_a, B, K, \{K, A\}_{K_b}\}_{K_a}$
3. $A \rightarrow B : \{A, K\}_{K_b}$	3. $M(A) \rightarrow B : \{A, K'\}_{K_b}$
4. $B \rightarrow A : \{N_b\}_K$	4. $B \rightarrow M(A) : \{N_b\}_{K'}$
5. $A \rightarrow B : \{N_b - 1\}_K$	5. $M(A) \rightarrow B : \{N_b - 1\}_{K'}$
6. $A \rightarrow B : \{Msg\}_K$	6. $M(A) \rightarrow B : \{Msg\}_{K'}$
the protocol narration	*a replay attack scenario*

The analysis result of Needhan-Schroeder Symmetric Key Protocol shows a violation, meaning that it is subject to a replay attack. This result corresponds to the replay attack reported by Denning & Sacco in [10]: the message in step 3 can be replayed with an old compromised session key by an active attacker and consequently B is forced to use the old key K' for communication. An example trace is shown above in the right.

To fix this problem, Denning & Sacco and Needham & Schroeder proposed different solutions but both make use of new nonces. Needham & Schroeder's solution is: having A ask B for another random value N_a' to be sent to the Server for return in $\{A, N_a', K\}_{K_b}$. After the correction, the first three steps become the followings and others keep unchanged.

$$
\begin{array}{lll}
1. & A \to S: & A, B, N_a, N_a' \\
2. & S \to A: & \{N_a, B, K, \{A, N_a', K\}_{K_b}\}_{K_a} \\
3. & M(A) \to B: & \{A, N_a', K\}_{K_b}
\end{array}
$$

After applying the analysis to the above version, the result becomes: *no violations possible*, i.e. $\psi = \emptyset$, meaning that the attacker now cannot replay the message from step 3 and therefore no replay attack is possible to this corrected version.

6 Conclusion

In this paper we have introduced a sound way to detect replay attacks at static time. To do that, we extended the standard LYSA calculus with session identifiers and gave it a reduction semantics. The semantics ensures session identifiers are properly treated along the evolution of a process. On the static side, we extended the control flow analysis [3,4] to verify the freshness property of the extended processes. The static property ensures that, if the secret information received by a principal is in the right context, then a process is not subject to a run-external attack at execution time. As far as the attacker is concerned, we adopted the notion from Dolev-Yao threat model and extended it with session identifiers in order to fit it into our setting. The extended Dolev-Yao attacker is able to monitor the traffic over the network and actively generate messages within his knowledge. We implemented the analysis and used our tool to check some significant protocols, including classical protocols, e.g. Wide Mouthed Frog, Yahalom, Andrew Secure RPC, Otway-Rees, Needham-Schroeder, Amended Needham-Schroeder. Besides the classical protocols, at present, we are successfully applying our analysis to other kinds of protocols, like the ones in the family of IEEE 802.16 [17]. The tool confirmed that we can successfully detect potential replay attacks on the protocols.

The original LYSA calculus and the control flow analysis [3,4] are designed to validate authentication property of security protocols. In this paper, they are extended systematically such that we are able to address an orthogonal property, freshness. The way we validate freshness is inspired by BAN logic [7], which is actually a set of rules for defining and analysing security protocols, namely "if one part of a formula is known to be fresh, then the entire formula must also be fresh". We also prove that analysing two copies of a process in our framework is sufficient for capturing run-external replay attacks. The experiments conducted also confirmed this. The literature already has similar results, e.g. Comon & Cortier [8] and Millen [19].

Several papers deal with replay attacks and freshness. Because of lack of space, we only mention the closest to ours, i.e. [14,15,16] and [6], where the approach is based on type (and effects) systems that statically guarantee entity authentication of protocols. Gordon and Jeffrey [14,15,16] defined type (and effects) systems that statically guarantee authentication of protocols specified in a Spi-calculus enriched with assertions à la Woo-Lam. In [6], Bugliesi, Focardi, Maffei still use a type and effect system, but use a different technique and a different calculus (the ρ-spi calculus).

The analysis presented in this paper is part of a project, analysing various security properties of communication protocols using annotations. It can be easily combined with other kinds of annotations from the same framework, e.g. the one from [13] for confidentiality, and the one from [5] for simple type flaw attacks, and hence gives a more comprehensive analysis result.

References

1. Abadi, M., Gordon, A.D.: A Calculus for Cryptographic Protocols: The Spi Calculus. Information and Computation 148(1), 1–70 (1999)
2. Blanchet, B.: An efficient cryptographic protocol verifier based on prolog rules. IEEE Computer Society Press, Los Alamitos (2001)
3. Bodei, C., Buchholtz, M., Degano, P., Nielson, F., Riis Nielson, H.: Automatic Valication of Protocol Narration. In: Proceeding of Computer Security Foundations Workshop, pp. 126–140. IEEE Press, Los Alamitos (2003)
4. Bodei, C., Buchholtz, M., Degano, P., Nielson, F., Riis Nielson, H.: Static Validation of Security Protocols. Journal of Computer Security 13(3), 347–390 (2005)
5. Bodei, C., Degano, P., Gao, H., Brodo, L.: Detecting and Preventing Type flaws: a Contro Flow Analysis with tags. In: Proceeding of 5th International Workshop on Security Issues in Concurrency. ENTCS (to appear)
6. Bugliesi, M., Focardi, R., Maffei, M.: Authenticity by Tagging and Typing. In: Proceeding of 2nd ACM Workshop on Formal Methods in Security Engineering, ACM Press, New York (2004)
7. Burrows, M., Abadi, M., Needham, R.: A Logic of Authentication. ACM Transactions in Computer Systems 8(1), 18–36 (1990)
8. Comon-Lundh, H., Cortier, V.: Tree automata with one memory set constraints and cryptographic protocols. Theoretical Computer Science 331(1), 143–214 (2005)
9. Curti, M., Degano, P., Tatiana Baldari, C.: Causal π-Calculus for Biochemical Modelling. In: Priami, C. (ed.) CMSB 2003. LNCS, vol. 2602, pp. 21–33. Springer, Heidelberg (2003)
10. Denning, D.E., Maria Sacco, G.: Timestamps in Key Distribution Protocols. Communications of the ACM 24(8), 533–536 (1981)
11. Dolev, D., Yao, A.C.: On the Security of Public Key Protocols. IEEE TIT, IT 29(12), 198–208 (1983)
12. Nielson, F., Seidl, H., Riis Nielson, H.: A Succinct Solver for ALFP. Nordic Journal of Computing 9, 335–372 (2002)

13. Gao, H., Riis Nielson, H.: Analysis of LYSA-calculus with explicit confidentiality annotations. In: Proceeding of Advanced Information Networking and Applications, IEEE Computer Society, Los Alamitos (2006)
14. Gordon, A.D., Jeffrey, A.: Authenticity by Typing for Security Protocols. In: Proceeding of Computer Security Foundations Symposium, IEEE, Los Alamitos (2001)
15. Gordon, A.D.: Typing Correspondence Assertions for Communication Protocols. In: Proceeding of Mathematical Foundations of Programming Semantics (2001)
16. Gordon, A.D., Jeffrey, A.: Types and Effects for Asymmetric Cryptographic Protocols. In: Proceeding of Computer Security Foundations Symposium, IEEE, Los Alamitos (2002)
17. IEEE Std 802.16e-2005, Standard for Local and metropolitan area networks Part 16: Air Interface for Fixed and Mobile Broadband Wireless Access Systems Amendment 2: Physical and Medium Access Control Layers for Combined Fixed and Mobile Operation in Licensed Bands and Corrigendum 1, IEEE, New York, USA (2006)
18. Meadows, C., Syverson, P., Cervesato, I.: Formal Specification and Analysis of the Group Domain of Interpretation Protocol Using NPATRL and the NRL Protocol Analyzer. Journal of Computer Security 12(6), 893–931 (2004)
19. Millen, J.K.: Term Replacement Algebra for the Interrogator. The MITRE Corporation, MP 97B65 (1997)
20. Milner, R.: Communicating and mobile systems: the π-calculus. Cambridge University Press, Cambridge (1999)
21. Needham, R., Schroeder, M.: Using encryption for authentication in large networks of computers. Communications of the ACM 21(12) (December 1978)
22. Otway, D., Rees, O.: Efficient and Timely Mutual Authentication. Operating Systems Review 21(1), 8–10 (1987)
23. Paulson, L.C.: Inductive Analysis of the Internet Protocol TLS. ACM Transactions on Computer and System Security 2(3), 332–351 (1999)
24. Paulson, L.C.: The foundation of a generic theorem prover. Automated Reasoning 5, 363–397 (1989)
25. Syverson, P.: A Taxonomy of Replay attacks. In: Proceeding of Computer Security Foundations Symposium, IEEE Computer Society Press, Los Alamitos (1994)

An Abstraction and Refinement Framework for Verifying Security Protocols Based on Logic Programming

MengJun Li[1,*], Ti Zhou[1], ZhouJun Li[2,*], and HuoWang Chen[1,*]

[1] School of Computer Science, National University of Defense Technology,
ChangSha, 410073, China
[2] School of Computer Science & Engineering, Beihang University, BeiJing 100083, China
mengjun_li1975@yahoo.com.cn

Abstract. Using depth(k) abstract domain, we present an abstraction and refinement framework for verifying security protocols based on logic programming. The solved-form fixpoint of the logic program model is abstracted by
depth(k) abstract domain, which guarantees termination of the verification algorithm; If the result of the verification algorithm with the abstract solved-form
fixpoint shows there exists counterexamples, but the result of the verification
algorithm with the logic rules in abstract solved-form fixpoint which are not abstracted shows there exists no counterexamples, then the abstracted solved-form
fixpoint is refined by increasing the value of term depth bound k. With this
framework, all of the verification, constructing counterexamples and refinement
can be implemented in a mechanized way.

Keywords: abstraction and refinement; security protocol.

1 Introduction

The verification of security protocols is an active research area. Bruno Blanchet and
Martin abadi present the verification technique based on logic program model and
resolution[1-5]. The verification technique consists of translating security protocol
into logic program model, followed by a resolution-based verification algorithm. It
has the following characteristics:

- It can verify protocols with an unbounded number of sessions.
- It can easily handle a variety of cryptographic primitives, including shared key and
  public-key cryptography, hash functions, message authentication codes, etc.
- It is efficient in practice.

However, the resolution-based verification algorithm does not terminate in general. In
fact, the algorithm did not terminate (went into an infinite loop) when it was applied
to the Needham-Schroeder shared-key protocol and several versions of the Woo-Lam
shared-key one-way authentication protocol[5].

---

* Supported by the National Natural Science Foundation of China under Grant Nos.
60473057,90604007,60703075.

I. Cervesato (Ed.): ASIAN 2007, LNCS 4846, pp. 166–180, 2007.

This paper presents an abstraction and refinement framework for verifying security protocol based on abstraction of fixpoint of its logic program model. The solved-form fixpoint of the logic program model is abstracted by depth(k) abstract domain[6], it is abstracted into finite solved-form logic rules, which would guarantee termination of the resolution-based verification algorithm. If the verification algorithm with the abstract solved-form fixpoint shows there exists counterexamples, but the verification algorithm with logic rules in abstract solved-form fixpoint which are not abstracted shows there exists no counterexamples, then the abstracted solved-form fixpoint is refined by increasing the value of term depth bound k. With this abstraction and refinement framework, security protocols can be verified iteratively: if the resolution-based verification algorithm with abstract fixpoint shows protocol satisfies the security properties, then the protocol satisfies the security properties since the abstraction is a safe approximation; Otherwise, if the counterexamples can be constructed using those logic rules which are not abstracted, then the constructed counterexamples are actually attacks against protocol. If the counterexamples can not be constructed using those logic rules which are not abstracted, then the abstraction of fixpoint should be refined. With this abstraction and refinement framework, all of the verification, constructing counterexample and refinement can be implemented in a mechanized way.

Related Work. Although the problem of deciding correctness of security protocol is undecidable[7], verifying it based on abstract interpretation[8] is a feasible and effective approach. L. Bozga, Y. Lakhnech and M. Perin present a pattern-based abstraction method for verifying secrecy property[9], they use the sets of pattern-terms as abstract domain, and they implement a verification tool HERMES[10].Given a protocol and a secret property, HERMES computes conditions on the initial intruder knowledge that guarantee the secret is never going to be revealed. Frédéric Oehl, Gérard Cécé, Olga Kouchnarenko and David Sinclair present an approximation function developed for the verification of security protocols. The approximation function can be build automatically and its computation is guaranteed to terminate. Given an initial tree automaton A (recognizing the initial configuration of the network where everybody wants to communicate with everybody), a term rewriting system R(modeling the protocol steps and the intruder abilities), by the approximation function, an tree automaton $TR \mathit{f}(A)$ recognizing an approximation of the possible configurations of the network reachable by R from A is built, moreover $R^{*}(L(A)) \subseteq L(TR \mathit{f}(A))$, where $L(A)$ is the language accepted by A and $*$ be the closure operator. Recently, Michael Backes, Matteo Maffei, and Agostino Cortesi present a novel technique for analyzing security protocols based on an abstraction of the program semantics[12], the technique is based on a novel structure called causal graph which captures the causality among program events within a finite graph. A core property of causal graphs is that they abstract away from the multiplicity of protocol sessions, hence constituting a concise tool for reasoning about an even infinite number of concurrent protocol sessions, and deciding security only requires a traversal of the causal graph.

Comparing with their work, our approach supports the abstraction and refinement iteration verification framework. There exists no explicit refinement ways for pattern-terms abstract domain[9],, tree automaton[11], and causal graphs abstract domain[12], whereas the depth(k) abstract domain is prone to be refined by only increasing the value of term depth bound k. And abstracting fixpoint by depth(k) abstract domain is also fit for the verification technique[1-5], many optimization techniques still can be used to improve computation efficiency.

The paper is organized as follows: in section 2, the logic program model of security protocol is presented; And in section 3, the resolution-based verification algorithm is presented; Both the extended model and the verification algorithm presented in [13][14] are variants corresponding to the model and the resolution-based verification algorithm in [1][2]; In section 4, the abstraction and refinement framework of the solved-form fixpoint is presented; In section 5, we demonstrate the effectiveness of the abstraction and refinement framework by the version Π_3 of the Woo-Lam Shared-key one way authentication protocol[16]. In section 6, we conclude this paper.

2 Security Protocols' Logic Program Model

A protocol is represented by a set of logic rules, whose syntax is given in Table1.

Table 1. Syntax of the Logic Program Model

tag::=	Tag
true, false	Bool
M,N,U,V,S,T::=	Terms
x, y, z	Variable
$a[M_1,\ldots, M_n]$	Name
$f(M_1,\ldots, M_n)$	Function

F,C,A::=	Atom, Fact
attacker(role(<M,N,tag>,M'))	Attacker predicate
begin(M,M')	begin predicate
end(M,M')	end predicate
R,R'::=	Rules
$F_1 \wedge \ldots \wedge F_n \rightarrow F$	Logic rules

The atoms attacker(role(<M,N,tag>),M'), begin(M,M') and end(M,M') are called closed atoms if M' does not contain any variables.

2.1 The Honest Roles' Model

The model of honest roles in security protocol is a group of logic rules. For each role A, a logic rule is generated when he sends a message M, the head of the rule is attacker(role(<A,N,true>,M)) if he believes N is the receiver(ideal receiver) of M; The body of the rule is attacker(role(<M_1,A, true>,M_1')) $\wedge \ldots \wedge$ attacker(role(<Mn,A,true>,Mn')), where $M_1',\ldots,$ Mn' are messages that A have received before he sends M, and he believes that M_i is the sender(ideal sender) of the message

$M_i'(i=1,...,n)$. For example, the logic rules are the representation of the honest role A in the simplified Needham-Schroeder public-key authentication protocol are described as follows:

$\rightarrow$attacker(role(<host(k_A[]),host(v_1),true>,encrypt(2tuple($N_A[i_A^1]$,host(k_A[])), pub(v_1))));
attacker(role(<host(v_4),host(k_A[]),true>,encrypt(2tuple(v_5,$N_A[i_A^2]$)),pub(k_A[]))))
$\rightarrow$attacker(role(<host(k_A[]),host(v_4), true>, encrypt(v_5, pub(v_4)))) ;

In the above logic rules, k_A[] is the private-key of A, pub(k_A[]) is the public-key of A, host(k_A[]) denotes A, the fresh nonce N_A is Skolemized to $N_A[i_A^1]$, i_A^1 is a session identifier variable, ntuple(M_1,..., M_n) is the composition message obtained from M_1,..., M_n, and encrypt(M,k) is the ciphertext constructed from the plaintext M and the key k. Generally speaking, similar to Bruno Blanchet's security protocol model, the fresh nonces and the fresh encryption keys in security protocols are all Skolemized: the parameters of the Skolem functions consist of a session identifier variable and the messages received before the fresh nonces or encryption keys are generated. In the honest roles' model, the value of tag in atoms attacker(role (<M,N,tag>, M')) is true.

2.2 The Intruder's Model

The intruder's Dolev-Yao model is characterized by the following logic rules:

(1)For each $M \in S$, where S is the public knowledge set of security protocol, the rule $\rightarrow$attacker(role(<host(k_I[]), host(v), false>,M)) is generated;
(2)For each n-ary constructor f in security protocol , the rule attacker(role (<host(v_1), host(k_I[]),false>,x_1))$\wedge$...$\wedge$attacker(role(<host(v_n),host(k_I[]),false>,x_n))$\rightarrow$attacker(role (<host(k_I[]), host(v), false>, f(x_1,...,x_n))) is generated;
(3)For every n-ary destructor g in security protocol and for each reduction g(M_1,...,M_n)=M of g, the rule attacker(role(<host(v_1),host(k_I[]),false>, M_1))$\wedge$...$\wedge$ attacker(role(<host(v_n),host(k_I[]),false>,M_n))$\rightarrow$ attacker (role (<host(k_I[]),host(v),false>, M)) is generated.
In the above model, host(k_I[]) denotes the intruder, and in all atoms attacker(role (<M,N,tag>,M')) of the Dolev-Yao model, the value of tag is false.

2.3 Security Property

Def1(Rule Implication). Let $R_1=H_1^1\wedge...\wedge H_m^1\rightarrow C_1$ and $R_2=H_1^2\wedge...\wedge H_n^2\rightarrow C_2$ be two logic rules, if C_1=attacker(role(<M_1,N_1,tag_1>, M^1)), C_2=attacker(role(<M_2, N_2,tag_2>, M^2)), or C_1=end(M,M^1) and C_2=end(M,M^2), define rule implication $R_1 \Rightarrow R_2$ if and only if there exists a substitution θ such that: $M^1\theta=M^2$, and for each H_i^1=attacker (role(<M_i^1,N_i^1,tag_i^1>,M_i'))$\in${H_1^1,...,H_m^1}, there exists H_j^2= attacker(role(<M_j^2,N_j^2, tag_j^2>,M_j'')) $\in${H_1^2,...,H_n^2}, and for each H_i^1=begin(M,M_i')$\in${H_1^1,...,H_m^1}, there exists H_j^2=begin (M,M_j'')$\in${H_1^2,...,H_n^2},such that $M_i'\theta=M_j''$. The substitution θ is called the implication substitution of $R_1 \Rightarrow R_2$.

Def2(Derivability). Let F be a closed atom, let B be a logic rule set, F is derivable from B if and only if there exists a finite tree defined as follows:

(1)Its nodes(except the root node) are labeled by rules R∈B, and its edges are labeled by closed atoms.

(2)If the tree contains a node labeled by R with an incoming edge labeled by F_0 and n outgoing edges labeled by $F_1,...,F_n$, then $R \Rightarrow F_1 \wedge ... \wedge F_n \rightarrow F_0$.

(3)The root node has only one outgoing edge labeled by F.

such a tree is called a derivation tree of F from B.

Def3(Secrecy). Let P be the logic program model of security protocol, F=attacker(role (<M, N,tag>,M')) be a closed atom, if F can not be derivable from P, then we say the security protocol satisfies the secrecy property with respect to M'.

The authentication property is characterized by the correspondence assertions begin(M,M') and end(M,M'), let B_b={→begin(M_1,M_1'), ..., →begin(M_n, M_n')}.

Def4(Authentication). Let P be the logic program model of security protocol, begin(M, M'),end(M,M') be correspondence assertions, and end(M,M') be a closed atom, if end(M,M') is derivable from $P \cup B_b$, then →begin (M, M')∈B_b, we say the security protocol satisfies the authentication property with respect to begin(M,M') and end(M,M').

3 Verification Approach

Def5(Resolution) Let R=H→F and R'=H'→F' be two logic rules, F=attacker(role (<M_1, N_1, tag_1>, M_1')), let F_0=attacker(role(<M_2,N_2,tag_2>,M_2')) be an atom in H' such that M_1' can be unified with M_2', then the resolution R'·R between R and R' is (H∧(H'-F_0))θ→F'θ, θ=mgu(M_1',M_2') is the most general unifier of M_1' and M_2', F_0= selectedAtom(R') is called the selected atom of R', θ=sub(R,R') is called the substitution of the resolution R'·R.

In fact, the resolution R'·R between R and R' describes a message exchange procedure: the exchanged message is M_1'θ(=M_2'θ), the sender is M_1θ and M_1θ believes that the receiver(ideal receiver) of M_1'θ is N_1θ, the receiver is N_2θ and N_2θ believes that the sender(ideal sender) of M_1'θ is M_2θ.

Def6(Goal). Atoms in the body of a logic rule which is in the form attacker(role (<M,N,tag>,x)(x is arbitrary a variable) and begin(M,M') are called false goals, atoms in the form attacker(role(<M,N,tag>,M')(M' is not a variable) and end(M,M') are called goals.

Def7 (Solved Form). Let H→C be a logic rule, if the atoms in H are all false goals, then we say H→C is in solved form.

Let SolvedForm denotes the set of logic rules those are in solved form, and UnSolvedForm denotes the set of logic rules those are not in solved form.

Def8(X-resolution). Let R=H→F and R'=H'→F' be two logic rules, R∈SolvedForm, R'∈UnSolvedForm,F=attacker(role(<M_1,N_1,tag_1>,M_1')),let F_0=attacker(role(<M_2, N_2, tag_2>, M_2')) be a goal in H' such that M_1' can be unified with M_2', then the X-resolution R'∘R between R and R' is $(H \wedge (H'\text{-}F_0))\theta \to F'\theta$, θ=mgu(M_1', M_2') is the most general unifier of M_1' and M_2', F_0=selectedGoal(R') is called the selected goal of R', θ=sub(R,R') is called the substitution of the X-resolution R'∘R.

Let R be a logic rule and B be a logic rule set, define addRule(R, B) as:

If $\exists$R'∈B, R'$\Rightarrow$R, then addRule(R,B)=B;

else addRule(R,B)={R}∪{R'| R'∈B ,R$\not\Rightarrow$R'} ∪ {marked(R'')| R''∈B,R$\Rightarrow$R''}

where marked(R'') denotes that R'' will not be used to compute X-resolutions. Let Marked denote the set of logic rules those will not be used to compute X-resolutions, and UnMarked denote the set of logic rules those are not in Marked.

Let R=$F_1 \wedge ... \wedge F_n \to C$ be a logic rule, F_i=attacker(role(<M_i,N_i,tag_i>,M_i'))(i= 1...,n), the unary function elimdup(R) returns a rule R' such that: (1)In {$F_1,...,F_n$}, only those atoms that satisfies the following conditions will occurs in the body of R': if j<i, then $M_i' \neq M_j'$; (2) C is the head of the rule R' ;

Let B be a logic rule set, define addRule({$R_1,...,R_m$},B)=addRule({$R_2,...,R_m$}, addRule (R_1, B)).Let P be the logic program model of security protocol, define:

Rule$^{(0)}$ (P)={elimdup(R)|R∈P}

$T^{(0)}$(P)=Rule$^{(0)}$ (P)∩SolvedForm $C^{(0)}$(P)= Rule$^{(0)}$ (P)∩UnSolvedForm

X_Resolution$^{(1)}$(P)={elimdup(R)|R=R'∘R'',R'∈$T^{(0)}$ (P),R''∈$C^{(0)}$(P)}

Rule$^{(n+1)}$(P)=addRule(X-Resolution$^{(n+1)}$(P),Rule$^{(n)}$ (P))

$T^{(n+1)}$(P)=Rule$^{(n+1)}$ (P)∩SolvedForm

$C^{(n+1)}$(P)=Rule$^{(n+1)}$ (P)∩UnSolvedForm

X_Resolution$^{(n+1)}$ (P)={elimdup(R)|R=R'∘R'',R'∈$T^{(n)}$ (P),R''∈$C^{(n)}$(P)}

Def9(solved-form fixpoint). Let P be the logic program model of security protocol, define fixpoint(P)={$T^{(n)}$(P)|n≥0}∩UnMarked,fixpoint(P) is called the solved-form fixpoint of P.

Let R be a logic rule and B be a logic rule set, for the secrecy property, define derivablerec(R,B,P) as:

if $\exists$R'∈B, R'$\Rightarrow$R, then derivablerec(R,B,P)= ϕ

else if R=$\to$C, then derivablerec(R,B,P)={$\to$C}

else derivablerec(R,B,P)={derivablerec(elimdup(R'·R),{R}∪B,P)| R'∈fixpoint(P)}

For the authentication property, define derivablerec(R,B,P) as:

if $\exists$R'∈B, R'$\Rightarrow$R, then derivablerec(R,B,P)=ϕ

else if R= begin(M_1,M_1')$\wedge ... \wedge$begin(M_n,M_n')$\to$end(M,M'),

then derivablerec(R,B,P) ={R}

else derivablerec(R,B,P)={derivablerec(elimdup(R'·R),{R}∪B,P)|

R'∈ fixpoint(P)}

And define derivable(F, P)=derivablerec(F$\to$F, ϕ,P).

Theorem1. If R·R' is defined, $R_1 \Rightarrow$R and $R_1' \Rightarrow$R', then either $R_1 \cdot R_1'$ is defined and $R_1 \cdot R_1' \Rightarrow$R·R', or $R_1' \Rightarrow$R·R'.

Theorem2. Let P be the logic program model of security protocol and F be a closed atom, then derivable(F, P) terminates.

Theorem3. Let P be the logic program model of security protocol and F be a closed atom, then F is derivable from P if and only if F is derivable from fixpoint(P).

Theorem4. Let P be the logic program model of security protocol,
1.(Secrecy Property) let F be a closed atom like attacker (role(<M,N, tag>, M')), then F is derivable from fixpoint(P) if and only if $\rightarrow$F$\in$derivable(F,P).
2.(Authentication Property) Let F be a closed atom like end(M,M'),then F is derivable from fixpoint(P)$\cup$B$_b$ and begin(M,M')$\in$B$_b$ if and only if: there exists $H_1 \wedge ... \wedge H_n \rightarrow F$ $\in$derivable(F, P) and begin(M,M')$\in$B$_b$, where H_i is in the form of begin(M_i,M_i') and $H_i \in B_b$.

The above four theorems[13][14] are variants of the corresponding theorems in [1][2].

4   Fixpoint Abstraction and Refinement

4.1   Fixpoint Abstraction

The abstraction of solved-form fixpoint is based on two abstraction functions: the abstraction function β_k over terms and the abstraction function α_k over logic rules in SolvedForm.

The abstraction function β_k over terms are defined inductively as follows:

if k=0, define β_k(t)=z for each term t, where z is a new fresh variable;
if k>0, define:
$\beta_k(a[M_1,..., M_n])= a[M_1,..., M_n]$, if $a[M_1,..., M_n]$ is a name;
$\beta_k(x)=x$, if x is a variable;
$\beta_k(f(t_1, ...,t_n))=f(\beta_{k-1}(t_1) , ..., \beta_{k-1}(t_n))$, if f is a function symbol.

The abstraction function β_k abstracts terms using new fresh variables into terms whose depth is less than or equal to k+1, limits the unbounded increase of depths of terms, where k is called the term depth bound. In this paper, we assume that the selected value of term depth bound k is larger or equal to the largest term depth of the terms in logic program model of protocol. The abstraction function α_k over logic rules in solved form is defined using β_k. Let R=H$\rightarrow$attacker(role(<M,N,tag>,M')) be arbitrary a logic rule in SolvedForm, α_k is defined as follows:

if β_k(M')=M', then α_k(R)= R;

if β_k(M')$\neq$M', then α_k(R)= $\rightarrow$attacker(role(<M,N,tag>,β_k(M'))).

The function α_k maintains R if the depth of M' is less than or equal to k, deletes the body of R and abstract the term M' using β_k if β_k(M')$\neq$M'. For each logic rule R in SolvedForm, by the definition of rule implication, α_k(R)$\Rightarrow$R always holds.

Let P be the logic program model of security protocol, define:
$\alpha^k T^{(0)}(P)=\{\alpha_k(elimdup(R))|R \in P \cap SolvedForm\}$
$\alpha^k T^{(0)}(P)=\{\alpha_k(elimdup(R))|R \in P \cap SolvedForm\}$
$\alpha^k Rule^{(0)} (P)= \alpha^k T^{(0)}(P) \cup \alpha^k C^{(0)}(P)$

$\alpha^k X\_Resolution^{(1)}(P)=\{elimdup(R)|R=R'\circ R'', R'\in\alpha^k T^{(0)}(P), R''\in\alpha^k C^{(0)}(P)\}$

$\alpha^k T^{(n+1)}(P)=\{\alpha_k(R')|R'\in addRule(\alpha^k X\_Resolution^{(n+1)}(P),\alpha^k Rule^{(n)}(P))\cap SolvedForm\}$

$\alpha^k C^{(n+1)}(P)=\{R'|R'\in addRule(\alpha^k X\_Resolution^{(n+1)}(P),\alpha^k Rule^{(n)}(P))\cap UnSolvedForm\}$

$\alpha^k Rule^{(n+1)}(P)= \alpha^k T^{(n+1)}(P)\cup\alpha^k C^{(n+1)}(P)$

$\alpha^k X\_Resolution^{(n+1)}(P)=\{elimdup(R)|R= R'\circ R'',R'\in\alpha^k T^{(n)}(P),R''\in\alpha^k C^{(n)}(P)\}$

Def10(abstract solved-form fixpoint). Let P be the logic program model of security protocol, define $\alpha^k fixpoint(P)=\{\alpha^k T^{(n)}(P)|n\geq0\}\cap UnMarked$, $\alpha^k fixpoint(P)$ is called the abstract solved-form fixpoint of P.

By the definition of α_k ,all rules R=H→attacker(role(<M, N, tag>,M')) in fixpoint(P) are maintained in $\alpha^k fixpoint(P)$ if the depth of M' is less than or equal to k, which are very fit for constructing attacks since many attacks are the interleaving of finite protocol sessions.

Theorem7. Let P be the logic program model of security protocol, then $\alpha^k fixpoint(P)$ terminates.
Proof: The function symbols and the names occurring in P are finite, if those terms with variable renaming are considered identical, then the terms constructed from the function symbols, the names occurring in P and variables whose depth is less than or equal to k+1 are finite. Let M be a term whose depth is less than or equal to k+1, let Var(M) denote the set of variables occurring in M, if the appendices M_i,N_i,tag_i in all atoms attacker(role(<M_i,N_i,tag_i>,M)) are ignored, then $\alpha^k fixpoint(P)\subseteq\cup$ $_{depth(M)\leq k+1}\cup_{i=1}^{|var(M)|}\{attacker(role(<M_1,N_1,tag_1>,x_1))\wedge...\wedge attacker(role(<M_i,N_i,tag_i>,x_i$))→attacker(role (<M_i',N_i',tag_i'>,M))\}\cup\{→attacker(role(<M_i', N_i',tag_i'>,M))\}$, where $x_j\in Var(M)$. Since the terms whose depth is less than or equal to k+1 are finite and the variables occur in these terms are finite, then $\alpha^k fixpoint(P)$ is a set whose elements are finite, thus $\alpha^k fixpoint(P)$ terminates.

Lemma8. Let P be the logic program model of security protocol, for each $R\in Rule^{(n)}(P)$, there exists $R'\in\alpha^k Rule^{(n)}(P)$ such that $R'\Rightarrow R$.
Proof: (1)if n=0, $\alpha^k Rule^{(0)}(P)=\alpha^k T^{(0)}(P)\cup\alpha^k C^{(0)}(P)$, since $\Rightarrow$ is reflexive and $\alpha_k(R)\Rightarrow R$, then the conclusion holds;
(2) Assume that the conclusion holds when n=m≥0, in the case of n=m+1, for each $R\in Rule^{(m+1)}(P)$, since $Rule^{(m+1)}(P)=addRule(X\text{-}Resolution^{(m+1)}(P),Rule^{(m)}(P))$, if $R\in Rule^{(m)}(P)$,then the conclusion holds by the induction assumption; if $R\in X\text{-}Resolution^{(m+1)}(P)$, then there exists $R_1\in T^{(m)}(P)\subseteq Rule^{(m)}(P)$ and $R_2\in C^{(m)}(P)\subseteq Rule^{(m)}(P)$ such that $R=elimdup(R_1\circ R_2)$, by the induction assumption, there exist R_1', $R_2'\in\alpha^k Rule^{(m)}(P)$ such that $R_1'\Rightarrow R_1$, $R_2'\Rightarrow R_2$, since $R_1'\Rightarrow R_1$ and R_1 is in SolvedForm, then $R_1'\in\alpha^k Rule^{(m)}(P)\cap SolvedForm$, by theorem 1, then $R_1'\Rightarrow R_1\circ R_2$ or $R_1'\circ R_2'\Rightarrow R_1\circ R_2$, since $\alpha_k(R_1')\Rightarrow R_1'$, then $\alpha_k(R_1')\Rightarrow R_1\circ R_2$ or $\alpha_k(R_1')\circ R_2'\Rightarrow R_1\circ R_2$, and $\alpha_k(R_1')\Rightarrow elimdup(R_1\circ R_2)$ or $elimdup(\alpha_k(R_1')\circ R_2')\Rightarrow elimdup(R_1\circ R_2)$. If there exists $R''\in\alpha^k X\_Resolution^{(m+1)}(P)$ such that $R''\Rightarrow R_1'$, then $\alpha_k(R'')\Rightarrow R_1'\Rightarrow elimdup(R_1\circ R_2)$ and $\alpha_k(R'')\in\alpha^k T^{(m+1)}(P)\subseteq\alpha^k Rule^{(m+1)}(P)$;
If there exists no $R''\in\alpha^k X\_Resolution^{(m+1)}(P)$ such that $R''\Rightarrow R_1'$, then

$\alpha_k(R_1') \in \alpha^k T^{(m+1)}(P) \subseteq \alpha^k Rule^{(m+1)}(P)$. Since $elimdup(\alpha_k(R_1') \circ R_2') \in \alpha^k X\_Resolution^{(m+1)}(P)$, if there exists no $R'' \in \alpha^k Rule^{(m)}(P)$ such that $R'' \Rightarrow elimdup(\alpha_k(R_1') \circ R_2')$, then $elimdup(\alpha_k(R_1') \circ R_2') \subseteq \alpha^k T^{(n+1)}(P) \cup \alpha^k C^{(n+1)}(P) = \alpha^k Rule^{(m+1)}(P)$;if there exists $R'' \in \alpha^k Rule^{(m)}(P)$ such that $R'' \Rightarrow elimdup(\alpha_k(R_1') \circ R_2')$, then $R'' \Rightarrow elimdup(\alpha_k(R_1') \circ R_2') \Rightarrow elimdup(R_1 \circ R_2)$ and $R'' \in \alpha^k Rule^{(m)}(P) \subseteq \alpha^k Rule^{(m+1)}(P)$. Thus the conclusion holds for n=m+1.

Theorem9 Let P be the logic program model of security protocol and F be a closed atom, if F is derivable from fixpoint(P), then F is also derivable from α^kfixpoint(P).

Proof: F is derivable from fixpoint(P), then there exists a derivable tree T of F from fixpoint(P). For each node m in T, assume the node m is labeled by $R \in$fixpoint(P) with an incoming edge labeled by F_0 and n outgoing edges labeled by $F_1,...,F_n$, then $R \Rightarrow F_1 \wedge ... \wedge F_n \rightarrow F_0$, since $R \in$fixpoint(P)= $\{T^{(n)}(P)|n \geq 0\} \cap UnMarked$, by lemma8, there exists $R' \in \{\alpha^k Rule^{(n)}(P)|n \geq 0\}$ such that $R' \Rightarrow R \Rightarrow F_1 \wedge ... \wedge F_n \rightarrow F_0$, since $R' \Rightarrow R$ and $R \in$SolvedForm, then $R' \in$SolvedForm and $R' \in \{\alpha^k T^{(n)}(P)|n \geq 0\}$, if $R' \in \alpha^k$fixpoint(P), then replace R by R' in T, if $R' \notin \alpha^k$fixpoint(P), by the definition α^kfixpoint(P) $=\{\alpha^k T^{(n)}(P)|n \geq 0\} \cap UnMarked$, then there exists $R'' \in \alpha^k$fixpoint(P) such that $R'' \Rightarrow R'$, replace R by R'' in T, repeat this procedure until all the rules in fixpoint(P) are replaced by rules in α^kfixpoint(P), then the derivation tree of F from α^kfixpoint(P) is constructed, thus F is derivable from α^kfixpoint(P).

Theorem9 shows that α^kfixpoint(P) is a safe approximation of fixpoint(P). Thus fixpoint(P) can be replaced by α^kfixpoint(P) in the resolution-based verification algorithm as follows:

for the secrecy property, define derivablerec(R,B,P) as:

if $\exists R' \in B$, $R' \Rightarrow R$, then derivablerec(R,B,P)=ϕ

else if $R= \rightarrow C$, then derivablerec(R,B,P)=$\{\rightarrow C\}$

else derivablerec(R,B)=$\{$derivablerec(elimdup(R'·R),$\{R\} \cup B$,P)$|$ R'$\in \alpha^k$fixpoint(P)$\}$

for the authentication property, define derivablerec(R,B,P) as:

if $\exists R' \in B$, $R' \Rightarrow R$, then derivablerec(R,B,P)=ϕ

else if R= $begin(M_1,M_1') \wedge ... \wedge begin(M_n,M_n') \rightarrow end(M,M')$,

then derivablerec(R,B,P)=$\{R\}$

else derivablerec(R,B)=$\{$derivablerec(elimdup(R'·R),$\{R\} \cup B$,P)$|$R'$\in \alpha^k$fixpoint(P)$\}$

4.2 Fixpoint Refinement

If the result of the resolution-based verification algorithm with α^kfixpoint(P) shows protocol satisfies the security properties, then the protocol satisfies the security properties since α^kfixpoint(P) is a safe approximation of fixpoint(P). If the result of the resolution-based verification algorithm with α^kfixpoint(P) shows protocol does not satisfy the security properties, according to the counterexample-driven abstract refinement iteration verification framework, the counterexample would be constructed and decided whether it is a false-counterexample or not, if it is, then α^kfixpoint(P) should be refined and the resolution-based verification algorithm should be run again, otherwise, the counterexample is actually an attack against the protocol.

In this subsection, we describe the refinement approach for α^kfixpoint(P): if the resolution-based verification algorithm with α^kfixpoint(P) shows protocol does not satisfy the security properties, then we run the resolution-based verification algorithm with those logic rules in α^kfixpoint(P) which are not abstracted by the abstraction function α_k, if the result shows that protocol does not satisfy security properties, then we construct the counterexamples from the verification procedure, which are actually attacks against the protocol since the derivations of all the logic rules are not abstracted by α_k. If the result shows that protocol satisfies security properties, then α^kfixpoint(P) should be refined by increasing the value of the term depth bound k.

Let P be the logic program model of security protocol and α^kfixpoint(P) be the abstract solved-form fixpoint, the set of logic rules which are not abstracted by α_k, denoted by UnAbstract, is defined inductively as follows:

(1)Let R=H$\rightarrow$attacker(role(<M,N,tag>,M'))$\in$P$\cap$SolvedForm, if β_k(M')=M', then α_k(elimdup(R))$\in$UnAbstract;

(2)If R$\in\alpha^k$C$^{(0)}$(P), then R$\in$UnAbstract;

(3)If there exists R'$\in\alpha^k$T$^{(n)}$(P)$\cap$UnAbstract and R''$\in\alpha^k$C$^{(n)}$(P)$\cap$UnAbstract such that R=elimdup(R'$\circ$R''), then R$\in$UnAbstract;

Def11(partial solved-form fixpoint). Let P be the logic program model of security protocol, define α^kpartialfixpoint(P)={α^kT$^{(n)}$(P)|n$\geq$0}$\cap$UnAbstract, α^kpartialfixpoint(P) is called the partial solved-form fixpoint of P.

The partial solved-form fixpoint α^kpartialfixpoint(P) of P consists of all the logic rules in SolvedForm whose derivations are all not be abstracted by the abstract function α_k.

If the resolution-based verification algorithm with α^kfixpoint(P) shows protocol does not satisfy the security properties, we run the resolution-based verification algorithm with α^kpartialfixpoint(P) as follows:

For the secrecy property, define derivablerec$_1$(R,B,P) as:

if $\exists$R'$\in$B, R'$\Rightarrow$R, then derivablerec$_1$ (R,B,P)= ϕ

else if R=$\rightarrow$C, then derivablerec$_1$(R,B,P)={$\rightarrow$C}

   else derivablerec(R,B,P)={derivablerec$_1$(elimdup(R'·R),{R}$\cup$B,P)|

   R'$\in\alpha^k$partialfixpoint(P)}

For the authentication property, define derivablerec$_1$ (R,B,P) as:

if $\exists$R'$\in$B, R'$\Rightarrow$R, then derivablerec$_1$(R,B,P)=ϕ

else if R= begin(M$_1$,M$_1$')$\wedge$...$\wedge$begin(M$_n$,M$_n$')$\rightarrow$end(M,M'),
    then derivablerec$_1$(R,B,P)={R}

   else derivablerec$_1$(R,B)={derivablerec$_1$(elimdup(R'·R),{R}$\cup$B,P)|

   R'$\in \alpha^k$partialfixpoint(P)}

And define derivable$_1$(F, P)=derivablerec$_1$(F$\rightarrow$F, ϕ, P).

By the theorem4, if the result shows that protocol does not satisfy security properties, the counterexamples can be constructed from α^kpartialfixpoint(P) by the approach presented in [15],which is similar to the approach presented in [4], since the logic rules in α^kpartialfixpoint(P) whose derivations are all not abstracted by α_k, the constructed counterexamples are attacks against the protocol.

If the result of the resolution-based verification algorithm with α^kfixpoint(P) shows protocol does not satisfy the security properties, but the result of the resolution-based verification algorithm with α^kpartialfixpoint(P) shows protocol satisfies the security properties, we increase the value of the term depth bound k, compute the abstract solved-form fixpoint α^{k+1}fixpoint(P), and run the resolution-based verification algorithm with α^{k+1}fixpoint(P) again.

Theorem10. Let P be the logic program model of security protocol, then for each $s \geq 0$, α^kpartialfixpoint(P)$\subseteq\alpha^{k+s}$partialfixpoint(P).

Proof: For each $n \geq 0$, we prove that $\alpha^k T^{(n)}(P) \cap$UnAbstract$\subseteq\alpha^{k+s}T^{(n)}(P) \cap$UnAbstract and $\alpha^k C^{(n)}(P) \cap$UnAbstract$\subseteq\alpha^{k+s}C^{(n)}(P) \cap$UnAbstract. If n=0, by the definition of α_k, $\alpha^k T^{(0)}(P) \cap$UnAbstract $=\alpha^{k+s}T^{(0)}(P) \cap$UnAbstract, $\alpha^k C^{(0)}(P) \cap$UnAbstract$=\alpha^{k+s}C^{(0)}(P) \cap$ UnAbstract, the conclusion holds. Assume that the conclusion holds when n=m$\geq$0, in the case of n=m+1, let R$\in\alpha^k T^{(m+1)}(P)$ $\cap$UnAbstract, then R$\in\alpha^k T^{(m)}(P) \cap$UnAbstract or R$\in\alpha^k$X_Resolution$^{(m+1)}(P) \cap$UnAbstract. If R$\in$ $\alpha^k T^{(m)}(P) \cap$UnAbstract, by the induction assumption, R$\in\alpha^{k+s}T^{(m)}(P) \cap$UnAbstract. If R$\in\alpha^k$X_Resolution$^{(m+1)}(P) \cap$ UnAbstract, then R=elimdup(R'∘R''), where R'$\in\alpha^k T^{(m)}(P) \cap$UnAbstract, R''$\in\alpha^k C^{(m)}(P)$ $\cap$UnAbstract, by the induction assumption, R'$\in\alpha^{k+s}T^{(m)}(P) \cap$UnAbstract, R''$\in$ $\alpha^{k+s}C^{(m)}(P) \cap$ UnAbstract, thus R$\in\alpha^{k+s}$X_Resolution$^{(m+1)}(P) \cap$UnAbstract. By the fact R$\in\alpha^{k+s}T^{(m)}(P) \cap$UnAbstract   or   R$\in\alpha^{k+s}$X_Resolution$^{(m+1)}(P) \cap$UnAbstract,   then R$\in\alpha^{k+s}T^{(m+1)}(P) \cap$UnAbstract. The fact that $\alpha^k C^{(n)}(P) \cap$UnAbstract$\subseteq\alpha^{k+s}C^{(n)}(P) \cap$ UnAbstract can be proved in the similar way.

Theorem10 shows that α^{k+s}partialfixpoint(P)(s$\geq$0) is actually a refinement of α^kpartialfixpoint(P). Since fixpoint(P)$\subseteq\cup_{k \geq 0}\{\alpha^k T^{(n)}(P)\}$ and fixpoint(P)$\subseteq$UnAbstract, it is easy to see that fixpoint(P) $\subseteq\cup_{k \geq 0}\{\alpha^k$partialfixpoint(P)$\}$, which means that the attacks against protocol can also be constructed from α^kpartialfixpoint(P) if the value of k is large enough.

Comparing with the refinement approach obeying the counterexample-driven abstraction refinement iteration verification framework, our framework needn't decide whether the constructed counterexample is a false-counterexample or not, all of the verification, constructing counterexamples and refinement of the abstracted solved-form fixpoint can be implemented in a mechanized way.

5   Example

We demonstrate the effectiveness of the presented abstraction and refinement framework for verifying security protocols with the version Π_3 of the Woo-Lam Shared-key one way authentication protocol[16]. Π_3 is described as follows:

$$A \rightarrow B: A$$
$$B \rightarrow A: N$$
$$A \rightarrow B: \{N\}_{kAS}$$
$$B \rightarrow S: \{ A, \{N\}_{kAS}\}_{kBS}$$
$$S \rightarrow B: \{A,N\}_{kBS}$$

Its logic program model P is described as follows:

(1)→attacker(role(<host(k_{IS}[]),host(k_{IS}[]),false>,k_{IS}[]));

(2)→attacker(role(<host(k_{IS}[]),-,false>,host(k_{IS}[])));

(3)→attacker(role(<host(k_{IS}[]),-,false>,host(k_{AS}[])));

(4)→attacker(role(<host(k_{IS}[]),-,false>,host(k_{BS}[])));

(5)attacker(role(<-,host(k_{IS}[]),false>,M)) ∧attacker(role(<-,host(k_{IS}[]),false >,k))
    →attacker(role(<host(k_{IS}[]),-,false>,encrypt(M,k)));

(6)attacker(role(<-,host(k_{IS}[]),false>,encrypt(M,k))) ∧attacker(role(<-,host(k_{IS}[]),
    false>,k)) →attacker(role(<host(k_{IS}[]),-,false>,M)) ;

(7)attacker(role(<-,host(k_{IS}[]),false>,x_1))∧ ··· ∧attacker(role(<-,host(k_{IS}[]),false>,
    x_n))→attacker(role(<host(k_{IS}[]),-,false>,ntuple(x_1,···,x_n))) ;

(8)attacker(role(<-,host(k_{IS}[]),false>,ntuple(x_1,···,x_n)))→attacker(role(<-,host
    (k_{IS}[]),false>,x_i)),i=1,...,n;

(9)begin(host(k_{AS}[]),host(v_1))→attacker(role(<host(k_{AS}[]),host(v_1), true >,
    host(k_{AS}[])));

(10)attacker(role(<host(v_2),host(k_{BS}[]),true>,host(v_2)))→
    attacker(role(<host(k_{BS}[]),host(v_2), true>,N[i_B^1,host(v_2)])) ;

(11)begin(host(k_{AS}[]),host(v_3))∧attacker(role(<host(v_3),host(k_{AS}[]),true>,v_4))→
    attacker(role(<host(k_{AS}[]),host(v_3), true >,encrypt(v_4,k_{AS}[])));

(12)attacker(role(<host(v_5),host(k_{BS}[]),true>,host(v_5)))∧attacker(role(<host(v_5),
    host(k_{BS}[]),true>,v_6)→attacker(role(<host(k_{BS}[]),host(k_{SS}[]),true>, encrypt
    (2tuple(host(v_5), v_6),k_{BS}[])));

(13)attacker(role(<host(v_8),host(k_{SS}[]),true >,encrypt(2tuple(host(v_7),encrypt
    (v_9,v_7)), v_8)))→attacker(role(<host(k_{SS}[]),host(v_8), true >,encrypt(2tuple
    (host(v_7) , v_9), v_8))) ;

(14)attacker(role(<host(v_{10}),host(k_{BS}[]),true>,host(v_{10}))) ∧attacker(role
    (<host(v_{10}),host(k_{BS}[]),true>,v_{11}))∧attacker(role(<host(k_{SS}[]),host(k_{BS}[]),
    true>,encrypt(2tuple(host(v_{10}),N[i_B^2,host(v_{10})]),k_{BS}[])))→end(host(v_{10}),
    host(k_{BS}[]));

In the above model, the logic rules from (1) to (8) are the intruder's model, and the
logic rules from (9) to (14) are the honest roles' model. The assertion be-
gin(host(k_{AS}[]),host(v_1)) asserts that the honest role A initiates a protocol session with
the role host(v_1), the assertion end(host(v_{10}),host(k_{BS}[])) asserts that the honest role B
ends up a protocol session with the role host(v_{10}).

The solved-form fixpoint of Π_3 does not terminate. In fact, compute the X-
resolution between the 3th rule and the 13th rule, we get the 15th rule:

(15)attacker(role(<host(k_{AS}[]),host(k_{BS}[]),true>,v_6)→attacker (role(<host(k_{BS}[]),
    host (k_{SS}[]), true>,encrypt (2tuple(host(k_{AS}[]),v_6),k_{BS}[])));

Computing the X-resolution between the 15th rule and the 13th rule, we get the 16th rule:

(16)attacker(role($<$host($k_{AS}[]$),host($k_{BS}[]$),true$>$,encrypt(v_9,v_7)))$\rightarrow$attacker(role

($<$host($k_{SS}[]$),host($k_{BS}[]$),true $>$,encrypt(2tuple(host($k_{AS}[]$),v_9),$k_{BS}[]$)));

Computing the X-resolution between the 15th rule and the 16th rule, we get the 17th rule:

(17)attacker(role($<$host($k_{AS}[]$),host($k_{BS}[]$),true$>$,v_6))$\rightarrow$attacker(role($<$host($k_{SS}[]$),

host($k_{BS}[]$),true$>$,encrypt(2tuple(host(k_{AS} []),2tuple(host($k_{AS}[]$),v_6)),$k_{BS}[]$)));

Computing the X-resolution between the 17th rule and the 16th rule, we get the 18th rule:

(18)attacker(role($<$host($k_{AS}[]$),host($k_{BS}[]$),true$>$,v_6))$\rightarrow$attacker(role($<$host($k_{SS}[]$),

host($k_{BS}[]$),true$>$, encrypt(2tuple(host(k_{AS} []),2tuple(host($k_{AS}[]$),v_6)),$k_{BS}[]$)));

We can also compute the X-resolution between the 18th rule and the 16th rule. By repeating this procedure, we get an infinite sequence of logic rules in SolvedForm, this infinite sequence shows the solved-form fixpoint of Π_3 does not terminate.

Now we choose k=4 as the term depth bound, then by theorem 7, α^4fixpoint(P) terminates. Computing the X-resolution between the 3th rule and the 14th rule, we get the 19th rule:

(19)attacker(role($<$host($k_{AS}[]$),host($k_{BS}[]$),true$>$,v_{11}))$\wedge$attacker(role($<$host($k_{SS}[]$),

host($k_{BS}[]$),true$>$,encrypt(2tuple(host($k_{AS}[]$),N[i_B^2,host($k_{AS}[]$)]),$k_{BS}[]$)))$\rightarrow$
end(host($k_{AS}[]$),host($k_{BS}[]$));

Computing the X-resolution between the 3th rule and the 12th rule, we get the 20th rule:

(20)attacker(role($<$host($k_{AS}[]$),host($k_{BS}[]$),true$>$,v_6)$\rightarrow$attacker(role($<$host($k_{BS}[]$),

host($k_{SS}[]$),true$>$,encrypt(2tuple(host($k_{AS}[]$),v_6),$k_{BS}[]$)));

Computing the X-resolution between the 20th rule and the 19th rule, we get the 21th rule:

(21)attacker(role($<$host($k_{AS}[]$),host($k_{BS}[]$),true$>$,v_{11}))$\wedge$attacker(role($<$host($k_{AS}[]$),

host($k_{BS}[]$),true$>$, N[i_B^2,host($k_{AS}[]$)]))$\rightarrow$end(host($k_{AS}[]$),host($k_{BS}[]$));

Computing the X-resolution between the 3th rule and the 10th rule, we get the 22th rule:

(22)$\rightarrow$Attacker(role($<$host($k_{BS}[]$),host($k_{AS}[]$), true$>$,N[i_B^1,host($k_{AS}[]$)])) ;

Computing the X-resolution between the 22th rule and the 21th rule, we get the 23th rule:

(23)attacker(role($<$host($k_{AS}[]$),host($k_{BS}[]$),true$>$,v_{11})) $\rightarrow$end(host($k_{AS}[]$),
host($k_{BS}[]$));

Let F=end(host($k_{AS}[]$),host($k_{BS}[]$)), since the 23th rule is in α^4fixpoint(P), then the logic rule $\rightarrow$end(host($k_{AS}[]$),host($k_{BS}[]$))$\in$derivable(F,P), which means the honest role B ends up a protocol session with the honest role A, but A does not initiate a protocol session with B, thus there exists a counterexample against the protocol Π_3 on the authentication property characterized by the correspondence assertations begin(host

$(k_{AS}[])$,host$(k_{BS}[]))$ and end(host$(k_{AS}[])$, host$(k_{BS}[]))$.Since all the logic rules from (19) to (23) are in UnAbstract, we have $\rightarrow$end(host$(k_{AS}[])$, host$(k_{BS}[]))\in$ derivable$_1$(F, P). Using the approach presented in [15], we can construct the counterexample against the protocol Π_3 from α^4partialfixpoint(P) as follows:

host$(k_{IS}[])$ (host$(k_{AS}[]))\rightarrow$host$(k_{BS}[])$:host$(k_{AS}[])$;

host$(k_{BS}[])\rightarrow$host$(k_{IS}[])$ (host$(k_{AS}[]))$:N$[i_B^1$,host$(k_{AS}[])]$;

host$(k_{IS}[])$ (host$(k_{AS}[]))\rightarrow$host$(k_{BS}[])$:N$[i_B^1$,host$(k_{AS}[])]$;

host$(k_{BS}[])\rightarrow$host$(k_{IS}[])$(host$(k_{SS}[]))$:encrypt(2tuple(host$(k_{AS}[])$,N$[i_B^1$,host$(k_{AS}[])])$),

$k_{BS}[])$;

host$(k_{IS}[])$(host$(k_{SS}[]))\rightarrow$host$(k_{BS}[])$:encrypt(2tuple(host$(k_{AS}[])$,N$[i_B^1$,host$(k_{AS}[])])$),

$k_{BS}[])$;

The above counterexample is the attack of Π_3 described in [16].

6 Conclusions

In this paper we present a an abstraction and refinement framework for verifying security protocols based on logic programming, with this framework all of the verification, constructing counterexample and refinement can be implemented in a mechanized way. We believe that our approach is more practical for verifying security protocols since the problem of deciding correctness of security protocol is undecidable and our approach supports the abstraction and refinement iteration verification framework.

Directions for further work include implementing the verifier Spvt[13] with the abstraction and refinement framework presented in this paper and using it to verify more security protocols.

References

1. Blanchet, B.: An Efficient Cryptographic Protocol Verifier Based on Prolog Rules. In: 14th IEEE Computer Security Foundations Workshop, pp. 82–96. IEEE Press, Cape Breton, Nova Scotia (2001)
2. Blanchet, B.: From Secrecy to Authenticity in Security Protocols. In: Hermenegildo, M.V., Puebla, G. (eds.) SAS 2002. LNCS, vol. 2477, pp. 242–259. Springer, Heidelberg (2002)
3. Abadi, M., Blanchet, B.: Analyzing security protocols with secrecy types and logic programs. In: 29th ACM Symposium on Principles of Programming Languages, pp. 33–44. ACM Press, Portland (2002)
4. Allamigeon, X., Blanchet, B.: Reconstruction of Attacks against Cryptography Protocols. In: 18th IEEE Computer Security Foundations Workshop, pp. 140–154. IEEE Press, Aix-en-Provence (2005)
5. Blanchet, B., Podelski, A.: Verification of cryptographic protocols: tagging enforces termination. Theor. Comput. Sci. 333(1-2), 67–90 (2005)
6. Gori, R., Lastres, E., Moreno, R., Spot, F.: Approximation of the Well-Founded Semantics for Normal Logic Programs using Abstract Interpretation. In: Freire-Nistal, J.L., Falaschi, M., Villares-Ferro, M. (eds.) Proceedings of the APPIA-GULP-PRODE 1998 Conference, A Coruña, Spain, pp. 433–441 (1998)

7. Durgin, N., Lincoln, P., Mitchell, J., Scedrov, A.: Undecidability of bounded security protocols. In: Heintze, N., Clarke, E. (eds.) Proceedings of the Workshop on Formal Methods and Security Protocols, Trento (1999)
8. Cousot, P., Cousot, R.: Abstract Interpretation: a unified lattice model for static analysis of programs by construction or approximation of fixpoints. In: 4th ACM Symposium on Principles of Programing Languages, pp. 238–252. ACM Press, Los Angeles (1977)
9. Bozga, L., Lakhnech, Y., Périn, M.: Pattern-Based Abstraction for Verifying Secrecy in Protocols. In: Garavel, H., Hatcliff, J. (eds.) ETAPS 2003 and TACAS 2003. LNCS, vol. 2619, pp. 299–314. Springer, Heidelberg (2003)
10. Bozga, L., Lakhnech, Y., Périn, M.: HERMES: An Automatic Tool for Verification of Secrecy in Security Protocols. In: Hunt Jr., W.A., Somenzi, F. (eds.) CAV 2003. LNCS, vol. 2725, pp. 219–222. Springer, Heidelberg (2003)
11. Oehl, F., Cécé, G., Kouchnarenko, O., Sinclair, D.: Automatic Approximation for the Verification of Cryptographic Protocols. In: Pezzé, M. (ed.) ETAPS 2003 and FASE 2003. LNCS, vol. 2621, pp. 34–48. Springer, Heidelberg (2003)
12. Backes, M., Maffei, M., Cortesi, A.: Causality-based Abstraction of Multiplicity in Security Protocols. In: 20th IEEE Computer Security Foundation Symposium, pp. 355–369. IEEE Press, Venice (2007)
13. Li, M., Li, Z., Chen, H.W.: Spvt: An efficient verification tool for security protocol. Chinese Journal of Software 17(4), 898–906 (2006)
14. Li, M., Li, Z., Chen, H.W.: Security protocol's extended horn logic model and its verification method. Chinese Journal of Computers 29(9), 1667–1678 (2006)
15. Zhou, T., Li, M., Li, Z., Chen, H.W.: Automatically Constructing Counter- examples of Security Protocols based on the extended Horn Logic Model. Chinese Journal of computer research and development 44(9), 1518–1531 (2007)
16. Clark, J., Joacob, J.: A survey on authentification protocol (1997), http://www.cs.york.ac.uk/jac/papers/drareviewps.ps

Secure Verification of Location Claims with Simultaneous Distance Modification

Vitaly Shmatikov and Ming-Hsiu Wang

The University of Texas at Austin

Abstract. We investigate the problem of verifying location claims of mobile devices, and propose a new property called *simultaneous distance modification* (SDM). In localization protocols satisfying the SDM property, a malicious device can lie about its distance from the verifiers, but all distances can only be altered by the same amount. We demonstrate that the SDM property guarantees secure verification of location claims with a small number of verifiers even if some of them maliciously collude with the device. We also present several lightweight localization protocols that satisfy the SDM property.

1 Introduction

In wireless networks, the physical location of a mobile device such as a sensor, a mobile phone, or a small computer often has implications for location-based access control and security of the nearby devices. A malicious device may lie about its location in an attempt to appear either farther away than its true location (*e.g.*, in order to intercept other devices' communications), or closer than it really is (*e.g.*, to subvert a location-based access control mechanism). In this paper, we study the problem of verifying location claims of potentially malicious mobile devices in an environment where some parts of the localization infrastructure may have been compromised.

To verify location claims of mobile devices, most existing protocols employ *distance bounding* [BC93]. A verifying "beacon" challenges the device and measures the time elapsed until the receipt of its response. This gives a lower bound on the distance to the device, which therefore cannot claim to be closer than it really is. Measurements from multiple beacons can then be combined to estimate the device's location.

Our contributions. We define a new property called *simultaneous distance modification* (SDM). In distance estimation protocols with the SDM property, a malicious device being interrogated by multiple verifiers can increase its claimed distance from the verifiers, but all distances can only be altered by the same amount. The SDM property enables secure verification of location claims with a small number of verifiers. In contrast to previously proposed protocols, the device's location can be verified *anywhere* on the two-dimensional plane and not just in the area enclosed by the verifiers.

In addition to the generic security argument for protocols with the SDM property, we present two practical protocols satisfying this property: (1) a challenge-response protocol based on hash chains and time-of-flight estimation, and (2) a hyperbolic localization protocol based on time difference of arrival. In contrast to the previous work, we analyze security of both protocols in the presence of malicious verifiers.

I. Cervesato (Ed.): ASIAN 2007, LNCS 4846, pp. 181–195, 2007.

Model. We use the standard model for location verification [WF03, SSW03, ČH05]. The goal of a malicious device is to be localized in a place other than its true location. Therefore, it participates in the protocol, but tries to mislead the verifiers. This model matches practical wireless security scenarios such as location-based access control, in which a device that refuses to respond to distance estimation requests is simply denied access. Our desired security property is as follows: *if the protocol produces a location for the device, then this location must be correct.*

The device is located on a two-dimensional coordinate grid. We will sometimes refer to the device's location as a *point*, even though in reality it is a small region rather than a point due to imprecision of distance measurements.

Several verifying *beacons* are located on the grid and exchange messages with the device. We assume that signals can be linked to the device that emitted them, *i.e.*, devices have "identities." This does not imply strong authentication; the device may have a unique code or dedicated frequency. The signal recognition assumption is essential, and is made by all localization protocols in the literature. In section 6, we discuss possible attacks if a signal cannot be linked to a particular device.

All beacons are connected to a trusted central processor, or the *base station*, which computes the location of the mobile device from the beacons' reports. We assume that the only way for the base station to communicate with the device is via the beacons, *i.e.*, localization must rely entirely on the information supplied by the (potentially malicious) beacons. By default, we assume that if the protocol detects an inconsistency in the device's responses to different beacons, it will not produce a location. Denial of service attacks are beyond the scope of this paper.

We abstract from the details of physical communication between the beacons and the device. It can be based on radio [BC93, WF03], ultrasound [SSW03], or any other suitable technology. An honest beacon's correct location is known to the base station via either static pre-configuration, or an on-board GPS, or from a previous instance of localization where the beacon itself acted as the device.

We will consider both honest and malicious beacons, but assume that there is a secure communication channel (*e.g.*, a secure wire) between each beacon and the base station. In particular, we assume that a malicious device cannot interfere with the information sent by an *honest* beacon to the base station. This is a realistic assumption for many sensor and mobile networks, where devices are low-powered and have no physical access to the communication network between the beacons and the base station.

Related work. Distance and angle estimation techniques include Time Difference of Arrival (TDoA) [PCB00, SHS01, LOR06], Time of Arrival [HWLC97, SHS01], Received Signal Strength [BP00], and Angle of Arrival [NN03a]. These methods are *not* designed to be secure in the presence of malicious devices and beacons. Range-free protocols [BHE00, NN03b, HHB+03] do not require distance or angle measurements, but are also insecure in adversarial environments.

In radio-based secure distance bounding by Brands and Chaum [BC93], the prover cannot pretend to be closer to the verifier than it really is. Similar protocols based on ultrasound and ultra-wideband appear in, respectively, [SSW03] and [HK05]. Variations include authenticated challenge-response [MSC06]. Distance bounding, however, does not prevent a device from enlarging the distance, *i.e.*, claiming to be farther away than it really is, because a malicious device can delay its responses. Furthermore, standard distance bounding can be subverted by guessing attacks or by exploiting the relatively high latency of communication channels [CHKM06].

Verification of location claims typically involves combining distance bounds from multiple verifiers. In previously proposed protocols [WF03, SSW03, ČH05], a malicious device can easily enlarge the distance in each instance of the distance-bounding protocol, and pretend to be *outside* the area enclosed by the verifiers. This is a serious security risk. For example, an untrusted device may claim to be far away from a wireless network, while locating itself in the middle in order to eavesdrop on messages.

All existing location verification protocols also assume that the verifiers are trusted. For example, the TDoA-based protocol of [ČČS06], which is superficially similar to one of our protocols, is insecure when some of the beacons (called "base stations" in [ČČS06]) are malicious. By contrast, we explicitly analyze the case when some of the beacons maliciously collude with the device whose location claims are being verified.

A complementary problem to location verification is *location discovery*: how to enable an *honest* device to determine its own location in the presence of malicious beacons [LP05, LND05a, LND05b, DFN06]. None of these protocols consider a malicious device colluding with malicious beacons to lie about its location. The only exception is the claim verification protocol of [LPČ05], which does not prevent a malicious device from pretending to be farther away than it really is.

Organization of the paper. We define the simultaneous distance modification (SDM) property and show how it guarantees secure localization in section 2. In section 3, we investigate which geometry of verifier placement prevents false location claims. In section 4, we present our protocols with the SDM property, and analyze their security in the presence of malicious beacons in section 5. In section 6, we survey attacks on the SDM property. Conclusions are in section 7.

2 Simultaneous Distance Modification (SDM)

Range measurement involves estimating the distance between a beacon and the mobile device from measurements of time, angle, or signal strength, then combining measurements from multiple beacons to localize the device. Intuitively, a range measurement protocol satisfies the *simultaneous distance modification* (SDM) property if a malicious device, by giving false responses to multiple beacons, can change each beacon's distance estimate, but all estimates can only be changed by the same amount.

Let s be the mobile device, and let $b_0, \ldots, b_n$ be the beacons within its broadcast range. Let d_i be the actual distance between s and b_i, and d'_i be the distance (possibly incorrect, due to malicious responses by s) as reported by the range measurement protocol. The $d_i - d'_i$ value is the *reported distance error* for beacon b_i. The SDM property states that, regardless of what s does, there is some constant k such that $d'_i - d_i = k$ for every honest beacon b_i. In other words, if the adversary changes the reported distance between s and some beacon by k, then he must also change the reported distance between s and every other beacon by k, or else the measurements will be inconsistent and the attack will be detected.

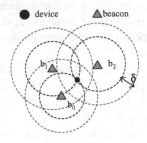
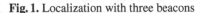

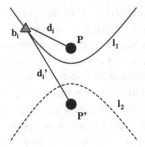

Fig. 1. Localization with three beacons   **Fig. 2.** Distance modification

For the rest of this section, assume that all beacons are honest (we consider the case of malicious beacons in section 5). Recall that the goal of the malicious device is to convince the base station of a false location, *i.e.*, the reports of all beacons should be *consistent*, yet the resulting location should *not* be the device's true location.

The following lemma gives the sufficient and necessary conditions under which a false location claim by a malicious device may successfully pass verification.

Lemma 1 (Security of SDM). *Consider an honest-beacon localization protocol based on range measurement which satisfies the SDM property. A malicious device located at position p can cause the localization protocol to compute its location as p', where $p' \neq p$, if and only if all of the following conditions hold:*

1. All beacons within the device's range lie on the same lobe l of some hyperbola h.

2. Positions p and p' are the foci of the hyperbola h.

3. If distance bounding is used, l must be the lobe closest to p.

Proof sketch: Localization with three honest beacons is shown in fig. 1. Each circle represents a distance between the beacon and the device, as reported by the range measurement protocol. The three circles corresponding to the actual distances intersect in the device's true location. Due to imprecise measurements, the intersection is a small region rather than a single point (this does not affect our analysis). We say that two curves "intersect" if they pass within the measurement error of each other (see section 5.1). The simplest protocol is to take the intersection of the three circles corresponding to the reported distances as the device's location. If the circles don't intersect in a single location, report an inconsistency.

If the protocol for measuring the distances between the individual beacons and the device satisfies the SDM property, the device can alter each reported distance by $|d'_i - d_i| = \delta$. Intuitively, the radiuses of all three circles must expand or contract by the same δ. The protocol produces a false location if and only if the new circles "intersect" in a region other than the device's true location.

Fig. 2 shows a malicious device in position p. Let d_i be the true distance between p and beacon b_i. For the device to be localized in some $p' \neq p$, it is necessary (but not sufficient) to modify the distance reported by b_i so that d'_i is equal to the distance between b_i and p'. This must hold for *every* beacon b_i. Therefore, all beacons must lie on the same lobe of a hyperbola whose foci are p and p'. (A *hyperbola* is the set of all locations x on a plane such that the absolute value of the difference between the distances from x to the two foci is a constant.) In fig. 2, the l_1 lobe is the set of all locations for which this difference is negative, the l_2 lobe is the set of all locations for which the difference is positive. With distance bounding (see section 1), a malicious device can pretend to be farther away, but not closer than it really is. Therefore, $d'_i > d_i$. In this case, the *only* situation in which a device located at p can successfully pretend to be located at p' is if all beacons lie on l_1, *i.e.*, the lobe of the hyperbola closest to p.

Lemma 1 says that a malicious device cannot choose an arbitrary false location. Its false location claim will pass verification *only* in the following case: if all beacons lie on a hyperbola and the device happens to be located in its focus, then it can successfully pretend to be located in the other focus. If any of the three conditions of lemma 1 is violated, the reported distances will be inconsistent, and the attack will be detected.

3 Preventing False Location Claims

We now investigate how many beacons and which placement geometry are sufficient to ensure that the conditions of lemma 1 can never be satisfied and, therefore, a false location claim by a malicious device can never pass verification.

Random beacon placement and pre-measurement selection. This is the most general scenario. Beacons are randomly scattered on the localization plane, and a subset of beacons must be chosen *before* the device's location claims are known. Beacon placement must be such that the chosen beacons cannot all lie on the same lobe of some hyperbola. Then, by the contrapositive of lemma 1, a false location claim cannot pass verification.

The straightforward approach is to start with the minimum number of beacons which uniquely identify a hyperbola lobe, then select one more beacon which does *not* lie on this lobe. In our setting, the lobe can lie at an arbitrary angle to the coordinate grid. To capture all possible rotations of the hyperbola, we resort to the general conic section equation, where A, B, C, D, E, F are constants:

$$Ax^2 + Bxy + Cy^2 + Dx + Ey + F = 0$$

Since the base station knows the coordinates of all beacons, six randomly selected beacons uniquely determine some conic section. The base station solves the system of six equations and checks whether $B^2 - 4AC > 0$, *i.e.*, whether the resulting section is a hyperbola. If not, the selected set is sufficient for secure localization.

If the chosen beacons do lie on a hyperbola, the base station randomly selects the 7th beacon. With high probability, it will not lie on the same lobe, or else the base station chooses a different beacon. The minimal set for preventing false location claims thus consists of seven beacons. If the size of the beacon set must be minimized, the base station can re-sample the six beacons until they do not form a hyperbola.

Random beacon placement with post-measurement selection. In this scenario, each beacon reports its distance from the device, and the base station selects a subset of the beacons *after* receiving all distance reports. A different set of beacons can thus be

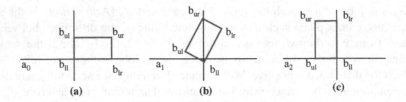

Fig. 3. Rectangular arrangement of beacons

used for each device. For each set, the base station computes the device position p' as the "intersection" of the circles whose centers are the beacons and the radiuses are the reported distances. Three beacons are sufficient.

If the beacons' reported distances are inconsistent, *i.e.*, the circles do not intersect in a single location, then the base station aborts the protocol. Otherwise, the base station assumes that p' is a *false* location and attempts to derive a contradiction. If the latter succeeds, it concludes that p' is the device's true location.

The polar-coordinate equation for a hyperbola with a focus at the origin is:

$$r = \frac{a(e^2 - 1)}{1 - e * cos(\theta + \phi)}$$

By setting p' as the origin and using the beacons' polar coordinates with respect to that origin, this system can be solved for a, e, ϕ, uniquely identifying some hyperbola h. As before, the base station checks whether the three beacons all lie on the same lobe of h, and, if distance bounding is used, that this is *not* the lobe closest to p'. If either condition fails, p' cannot be a false location, and the device is securely localized.

If the three beacons all lie on the same hyperbola lobe, then the base station randomly selects a 4th beacon which does not lie on the lobe, and checks whether its distance report is consistent with those of the three original beacons. If it is, then p' cannot be a false location, and the device's location claim is securely verified.

Controlled beacon placement. If placement of beacons on the localization grid is not random, but controlled by some trusted entity, then the *same set of four beacons* can be used to securely verify the claims of any device. It is sufficient to find a placement topology such that the beacons cannot all lie on the same hyperbola lobe. Consider a rectangle. Observe that for every hyperbola lobe, there exists some Cartesian coordinate system such that (1) the hyperbola lobe is a function in this coordinate system, and (2) the derivative of this function changes sign only once. In any Cartesian coordinate system, a curve that passes through the four points forming the corners of a rectangle is either not a function, or requires more than one sign change in the derivative. Therefore, four beacons placed in a rectangle cannot lie on the same hyperbola lobe.

Lemma 2 (Rectangular topology prevents false localization). *If the localization protocol satisfies the SDM property, and four verifying beacons are placed in a rectangular grid, then a false location claim can never pass verification.*

Proof sketch: Denote the four beacons as b_{ll} (lower left), b_{lr} (lower right), b_{ul} (upper left), and b_{up} (upper right) and let $b_i.x$ and $b_i.y$ be, respectively, the x and y coordinates

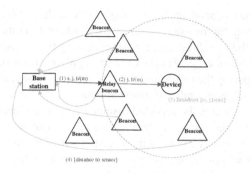

Fig. 4. SDM protocol based on hash chains

of beacon b_i. Consider the family of Cartesian coordinate systems with the origin at b_{ll}. Fig. 3 shows some of the rotations (technically, we are rotating the coordinate system, but it is easier to visualize the rotations of the beacon rectangle around the b_{ll} origin). Denote these rotations as a_0, a_1, a_2, respectively. In all of them, two of the beacons lie on the y-axis. Therefore, no curve that goes through all four beacons can be a function.

Now consider all coordinate systems where the (rotated) principal axis lies between that of a_0 and that of a_1. In all of these systems, $b_{ul}.x < b_{ll}.x < b_{ur}.x < b_{lr}.x$. Similarly, $b_{ul}.y > b_{ll}.y$ and $b_{ll} < b_{ur}$, implying one sign change in the derivative. And $b_{ll}.y < b_{ur}.y$ and $b_{ur} > b_{lr}$, implying another sign change in the derivative. Therefore, no hyperbola lobe can pass through all four beacons in this coordinate system.

A similar argument applies to all coordinate systems where the rotated principal axis lies between a_1 and a_2. Therefore, no hyperbola can pass through all four beacons in any coordinate system rotated between 0 and 90 degrees. The proof for rotations between 90 and 360 degrees is similar. Since any Cartesian coordinate system can be x- and y-translated into a system in the above family, this completes the proof.

4 Protocols with the SDM Property

4.1 Challenge-Response with Hash Chains

We present a localization protocol based on hash chains, in which the SDM property is achieved by a simple challenge-response mechanism. The protocol can be ultrasound-based as in [SSW03] or radio-based as in [BC93, ČH05] (the latter requires extremely precise clocks in order to measure propagation time of speed-of-light signals, and cannot be used in many practical scenarios).

The base station sets up a hash chain $h^k(m)$, where m is a secret, k is a parameter (how many localizations can be performed before a new chain must be created), and h is a cryptographic hash function. The $h^k(m)$ value is distributed to all beacons. Each beacon must maintain the current chain counter c (initialized to k) and $h^c(m)$ value.

The protocol is shown in fig. 4. To localize a device, the base station sends the message $\langle j, h^j(m) \rangle$ to a randomly chosen *relay* beacon, along with a future time t_0. The only requirement on j is that it has to decrease from one instance of the protocol to the next (*i.e.*, the hash chain should be monotonically unrolled).

At time t_0, the relay beacon challenges the device with $\langle j, h^j(m) \rangle$. The device responds by broadcasting the message $\langle t_d, j, h^j(m) \rangle$ where t_d is its current timestamp. Each beacon within the broadcast range, upon receiving this message, records the current time t_i and verifies the $\langle j, h^j(m) \rangle$ value by applying hash function h to $h^j(m)$ $c - j$ times and comparing the result to $h^c(m)$. If verification succeeds, the beacon sets $c = j$, $h^c(m) = h^j(m)$, and sends the timestamp pair $\langle t_d, t_i \rangle$ to the base station.

The base station computes the reported distance from each beacon to the device as $d'_i = \frac{t_i - t_d}{v}$, where v is the speed of signal propagation. The base station constructs a circle for each beacon, with the beacon in the center and d'_i radius. If the circles do not "intersect" (*i.e.*, pass within the measurement error of each other) in a single location, the protocol is aborted, and the location claim does not pass verification. Otherwise, the device is considered localized in the small region where all circles intersect. The case of malicious beacons is discussed in section 5.

An important property of this protocol is that the device cannot broadcast a valid response *before* receiving the challenge, since this requires finding a pre-image of $h^c(m)$. Instead of $\langle t_d, j, h^j(m) \rangle$, the device can broadcast, for example, $\langle t_d, j+i, h^{j+i}(m) \rangle$ for some i such that $j+i < c$, but this can only happen *after* the device has received $h^j(m)$. Therefore, elapsed time can be artificially increased by delaying the response, but not shortened. Furthermore, because localization is based on a *single* message emitted by the device, the reported distances will change by the same amount for each beacon (under the assumption that distance is linear in time). Therefore, the protocol satisfies the SDM property. Its security then follows directly from lemmas 1 and 2.

This protocol assumes that the clocks of the beacons and the device are synchronized. (Changing the timestamp cannot help a false location claim to pass verification, but clock skew can prevent an honest claim from being verified.) To remove this requirement, the protocol can be slightly modified so that both challenge and response include t_0. The base station can then compute t_d as $\frac{t_r - t_0}{2v}$, where t_r is the time the device's response was received at the relay beacon.

4.2 Time Difference of Arrival

Time difference of arrival (TDoA) inherently possesses the SDM property. The device broadcasts an identifying signal. All beacons within range record the time of signal arrival and relay it to the base station. For each pair of beacons, the base station computes the hyperbola corresponding to the difference between their timestamps (for any two beacons A and B, all locations whose distances from A and B differ by a constant form a hyperbola). The "intersection" of all hyperbolas is the location of the device.

This assumes that a constant difference in *time* (of signal arrival) implies a constant difference in *distance* (to the location from which the signal was emitted). The signal must travel at a constant speed v, as is the case for radio or ultrasound signals. Distance d_i between the device and a beacon is v multiplied by the time difference between the (unknown) time t_0 when the signal was sent and the time it was received.

Let t_{bi} be the time when beacon b_i received the signal. Then $v \cdot (t_{bi} - t_0) = d_i$. Even though t_0 is not known, given two timestamps t_{bi} and t_{bj} from different beacons, the

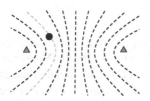

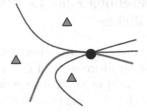

Fig. 5. Family of hyperbolas between two beacons

Fig. 6. Intersection of three hyperbolas

base station can subtract it out to obtain the equation $v \cdot (t_{bi} - t_{bj}) = d_i - d_j$. This equation defines a hyperbola on which the signal-emitting device must be located, as shown in figure 5. Given multiple hyperbolas (one per each pair of beacons), they must "intersect" in the device's true location (see fig. 6).

TDoA-based localization satisfies the SDM property because all beacons' measurements are based on a *single* signal broadcast by the device. Observe that the time of signal emission does not enter into the TDoA calculation. Therefore, unlike distance bounding protocols, TDoA localization is not vulnerable to the distance enlargement attack, in which the device delays its response to a challenge in order to pretend that it is located farther than it really is.

4.3 Signal Strength

Signal strength drops off as the inverse square of the distance [SHS01, Rap96]. A constant difference between the relative strengths of received signals does not imply that the device lies on a certain hyperbola, and the protocol of section 4.2 does not work.

The protocol based on hash chains from section 4.1 can still be used. All that is needed is some way of converting the received signal into distance. Suppose that the malicious device artificially modifies its response, *e.g.*, emits at a lower than normal signal strength in order to pretend that it is located farther away than it really is. As long as the modification is the same for all receiving beacons, as will be the case when localization is based on a single broadcast response, the protocol works.

Technically, this is not the same property as SDM, as the error in reported distances is not constant across all beacons (a constant difference in signal strength does not imply a constant difference in distance). Nevertheless, the same general principle applies. For all beacons which receive the same signal, the reported distance will differ from the true distance by a fixed amount, which depends on the true distance. Therefore, the adversary cannot pass verification for an arbitrary false location claim.

All of the above protocols assume that the signal sent by the device which is being localized cannot be modified or delayed before reaching the beacons. For example, if signal strength is artificially boosted in transit by some colluding device, localization will be incorrect. Similarly, if a non-radio signal is used, it can be artificially "speeded up" by one or more colluding devices who talk to each other by radio. Finding effective defenses against these attacks is an interesting topic for future research.

5   Preventing False Location Claims When Beacons Can Be Malicious

We now consider verification of location claims of a potentially malicious device in the scenario where some of the beacons may collude with it. The SDM property improves security of localization in this case, too. We emphasize that none of the existing protocols for verifying location claims provide any security guarantees in this scenario.

Naturally, even with the SDM property, secure verification of location claims is not guaranteed unless there is a bound on the number of malicious beacons. Let n be the number of beacons within the range of the device being localized, b the maximum number of malicious beacons, $g = n - b$ the minimum number of honest beacons.

We deliberately consider an extremely strong attack model. All malicious beacons collude and choose a false location for the device which is the *worst possible location* from the viewpoint of the localization protocol. In other words, the attack succeeds if malicious beacons can convince the base station that the device is located in *any* position other than its true location. In reality, a malicious device may wish to be localized in a *specific* false location, so "insecurity" in our model does not always imply insecurity in practice. Vice versa, if the protocol is secure in our model, then it is also secure in any realistic deployment scenario.

Depending on the beacon placement procedure, malicious beacons may not freely choose their own locations on the grid (*e.g.*, if the beacons' layout is configured by the base station). With static beacons, the topology may enable malicious beacons to produce false locations for some devices, but not others. It is much more difficult for a coalition of malicious beacons to convince the base station of false locations for multiple devices. We will further strengthen the attack model by assuming that the base station does not notice inconsistencies between multiple runs of the localization protocol. Finally, we will assume that malicious beacons can eavesdrop on all distance and time measurements reported by the honest beacons. This is too strong in many scenarios, *e.g.*, when each beacon is connected to the base station by a dedicated wire.

5.1   Challenge-Response

As before, we require that if the protocol produces a location, then the location must be correct. If the device is malicious, the protocol may fail to provide an answer. This is not a significant limitation, because in the standard location claim verification scenario [WF03, SSW03, ČH05], the objective of a malicious device is to convince the base station of a false location.

We add the following voting scheme to the protocol of section 4.1.

1. Let t be a threshold value, which is a parameter of the protocol. It is equal to the fraction of reported distances that must be consistent before the base station decides that the device has been localized.
2. For each beacon that reported distance d_i' to the device, the base station computes a circle of radius d_i' centered at that beacon.
3. Let P be the set of locations in which at least $t \cdot n$ distance circles "intersect" (*i.e.*, pass within the measurement error of each other).
4. If set P is empty, return a special symbol, indicating that the answer is inconclusive.

5. For each location $x_i \in P$, define $c(x_i)$ to be the number of distance circles "intersecting" in that location. Note that $c(x_i) \geq t \cdot n$.

   Let $X = \{x_i \in P \text{ s.t. } \forall j \neq i \; c(x_j) \leq c(x_i)\}$ be the set of locations where most circles "intersect."

6. If $|X| > 1$, the answer is inconclusive; else let p be the single location contained in X.

7. Return p as the device's location.

Security analysis (honest device, malicious beacons). If the device is honest, the base station will receive at least g correct distances from the good beacons. All corresponding circles intersect in the true location.

Can colluding malicious beacons produce a false location in which the number of intersecting circles exceeds the threshold as well? First, the malicious beacons have to find the region p' in which the second highest number of honest beacons' circles pass within the measurement error of each other (the region with the highest number of intersections is the true location). Note that (a) such a region may not exist, and (b) malicious beacons cannot freely choose an arbitrary point as the false location. Let m be the number of honest beacons' circles intersecting in p'. Each malicious beacon modifies its distance report so that the resulting circle passes through p'.

The number of votes for the false location p' is $b + m$, where b is the number of bad beacons. The number of votes for the correct location is at least g (some of the malicious beacons' circles may pass through the correct location in addition to the false location). Correct localization is only guaranteed if $g > b + m$.

Deriving a theoretical upper bound on m is difficult, as it depends on the layout of the beacons, device location, and precision of distance measurement. We use simulation instead. Our setup consists of a square grid, with the device being localized positioned in its center, and n beacons randomly scattered within the device's broadcast range. The hyperbolas or distance circles (depending on the localization protocol) are computed for each beacon and overlaid on the grid. Two curves are considered to intersect at position p if both pass within the distance measurement error of p. Our simulation parameters are consistent with the specification of PAL650 UWB Precision Asset Location system [FRB03]: the communication range between a device and a beacon is 200 feet (indoor) or 600 feet (outdoor), measured with 1-foot precision. By default, the device is falsely localized if the location produced by our protocol differs from the correct location by more than 20 feet.

Fig. 7 shows the number of circles intersecting in the false location p' with the second highest number of intersections, averaged across 5000 simulations, assuming a 200-feet communication range. It is much smaller than the number of intersections in the correct location, which is equal to the number of beacons.

Security analysis (malicious device, malicious beacons). This case is difficult because *all* reported distances, including those reported by the honest beacons, may be incorrect. The SDM property ensures, however, that the distances reported by the honest beacons are changed by the same amount viz. correct distances. Therefore, if the device attempts to alter its reported distance to one of the honest beacons, it has no control over the distances reported by the other honest beacons.

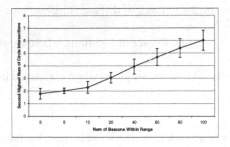 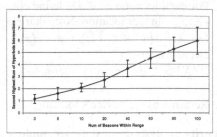

Fig. 7. Number of circles intersecting in the false location

Fig. 8. Number of hyperbolas intersecting in the false location

As explained in section 2, the number q of honest beacons' circles that will intersect in the false location is equal to the number of honest beacons that happen to lie on the same lobe of a hyperbola whose focus is the true location of the device, and whose other focus is the false location. This number is very small relative to the total number of beacons (see fig. 9 for beacons with 200-feet communication range).

The total number of circles that intersect in the false location is $b + q$. The protocol will output the false location if $\frac{b+q}{n} \geq t$. Therefore, our protocol guarantees secure localization of a malicious device even in the presence of malicious beacons as long as $g \geq b + max(m, q) + 1$.

5.2 Time Difference of Arrival

An important advantage of TDoA localization (see section 4.2) is that it doesn't matter whether the device is malicious or honest. We adopt the following voting protocol.

1. For each beacon b_i, the base station constructs $n - 1$ hyperbolas as described in section 4.2), one per each beacon b_j where $j \neq i$.
2. Let P be the set of locations in which at least two of the constructed hyperbolas "intersect," *i.e.*, pass within the measurement error of each other.
3. For each location $x_l \in P$, define $h(x_l)$ to be the number of hyperbolas "intersecting" in that location. Let $X = \{x_m \in P \text{ s.t. } \forall l \neq m \ h(x_l) \leq h(x_m)\}$ be the set of locations where most hyperbolas "intersect."
4. If $|X| > 1$, the beacon abstains. Otherwise, its vote is the single location contained in X.
5. The location with the most beacon votes is determined to be the device's location.

Security analysis. For each beacon pair when both beacons are honest, the hyperbola passes through the true location p. Therefore, for each honest beacon, at least $g - 1$ hyperbolas will intersect in the true location.

As in the challenge-response protocol, the worst possible false location p' is the region where the second highest number of hyperbolas intersect. Let m be this number. The only situation in which an honest beacon will abstain or vote for a false location is when $g - 1 \leq b + m$. The probability of this happening is very small when beacons are scattered randomly on the localization grid (see fig. 8). Therefore, as long as there are

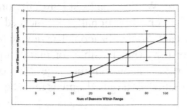
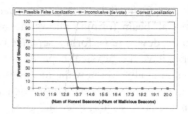

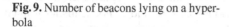

Fig. 9. Number of beacons lying on a hyperbola

Fig. 10. TDoA localization with malicious beacons (numbers for false localization are a conservative upper bound)

slightly more honest beacons than malicious beacons, each honest beacon will vote for the correct location.

The $b+m$ upper bound on the number of hyperbolas intersecting in the false location is very conservative. To achieve it, *every* malicious beacon must report the signal-receipt timestamp such that *all* of the resulting TDoA hyperbolas pass through p'. This can only happen if *all* honest beacons lie on the same lobe of a hyperbola whose foci are p and p'. The probability of this is very small (see fig. 9).

As long as $g > b$, and the vote of each honest beacon is correct, the protocol will produce the correct location. Even if some of the honest beacons' votes are incorrect, the protocol produces the correct location as long as fewer than $\frac{m}{2}$ of the honest beacons lie on a hyperbola whose foci are the true and false locations. Finally, the attack will fail completely if the false location is anything other than a focus of this hyperbola.

Simulation results with 200-feet communication range are shown in fig. 10. As mentioned above, these numbers are a very conservative upper bound on the attackers' ability to have a false location claim successfully pass verification.

Existence of more than one location with a non-trivial number of votes should be treated as an anomalous event. In particular, if location p received the highest number of votes v, location p' has the second-highest number of votes v', and v' is close to v, the base station should suspect that an attack is in progress and verify whether a large number of reporting beacons happen to lie on a hyperbola whose foci are p and p'. Once the attack is confirmed, all subsequent reports from these beacons should be ignored.

6 Attacks on the SDM Property

SDM property fundamentally relies on the assumption that all beacons' reports are based on a single signal sent by the device. To break the SDM property, a malicious device must be able to send different signals to different beacons. This requires the device to carry directional antennas, or else this can be achieved by device *cloning*, where multiple physical devices pretend to be the same device for the purposes of localization. Note that direct attacks on distance bounding, such as those described in [CHKM06], do not violate the SDM property.

One simple attack is to send multiple signals at different strength so that far-away beacons do not receive the weaker signals. This naive attack is easily detected by the honest beacons located close to the device because they will receive multiple signals.

A more sophisticated attack involves *beam forming*. While broadcast is usually omni-directional, beam forming allows the signal to be sent directionally. To succeed, the malicious device must form a separate beam for each honest beacon. The device must not only have the physical capacity for beam forming (not feasible for many mobile devices), but also to know the locations of all honest beacons within range. Moreover, if localization is based on time-of-flight measurements, all targeted signals must be sent within a relatively short interval.

Another attack involves colluding devices who jam and/or replay each other's signals. This requires a large number of malicious devices, and is not realistic in many practical scenarios. If multiple devices at different locations share the same identity, they can each send a different message to a subset of the honest beacons.

Defending against cloning and directional signals is a difficult challenge, and an interesting topic for future research. Proposed defenses include hiding locations of the beacons [ČČS06]. Our protocols are compatible with this defense, and the generic security argument given in sections 2 and 3 holds when the beacons' locations are hidden. The analysis in [ČČS06], however, does not consider the case of malicious beacons colluding with the device.

In this paper, we focused on verifying location claims of a single device. When multiple devices are being localized, interference and missed signals are possible. Because our protocols require that a sufficient number of honest beacons receive the device's signal, the protocol may need to be repeated several times. Each protocol session must include a unique session id so that different sessions can be distinguished.

We assumed that communication between the beacons and the base station is secure. If the adversary has the ability to block the reports of honest beacons, verification of location claims does not appear feasible since the base station will be computing the location solely from the reports of malicious beacons.

7   Conclusions

We proposed a new *simultaneous distance modification* property for distance estimation protocols, and demonstrated that this property enables secure verification of location claims of mobile devices with a small number of verifiers, and regardless of the device's position relative to the verifiers. We also presented two lightweight localization protocols based on, respectively, challenge-response and time difference of arrival. These protocols prevent false location claims even if some of the verifiers are malicious.

References

[BC93]   Brands, S., Chaum, D.: Distance-bounding protocols (extended abstract). In: Helleseth, T. (ed.) EUROCRYPT 1993. LNCS, vol. 765, Springer, Heidelberg (1994)

[BHE00]   Bulusu, N., Heidemann, J., Estrin, D.: GPS-less low cost outdoor localization for very small devices. Technical Report 00-729, Computer Science Department, University of Southern California (April 2000)

[BP00]   Bahl, P., Padmanabhan, V.: RADAR: An in-building RF-based user location and tracking system. In: INFOCOM (2) (2000)

[ČČS06]   Čapkun, S., Čagalj, M., Srivastava, M.: Secure localization with hidden and mobile base stations. In: INFOCOM (2006)

[ČH05]   Čapkun, S., Hubaux, J.-P.: Secure positioning of wireless devices with application to sensor networks. In: INFOCOM (2005)

[CHKM06]   Clulow, J., Hancke, G., Kuhn, M., Moore, T.: So near and yet so far: distance-bounding attacks in wireless networks. In: Buttyán, L., Gligor, V., Westhoff, D. (eds.) ESAS 2006. LNCS, vol. 4357, Springer, Heidelberg (2006)

[DFN06]   Du, W., Fang, L., Ning, P.: LAD: localization anomaly detection for wireless sensor networks. J. Parallel Distrib. Comput. 66(7), 874–886 (2006)

[FRB03]   Fontana, R., Richley, E., Barney, J.: Commercialization of an ultra wideband precision asset location system. In: IEEE Conf. on Ultra Wideband Systems and Technologies (2003)

[HHB+03]   He, T., Huang, C., Blum, B., Stankovic, J., Abdelzaher, T.: Range-free localization schemes for large scale sensor networks. In: MOBICOM (2003)

[HK05]   Hancke, G., Kuhn, M.: An RFID distance bounding protocol. In: SecureComm (2005)

[HWLC97]   Hofmann-Wellenhof, B., Lichtenegger, H., Collins, J.: Global Positioning System: Theory and Practice. Springer, Heidelberg (1997)

[LND05a]   Liu, D., Ning, P., Du, W.: Attack-resistant location estimation in sensor networks. In: IPSN (2005)

[LND05b]   Liu, D., Ning, P., Du, W.: Detecting malicious beacon nodes for secure location discovery in wireless sensor networks. In: ICDCS (2005)

[LOR06]   LORAN. LORAN-C general information (2006), http://www.navcen.uscg.gov/loran/

[LP05]   Lazos, L., Poovendran, R.: SeRLoc: Robust localization for wireless sensor networks. ACM Trans. Sensor Networks 1(1), 73–100 (2005)

[LPČ05]   Lazos, L., Poovendran, R., Čapkun, S.: ROPE: Robust position estimation in wireless sensor networks. In: IPSN (2005)

[MSC06]   Meadows, C., Syverson, P., Chang, L.: Towards more efficient distance bounding protocols for use in sensor networks. In: SecureComm (2006)

[NN03a]   Niculescu, D., Nath, B.: Ad hoc positioning system (APS) using AoA. In: INFOCOM (2003)

[NN03b]   Niculescu, D., Nath, B.: DV based positioning in ad hoc networks. J. Telecommunication Systems (2003)

[PCB00]   Priyantha, N., Chakraborty, A., Balakrishnan, H.: The Cricket location-support system. In: MOBICOM (2000)

[Rap96]   Rappaport, T.: Wireless Communications: Principle and Practice. Prentice-Hall, Englewood Cliffs (1996)

[SHS01]   Savvides, A., Han, C.-C., Srivastava, M.: Dynamic fine-grained localization in ad-hoc networks of sensors. In: Mobile Computing and Networking, pp. 166–179 (2001)

[SSW03]   Sastry, N., Shankar, U., Wagner, D.: Secure verification of location claims. In: WiSe (2003)

[WF03]   Waters, B., Felten, E.: Secure, private proofs of location. Technical Report 667-03, Department of Computer Science, Princeton University (January 2003)

Modeling and Virtualization for Secure Computing Environments

Kazuhiko Kato

Department of Computer Science
University of Tsukuba
Tennodai 1-1-1, Tsukuba, Ibaraki 305-8573, Japan
kato@cs.tsukuba.ac.jp
http://www.osss.cs.tsukuba.ac.jp/kato/

Modeling and virtualization are typical methodologies used to develop efficient security enhancement techniques. Modeling approximates complex human or software behaviors with limited resources and enables effective analysis of usage patterns. Virtualization allows simulating existing computing resources, adding some capabilities such as access control and/or modifying semantics. Thus entities accessing computer resources are handled by modeling, whereas the resources themselves can be managed through virtualization. This invited talk describes our approaches and experiences that takes advantage of both methodologies.

By modeling software or user behavior, the system can make approximations that capture the "normal" behaviors with limited resources. Once we obtain an approximation, it can be utilized to detect anomalies that an intruder would likely perform. Conventional modeling approaches for anomaly-based intrusion detection can be classified as either vector space-based methods or network-based methods. The advantages of these two types of methods are complementary to each other. The vector space-based methods can automatically generate a model from an event sequence, but the relations between the events cannot be represented, whereas the network-based methods can represent the relations between the events, but a domain specific knowledge is often required to define the topology of the network. We show that it is possible to develop a method that combines the advantages of the two types [3]. The idea behind this method is to regard an event sequence as a serialized sequence that originally had structural relations and to extract the embedded dependencies of the events.

Most modeling methods of anomaly-based intrusion detection requires a "learning" phase of normal behavior, including the above-mentioned technique. Determining what data should be used for the learning stage is a nontrivial issue and careful selection is required. David Wagner and Drew Dean proposed an interesting approach that directly extracts a model by statically analyzing program codes [5]. Unfortunately, the proposed method inherently incorporates nondeterministic search at runtime, so it suffers significant runtime overhead. We found that the overhead can be drastically reduced by combining two techniques [1]. One technique is to examine calling sequences stored in the execution stack and the other is to reuse searching results stored in a caching table.

I. Cervesato (Ed.): ASIAN 2007, LNCS 4846, pp. 196–197, 2007.

Virtualization, on the other hand, abstracts computing resources and enables one to control access to resources and/or to modify the semantics of the resources. Such capabilities are useful to protect the system's resources even when an intrusion detection system cannot recognize malicious programs or masqueraders. Our research group has two approaches to utilize such virtualization techniques: operating-system-level virtualization and processor-level virtualization.

The SofwarePot system [2,4] adopts operating-system-level virtualization. It provides an interface similar to existing Unix system-call interfaces, but its access is controlled by a specified security policy. Furthermore, semantics of system-calls are flexibly changed according to the policy.

In regards to a processor-level virtual machine system, we are currently developing a government-sponsored Secure Virtual Machine system. Transparent to commodity guest operating systems such as Windows and Linux, it provides virtualized devices including network, storage, and IC cards. The virtualization includes an encryption technology so that a certain level of security specified by security polices are guaranteed regardless of the guest operating system's settings.

References

1. Abe, H., Oyama, Y., Oka, M., Kato, K.: Optimization of intrusion detection system based on static analyses. IPSJ Transactions on Advanced Computing Systems(In Japanese) 45(SIG 3(ACS 5)), 11–20 (March 2004)
2. Kato, K., Oyama, Y.: Softwarepot: An encapsulated transferable file system for secure software circulation. In: Okada, M., Pierce, B.C., Scedrov, A., Tokuda, H., Yonezawa, A. (eds.) ISSS 2002. LNCS, vol. 2609, pp. 112–132. Springer, Heidelberg (2003)
3. Oka, M., Oyama, Y., Abe, H., Kato, K.: Anomaly detection using layered networks based on eigen co-occurrence matrix. In: Jonsson, E., Valdes, A., Almgren, M. (eds.) RAID 2004. LNCS, vol. 3224, pp. 223–237. Springer, Heidelberg (2004)
4. Oyama, Y., Kanda, K., Kato, K.: Design and implementation of secure software execution system softwarepot. Computer Software(In Japanese) 19(6), 2–12 (2002)
5. Wagner, D., Dean, D.: Intrusion detection via static analysis. In: Proc. IEEE Symposium on Security and Privacy, pp. 156–168 (May 2001)

Empirical Study of the Impact of Metasploit-Related Attacks in 4 Years of Attack Traces

E. Ramirez-Silva and M. Dacier

Eurecom Institute
Sophia Antipolis, France
{ramirez, dacier}@eurecom.fr

Abstract. For several years, various projects have collected traces of malicious activities thanks to honeypots, darknets and other Internet Telescopes. In this paper, we use the accumulated four years of data of one such system, the Leurré.com project, to assess quantitatively the influence, in these traces, of a very popular attack tool, the Metasploit Framework. We identify activities clearly related to the aforementioned exploitation tool and show the fraction of attacks this tool accounts for with respect to all other ones. Despite our initial thinking, the findings do not seem to support the assumption that such tool is only used by, so called, script kiddies. As described below, this analysis highlights the fact that a limited, yet determined, number of people are trying new exploits almost immediately when they are released. More importantly, such activity does not last for more than one or two days, as if it was all the time required to take advantage of these new exploits in a systematic way. It is worth noting that this observation is made on a worldwide scale and that the origins of the attacks are also very diverse. Intuitively, one would expect to see a kind of a Gaussian curve in the representation of the usage of these attacks by script kiddies over time, with a peak after one or two days when word of mouth has spread the rumor about the existence of a new exploit. The striking difference between this idea and the curves we obtain is an element to take into account when thinking about responsible publication of information about new exploits over the Internet.

1 Introduction

In this paper, we present a thorough analysis of 4 years of data collected by a number of honeypots distributed all over the world. The initial goal of this effort was to see i) if script kiddies activities were captured by honeypots and, if yes, ii) what relative importance such traffic had in the bulk of the collected dataset. Since, a priori, nothing distinguishes the attack traffic generated by a script kiddie from the one due to a botnet or an organized crime organization, our first task was to formulate the problem in a tractable way. Therefore, we have reduced the problem to the identification and quantification of the traces due to

I. Cervesato (Ed.): ASIAN 2007, LNCS 4846, pp. 198–211, 2007.
© Springer-Verlag Berlin Heidelberg 2007

a specific tool that most script kiddies, without any expertise at all, could use to run attacks. There is a consensus in the security community to say that the Metasploit Framework is probably "the" tool that matches this criteria. Thus, the analysis presented here after focuses on the identification of attack traces due to that specific tool.

Much to our surprise not only did this attack tool left clear traces on our honeypots, a little bit all over the world but, more importantly, the discussion presented at the end of this paper seems to indicate that this tool is used in a very systematic way by well organized people who use the very latest exploit within the 24 first hours of their release. Such activity profile does not really match the expected behavior of script kiddies and this finding should be taken into serious consideration by the security community at large and by those who produce and publish such exploit code in particular.

The structure of the paper is as follows. In Section 2, we present the Leurré.com environment and the data set used in this experiment. We introduce the key notion of clusters, as defined within the Leurré.com project and we offer a brief presentation of the Metasploit Framework. We invite the reader who would already be familiar with these notions to skip this Section and immediately continue with the next one. Section 3 describes the experimental setup we have built to systematically identify all traces of potential interest in our database. We conclude that Section by explaining why the identified traces are likely to contain traffic not related to the Metasploit attacks. Section 4 proposes various strategies to filter out this noise and discuss the results obtained with this cleaned dataset. Section 5 concludes the paper with some discussion on the most surprising results.

2   Data Collection Environment

2.1   The Leurré.com Project

For almost 4 years, the people coordinating the Leurré.com project [4] have deployed and maintained a distributed system of identical honeypots all over the world. As of today, the system is made of approximately 50 platforms located in 30 different countries. Each platform monitors 3 distinct IP addresses, using the honeyd application developed by Niels Provos [13]. Each platform captures, by means of a tcpdump file, all packets sent to and from these three virtual machines. All captured tcpdump files are parsed and stored in an SQL database, enriched with data such as the geographical location of each attacking IP, the identification of its operating system (obtained thanks to p0f and disco, two passive OS fingerprinting techniques [14],[15]), etc. The interested reader is invited to look at [12],[7],[8],[9],[11] for more information on the various findings obtained thanks to this infrastructure.

2.2   The Leurré.com Notion of "Cluster"

The notion of "cluster of traces", as defined within the Leurré.com project [9],[10],[12], is a key concept used throughout the rest of this paper. To make a long story short, one can say that a "cluster" is nothing else but a group of IP addresses that have interacted with the virtual machines of a given platform in a very similar way. Therefore, one can imagine that all these traces are likely to be due to the execution of the same attack tool on each of these attacking IPs. In other words, that the same tool has been launched from all IPs found in a cluster, or, similarly, that all IPs found in a given cluster are likely compromised by the same tool. It is clear that the semantic attached to the notion of cluster is, by far, not an exact one. The same tool can leave different traces [10], leading to the creation of several clusters that, actually, relate to a single tool. Similarly, distinct tools may leave the same fingerprint against a platform resulting in impure clusters where IPs corresponding to machines infected by different tools are grouped together. Nevertheless, introduced in [9], this notion has been validated and used in several publications, highlighting the fact that, in many cases, it was a meaningful way to group traces together.

We invite the interested reader to refer to [9] for the details of the algorithm used to build the clusters.

2.3   Metasploit Framework

Metasploit [5], according to the latest survey conducted by Fyodor [2], is the most popular vulnerability exploitation tool [3] and comes at the fifth position for the most popular security tool, according to the same study. Quoting that study: *"Metasploit took the security world by storm when it was released in 2004. No other new tool even broke into the top 15 of this list, yet Metasploit comes in at #5, ahead of many well-loved tools that have been developed for more than a decade. It is an advanced open-source platform for developing, testing, and using exploit code. The extensible model through which payloads, encoders, no-op generators, and exploits can be integrated has made it possible to use the Metasploit Framework as an outlet for cutting-edge exploitation research. It ships with hundreds of exploits, as you can see in their online exploit building demo. This makes writing your own exploits easier, and it certainly beats scouring the darkest corners of the Internet for illicit shellcode of dubious quality. Similar professional exploitation tools, such as Core Impact and Canvas already existed for wealthy users on all sides of the ethical spectrum. Metasploit simply brought this capability to the masses."* [3].

The Metasploit Framework can be invoked in different ways to launch attacks (msfconsole, msfcli interface or the msfweb interface). When using the graphical interface, the user can not easily launch attacks against a large number of hosts but, by using the msfcli command, one obtains a command line interface which is well suited to automatize campaigns of attacks against large numbers of hosts using so called Metasploit plugins, ie vulnerability exploitation tool. This command is simply invoked as follows: *"msfcli match_string options(VAR=VAL) action_code"* where match_string is the plugin (exploit) name to be launched. The action_code is a single letter used to specify what should be done; S for summary, O for options, A for advanced options, P for payloads, T for targets, C to try a vulnerability check, and E to exploit [6].

For instance, to launch the execution of the so called *"backupexec_dump"* plugin against the host 192.168.1.11, one would issue the following command:

"./msfcli   backupexec_dump   PAYLOAD=win32_exec   RHOST=192.168.1.11 TARGET=0 E"

Released at the end of 2003, the framework has evolved over the years incrementally. In early 2007, version 3.0 has been produced which is a complete rewrite of the whole framework using the Ruby language with new features and interfaces that distinguishes it completely from the previous releases. Version 2.x, written in Perl, was also different from 1.0 and has been through 8 releases; each release came with new plugins (exploit modules). For the sake of consistency and also for practical reasons, we restrict ourselves to these 8 versions (version 2.0 to 2.7), out of 10, of the Metasploit Framework to analyze its impact on our dataset.

3   Experimental Setup

3.1   Introduction

The analysis we have carried out is made of two distinct steps. In the first step, we have experimentally produced the partial definition of clusters that a Metasploit attack against our platforms would have left. Then, in a second phase, we have identified in our database all clusters whose definition was matching the one of any of those produced in the first step. Last but not least, we have applied various filters to ensure that the found clusters were, with a very high probably, linked to a real Metasploit attack and not to another attack which would have left the same fingerprint on the attacked platform. In this section, we present, step by step, the process followed to create the various partial definitions of "Metasploit" clusters. Section 4 presents the various filtering strategies applied on them.

Fig. 1 gives a high level description of the process that leads to the creation of potential candidate definitions of Metasploit-related clusters. Two distinct functional modules appear. The one on the left is responsible for launching all possible attacks against one of our platforms, in a laboratory. Traces of the attacks are saved, labeled and provided to the second module, on the right, which extracts, for each attack, the characteristics common to all clusters that would contain the same kind of traces. It also searches the database for all matching clusters, if any, and produces, as an output, a list of clusters found in the database that matches the signature of a Metasploit-related attack.

These two modules are described in more detail here below.

3.2   Launching All Possible Attacks

We wrote a perl script that iterates through all attacks available in the Metasploit Framework and that targets the virtual machines on the platform using

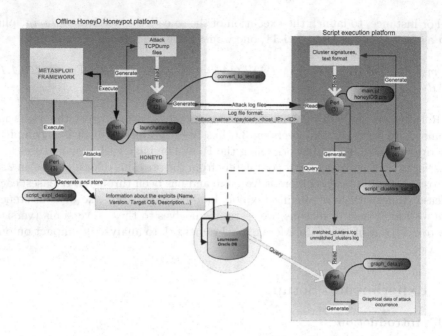

Fig. 1. High level presentation of the signatures generation process

all possible combinations, ie targeting Machine 1 only (resp 2, or 3 only), Machines 1 and 2 (resp. 1 and 3, 2 and 3), machines 1, 2 and 3. The order of the attack, 1-2-3 or 1-3-2 or ..., is one of the seven attributes that defines a cluster, as described in Section 2. We have not taken this element into consideration in our experiment as it would have dramatically increased the number of traces produced without adding any discriminant information, since all sequences must be seen as valid.

Our script invokes the msfcli command to launch the Metasploit attacks on the three honeypot IPs. It consists of iterative loops that start by querying Metasploit for all available attacks and then runs each attack, with all possible payloads, against the various combinations of the three available honeypots. This script also starts and stops the honeyd service and generates a tcpdump in order to be able to generate a tcpdump file for each attack.

The different steps the script goes through are:

1. Query Metasploit for all available attacks
2. For each attack, query Metasploit for all available payloads
3. For each honeypot IP and combination of IPs, launch the attack and the specific payload as follows:
   (a) Start the honeyd service.
   (b) Start the tcpdump monitor.
   (c) Launch the attack using the msfcli shell command with specific attack and payload and default options.
   (d) When the attack is over, stop the honeyd service and stop tcpdump.

(e) Rename the generated log file.

(f) Go to step (a) until all attacks are carried out.

3.3   Data Processing: Labeling Clusters with Attack Signatures

The role of the second functional module is to search for all clusters in the database that contain traces similar to the ones generated in the first phase of the experiment. To do this, we extract from each tcpdump file generated in the first phase, the values of the four first attributes used to define a cluster. As explained before, we ignore the order in which the virtual machines have been hit. We also ignore the total duration of the attack as well the average inter arrival time of the packets as these two factors could vary depending on the way the attacker has automatized the launching of the Metasploit plugin. Indeed, suppose that two attackers are scanning, e.g., the class C where one of our platforms is located. The first one does the scan randomly whereas the other does it sequentially. Both traces will end in clusters that will vary only on the basis of the last 3 attributes. As we are interested in finding these clusters, as well as all the others, we simply ignore the last 3 attributes when generating the signatures of our traces. To do this, we have a script that converts each attack dump file, obtained in 3.1, into an attack signature which has the following format:

```
Attack=<attack name> ports=<ports sequence> T=<No. targeted virtual
machines> N=<Total No. packets sent> n1=<packets sent to machine1>
n2=<packets sent to machine2> n3=<packets sent to machine3>
```

Last but not least, we extract from the Leurré.com database all the cluster identifiers the four first attributes of which match one of the attack signatures generated before. More precisely:

– Compare each attack signature to all the cluster signatures and declare a match if all of the following are true:
    1. $n1(min)Cluster \leq n1Attack \leq n1(max)Cluster$[1]
    2. $n2(min)Cluster \leq n2Attack \leq n2(max)Cluster$
    3. $n3(min)Cluster \leq n3Attack \leq n3(max)Cluster$
    4. $Ports\_sequence\_Cluster = Ports\_sequence\_Attack$
    5. $number\_of\_targeted\_IPs\_Cluster = number\_of\_targeted\_IPs\_Attack$
    6. $N(min)Cluster \leq NAttack \leq N(max)Cluster$

3.4   Preliminary Results

When we ran the attack script with all the exploit modules found in release 2.7, we obtained approximately 4000 distinct tcpdump files. It should be noted that certain Metasploit attacks require a connection from the target (to download a

---

[1] In the definition of a cluster, the number of packets sent against a given machine is not an absolute value but a range of values -to take into account duplicates and lost packets, among other things.

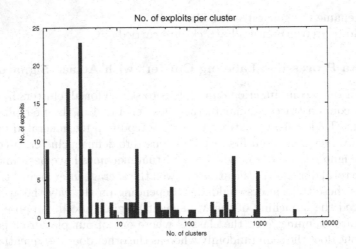

Fig. 2. Distribution of the number of exploits wrt number of clusters

file for example), whereas others wait for a connection from a user (SSL attack). These exploits have therefore been omitted from the analysis since they do not generate any traffic at all.

At the time of the experiment, the Leurré.com database did contain approximately 150.000 distinct clusters.

When we matched the derived 4000 signatures with each of these 150.000 cluster definitions, we end up with around 19'000 distinct cluster IDs. In other words there are 19'000 groups of traces in the database that are similar to traces generated artificially in the laboratory by running Metasploit plugins against a similar platform. Fig. 2 shows the distribution of the amount of exploits "per cluster". The figure shows that among the 132 exploits, there are 9 exploits that have matching characteristics in a single cluster, 17 for which 2 clusters where identified for each, 23 with three clusters, etc. In other words, almost half of the exploits are mapped with a single or a couple of clusters in the DB. We also see that a few exploits are mapped to a very large number of clusters (up to 3287 distinct ones !). It is quite likely that, among these clusters, many are not related at all to the Metasploit attack but simply target the same port in a similar way (e.g., port 445 or 139 or ...). We can, therefore, not rely on this first extraction method to look at the observed activities. In the next Section, we explain how we can filter out all the clusters that are likely due to other phenomena.

4   Analysis Results

4.1   Logic of the Experiment

From the previous Section, it is quite clear that the procedure we have followed may have helped identifying traces in our database that are linked to the manifestation of Metasploit related attacks but it is also clear that these traces are mixed with a large number of traces that have nothing to do with the phenomena we are interested in.

To isolate the interesting traces, we are going to follow a three stage process. In the first phase, Section 4.2, we filter out a very large number of traces to keep only those for which we are almost certain that they correspond to the phenomena we are interested in. This first result ensures us that there is, indeed, something to be found in the dataset. In the second phase, Section 4.3, we relax some of the constraints used in the first filtering process and we verify that the characteristics of this second result are consistent with the first one. This suggests that we have captured again, in this second filtering, traces related to the Metasploit related phenomena. Last but not least, in the third phase, Section 4.4, we apply some heuristics that we believe could also capture other interesting traces and, hereto, we verify that the characteristics of this new experiment are consistent with those corresponding to well identified Metasploit traces.

4.2 Selection on the Basis of the Original Date

In order to define the traces we are interested in, we impose some reasonable constraints on them and we select only those clusters that fulfill all criteria. The basic underlying idea is that a cluster contains traces related to a given Metasploit plugin if the number of attacks observed for that cluster around the date of the release of the plugin is significantly different than before or after. To select clusters that satisfy this property, we apply the following algorithm:

1. For each of the 19000 selected clusters in the previous phase do:
   - Obtain the original plugin release date corresponding to the cluster under consideration.
   - Compute the number of attacks, per day, observed for that cluster in the period going from -30 days until +30 days after the found release date.
   - If this cluster had never been observed before the release day minus 3 day, select the cluster and go to step 2.
   - Compute the average number of attacks for that cluster for the period [release date - 30 days, release date + 30 days]. Compute the standard deviation for the same period.
   - Select the cluster and go to step 2 if, within the period [release date - 5 days, release date + 5 days], we observe days where the number of attacks is greater than the average value + 2 times the standard deviation.
   - If no such point exists, discard the cluster and move to step 1 with the next cluster in the list.
2. Search for the maximal value of attacks per day observed for the selected cluster over the whole lifetime of the cluster.
3. If the found maximal value does not appear within the period [release date - 5 days, release date + 5 days], discard the cluster as we are interested in clusters that should normally be more active around the period of the plugin release. Continue to step 1 with a new cluster.
4. If the maximal value is within the expect boundaries, mark this cluster as being a good candidate.

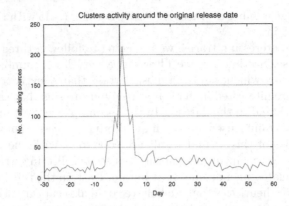

Fig. 3. First phase, number of attacks observed around day 0

The information concerning the original release date we have used is the one published officially in the Metasploit website, and is the date of the first appearance of the exploit module in the Framework. The execution of this algorithm against the 19000 selected lectures leads to the selection of only 700 of them! By having been very selective, we are quite confident that these clusters do indeed correspond to activities linked to the Metasploit Framework.

Fig. 3 represents the number of attacks observed for these 700 clusters where the X axis represents the number of day before and after the original plugin release. It highlights the fact that the peak activity occurs between -1 day and up to 2 days after the exploit release date with a maximal value in day 1. Two conclusions can be derived from this picture:

1. some exploits are tried out in the wild a few days before being officially published
2. the new plugins are very rapidly tried out and abandoned, as highlighted by the burst of attacks observed on day +1.

It is interesting to note that these attacks have been observed against platforms located all over the world and that they did originate from machines found in many different countries as well. This is a general phenomenon, not restricted to some countries or some platforms. This is represented in Fig. 4 and 5. Fig. 4 shows the geographical location of the attack sources. In Fig. 5, the horizontal axis presents the top 10 countries where attackers are coming from, for the selected clusters. The vertical axis gives the number of associated attacking sources. The other countries are grouped in the 'others' category (62 countries).

Fig. 6 shows the distribution of the attacks per environment[2]. We can observe that the attacks are not limited to a particular environment, at the contrary, they

---

[2] All Leurré.com partners are bound by an NDA that forbids them from communicating to the outside neither the IPs of the attackers or the IPs of the attacked platforms. This is why we anonymize the names of the platforms by replacing them by the name of the country where they are located.

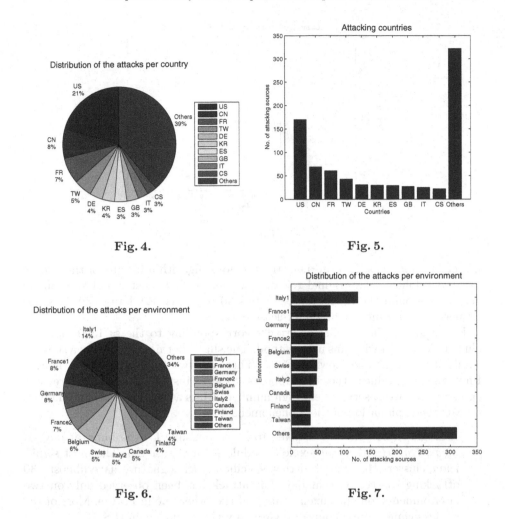

Fig. 4.

Fig. 5.

Fig. 6.

Fig. 7.

are well distributed. We only present the 10 most frequently attacked environments. The data series labelled *others* correspond to all other Metasploit related attacks observed on the remaining 38 environments.

4.3 Selection on the Basis of All Release Dates

So far, the algorithm described before has been applied for each cluster for a single date, the date of the original release of the plugin linked to the cluster under consideration. However, it is reasonable to expect that an "old" plugin published, e.g., in 2005, would suddenly be reused intensively simply because, e.g., a new releases of the framework is published. This could be a side effect of the publicity surrounding the publication of the new release. To take this element into account, we rerun the algorithm on the 19000 clusters, minus the 700 found before, by taking into account not only the original release date of the plugin but all other dates of plugin releases coming after that. In other words,

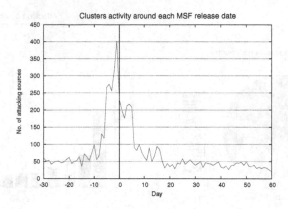

Fig. 8.

if a cluster matches the criteria of the previous algorithm for any of the release date that follows the original release[3], we select that cluster and sum all its activities around the range [release date - 30 days, release date + 30 days] for all periods following the original release date.

Fig. 8 shows the number of attacks corresponding to the ≈ 1300 matched clusters identified with this new method. The shape of this curve shows a striking similarity with the one shown in Fig. 3. There are two major differences though. First, the peak value of the curve appears at day -1 instead of +1, in the previous case. Second, we observe a very high number of hits at day -2. A deeper analysis reveals the explanation of these phenomena:

- A single exploit module appears to be responsible for the burst at day -1: *msasn1_ms04_007_killbill* exploit module from release 2.5. The most significant clusters that matched that specific attack signature have almost 230 attacking sources on that day. The attack has been observed only on two environments: one in Luxembourg and the other one in France. Most of the attacks came from 2 countries: Germany (DE) and Spain (ES).
- A single exploit module appears to be responsible for the burst at day -2: *mssql2000_preauthentication* exploit module from release 2.6. The most significant clusters that matched that specific attack signature have almost 100 attacking sources on that day. The attack has been observed a little bit all over the world and most of the attacks came from 1 country: China (CN).

So, in this case, the filtering has identified new traces that are, quite likely, linked to the Metasploit Framework and that also revealed some specific behavior on behalf of the attackers.

4.4 Clusters Without Activity Before Day -2 Filter

The two preceding filters are very good to select clusters that are, with a very high probability, linked to Metasploit related activities. However, they are probably

---

[3] Dates of releases 2.1 to 2.7.

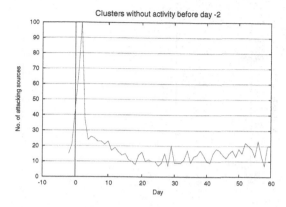

Fig. 9.

too restrictive and may have discarded clusters that could have been of interest. As a sanity check, we have decided to select all clusters for which the very first manifestation had been observed in a window of -2 to +2 days around any of the 8 possible release dates. In this last filtering approach, we do not discard clusters fulfilling this property if their maximal value appears in a period of time unrelated to any important Metasploit dates. Our hope is to identify, by doing so, clusters that are linked to the Metasploit exploit around one or several release dates but that got mixed with another, more important activity, later on.

The application of this algorithm to the remaining clusters not yet selected, we obtain 80 new clusters. Fig. 9, represents the number of attacks per day, reported relatively to any release date. Here to, we obtain a very bursty curve, just after the release which seems to indicate that the clusters we have selected are behaving similarly than the other ones and, therefore are also due to the Metasploit plugin releases.

4.5 Discussion

Fig. 10 offers the sum of all activities linked to the clusters identified in the three previous methods. The refined approach confirmed the first observations made:

1. the exploits are used extremely rapidly once they have been released.
2. some exploits are used in the wild before being made public.

It is also worth noting that the amount of attacks observed is actually fairly small. This, of course, has to be put in relation with the very limited number of addresses we are observing and, furthermore, the fact that these honeypots are low interaction ones. One can assume that we only see attacks that do participate to a very large, potentially worldwide, scan of the internet for specific exploit. Therefore, the hits we see do simply represent the tip of the iceberg and it means that there are people in the world who, as soon as plugins are released, immediately launch a worldwide scale attack against all possible platforms thanks to the new plugin, or new release. It is also important to notice

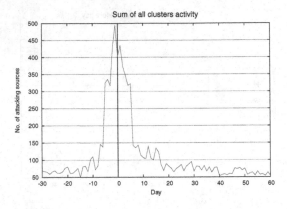

Fig. 10.

that these phenomena last for a very limited amount of time, one or two days. This is not at all what one would expect from a large population of script kiddies, scattered all over the world, with different skills and equipments at their disposal. As for every activity involving a large number of participants, it should rather be represented by a Gaussian curve highlighting the fact that a few ones see the new release immediately, spread the news, more script kiddies try it out as well, reaching a peak and, then, the number of attacks slowly decreases over the course of several days or weeks. The fact that none of our curves matches this description is a strong indication that new Metasploit releases are used by a very different population of users. These ones keep a close eye on new releases and have, probably, bots at their disposals to try them out on a very large scale immediately. Security administrators should be aware of that fact and, similarly, keep the publication of new exploits within Metasploit under close scrutiny as they can represent significant threats for their systems.

Whereas we are certainly not advocating that "security by obscurity" is a paradigm that should be promoted, at the same time we consider that those who publish new exploit plugins for the Metasploit Framework should be made aware of the fact that they help well organized entities who are not maneuvering for the good of the humanity.

5   Conclusion

In this paper, we have proposed a method to systematically identify in a very large dataset all the traces that were likely due to the Metasploit Framework (releases 2.0 to 2.7). We have shown that new plugins and new releases, are used by an important population, all over the world, that seems eager to run these exploits against as many machines as fast as possible. Quantitative examples are given throughout the text that show the validity of the approach as well as the impact of that tool on the community at large.

References

1. Arbaugh, W.A., Fithen, W.L., McHugh, J.: Windows of Vulnerability: A Case Study Analysis. IEEE Computer 33, 52–59 (2000)
2. Fyodor.: Top 100 Network Security Tools (last visited, July 25, 2007), available on line on http://sectools.org
3. Fyodor.: Top 3 Vulnerability Exploitation Tools (last visited, July 25, 2007), available on line on http://sectools.org/sploits.html
4. Leurré.com Project web page (last visited, July 25, 2007),
   http://www.leurrecom.org
5. Metasploit Project web page (last visited, July 25, 2007),
   http://www.metasploit.com
6. Metasploit Framework User Guide. Version 2.5., http://metasploit.com/projects/Framework/docs/userguide.pdf
7. Pouget, F., Dacier, M., Debar, H., Pham, V.H.: Honeynets: foundations for the development of early warning information systems. In: The Cyberspace Security and Defense: Research Issues - NATO Advanced Research Workshop, Gdansk, Poland (September 6-9, 2004)
8. Pouget, F., Dacier, M., Debar, H.: Honeypots, a practical mean to validate malicious fault assumptions. In: PRDC 2004. 10th International symposium Pacific Rim dependable computing Conference, Tahiti, French Polynesia (March 3-5, 2004)
9. Pouget, F., Dacier, M.: Honeypot-based Forensics. In: Proc. AusCERT Asia Pacific Information Technology Security Conference, Brisbane (2004)
10. Pouget, F., Dacier, M.: Honeypot Platform: Analyses and Results. Rapport de recherche RR-04-104 (October 30, 2004)
11. Pouget, F., Dacier, M., H., Pham, V.H.: Leurre.com: on the advantages of deploying a large scale distributed honeypot platform. In: ECCE 2005. E-Crime and Computer Conference, Monaco (March 29-30, 2005)
12. Pouget, F.: Distributed System of Honeypots Sensors: Discrimination and Correlative Analysis of Attack Processes. PhD thesis, Institut Eurecom (2006)
13. Provos, N.: A virtual honeypot framework. In Proceedings of the 12th USENIX Security Symposium, pp. 1-14 (August 2004)
14. Disco tool web page, http://www.altmode.com/disco/
15. p0f passive fingerprinting tool web page,
    http://lcamtuf.coredump.cx/p0f-beta.tgz

A Logical Framework for Evaluating Network Resilience Against Faults and Attacks

Elie Bursztein* and Jean Goubault-Larrecq

LSV, ENS Cachan, CNRS, INRIA
{eb,goubault}@lsv.ens-cachan.fr

Abstract. We present a logic-based framework to evaluate the resilience of computer networks in the face of incidents, i.e., attacks from malicious intruders as
well as random faults. Our model uses a two-layered presentation of *dependencies* between files and services, and of *timed games* to represent not just incidents,
but also the dynamic responses from administrators and their respective delays.
We demonstrate that a variant TATL◊ of timed alternating-time temporal logic
is a convenient language to express several desirable properties of networks, including several forms of survivability. We illustrate this on a simple redundant
Web service architecture, and show that checking such timed games against the
so-called TATL◊ variant of the timed alternating time temporal logic TATL is
EXPTIME-complete.

1 Introduction

Computer networks are subject to random faults, i.e., a server may fail because of a
bug or due to preventive maintenance. They are also subject to attacks by malicious
adversaries. Both are growing concerns. We propose a logic and a simple model to
evaluate the resilience of networks to such faults. While this model is still far from
being a complete one—it does not include probabilistic transitions, does not take into
account the financial and human cost of patching, and ignores some other intricacies of
the real world—it has the nice feature of taking into account the *time* needed to mount
attacks, to crash, or to patch systems.

Incidents may have dramatic consequences: on Nov. 04, 2004, the 7 million sub-
scribers to French mobile phone (GSM) network operator Bouygues remained unable
to make a call for several hours [8]. This incident made the headlines of national news-
papers and news reports on television and radio, and was felt as outrageous by many.
(Financial loss by Bouygues was not documented.) It was later discovered that this incident was caused by the simultaneous failure of two redundant central servers. That
this could happen, and would cause a disaster, had remained unforeseen by software
architects and security experts.

The Bouygues incident does not imply any malicious activity. Nonetheless, it is
equally important to predict the impact of malicious attacks, too, on computer networks. Real-world attacks are often a combination of successful exploitation of several
vulnerabilities, used as stepping stones.

---

* PhD student at LSV, supported by a DGA grant.

I. Cervesato (Ed.): ASIAN 2007, LNCS 4846, pp. 212–227, 2007.
© Springer-Verlag Berlin Heidelberg 2007

Contribution. We are interested in evaluating the *resilience* of networks in the face of both intended and unintended incidents, i.e., whether the network is able to survive attacks and faults, and to recover from them. This implies new aspects that are not covered by previous models.

First, our level of abstraction of the network is that of *dependencies* between files and services. In the Bouygues example, the important point is that each mobile phone on the network depends on the user database served by the two redundant servers, in the sense that if the latter fail, then each mobile phone fails, too. But the actual topology of the network is unimportant. Another benefit of considering dependencies is that we can anticipate *collateral* damage. E.g., while the Bouygues incident targets the servers, the mobile phones were affected as a consequence.

Second, it is futile to evaluate resilience by modeling incidents only. We also need to model responses, typically by administrators. E.g., it is important to know whether administrators will be able to patch system services before they fail (or are attacked), or shortly after they fail. Accordingly, we shall examine properties of the network modeled in a *game* logic, where the players are I (incident) and A (administrator). At this point we must say that our approach is inspired from biological models, and in particular from the SIR (Susceptible-Infected-Recovered) model [6]. The I player conducts actions so as to infect susceptible nodes, and A plays so as to heal infected nodes.

Third, *time* plays a key role in modeling network evolution. I and A will indeed compete in pursuing their goals, and the faster will usually gain a decisive advantage. E.g., patching a service is usually slower than launching an exploit against it. Windows of vulnerability are another case in point [14]: a vulnerable service actually cannot be patched until an official patch is released. Our model will deliberately include delays.

Accordingly, our game logic TATL$\Diamond$ will be an extension of *timed alternating-time temporal logic* (TATL) [9]. We shall see (Theorem 1) that, despite the fact that our anticipation games are exponentially more succinct than the timed automaton games they represent, and despite the fact that the natural translation from TATL$\Diamond$ formulae to TATL formulae suffers an exponential size blowup, the model-checking problem for TATL$\Diamond$ has the same complexity as that of TATL, i.e., is EXPTIME-complete.

An unusual feature of our model is that it consists of two layers. The lower layer— *dependency graphs*—models the dependencies, vulnerabilities, availability, etc., of files and services at a given time. The upper layer models the evolution over time of dependency graphs, through a set of timed rules. The semantics of timed rules is given as a timed automaton game [4], on which we can then define properties through a variant of TATL [9]. Timed automaton games are also interesting because they include a so-called *element of surprise*: the administrator A must react while not knowing what the other player I's next move is (and conversely); see Section 5 for an illustration of this. The properties we can describe are also far more general than simple reachability properties: see the example of the *service level agreement* property in Section 4.

Outline. After reviewing related work, we describe an example of a redundant Web service in Section 2, inspired from [17], and which we shall use for illustration purposes in the rest of the paper. We then describe the lower layer of our model, dependency graphs, in Section 3, as well as some base rules governing their evolution. Our framework is extensible: other, context-specific rules can always be added, and we shall illustrate this on our example. We then proceed to the upper layer in Section 4, where the semantics of dependency graphs over time is given as timed automaton games (of exponential size), which we dub *anticipation games*. This allows us to define a variant of the TATL logic on such games, TATL◊, to give a sampler of properties that can be expressed in this logic (including service level agreement, as mentioned above), and prove that model-checking properties in this logic is EXPTIME-complete. We illustrate some fine points of our model in Section 5, and conclude in Section 6.

Related Work. A successful model of malicious activity is given by *attack graphs* [12], modeling the actions of an intruder on a given network. Edges in attack graphs are actions (mostly exploits) that the intruder may undertake, and vertices are states of the network. It is then possible to detect, using reachability analyses, whether a state where a target host is compromised is reachable from an initial state. These were pioneered by Schneier [19,20] under the form of so-called tree graphs, are the closest model to our dependency graph. Ammann and Ritchey [17] considered model checking attack graphs to analyze network security [2,11]. There is an abundant literature on these, which we shall omit. Attack graphs represent states of the network and possible attacks explicitly, while dependency graphs represent the logical dependencies between files and services on a network, which may or may not be represented in the graph. The automatic discovery of such dependencies will be dealt with elsewhere.

We have briefly mentioned the SIR model in the study of propagation of epidemics in biology. This has a long history [6]. Biological models for computer security were proposed recently [18]. As in computer virus propagation research [3,21], biological models are an inspiration to us. The antibody (A) fights the disease (I) to maintain the body alive (the network). Following this intuition, using games to capture this fight interaction appears natural.

Games have become a central modeling paradigm in computer science. In synthesis and control, it is natural to view a system and its environment as players of a game that pursue different objectives [5,16]. In our model, I attempts at causing the greatest impact on the network whereas A tries to reduce it. Such a game proceeds for an infinite sequence of rounds. At each round, the players choose actions to play, e.g., patching a service, and the chosen actions determine the successor state. For our anticipation games we need, as in any *real-time* system, to use games where time elapses between actions [15]. This is the basis of the work on timed automata, timed games, and timed alternating-time temporal logic (TATL) [9], a timed extension to alternating-time Kripke structures and temporal logic (ATL) [1]. The TATL framework was specifically introduced in [7]. Timed games differs from their untimed counterpart in two essential ways. First, players have to be prevented from winning by stopping time. More important to us is that players can take each other by *surprise*: imagine A attempts to patch a vulnerable service, and this will take 5 minutes, it may happen that I is in fact currently conducting an attack, which will succeed in 5 seconds, nullifying A's action.

2   Example: A Simple Redundant Web Server

To illustrate our model, we choose to present a simplified redundant Web service (Figure 1). This is typical of Web services such as *Amazon*'s, *Google*'s, *MSN*'s. The objective is to provide clients with a reliable and responsive service, in particular to limit service downtime.

The two HTTP nodes *HTTP[1]:1*, *HTTP[1]:2* serve the Web pages *index.php[1]:1*, and *index.php[1]:2* respectively. Node names are not really important for our approach, however we have chosen the following naming convention for clarity: each node name is composed of the the service or file name first (e.g., HTTP), then an equivalence class number between square brackets, finally an optional unique identifier after the semicolon. Two node names with the same name and the same equivalence class number are meant to be *equivalent*, i.e., to provide the same service, and to be freely interchangeable. For example, *HTTP[1]:1* and *HTTP[1]:2* both have equivalence class number 1, and indeed serve the same files — or rather, files which are again equivalent, in the sense that they have the same contents. We shall use a more abstract equivalence relation $\equiv$ and modal operator $\Diamond_\equiv$ later for the same purpose.

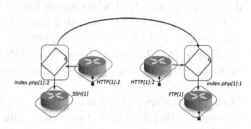

Fig. 1. Dependency Graph Exemple

Edges are used to represent dependencies. The *index.php[1]:1* file depends of the *FTP[1]* service for being updated. The *HTTP[1]:1* service depends on *index.php[1]:1*, as (according to a deliberately simplified server policy) the service will fail if the file *index.php* to be served does not exist. We take *index.php[1]:2* to depend on *index.php[1]:1*, for updating purposes: *index.php[1]:2* is copied from *index.php[1]:1*. We assume the copy is performed by using some secure replication software using SSH, e.g., rsync, unison, svn, or cvs, so that *index.php[1]:2* also depends on *SSH[1]*.

We shall represent dependencies as edges in a graph, modeling the one-step impact of an incident. For example, reading Figure 1, if the *SSH[1]* service is offline due to a failure, then the contents of *index.php[1]:2* will sooner or later be inconsistent with that of *index.php[1]:1*, and consequently the page served by *HTTP[1]:2* will also be inconsistent with the one served by *HTTP[1]:1*. Note how time is important here—until the contents of *index.php[1]:1* is updated, the impact of the failure of *SSH[1]* is limited. We assume that *index.php[1]:1* is updated every 5 minutes, so that the administrator has a window of 5 minutes to bring *SSH[1]* online before the impact of the failure expands.

3   Lower Layer: Dependency Graphs

Definition. *Dependency graphs* (e.g., Figure 1) are tuples $G = (V, \rightarrow, \equiv)$ where V is a finite set of so-called *vertices*, $\rightarrow$ is a binary relation on V (the *dependency* relation), $\equiv$ is an equivalence relation on V. For example, the *HTTP[1]:1* server depends on *index.php[1]:1*, whence there is an edge *HTTP[1]:1* $\rightarrow$ *index.php[1]:1*.

The role of $\equiv$ is to equate two services that play the same role in the actual network whose dependencies we are trying to capture. In the example of Section 2, two nodes are equivalent if and only if they have the same name and the same equivalence class number, between square brackets. That is, *HTTP[1]:1$\equiv$HTTP[1]:2*, and *index.php[1]:1$\equiv$index.php[1]:2*, but *HTTP[1]:1$\not\equiv$FTP[1]* for example.

In general, $\equiv$ is used to specify such configurations as n servers that serve the same data for efficiency (load balancing) or fault-tolerance (failover) reasons. Redundancy is a common recipe for implementing network resilience: provided not too many servers fail, clients should be able to obtain the intended service. Several protocols, such as the *Simple Mail Transfert Protocol* (SMTP) [13] protocol, are designed to work with multiple delivery servers for failover and balancing purpose.

States. Dependency graphs are meant to remain fixed over time. We use *states* to model information that does evolve over time. Intuitively the state describes which services and files are currently available, compromised, defunct, and so on. For example, a service may be *public* or not—a service is typically not public when behind a firewall that prevents access to the server from the outside.

Formally, let $\mathcal{A}$ be a finite set of so-called *atomic propositions* $A_1, \dots, A_n, \dots$, denoting each base property. Each atomic proposition is true or false at each vertex. E.g., Avail is true at each vertex that is available, File is true of those vertices that are files, Service is true of vertices that are services, Compr denotes compromised vertices, Vuln denotes remotely exploitable services, VulnLocal locally exploitable services (e.g., we assume that the HTTP servers of Figure 1 are locally exploitable), Patch denotes patchable services [14], Pub public services (i.e., possible starting points from an outside attack; in our example, only SSH is not assumed to be public; services behind firewalls would also typically assumed not to be public), MayDefunct identifies those vertices that can become unavailable (for whatever reason, including bugs), Crypt holds of encrypted files (e.g., encrypted password files; one may estimate that attackers will need a long time to access and exploit encrypted files, and a short time for others). This list can be extended at will. In the example of Section 2, Synced denotes files that are produced as the result of a replication process—namely, *index.php[1]:2*.

States on G are then simply functions $\rho : \mathcal{A} \to \mathbb{P}(V)$ mapping each atomic proposition to the set of vertices that satisfies it. We describe ρ in a finite way, as a table of all pairs $(A, v) \in \mathcal{A} \times \mathbb{P}(V)$ such that $v \in \rho(A)$; hence there are finitely many states.

Modeling the Evolution of Dependency Graphs. We now need to model actions that modify the state. These can be the result of faults (disk crashes, power failures), malicious attacks, or corrective actions by an administrator. This is done through *rules* of the form $\mathbf{Pre}\ F \longrightarrow^{\Delta,p,a} P$ where F is the *precondition*, stating when the rule applies, Δ is the least amount of time needed to fire the rule, p is the name of the player that originates the rule, a is an action name, and P is a *command*, stating the effects of the rule. The latter sentence contains an ambiguity: we require the precondition F to hold not just at the beginning of the rule, but during the whole time it takes the rule to actually complete (at least Δ time units). For example, a patching rule can only be triggered on a patchable vertex in the dependency graph, and we consider that it has to remain patchable for the whole duration of the patching action.

It is convenient to use a simple modal logic to specify preconditions F. The $\Diamond$ modality embodies the concept of dependency, while $\Diamond_\equiv$ models the equivalence of services. Other connectives are defined as usual: $F \vee F'$ is $\neg(\neg F \wedge \neg F')$, $F \Rightarrow F'$ is $\neg(F \wedge \neg F')$, and $\Box F$ is $\neg\Diamond\neg F$ for example.

$$F ::= A \qquad \text{atomic propositions, in } \mathcal{A}$$
$$\mid \top \qquad \text{true}$$
$$\mid \neg F \qquad \text{negation}$$
$$\mid F \wedge F \quad \text{conjunction}$$
$$\mid \Diamond F$$
$$\mid \Diamond_\equiv F$$

The semantics is a Kripke semantics for mixed K ($\Diamond$) and S5 ($\Diamond_\equiv$) operators. We define a predicate $G, \rho, v \models F$ by induction on F: $G, \rho, v \models \Diamond F$ iff there is a vertex w in G such that $v \to w$ and $G, \rho, w \models F$; $G, \rho, v \models \Diamond_\equiv F$ iff there is a vertex w in G such that $v \equiv w$ and $G, \rho, w \models F$. The semantics of the other connectives is standard, e.g., $G, \rho, v \models F_1 \wedge F_2$ iff $G, \rho, v \models F_1$ and $G, \rho, v \models F_2$. In the example of Figure 1, if the file *index[1]:1* becomes unavailable then *HTTP[1]:1* will become defunct after some time. This effect is expressed by the rule : "If there is a successor of *HTTP[1]:1* that is not available, then *HTTP[1]:1* becomes defunct after a delay of at least Δ_2 time units". The precondition is therefore $\Diamond\neg$Avail, interpreted at vertex *HTTP[1]:1*.

On the other hand, commands P are finite lists of assignments $A \leftarrow \top$ or $A \leftarrow \bot$, where A is an atomic proposition. This is interpreted at each vertex v. Formally, write $\rho[A \mapsto S]$ the state mapping A to set S, while mapping every other atomic proposition A' to $\rho(A')$. Let $\rho[A@v \mapsto \top]$ be $\rho[A \mapsto \rho(A) \cup \{v\}]$, $\rho[A@v \mapsto \bot]$ be $\rho[A \mapsto \rho(A) \setminus \{v\}]$. Then we let $\rho \models_v P \Rightarrow \rho'$ be defined by: $\rho \models_v \epsilon \Rightarrow \rho$ (where ϵ is the empty command), and $\rho \models_v A \leftarrow b, P \Rightarrow \rho'$ provided that $\rho[A@v \mapsto b] \models_v P \Rightarrow \rho'$.

Let us give a few examples of rules of common use. We use two sets of rules: one to model the incident/intruder actions and the other to model administrator actions. Rules are prefixed with their names. We start with the incident/intruder rules:

Defunct :	**Pre** Avail $\wedge$ MayDefunct $\longrightarrow$ Avail $\leftarrow \bot$
DefunctProp :	**Pre** $\Diamond\neg\Diamond_\equiv$Avail $\wedge$ Avail $\longrightarrow$ Avail $\leftarrow \bot$
Comp$_1$:	**Pre** Avail $\wedge$ Pub $\wedge$ Vuln $\longrightarrow$ Compr $\leftarrow \top$
Comp$_2$:	**Pre** Avail $\wedge$ Pub $\wedge$ Vuln $\longrightarrow$ Avail $\leftarrow \bot$
CServProp$_1$:	**Pre** $\Diamond$Compr $\wedge$ VulnLocal $\wedge$ Avail $\wedge$ Service $\longrightarrow$ Compr $\leftarrow \top$
CServProp$_2$:	**Pre** $\Diamond$Compr $\wedge$ VulnLocal $\wedge$ Avail $\wedge$ Service $\longrightarrow$ Avail $\leftarrow \bot$
CFileProp$_1$:	**Pre** $\Diamond$Compr $\wedge$ Avail $\wedge$ File $\wedge$ $\neg$Crypt $\longrightarrow$ Compr $\leftarrow \top$
CFileProp$_2$:	**Pre** $\Diamond$Compr $\wedge$ Avail $\wedge$ File $\wedge$ Crypt $\wedge$ VulnLocal $\longrightarrow$ Compr $\leftarrow \top$

We have omitted the subscript on arrows, which should be of the form Δ, I, a for some delay Δ and some action name depending on the rule. Defunct is a typical accidental fault: any file or service that is subject to faults (e.g., bugs) and is available can become unavailable. We may naturally vary the set of vertices that make MayDefunct to study the impact of buggy software of the health of the network. DefunctProp states that a vertex may crash when all vertices it depends on crashed, taking into account equivalent vertices. For example, most Internet connections depend on DNS root servers to perform address lookup. While there remain available DNS root servers, Internet connections are not or at least only partially affected by the failure of some of them. E.g., this is is why the attack of February 6, 2007, against 6 of the 13 root DNS servers remained mostly unnoticed by Internet users [10].

On the other hand, rules Comp_1 and Comp_2 model remote attacks on vulnerable, public services or files. While Comp_1 models the case where the attack is completely successful, and the target vertex is compromised, Comp_2 models a typical case where, e.g., the attack is by code injection, but the attack fails and instead the target service crashes (e.g., because of address space randomization).

The remaining rules represent incident propagation. CServProp_1 states how locally vulnerable services depending on compromised files (e.g., password files or route tables) can themselves become compromised, and CServProp_2 is the case where the service crashed instead (as above). CFileProp_1 states that non-encrypted files depending on (e.g., served by) compromised vertices may get compromised. This is a typical rule with a small delay Δ. The CFileProp_2 rule here would have a larger delay, and represents compromission of encrypted (Crypt) files with a weak key (VulnLocal).

Let's get on to administrator rules, with implicit superscripts of the form Δ, A, a:

Patch :	**Pre** Avail $\wedge$ (Vuln $\vee$ VulnLocal) $\wedge$ Patch $\longrightarrow$ Vuln $\leftarrow \perp$, VulnLocal $\leftarrow \perp$, Patch $\leftarrow \perp$
Deny :	**Pre** Pub $\wedge$ Service $\longrightarrow$ Pub $\leftarrow \perp$
Allow :	**Pre** ¬Pub $\wedge$ Service $\longrightarrow$ Pub $\leftarrow \top$
ORest :	**Pre** ¬Avail $\longrightarrow$ Avail $\leftarrow \top$
OReco :	**Pre** Compr $\longrightarrow$ Compr $\leftarrow \perp$
PReco :	**Pre** Compr $\wedge \Diamond_\equiv$(Avail $\wedge$ ¬Compr) $\longrightarrow$ Compr $\leftarrow \perp$
PRest_1 :	**Pre** ¬Avail $\wedge \Diamond_\equiv$(Avail $\wedge$ ¬Compr) $\longrightarrow$ Avail $\leftarrow \top$, Compr $\leftarrow \perp$
PRest_2 :	**Pre** ¬Avail $\wedge \Diamond_\equiv$(Avail $\wedge$ Compr) $\longrightarrow$ Avail $\leftarrow \top$, Compr $\leftarrow \top$

The rules shown are meant to illustrate that A may update services (rule `Patch`), configure network devices so as to make a service unreachable (`Deny`) or reachable (`Allow`), or directly repair incidents. The optimistic repair rule `ORest` states that A can always repair the damage. We may think of using variants of this rule with varying delays, representing how easy it is to make the vertex available again. Similarly, `OReco` is an optimistic vertex recovery rule. More pessimistic recovery rules are given as `PReco` (where a compromised vertex is recovered thanks to an available, uncompromised equivalent vertex), PRest_1 (where the vertex is also made available), and PRest_2 (where the vertex is unfortunately recovered from another compromised vertex).

4 Upper Layer: Anticipation Games

The rules of the last section give rise to a semantics in terms of timed automaton games [4], which we now make explicit. This can also be seen as a translation to such games, although the resulting games will have exponential size in general. We shall call these games *anticipation games*.

We assume that the rules of an anticipation graph are finitely many, and are given names that identify them in a unique way, as in Section 3. Moreover, we assume given a table Trig such that for each rule name R (for a rule **Pre** $F \longrightarrow^{\langle \Delta, p, a \rangle} P$), $\text{Trig}[R] = \Delta$ returns the least time needed to actually trigger the effect of rule R, a table Act such that $\text{Act}[R] = a$, a table Prog such that $\text{Prog}[R] = P$, and a table **Pre** such that $\textbf{Pre}[R] = F$.

For any set S, write $S_\perp$ the set S with a fresh element $\perp$ added. E.g., letting $\mathcal{R}$ be the (finite) set of all rule names of a given anticipation graph, $(\mathcal{R} \times V)_\perp$ denotes either the absence of a rule name ($\perp$), or some specific pair (R, v), typically denoting a rule named R that we try to apply to vertex v. Such pairs (R, v) are called *targeted rules*, and elements of $(\mathcal{R} \times V)_{\perp}$ are *optional* targeted rules.

A *timed automaton game* is a tuple $\mathcal{T} = (L, \Sigma, \sigma, C, A_{\mathsf{I}}, A_{\mathsf{A}}, E, \gamma)$ satisfying some conditions [4, Section 2.2]. We recapitulate these conditions while showing how we define the timed automaton game associated with an anticipation graph, explaining the semantics intuitively along the way. • L is a finite set of *locations*. We take L to be $(\mathcal{A} \to \mathbb{P}(V)) \times V \times (\mathcal{R} \times V)_{\perp} \times (\mathcal{R} \times V)_{\perp}$ consisting of tuples $(\rho, v, trg_{\mathsf{I}}, trg_{\mathsf{A}})$ of a state ρ, a vertex $v \in V$, and two optional targeted rules $trg_{\mathsf{I}}, trg_{\mathsf{A}}$ stating which rule is currently executed, if any, and targeting which vertex, by the intruder (launching an attack or causing some failure), resp. the administrator (doing a corrective action). The vertex v plays no role in the semantics of the anticipation graph per se, but will be useful in the semantics of the TATL logic we shall define next; v is the *vertex under focus* of an observer external to the anticipation graph.

• Σ is a finite set of *propositions*. We take Σ to be $\mathcal{A}$.

• $\sigma : L \to \mathbb{P}(\Sigma)$ assigns to each location the set of propositions true at this location. We define naturally $\sigma(\rho, v, trg_{\mathsf{I}}, trg_{\mathsf{A}}) = \{A \in \mathcal{A} | v \in \rho(A)\}$.

• C is a finite set of so-called *clocks* (a.k.a., clock variables). There should be a distinguished clock z, which is used to measure global time. We define $C = \{z, z_{\mathsf{I}}, z_{\mathsf{A}}\}$. The clock z_{I} measures the time elapsed since the start of the last attack launched by the intruder (or the last event that will eventually cause a failure, more generally), if any, that if, if $trg_{\mathsf{I}} \neq \perp$. Similarly, z_{A} measures the time elapsed since the start of the last (hopefully) corrective action by the administrator, if any. We allow I and A to launch concurrent actions, with possible different starting dates, and delays.

• A_{I} and A_{A} are two disjoint sets of events for the intruder I and the administrator A respectively. (Such events are usually called actions, but this would be in conflict with our own so-called actions.) We take the elements of A_p to be the pairs $\langle p, \mathbf{Launch}\ a \rangle$ and $\langle p, \mathbf{Complete}\ a \rangle$, where a is any action name, for any $p \in \{\mathsf{I}, \mathsf{A}\}$. An event $\langle \mathsf{I}, \mathbf{Launch}\ a \rangle$ means that the intruder has just launched an attack with action name a. This attack will succeed, possibly, but no earlier than some delay. When it succeeds, this will be made explicit by an action $\langle \mathsf{I}, \mathbf{Complete}\ a \rangle$.

• $E \subseteq L \times (A_{\mathsf{I}} \cup A_{\mathsf{A}}) \times \mathsf{Constr}(C) \times L \times \mathbb{P}(C \setminus \{z\})$ is the *edge relation*, and embodies the actual semantics of the timed automaton game. $\mathsf{Constr}(C)$ is the set of all *clock constraints*, generated by the grammar $\theta ::= x \leq d | d \leq x | \neg\theta | \theta_1 \wedge \theta_2 | \mathrm{TRUE}$ where x ranges over clocks in C, and d over $\mathbf{N}$. The idea is that, if $(l, \alpha, c, l', \lambda) \in E$, then the timed automaton game may go from location $l \in L$ to location l' by doing action α, provided all the clocks are set in a way that c is true; then all the clocks in λ are reset to zero. (Additionally, a timed automaton game may decide to remain idle for some time, i.e., not to follow any edge, provided the invariant $\gamma(l)$ remains satisfied throughout; see below.)

In our case, E is the set of all tuples (i.e., *edges*) of one of the following forms:

- $((\rho, v, trg_{\mathsf{I}}, trg_{\mathsf{A}}), \langle \mathsf{I}, \mathbf{Launch}\ a \rangle, \mathrm{TRUE}, (\rho, v, (R, v'), trg_{\mathsf{A}}), \{z_{\mathsf{I}}\})$, where v' is any vertex of G, and R is the name of a rule $\mathbf{Pre}\ F \longrightarrow^{\langle \Delta, \mathsf{I}, a \rangle} P$ with $G, \rho, v' \models F$. (And v is arbitrary.) In other words, the intruder may decide to launch the rule named R on any vertex v' at any time, provided its precondition F holds in the current state ρ at v'. Launching it does not modify the ρ part, which will only change when the rule is complete. This can only happen after at least Δ time units. Note that once a new rule is launched, the clock z_l is reset. This restarts this clock, so that the next rule knows when it is allowable to complete the rule

- $((\rho, v, (R, v'), trg_\mathsf{A}), \langle\mathsf{l}, \mathbf{Complete}\ a\rangle, z_\mathsf{l} \geq d, (\rho', v, \bot, trg'_\mathsf{A}), \emptyset)$, where $a = \mathsf{Act}[R]$ and $d = \mathsf{Trig}[R]$, and ρ' is given by $\rho \models_{v'} \mathsf{Prog}[R] \Rightarrow \rho'$. Then, $trg'_\mathsf{A} = trg_\mathsf{A}$ if $trg_\mathsf{A} = \bot$, or if trg_A is of the form $(R_\mathsf{A}, v_\mathsf{A})$ where $G, \rho', v_\mathsf{A} \models \mathbf{Pre}[R_\mathsf{A}]$; otherwise $trg'_\mathsf{A} = \bot$.

In other words, the rule named R at vertex v' completes at any time provided at least d units of times have elapsed since the attack was launched (the constraint $z_\mathsf{l} \geq d$). Then the state ρ is changed to ρ', that is, the result of executing program $P = \mathsf{Prog}[R]$ from state ρ at state v'. The fact that trg_A may change to trg'_A reflects the fact that as a result of an action by l, the precondition $\mathbf{Pre}[R_\mathsf{A}]$ of the rule that was in the process of being launched by A may suddenly become false, foiling A's action.

- and similar rules obtained by exchanging the roles of l and A.

• $\gamma : L \to \mathsf{Constr}(C)$ is a function mapping each location l to an *invariant* $\gamma(l)$. When at location l, each player (l or A) must propose a move out of l before the invariant $\gamma(l)$ expires. We take $\gamma(l) = \mathrm{TRUE}$ for each l, i.e., we have no urgent transition: attacks, failures and repairs can always take longer than expected.

Informally [4], the game proceeds by jumping from configurations to configurations. A *configuration* is a pair (l, κ), where l is a location and κ is a *clock valuation*, that is, a function mapping each clock (here z, z_l, z_A) to a non-negative real. Timed automaton games may proceed by triggering an actual edge in zero time. They may also proceed by letting time pass, i.e., by remaining in the same location l while incrementing each clock by the same amount. Importantly, in any given configuration, there may be several options for the game to evolve, and in particular it may be the case that two edges have the same starting location. The semantics of timed automaton games states that only the one with the shortest completion time can be triggered (or one of the shortest ones, non-deterministically, if there are several shortest edges, with the same duration). This how the *element of surprise* that we have discussed before is implemented in the model.

It is convenient to define a logic that includes both TATL operators [9] and the operators of the modal logic of Section 3.

Let $x, y, z, \ldots$ be taken from a count-ably infinite set of *clock variables*, distinct from the clocks z, z_l, z_A. We reserve the notation d, d', d_1, d_2, $\ldots$, for non-negative integer constants. We let $\mathfrak{P}$ range over subsets of $\{\mathsf{A}, \mathsf{l}\}$. The syntax of our TATL-like logic TATL$\Diamond$ is shown on the right, where in clock constraints $x + d_1 \leq y + d_2$, x and y can be clock variables or zero. We abbreviate $\langle\!\langle\mathfrak{P}\rangle\!\rangle \mathrm{TRUE}\ \mathcal{U}\ \varphi$ as $\langle\!\langle\mathfrak{P}\rangle\!\rangle \blacklozenge \varphi$.

$$
\begin{aligned}
\varphi ::=\ & A & &\text{atomic prop., in } \mathcal{A} \\
\mid\ & \neg\varphi & & \\
\mid\ & \varphi \wedge \varphi & & \\
\mid\ & \Diamond\varphi & & \\
\mid\ & \Diamond_{\equiv v}\varphi & & \\
\mid\ & x + d_1 \leq y + d_2 & &\text{clock constraints} \\
\mid\ & x \cdot \varphi & &\text{freeze} \\
\mid\ & \langle\!\langle\mathfrak{P}\rangle\!\rangle \blacksquare \varphi & &\text{invariant} \\
\mid\ & \langle\!\langle\mathfrak{P}\rangle\!\rangle \varphi_1\ \mathcal{U}\ \varphi_2 & &\text{eventually}
\end{aligned}
$$

The semantics is again given as on any timed automaton game, by specifying when $l, t, \kappa \models \varphi$ holds for any configuration (l, κ) and time t. Recall that l is of the form

$(\rho, v, trg_\mathsf{I}, trg_\mathsf{A})$. We let $(\rho, v, trg_\mathsf{I}, trg_\mathsf{A}), t, \kappa \models A$ if and only if $\rho(A)$ is true. As in the modal logic of Section 3, we define $(\rho, v, trg_\mathsf{I}, trg_\mathsf{A}), t, \kappa \models \Diamond \varphi$ if and only if there is a vertex w in G such that $v \to w$ and $(\rho, w, trg_\mathsf{I}, trg_\mathsf{A}), t, \kappa \models \varphi$, and similarly for $\Diamond_\equiv, \neg, \wedge$. As in TATL, $l, t, \kappa \models x + d_1 \leq y + d_2$ if and only if $\kappa(x) + d_1 \leq \kappa(y) + d_2$, $l, t, \kappa \models x \cdot \varphi$ if and only if $l, \kappa[x \mapsto t] \models \varphi$. $\langle\!\langle \mathfrak{P} \rangle\!\rangle \blacksquare \varphi$ holds whenever the players in $\mathfrak{P}$ have a strategy so as to ensure that φ will hold at every instant in the future whatever the other players do. $\langle\!\langle \mathfrak{P} \rangle\!\rangle \varphi_1 \, \mathcal{U} \, \varphi_2$ holds whenever the players in $\mathfrak{P}$ have a strategy to ensure that φ_2 will eventually holds, and that φ_1 will hold at each time before that, whatever the other players do again. Moreover, a technical condition ensures that time diverges, so as to prevent a player from winning by stopping time for infinitely many (instantaneous) actions: see [9, Section 3.1] for details; we shall need to introduce it briefly as the winning condition $WC_\mathfrak{P}$ in the proof of Theorem 1 below.

TATL model-checking is decidable [9, Theorem 1], and EXPTIME-complete. It follows that model-checking anticipation games against TATL$\Diamond$ formulae is also decidable. The short argument is by noticing that any formula φ in our logic can be translated to an ordinary TATL formula φ_v^* such that $l, t, \kappa \models \varphi$ if and only if $l^*, t, \kappa \models \varphi_v^*$, where $l = (\rho, v, trg_\mathsf{I}, trg_\mathsf{A})$, and $l^* = (\rho, trg_\mathsf{I}, trg_\mathsf{A})$ is a location on a modified timed automaton game. The timed automaton game is given by a set of edges E^*, consisting of edges of the form $((\rho, trg_\mathsf{I}, trg_\mathsf{A}), \alpha, c, (\rho', trg_\mathsf{I}', trg_\mathsf{A}'), \lambda)$, where $((\rho, v, trg_\mathsf{I}, trg_\mathsf{A}), \alpha, c, (\rho', v, trg_\mathsf{I}', trg_\mathsf{A}'), \lambda)$ is an edge in E (for some v—we use the fact that the semantics actually does not depend on v). Translation φ to φ_v is essentially clear, e.g., $(\varphi_1 \wedge \varphi_2)_v^* = \varphi_1^* {}_v \wedge \varphi_2^* {}_v$, and similarly for all cases except when φ is of the form $\Diamond \varphi'$ or $\Diamond_\equiv \varphi'$. We then define $(\Diamond \varphi')_v^*$ as the disjunction over all w's such that $v \to w$ of φ'^*_w, and $(\Diamond_\equiv \varphi')_v^*$ as the disjunction over all w's such that $v \equiv w$ of φ'^*_w. We can refine this as follows.

Theorem 1. *Model-checking anticipation games against TATL$\Diamond$ formulae is EXPTIME-complete.*

Proof. Space does not permit us to include the algorithm in full. This is a combination of the above translation from TATL$\Diamond$ to TATL, and the TATL model-checking algorithm, whose details are sprinkled across [9,7,1]. Write $\langle\!\langle \mathfrak{P} \rangle\!\rangle$, $\blacksquare$ and $\blacklozenge$ the standard ATL* modalities. The latter two are usually written $\Box$ and $\Diamond$, but the latter should not be confused with our $\Diamond$, while the former is really the same as our $\blacksquare$.

Using [9, Lemma 1, 2], [7, Theorem 5], and [1, Section 3.2], we see that model-checking a TATL formula ϕ against a timed automaton game $\mathcal{T}$, i.e., checking whether $s \models_{td} \phi$, for some state s in $\mathcal{T}$, can be done in time $T = O((|Q| \cdot m! \cdot 2^m \cdot (2c + 1)^m \cdot h \cdot h_*)^{h_*+1})$, where Q is the set of locations in $\mathcal{T}$, m is the number of clock variables in $\mathcal{T}$ plus the number of freeze quantifiers in ϕ, c is the largest delay in $\mathcal{T}$ and in ϕ; finally, h is the number of states, and h_* is the order (i.e., half the number of possible priorities assigned to states) of a deterministic and total parity automaton H_{ϕ^Λ} computed from ϕ^Λ, where ϕ^Λ is itself obtained from ϕ by replacing each constraint α of the form $x + d_1 \leq y + d_2$ by a fresh atomic proposition p_α. By [7, Lemma 1], the values of h and h_* are polynomial in the size of ϕ. The (modified) timed automaton game $\mathcal{T}$ underlying a given anticipation game $\mathcal{G}$ has exactly as many clocks and the same upper bound c on clock values, but its number of locations is exponential, namely $|Q| = O(2^{|V| \cdot n} \cdot (r \cdot |V|)^2)$, where $|V|$ is the number of vertices in the dependency graph

G, n is the number of atomic propositions in $\mathcal{A}$, and r is the number of rule names. This still makes the time T given above a single exponential expression. However, the translation from TATL$\lozenge$ to TATL above builds a TATL formula $\phi = \varphi_v^*$ of size exponential in that of φ: this makes h an exponential of the size of φ. On the other hand, h_* essentially counts the number of nested uses of a winning condition called WC$_1$ in [7], or in general WC$_{\mathfrak{P}}$, for $\mathfrak{P} \subseteq \{\mathsf{I}, \mathsf{A}\}$: fix three distinct new atomic propositions $tick$, bl_{I} and bl_{A}, let $bl_{\{\mathsf{I}\}} = bl_{\mathsf{I}}$, $bl_{\{\mathsf{A}\}} = bl_{\mathsf{A}}$, $bl_{\emptyset}$ be false and $bl_{\{\mathsf{I},\mathsf{A}\}}$ be true, then for every ATL* formula ψ, WC$_{\mathfrak{P}}(\psi) = (\blacksquare\blacklozenge tick \Rightarrow \psi) \wedge (\blacklozenge\blacksquare\neg tick \Rightarrow \blacklozenge\blacksquare\neg bl_{\mathfrak{P}})$ states (informally) that either time diverges (we get infinitely many ticks) and ψ holds, or time is bounded (we only get finitely many ticks) and somebody from $\mathfrak{P}$ can be blamed for blocking time by triggering infinitely many (zero delay) actions. By [7, Lemma 1], the h_* value of a formula of the form WC$_{\mathfrak{P}}(\psi)$ is one plus that of ψ. The h_* value of a clock variable free TATL formula ϕ^Λ (gotten from a TATL formula ϕ in [9, Lemma 2]) is given through that of the ATL* formula $\psi = \mathsf{atlstar}(\phi)$ described in [9, Lemma 1]. It turns out that the crucial cases of the atlstar translation are $\mathsf{atlstar}(\langle\!\langle\mathfrak{P}\rangle\!\rangle\blacksquare\phi_1) = \langle\!\langle\mathfrak{P}\rangle\!\rangle(\mathrm{WC}_{\mathfrak{P}}(\blacksquare\mathsf{atlstar}(\phi_1)))$ and $\langle\!\langle\mathfrak{P}\rangle\!\rangle\phi_1 \, \mathcal{U} \, \phi_2 = \langle\!\langle\mathfrak{P}\rangle\!\rangle\mathrm{WC}_{\mathfrak{P}}(\mathsf{atlstar}(\phi_1) \, \mathcal{U} \, \mathsf{atlstar}(\phi_2))$, and no other case introduces a $\blacksquare$ or $\blacklozenge$ modality. So the h^* value of ϕ^Λ, or of ϕ for that matter, is exactly the nesting depth of game quantifiers in ϕ. In our translation $\phi = \varphi_v^*$, and although ϕ is exponentially larger than φ, the nesting depth of game quantifiers remains the same. So the time T is an exponential of the size of φ and the size of the given anticipation game.

EXPTIME-hardness does *not* follow from the EXPTIME-hardness of TATL model-checking, contrarily to e.g., [9, Theorem 1]: in this work, it is crucial to be able impose guards of the form $x = d$ in the automaton (where x is a clock), while we only have guards of the form $x \geq d$. EXPTIME-hardness will follow from the fact that the modal formulae can represent sets of environments in a concise way instead. To show this, we directly encore the reachability problem for alternating polynomial space Turing machines $\mathcal{M}$. Without loss of generality, we shall assume that $\mathcal{M}$ strictly alternates between $\forall$ and $\exists$ states, where $\exists$ states lead to acceptance if and only if some successor leads to acceptance, and $\forall$ states are those that lead to acceptance iff all of their successors lead to acceptance.

Let n be the size of the input, $p(n)$ the (polynomial) space available to $\mathcal{M}$. We represent IDs of $\mathcal{M}$ (tape contents, control state, head position) using $O(p(n))$ many atomic propositions A_i, one for each bit of the ID. We assume the head position is represented by $O(p(n))$ propositions of which exactly one will be true. We also assume a proposition accept that is true in exactly the accepting states. Build the (trivial) dependency graph G with exactly one vertex and no transition: on G, each variable is either true or false (at the unique vertex). For each transition $(q, \alpha, q', \alpha', dir)$ of $\mathcal{M}$ (from state q reading letter α, go to state q' while writing α' under the head and move the head in direction $dir \in \{-1, 0, 1\}$), write $O(p(n))$ rules, one for each possible position k of the head. If q is an $\exists$ state, the rules are of the form $\mathbf{Pre} \, F_{k,q,\alpha} \xrightarrow{1,\mathsf{l},a} P_{k,q',\alpha',dir}$ where $F_{k,q,\alpha}$ is a formula built on the A_i's that tests whether the head is at position exactly k, whether the state is exactly q, and whether the letter under the head is exactly α; and where $P_{k,q',\alpha',dir}$ sets and resets bits so as to write α' under the head, change the control state to q', and change the position of the head. If q is a $\forall$ state, the rules are of a similar form $\mathbf{Pre}\ F_{k,q,\alpha} \longrightarrow^{1,A,a} P_{k,q',\alpha',dir}$ (this time with A playing), and we require an additional *rush* rule $\mathbf{Pre}\ F_{k,q,\alpha} \longrightarrow^{2,l,a}$ accept $\leftarrow \top$ (played by l, but requiring 2 time units instead of 1). We then model-check this against the formula $F = \langle\!\langle l \rangle\!\rangle \blacklozenge$accept, starting from the initial location that codes the input to $\mathcal{M}$.

If $\mathcal{M}$ accepts, then there is an (untimed) strategy that chooses transitions from $\exists$ states such that whatever transition is picked from $\forall$ states, some accepting state is eventually reached. This transfers directly to a strategy for l against A in the anticipation game—in the case of $\exists$ states. For $\forall$ states q, the argument is slightly more subtle: without rhe rush rule, A may simulate taking any of the transitions from q, but may also decide to wait and never take any transition. Instead, we insist that l's strategy be to launch the rush rule, so that if A waits for more than 2 times units, then the rush rule completes and a location is reached where accept is true. (A is in a *rush* to take a transition.) In any case, F holds.

Conversely, if F holds, then there is a strategy for l that eventually will set accept to true, whatever A does. In $\forall$ states, note that A can always complete one of the non-rush rules in 1 time unit (which is less than the time needed by l to complete a rush rule), so that rush rules play no role. Note in particular that, because $\exists$ and $\forall$ states alternate in $\mathcal{M}$, and because our rules always check for being in the right state q in their precondition, no rush rule can have remained dangling, waiting since a previous $\forall$ state was reached: once a non-rush rule is taken, the precondition for the rush rule if any becomes false, and the trg_l field in the corresponding timed automaton game is reset to $\bot$. Clearly, this strategy of l leads to a strategy for picking transitions from $\exists$ states in $\mathcal{M}$ that will lead to acceptance whichever transitions are picked from $\forall$ states. $\qquad\square$

We finish this section by giving a few examples of properties that can be expressed in TATL$\Diamond$. Call *intrusion survivability* the property $\langle\!\langle A \rangle\!\rangle\blacksquare\Diamond_\equiv\neg$Compr, stating that there is a way for the administrator to make sure that any vertex is always backed up by an equivalent one, whatever the malevolent l does. Similarly, the *n-survivability property* $\langle\!\langle A \rangle\!\rangle\blacksquare\Diamond_\equiv$Avail states that each vertex is backed up by at least one available equivalent vertex. This is typically the property we would have desired of the Bouygues servers mentioned in the introduction. The following SLA property:

$$\langle\!\langle A \rangle\!\rangle\blacksquare x \cdot \neg\Diamond_\equiv\mathsf{Avail} \Rightarrow [\langle\!\langle A \rangle\!\rangle\blacklozenge y \cdot y \leq x + d \wedge \langle\!\langle A \rangle\!\rangle\blacksquare z \cdot z \leq y + d' \Rightarrow \Diamond_\equiv\mathsf{Avail}]$$

is one way to model the so-called *Service Level Agreement* property, which in a sense bounds service downtime. This is usually described informally by requiring the system, e.g., "not to suffer more than 5 min. of downtime per year". Formally, we cannot express this in TATL$\Diamond$, but this would also be meaningless: suffering from 1 ms. of downtime every minute would in principle account for 8.76 minutes of downtime a year, thus violating the specification, but would hardly be noticed. Instead, SLA specifies that whenever a service fails and has no equivalent backup, then the administrator should have a way to get one of the backups up again in time at most d (where d is typically small), so that it or an equivalent vertex remains up for at least d' time units (where d' is usually large).

5 An Anticipation Game for the Redundant Server Example

Let us illustrate anticipation games on the example of Section 2. This will have the virtue of illustrating what the element of surprise is all about in our context.

To model the fact that *index.php[1]:2* is synced with *index.php[1]:2*, we add a Synced variable which is true of just *index.php[1]:2* (and will never be modified). We model the system using rules $Comp_1$ (with delay $\Delta = 5$—delays are given for indication purposes only), $CServProp_1$ (delay 5), Deny (delay 20), Allow (delay 20), OReco (delay 30), Patch (delay 300), plus the following rules:

$$CFilePropNS : \quad Pre \ \Diamond Compr \wedge Avail \wedge File \wedge \neg Sync \wedge \neg Crypt \longrightarrow^{5,I,a} Compr \leftarrow \top$$
$$CFileSynProp : \quad Pre \ \Diamond Compr \wedge Avail \wedge File \wedge Sync \wedge \neg Crypt \longrightarrow^{300,I,a} Compr \leftarrow \top$$

$CFilePropNS$ is a variant on $CFileProp_1$, which only fires on non-synced files. The $CFileSynProp$ rule states that the replication of *index.php[1]:1* to *index.php[1]:2* is done on a regular basis, and we assume that this implies that compromising the first makes the second compromised only 300 time units later.

One Player Intrusion Scenario. We first examine the case where no administrator rule is present, i.e., we don't consider rules Deny, Allow, OReco, or Patch. Accordingly, I plays alone, and it is then not surprising that intrusion survivability fails at vertex *HTTP[1]*. The necessary intrusion steps are summarized in Figure 2.

Step	z	Rule	Node
1	5	$Comp_1$	*FTP[1]*
2	5	$CFilePropNS$	*index.php[1]:1*
3	5	$CServProp_1$	*HTTP[1]:1*
4	300	$CFileSynProp$	*index.php[1]:2*
5	5	$CServProp_1$	*HTTP[1]:2*

Fig. 2. Intrusion Single Player Example

In *Step 1*, the intruder I exploits the vulnerability present in the FTP server which is publicly available. Exploiting the vulnerability takes 5 seconds. Once I gets a remote shell, he alters the *index.php[1]:1* file, in *Step 2*, to add a code that will be used to exploit the remote vulnerability present in the *HTTP[1]:1* server. This action requires 5 seconds. This is accomplished in *Step 3* in 5 seconds. Then in Step 4, I waits 300 seconds until the changes done on *index.php[1]:1* are replicated to *index.php[1]:2*. Finally in *Step 5* the second HTTP server *HTTP[1]:2* is compromised, violating survivability for *HTTP[1]*.

Two Player Intrusion Scenario. In the general case, where both I and A play, administrator intervention can counter the above intrusion. This example displays the race that takes place between the incident player I and the administrator A. Figure 3 summarizes the actions taken by I (columns 3–5) and by A (columns 6–8). We indicate by an $\Rightarrow$ sign which action is chosen; remember that this is how the element of surprise is implemented in anticipation games: the fastest player wins. The z_I column gives the value of I's clock at the end of the considered action, z_A is A's clock, and z is the global clock. The format of the z_I and z_A columns is given as t/Δ, where t is the value of the clock at the end of the turn, and Δ is the least execution time of the action.

At each turn, if player p loses (no $\Rightarrow$ sign in the corresponding row), this does not mean that the action a that p was currently trying to do is stopped. Instead, the action continues to progress, because the precondition for a remains true despite changes done

Step	z	rule	node	z_I	z_A	rule	node
1	5	$\Rightarrow$ Comp$_1$	*FTP[1]*	5/5	5/20	Deny	*FTP[1]*
2	10	$\Rightarrow$ CFilePropNS	*index.php[1]:1*	5/5	10/20	Deny	*FTP[1]*
3	15	$\Rightarrow$ CServProp$_1$	*HTTP[1]:1*	5/5	15/20	Deny	*FTP[1]*
4	20	CFileSynProp	*index.php[1]:2*	5/300	20/20	$\Rightarrow$ Deny	*FTP[1]*
5	40	CFileSynProp	*index.php[1]:2*	25/300	20/20	$\Rightarrow$ Deny	*HTTP[1]:1*
6	70	CFileSynProp	*index.php[1]:2*	55/300	30/30	$\Rightarrow$ OReco	*FTP[1]*
7	100	CFileSynProp	*index.php[1]:2*	85/300	30/30	$\Rightarrow$ OReco	*index.php[1]:1*
8	130	(*)CFileSynProp	*index.php[1]:2*	115/300	30/30	$\Rightarrow$ OReco	*HTTP[1]:1*
9	315	(*)CFileSynProp	*index.php[1]:2*	300/300	185/300	$\Rightarrow$ Patch	*FTP[1]*
10	430	$\bot$	-	-	300/300	$\Rightarrow$ Patch	*FTP[1]*
11	730	$\bot$	-	-	300/300	$\Rightarrow$ Patch	*HTTP[1]:1*
12	750	$\bot$	-	-	20/20	$\Rightarrow$ Allow	*HTTP[1]:1*
13	780	$\bot$	-	-	20/20	$\Rightarrow$ Allow	*FTP[1]*

Fig. 3. Intrusion Two Player Example

by the other player. For example, in *steps 1, 2, 3, 4*, A is attempting to deny access to the FTP server by triggering rule Deny on *FTP[1]*. This takes 20 seconds, so this is too slow to complete at the end of *steps 1, 2,* or *3*. At each of these first three steps, I wins the turn, but the Deny action by A remains current.

The first three steps are identical to the one-player case, as I was faster. But at *step 4*, A is finally able to deny access to the FTP server, since the intruder must wait until the *index.php[1]:1* file is replicated to *index.php[1]:2*. This requires 300 seconds. Now A is faster, since she only needs 5 (remaining) seconds to complete the Deny action. During the 300 seconds required by replication, A performs *steps 4* through *8*. At *step 5*, she denies access to *HTTP[1]:1*. At *step 6*, she recovers *FTP[1]*. At *step 7*, she recovers *index[1]:1*, and finally at *step 8*, she recovers *HTTP[1]:1*. At this point (*step 9*), the file *index.php[1]:2* could have been compromised because the time required for file replication is shorter than the one needed to patch *FTP[1]*. However, since the administrator was able to recover *index.php[1]:1*, before the replication occurs (*step 6*), the precondition of the CFileSynProp rule is false, so I's CFileSynProp rule cannot fire—which we materialize in the table by a (*) sign. Again, this is the element of surprise that allows us to model such a crucial behaviour.

From this point on, I can only let time pass. A safely finishes to secure her network from *step 9* to *step 13*. Note that if the administrator had chosen to patch before denying access to servers, she would have lost.

6 Conclusion

We have presented a framework to evaluate the resilience of computer networks in the face of incidents, i.e., attacks from malicious intruders as well as random faults. Our model uses a two-layered presentation of *dependencies* between files and services, and of *timed games* to represent not just incidents, but also the dynamic responses from administrators and their respective delays. We have introduced a variant TATL$\Diamond$ of timed alternating-time temporal logic, as a convenient language to express several desirable properties of networks, including survivability and service level agreement. We have illustrated this on a simple redundant Web service architecture. Despite the fact that dependency graphs are exponentially more succinct than timed automaton games and TATL◊ expand to TATL formulae of exponential size, we have shown that model-checking dependency graphs against TATL◊ formulae is no more complex that model-checking timed automaton games against TATL formulae, i.e., EXPTIME-complete.

References

1. Alur, R., Henzinger, T.A., Kupferman, O.: Alternating-time temporal logic. J. ACM 49(5), 672–713 (2002)
2. Artz, M.: NetSPA : a Network Security Planning Architecture. PhD thesis, Massachusetts Institute of Technology. Dept. of Electrical Engineering and Computer Science (2002)
3. Balthrop, J., Forrest, S., Newman, M.E.J., Williamson, M.M.: Technological networks and the spread of computer viruses. science 304(23) (2004)
4. Brihaye, T., Henzinger, T.A., Raskin, J., Prabhu, V.: Minimum-time reachability in timed games. In: Asarin, E., Bouyer, P. (eds.) FORMATS 2006. LNCS, vol. 4202, Springer, Heidelberg (2006)
5. Church, A.: logic, arithmetics and automata. In: Congress of Mathematician, Institut Mittag-Leffler, pp. 23–35 (1962)
6. Colizza, V., Barrat, A., Barthelemy, M., Vespignani, A.: The modeling of global epidemics: stochastic dynamics and predictability. Bulletin of Mathematical Biology 68, 1893–1921 (2006)
7. de Alfaro, L., Faella, M., Henzinger, T., Majumdar, R., Stoelinga, M.: The element of surprise in timed games. In: Amadio, R.M., Lugiez, D. (eds.) CONCUR 2003. LNCS, vol. 2761, Springer, Heidelberg (2003)
8. du net, J.: Bouygues telecom privé de réseau (2004)
9. Henzinger, T., Prabhu, V.: Timed alternating-time temporal logic. In: Asarin, E., Bouyer, P. (eds.) FORMATS 2006. LNCS, vol. 4202, pp. 1–18. Springer, Heidelberg (2006)
10. ICANN. Dns attack factsheet. Technical report, ICANN (March 2007)
11. Jajodia, S.: Topological analysis of network attack vulnerability. In: ASIACCS 2007. Proceedings of the 2nd ACM symposium on Information, computer and communications security, Singapore, p. 2. ACM Press, New York (2007)
12. Jha, S., Sheyner, O., Wing, J.: Two formal analysis of attack graphs. In: CSFW 2002. Proceedings of the 15th IEEE Computer Security Foundations Workshop, Washington, DC, USA, p. 49. IEEE Computer Society Press, Los Alamitos (2002)
13. Klensin, J.: Rfc 2821 - simple mail transfer protocol. Technical report, IETF Network Working Group (2001)
14. Lippmann, R., Webster, S., Stetson, D.: The effect of identifying vulnerabilities and patching software on the utility of network intrusion detection. In: Wespi, A., Vigna, G., Deri, L. (eds.) RAID 2002. LNCS, vol. 2516, Springer, Heidelberg (2002)
15. Maler, O., Pnueli, A., Sifakis, J.: On the synthesis of discrete controllers for timed systems (extended abstract). In: STACS 1995, pp. 229–242 (1995)
16. Pnueli, A., Rosner, R.: On the synthesis of a reactive module. In: POPL 1989. Proceedings of the 16th ACM SIGPLAN-SIGACT symposium on Principles of programming languages, Austin, Texas, United States, pp. 179–190. ACM Press, New York (1989)

17. Ritchey, R.W., Ammann, P.: Using model checking to analyze network vulnerabilities. In: SP 2000. Proceedings of the 2000 IEEE Symposium on Security and Privacy, Washington, DC, USA, p. 156. IEEE Computer Society Press, Los Alamitos (2000)
18. Saffre, F., Halloy, J., Deneubourg, J.L.: The ecology of the grid. In: ICAC 2005. Proceedings of the Second International Conference on Automatic Computing, Washington, DC, USA, pp. 378–379. IEEE Computer Society Press, Los Alamitos (2005)
19. Schneier, B.: Attack trees: Modeling security threats. Dr. Dobb?s journal (December 1999)
20. Schneier, B.: Secrets & Lies: Digital Security in a Networked World. Wiley, Chichester (2000)
21. Williamson, M.M.: Throttling viruses: Restricting propagation to defeat malicious mobile code. acsac 00: 61 (2002)

Masquerade Detection Based Upon GUI User Profiling in Linux Systems

Wilson Naik Bhukya, Suneel Kumar Kommuru, and Atul Negi

Department of Computer & Information Sciences,
University of Hyderabad, Hyderabad, India
naikcs@uohyd.ernet.in, suneel.kommuru@gmail.com,
atulcs@uohyd.ernet.in
http://dcis.uohyd.ernet.in

Abstract. Masquerading or impersonation attack refers to the act of gaining access to confidential data or greater access privileges, while pretending to be legitimate users. Detection of masquerade attacks is of great importance and is a non-trivial task of system security. Detection of these attacks is done by monitoring significant changes in user's behavior based on his/her computer usage. Traditional detection mechanisms are based on command line system events collected using log files. In a GUI based system, most of the user activities are performed using either mouse movements and clicks or a combination of mouse movements and keystrokes. The command line data cannot capture the complete GUI event behavior of the users hence it is insufficient to detect attacks in GUI based systems. Presently, there is no frame work available to capture the GUI based user behavior in Linux systems. We are proposing a novel approach to capture the GUI based user behavior for Linux systems using our event logging tool. Our experimentation results shows that, the GUI based user behavior can be efficiently used for masquerade attack detection to achieve high detection rates with less false positives. We have applied One-class SVM on the collected data, which requires only training the user's own legitimate sessions to build up the user's profile. Our results on GUI data using One-class SVM gives higher detection rates with less false positives compared to a Two-class SVM approach.

Keywords: GUI based Profiling, Mouse events, Masquerade detection, Intrusion detection, Anomaly detection, One-class SVM, KDE, Linux Profiling.

1   Introduction

Masquerade attacks are among the most dangerous attacks posed to information systems today, not merely because they are so difficult to detect, but also because they have the ability to undermine some of the most advanced information security technologies available. In traditional masquerade attack, an attacker takes over the account of legitimate user to utilize the privileges and rights to carry out the malicious agenda. In a slight variant of masquerade attack known as insider

I. Cervesato (Ed.): ASIAN 2007, LNCS 4846, pp. 228–239, 2007.

attack, a legitimate user chooses to use legitimate user privileges for malicious or unauthorized purposes [5].

When an insider masquerades another person inside the organization most of his actions may be technically legal for the system and hence it is more difficult to detect such violations. Also, insider has enough knowledge about the system as well as the behavior of the victims so that he can escape detection for a longer period of time. The only information, which can be used to detect masquerade attacks is contained in the actions a masquerader performs. This set of actions is known as behavioral profile. Masquerade detection techniques are based on the premise that when a masquerader attacks the system, he will sufficiently deviate from the users behavior and thus be caught [1].

To be able to make a distinction between normal and malicious behavior, these detection systems collect and utilize data form user sessions to build user profiles. The user profiles can be build using command line sequences or GUI events captured for the particular user or by using both. This data is initially used to train the detection systems about what is normal, and later for detecting malicious activity. There have been several attempts by Schonalu [10] and other researchers to tackle the problem of detecting masqueraders using several techniques on same data set (SEA) [25][6][11][12] [27][29] that was created using Unix *acct* utility, which records users commands. These command sequences are then used to build the user profiles and detect their normal and abnormal behavior. There have been attempts to capture the user profiles using process table details and GUI event details for Windows Operating Systems [3][1][7]. However, little work has been done so far for capturing GUI user profile of Linux and other Unix variants, although these are widely used. Moreover, there are no data sets available for GUI events for these Operating Systems. This motivated us to work in this direction. In this paper, we have developed a Linux GUI event logger and used it for masquerade detection. Our main aim was to detect user abnormal deviation from users normal profile, rather than to know how user tried to deviate from his normal profile, therefore only binary classifier has been used to check the normal and abnormal user activities . We have used One-class SVM to build self profile with users legitimate sessions and detect masquerader when significant deviation occurs. Though One-Class SVM has been proven [2][13] best for binary classification, for comparison purpose we have also experimented with Two-class SVM, which is similar to the signature based detection system.

This paper is organized as follows: In section 2, we have discussed background and related work. In section 3, we described event logging and feature extraction. Section 4 describes our experimental setup. Results are presented in section 5. Finally, section 6 outlines conclusions and future work.

2   Background and Related Work

2.1   Detection Mechanisms Based on Command Line Data

There has been many techniques to tackle the problem of anomaly detection [28][16][18] [8][9][5] and masquerade detection using Unix commands collected at command line. Schonlau et al. [25] collected Unix command line data of 50 users for testing and comparing masquerade attack detection mechanisms [25][6][11][12][27][29]. In another work, Schonlau et al. [10] utilized various statistical techniques ("Uniqueness", "Bayes onestep Markov", "Hybrid multi-step Markov", "Compression", "IPAM" and "Sequence Match") and for evaluating their effectiveness in masquerade detection using above data. Naive Bayes Classifier was used by Maxion et al. [11] on a truncated user command dataset. They provide results to prove that their technique improves detection significantly giving very low false positives. In a later work [12] they claim that enriched command dataset results in a better detection accuracy. The disadvantage of above methods is that, they are not able to capture the user interactions, which could be the main discriminating factor for masquerade detection.

Li and Manikopoulos [3] investigated on Windows system users, utilizing real network data. This work primarily focuses on One-class support vector machine(SVM) masquerade detection. Their capturing procedure depends mainly on windows opened by the user and different process information and not on the user interactions.

However, these detection mechanisms are not able to accurately represent the behavioral profiles of users working on modern graphical user interface (GUI) systems such as Microsoft Windows and Linux. This is due to fact that in GUI based systems most of the actions are carried out by using either mouse movement and clicks or combination of mouse movements and key strokes. The command line data can not capture the complete GUI event behavior of the users. Hence command line data is insufficient to detect attacks in GUI based systems.

2.2   Masquerade Detection Based on GUI Data

Pausra and Brodley [7] focused on use of mouse while browsing the web pages in a browser, considering only mouse movements. This approach can be disadvantageous if a user uses an application other than the browser. The GUI based user behavior includes number of mouse clicks, mouse movements, mouse speed, keys pressed etc. This GUI behavior can be used for masquerade attack detection. For this purpose, Garg and Kwait [1] developed an active system logger using Microsoft .NET framework and C# language on Windows XP System. GUI event data is captured from users and useful parameters are extracted to construct the feature vectors. This profiling method was good to capture the user behavioral data. The disadvantage of this approach is that, they implemented it only for Microsoft GUI systems with much focus only on mouse usage. Their methodology is not scalable to Unix variants like(Linux, Sun and MacOS) GUI systems. Moreover, their detection rate was not impressive, since they used Two-class SVM approach with 16 features, which requires more training time, as they need to train both the positive and negative(illegitimate sessions).

2.3   Masquerade Detection Based on GUI Usage Analysis

The work of Imsand and John [4] is based on the notion of how the current user interacts with the graphical user interface. This method does not use mouse movements or keystroke dynamics, rather profiles how the user manipulates the windows, icons, menus, and pointers that comprise a graphical user interface.

This method has a number of disadvantages. Most of the user profiling seems to be manual then an automated process. This methodology is application specific rather than capturing overall system events and is not generalized for all users. The method of training the system is biased and it is much like a manual survey of the different users, which is very difficult in real world scenario. The use of time factor is not stated clearly in their work. The authors do not appear to consider time as a factor, which is crucial for intrusion analysis.

3   Proposed Method

We have proposed a novel approach to capture the GUI based user behavior for Linux Systems. This behavior includes amount of mouse clicks, different attributes of clicks like, which button was pressed, co-ordinates of mouse, different mouse movements, wheel rotations (horizontal or vertical), and keys pressed during a user session. As there are no publicly available GUI data sets, we have developed a logging tool to collect the GUI event details of KDE (K Desktop Environment). We have collected data from 8 different users in our lab using this tool. Our experimentation results shows that the GUI based behavior can be efficiently used for masquerade attack detection to achieve high detection rates with less false positives.

3.1   KDE Application Structure and Event Capturing

KDE or the K Desktop Environment, is a network transparent contemporary desktop environment for UNIX workstations. KDE seeks to fulfill the need for an easy to use desktop for UNIX workstations, similar to desktop environments found on Macintosh and Microsoft Windows operating systems. Figure 1 shows the architecture of a typical KDE application. *KApplication* is a class that provides low-level KDE application services, and *KTMainWindow* serves as a programmer-friendly base class for our main application window, *KMyMainWindow*. The classes *KMenuBar*, *KToolBar*, and *KStatusBar* are created, positioned, and resized by *KTMainWindow*, but we can customize them from within *KMyMainWindow* [26].

Widgets are graphical user-interface elements. Simple widgets can be controls or indicators such as a push button or a text label. In KDE, widgets are implemented using C++ classes. Usually there is a One-to-one widget-to-class correspondence. For example, a pushbutton is implemented by *QPushButton*. All widgets are ultimately derived from the *QWidget* base class. All these widgets ultimately interact with the user through the class *KApplication*. *KApplication* dispatches event messages that signal, for example, keypresses or mouse clicks to all the widgets used by an application. *KApplication* receives messages from X, the underlying windowing system, and distributes them to the widgets in your application.

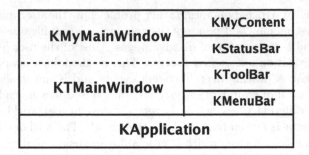

Fig. 1. KDE Application Structure

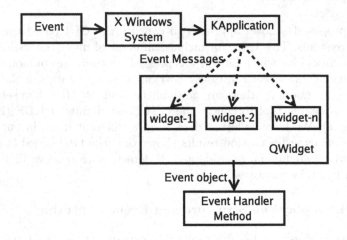

Fig. 2. Event capturing

System Events. Window system events tell the widget when it needs to re-paint, reposition, or resize itself, when mouse clicks or keystrokes have been directed toward that widget, when the widget receives or loses the focus, and so on. *QWidget* handles the events by calling a virtual method for each event. Each method get passed, as an argument, a class containing information about the event. To handle the event, the corresponding method must be reimplemented in the subclass of *QWidget*. Figure 2 shows the event capturing procedure.

3.2   Experimental Setup

Data Collection. We have collected real user behavior data for multiple users and extracted unique parameters to be able to construct the feature vectors. For this purpose, we have developed an *active event logger* for KDE (K Desktop Environment) in Linux. KDE is one of most powerful desktop environments for Linux. This logger is designed such that it is able to collect system events due to all possible user activities on the system. The logger collects events such as keyboard activity, mouse movement coordinates and mouse clicks, keyboard shortcuts, and wheel rotations.

All the GUI event details were logged to log file. Event details include name of the event, time of event occurrence, and different attributes of the event. The following are the some of the event details from the log file:

User Session Started ....
Event Occurred at:Fri Apr 6 23:34:49 2007
Event :: Mouse Cursor entered the Window
Event Occurred at:Fri Apr 6 23:34:53 2007
Event :: Mouse clicked
Window Coordinates:27 39
Global Coordinates:132 163
Button Pressed : Left
Key Board Shortcut : Alt+c

Feature Extraction. After collecting the real user data, we have extracted useful and unique parameters of the user behavior to be able to construct unique feature vectors for training and testing with SVM [1]. We have developed our own feature extraction engine to parse the logged data. We have extracted the following unique features from that of [1]
:

Mouse Clicks (lc, rc, dc): the average number of left, right, and double mouse clicks per user session as well as activity for each 10 minute window during the session.

Mouse Enter and Exit (en,ex): the average number of mouse entrance and exits in to the window per user session.

Wheel Rotations (wh, wv): the average number of horizontal and vertical wheel rotations per user session.

Key Pressed (kp): the average number of keys pressed per user session.

Keyboard shortcuts used (ks): the average number of keyboard shortcuts per user session.

Taking above features we have constructed the feature vectors for all the users.

Calculation of Features. Moreover, we have constructed 18 features for every user after extracting parameters as described in previous section. They are :
Mouse Clicks: *(lc,rc,dc)* = 3
Mouse Enter and Exit : *(en,ex)* = 2
Wheel Rotations : *(wh,wv)* = 2
Key Pressed : *(kp)* = 1
Keyboard shortcuts used: *(ks)*=1
The total of these raw features is 9. Additionally, we calculated the mean *'m'* and standard deviation *'sd'* for all the raw features above. This gives a total of 18 unique features represented as:
(lc,rc,dc,en,ex,wh,wv,kp,ks) * *(m,sd)*

we have applied sliding window technique on these features to generate the tuples. These tuples are given as input to the SVM [1], as SVMs have been known to be highly effective in text classification [21],[22].

4 Applying One-Class Masquerade Detection

In the previous section, we have used a Two-class SVM for which both the positive and negative training is required. To improve the detection rates, we have also applied *One-class Masquerade Detection*. One-class SVM requires only the user's legitimate sessions training to build up the user's profile and not the illegitimate sessions [2][13]. Therefore, when only user's legitimate sessions are available, one class training is the only viable approach.

4.1 Experimental Setup

Our main aim is to detect masquerades and for that we have checked that new sessions does or doesn't belongs to the real user (a "Positive" or "Negative"). We have used one target user's some sessions as "positive data" to train a One-class SVM without any negative training data. We have used remaining sessions of that user for testing purpose. For each target user (User A, User B, User C, User D, ...), a set of the sessions from the target user are trained as positive with out any negative training. Then the remaining sessions from the target user are used for testing with each other user's sessions as negative.

We have used the data set from 8 user's for this One-class SVM approach. User A (10 sessions), User B (8 Sessions), User C (9 sessions), User D (8 sessions), User E (6 sessions), User F (7 sessions), User G (6 sessions), User H (8 sessions)

5 Results and Discussion

We have collected data from 8 different users in our lab using the logging tool. This data was fed to the parsing engine, as described to obtain 18 features. These features were used to create tuples for providing input to the SVMs. The methodology to train and test the system was as follows:

- Data sets were obtained for four distinct users A(10 sessions), B(8 sessions), C(9 sessions), and D(8 sessions).
- The obtained data was split for training and testing as follows:
- Used the sliding window technique to generate feature vectors
- Used training and testing sets for SVM as described in previous section and calculated detection rates and false positives
- We have used SVM lite software, which implements Vapiniks Support vector machine[22].

We have calculated classification results and detection rates for four users. The results from this test are shown below.

Table 1. Training and Testing sessions

User	Training sessions	Testing sessions
A	5	5
B	4	4
C	5	4
D	4	4

Table 2. Result for Two Users

No.of Features	DR	FPR
8	85.57%	2.93%
9	85.57%	2.93%
10	85.57%	2.93%
16	85.09%	3.42%

We have compared our results with the previous work done in Microsoft Windows environment [3]. For 3 users and 8 features, their detection rate is 73.85% and false positive rate is 26.15% . For the same number of users(3) and features(8) $lc, rc, dc, en, ex, wh, wv, kp$ we obtained 86% detection rate and 2.23% false positive rate and 11.77% false negative rate. We have achieved comparatively, higher detection rates with a very low false positive rate for less number of features(8).

5.1   One-Class SVM Results

We have used the data set from 8 user's for this One-class SVM approach. User A (10 sessions), User B (8 Sessions), User C (9 sessions), User D (8 sessions), User E (6 sessions), User F (7 sessions), User G (6 sessions), User H (8 sessions).

For each target user, we have trained the SVM using only the legitimate training sessions. Note that when only the user's own legitimate sessions are available, One-class training is the only viable approach [2][13].

For example, consider the training and testing strategy for User D. The User D is trained as positive. 4 positive sessions from User D are used for training and the remaining 4 positive sessions are tested with each other user's sessions as negative.

The average hit rate is 94.88% for User D using One-class SVM approach.

5.2   Comparing with Two-Class SVM Approach

The same data set (8 users) is tested with the Two-class SVM. In this approach, we have trained both the positive and negative samples and the results are compared with the One-class SVM approach.

The average hit rate is only 53.08%, compared to 94.88% of one-class approach. We observed that, we can obtain higher detection rates using One-class SVM approach compared to Two-class approach. Moreover, One-class approach

Table 3. Result for three Users

No.of Features	Users	DR	FPR
	A-B,C	85.6%	7.09%
	A-C,B	*86%*	*2.23%*
	B-C,A	80.32%	17.64%
8	A-B,C	85.6%	7.09%
	A,(B-C)	80.32%	7.09%
	B,(A-C)	86%	11.76%
	C,(A-B)	85.6%	7.3%
	A-B,C	84.79%	8.31%
16	A-C,B	84.99%	3.04%
	B-C,A	78.3%	17.64%

Table 4. Result of One-class SVM for User-D

User	Hits(%)	FPR
User E	97.24%	2.75%
User F	95.00%	5.00%
User G	94.87%	5.12%
User H	92.42%	7.8%
Average	94.88%	5.16%

Table 5. Result of Two-class SVM for User-D

User	Hits(%)	FPR
User E	56.86%	8.49%
User F	52.48%	0.00%
User G	60.38%	0.00%
User H	42.61%	28.87%
Average	53.08%	9.34%

requires less training data because there is no need of training the masquerade sessions (illegitimate sessions).

5.3 ROC Scores for Different Users

To compare the performance of detection for different users, we have computed the ROC score for each user. The ROC score is the fraction of area under ROC curves. The larger the score, the better. An ROC score of 1 means perfect detection without any false positives.

The figure 3 shows the ROC curve for User B using Two-class SVM to detect User C as Masquerader.

The following table 6 shows the ROC scores for different targets and masqueraders.

Table 6. ROC scores for different targets

User	User A	User B	User C	User D	Average
A	-	0.7190	0.4890	0.5010	0.5696
B	0.7192	-	0.9051	0.8642	0.8295
C	0.4890	0.9051	-	0.2665	0.5535
D	0.5010	0.8643	0.2665	-	0.5439

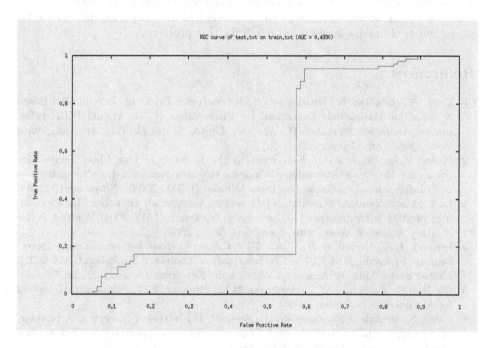

Fig. 3. ROC Score for User B(score=0.9051)

From the table 6, the ROC scores are in range from 0.2665 to 0.9051 when detecting different masqueraders from different targets. For example, ROC score for User B for identifying User C as masquerader is 0.9051.

6 Conclusions

We have designed and developed a new framework for capturing GUI based user behavior for Linux Systems. We have collected data from a Linux system using a logger developed for KDE(KDesktop Environment). After sanitizing this data to remove unnecessary or redundant information, we have used a parsing engine to extract parameters from this data. We have constructed feature vectors from these parameters and used support vector machine algorithms to first train and then classify the users using both One-class as well as Two-class SVMs. Our results demonstrate that One-class SVM is far better than Two-class SVM for this problem not only in terms of detection rates but also in terms of training and testing times.We have also computed ROC scores for different users from different targets. We have found that user behavior features based on mouse and keyboard activities on a GUI based system can be effectively used to uniquely identify users and thus provide better masquerade detection capability.

As part of our future work, we plan to generalize the event capturing for all the GUI applications. We would also like to test our system with more users and more features as the data becomes available. We have also observed that different events across the system can be arranged in various layers . There for we intend to develop a layered approach for this problem.

References

1. Garg, A., Rahalkar, R., Upadhyaya, S.: Kevin Kwait Profiling Users in GUI Based Systems for Masquerade Detection. In: Proceedings of 7th Annual IEEE Information Assurance Workshop (IAW 2006), United States Military Academy, West Point, New York (June 21-23, 2006)
2. Heller, K.A., Svore, K.M., Keromytis, A.D., Stolfo, S.J.: One Class Vector Machines for Detecting Anomalous Windows Registry Accesses. In: Proceedings of 2003 International conference on Data Mining- (ICDM 2003) (November19, 2003)
3. Li, L., Manikopoulos.: Windows NT One-class Masquerade Detection. In: Proceedings of 2004 IEEE,Information Assurance Workshop (IAW 2004), United States Military Academy, West Point, New York (June 2004)
4. Imsand, E.S., Hamilton Jr., J.A.: GUI Usage Analysis for Masquerade Detection. In: Proceedings of 2007 IEEE, Information Assurance Workshop (IAW 2007), United States Military Academy, West Point, New York (June 21-23, 2007)
5. Coull, S.E., Branch, J.W., Szymanski, B.K., Breimer, E.A.: Sequence Alignment for Masquerade Detection (2006)
6. Coull, S., Branch, J., Szymanski, B., Breimer, E.: Intrusion detection: A bioinformatics approach. In: 19th Annual Computer Security Applications Conferences, Las Vegas, Nevada (December 8-12, 2003)
7. Pusara, M., Brodley, C.: User Re-authentication via mouse movements. In: Proceedings of the 2004 ACM workshop on visualization and data mining for computer security, Washington D.C., USA (October 29, 2004)
8. Lane, T., Brodley, C.E.: An Application of Machine Learning to Anomaly Detection. In: Proceedings of Twentieth National Information Systems Security Conference, vol. 1, (Gaithersburgh, MD), pp. 366–380. The National Institute of Standards and Technology and the National Computer Security Center (1997)
9. Lane, T., Brodley, C.: Sequence Matching and Learning in Anomaly Detection for Computer Security. In: Proceedings of AAAI-97 Workshop on AI Approaches to Fraud Detection and Risk Management, pp. 43–49 (1997)
10. Schonlau, M., DuMouchel, W., Ju, W.-H., Karr, A.F., M.T., Vardi, Y.: Computer Intrusion: Detecting Masquerades. Statistical Science 16, 58–74 (2001)
11. Maxion, R.A., Townsend, T.N.: Masquerade Detection Using Truncated Command Lines. In: Proceedings of International Conference on Dependable Systems and Networks (DSN 2002), pp. 219–228 (2002)
12. Maxion, R.A.: Masquerade Detection Using Enriched Command Lines. In: Proceedings of International Conference on Dependable Systems and Networks (DSN 2003), San Francisco, CA (June 2003)

13. Wang, K., Stolfo, S.J.: One Class Training for Masquerade Detection. In: ICDM Workshop on Data Mining for Computer Security (DMSEC 2003) (2003)
14. Monrose, F., Rubin, A.: Authentication via Keystroke Dynamics. In: ACM Conference on Computer and Communications Security, pp. 48–56 (1997)
15. Pusara, M., Brodley, C.E.: User re-authentication via mouse movements. In: VizSEC/DMSEC 2004: Proceedings of the 2004 ACM workshop on Visualization and data mining for computer security, Washington DC, USA, pp. 1–8 (2004)
16. Hofmeyr, S., Forrest, S., Somayaji, A.: Intrusion Detection Using Sequences of System Calls. Journal of Computer Security 6(3), 151–180 (1998)
17. Forrest, S., Hofmeyr, S.A., Somayaji, A.: Computer Immunology. Communications of the ACM 40(10), 88–96 (1997)
18. Warrender, C., Forrest, S., Pearlmutter, B.: Detecting Intrusions using System Calls: Alternative Data Models. In: IEEE Symposium on Security and Privacy, Oakland, CA, pp. 133–145 (1999)
19. Wespi, A., Dacier, M., Debar, H.: Intrusion Detection Using Variable-Length Audit Trail Patterns, In Recent Advances in Intrusion Detection. In: Debar, H., Mé, L., Wu, S.F. (eds.) RAID 2000. LNCS, vol. 1907, pp. 110–129. Springer, Heidelberg (2000)
20. Feng, H., Kolesnikov, O., Fogla, P., Lee, W., Gong, W.: Anomaly Detection using Call Stack Information. In: Proceedings of IEEE Symposium on Security and Privacy, Oakland, California (May 2003)
21. Joachims, T.: Text Categorization with Support Vector Machines: Learning with many relevant features. In: Nédellec, C., Rouveirol, C. (eds.) Machine Learning: ECML 1998. LNCS, vol. 1398, pp. 137–142. Springer, Heidelberg (1998)
22. Joachims, T.: SVM light:Support Vector Machine (2004), http://www.cs.cornell.edu/People/tj/svmlight/index.html
23. Ghosh, A., Schwartzbard, A., Schatz, M.: Learning Program Behavior Profiles for Intrusion Detection. In: First USENIX Workshop on Intrusion Detection and Network Monitoring, pp. 51–62 (1999)
24. Levitt, K., Ko, C., Fink, G.: Automated Detection of Vulnerabilities in Privileged Programs by Execution Monitoring. In: Computer Security Application Conference (1994)
25. Schonlau, M.: Masquerading User Data (1998), http://www.schonlau.net/intrusion.html
26. http://developer.kde.org/documentation/books/kde-2.0-development
27. Dash, S.K., Reddy, K.S., Pujari, A.K.: Episode Based Masquerade Detection. In: Jajodia, S., Mazumdar, C. (eds.) ICISS 2005. LNCS, vol. 3803, pp. 251–262. Springer, Heidelberg (2005)
28. Kim, H.-s., Cha, S.-D.: Empherical evaluation of SVM-based masquerade detection using UNIX commands. Computers and Security 24, 160–168 (2005)
29. Bhukya, W.N., Kumar, S., Negi, A.: A study of effectiveness in masquerade detection IEEE TEN CON 2006 14-17, pp. 1–4 Digital Object Identifier 10.1109/TENCON.2006.344199 (November 2006)

One-Time Receiver Address in IPv6 for Protecting Unlinkability

Atsushi Sakurai, Takashi Minohara, Ryota Sato, and Keisuke Mizutani

Department of Computer Science, Takushoku University
815-1 Tatemachi, Hachioji, Tokyo 193-0985 Japan
{y6m314@st,minohara@cs}.takushoku-u.ac.jp

Abstract. Privacy is one of the most desirable properties in modern communication systems like the Internet. There are many techniques proposed to protect message contents, but it is difficult to protect message addresses because they should be clear to message router. In this paper we propose a mechanism of one-time receiver address in IPv6 for providing unlinkability against eavesdroppers. In our system, a pair of sender and receiver independently generate an identical sequence of addresses by using a secret key exchanged in advance. The sender changes the destination address every time when it initiates a transaction, and only the corresponding receiver can follow the change of the address. We have implemented the proposed mechanism on Linux systems. The prototype system hides relation between transactions with small overhead.

1   Introduction

Privacy is one of the most important properties in present-day life. It is desirable to protect privacy in modern communication systems like the Internet[1]. Many methods, for example IPsec[2], TSL[3], PGP[4], etc., are proposed for protecting privacy of message contents. However it is difficult to protect message addresses, since the information of the addresses is necessary to deliver the messages. One of the most important privacy issues concerning message addresses is the unlinkability[5]. Unlinkability is the property that messages cannot be linked together to assemble a profile of the sender or receiver of the messages. To keep message addresses away from being used for making relation, senders and receivers should change their address frequently.

One way to avoid continuous use of identical address is to use DHCP[6]. With DHCP, addresses are assigned dynamically from DHCP servers. Although servers often hand out the same address to the same client in current implementation, they could arrange to lease addresses that change over time. In IPv6, another method to realize temporarily changing addresses is defined in RFC 3041[7] as an extension to the stateless address autoconfiguration[8]. With stateless address autoconfiguration, IPv6 addresses are generated from a routing prefix portion and a interface identifier. RFC 3041 provides a method to randomize the interface identifier. Changing addresses with DHCP or RFC 3041 makes it more difficult to identify which packets in independent transactions correspond to the same node.

I. Cervesato (Ed.): ASIAN 2007, LNCS 4846, pp. 240–246, 2007.

Unfortunately such difficulty torments not only wiretapping but also proper communication. For initiating a communication, a sender node must know one of the valid addresses of a receiver node. It is required that the receiver node can change its address with preserving accessibility from proper senders.

Unlinkability differs from anonymity, since anonymity may provide relations between different actions, but some methods for anonymity also provide unlinkability. The onion routing[9] hides the receiver address by using numbers of relays. A message is multiply enclosed in addressed envelopes and each envelope is encrypted so that only the proper relay can open it. This method provides both anonymity and unlinkability, but it is required significant overhead. Heavy decrypting processes are imposed on relays, and length of initial packet rises in proportion to the number of relays.

Waters, et al. proposed an addressing method for receivers' anonymity using a special cryptographic primitive called Incomparable Public Key[10]. In their system, each message is sent to a multicast group, and all members of the group try to decrypt the message. Their cryptographic system is designed so that only one of members can succeed to decrypt the message, and the other members ignore it after failing in the decryption. Their system can preserve receiver anonymity even to the message sender itself, however all but one of the multicasted messages will be waisted. The overhead for delivering and decrypting useless messages is not negligible, since the considerable number of receivers is required for providing anonymity.

We consider that unlinkability about receiver addresses are required for a kind of closed community like a friend-to-friend (F2F) network[11,12], and we propose a mechanism for using one-time receiver address in IPv6 in this paper. In our system, a receiver maintains multiple addresses corresponded to registered sender. Each address is not used repeatedly over different transaction. The sender uses novel address when it initiates a transaction, and the receiver follows the change. Our method is targeted for unlinkability in the IP layer, and the relationship in the lower layer (ex. Ethernet address) or the upper layer is not concerned.

2   One-Time Receiver Address in IPv6

2.1   Secret Address Sequence for a Pair of Sender and Receiver

In order to change receiver address for every transaction, the sender and receiver must agree on a sequence of addresses used for transactions, and the sequence must be hidden from outsiders to provide unlinkability.

In our system, both sender and receiver generate a common sequence of addresses independently. Each receiver prepares individual address sequences for every potential senders. The sender draws a new address from the sequence when it initiates a transaction, and the receiver accept the transaction destined to an address in the sequence.

The sequence of addresses is genereted by using the secret encryption key exchanged between sender and receiver in advance. Even if an eavesdropper succeeded in wiretapping, it cannot guess future addresses from former addresses, and cannot judge whether two or more addresses are corresponded to the same receiver. An encryption key can be shared by the Diffie-Hellman algorithm[13]. Sender and receiver exchange their public key each other on a key server, and a common encryption key can be generated by the partner's public key and one's own secret key.

2.2   Generation of Address Sequence

Since IPv6 address is composed of a routing prefix and a interface identifier, a sequence of addresses can be generated from a sequence of interface identifiers. The algorithm described in RFC 3041 generates a random sequence of interface identifiers so that it is hard to predict past and future identifiers based on a current one. We modified the algorithm in order to generate identical sequences independently at sender and receiver under the condition that they share a secret key K. The following algorithm assumes that both sender and receiver have the same information about the routing prefix P of receiver and an initial interface identifier I_0, and provide the method for generating address sequence $A_i = < P : I_i(P, K, I_0) > (i = 1, 2, \cdots)$.

The receiver obtains the routing prefix from router advertisement(RA) in IPv6, and it is possible to generate random initial interface identifier. Those values are handed to the sender via the key exchange server.

1. Take the history value J_{i-1} from the previous iteration (the initial value J_0 is set to interface identifier I_0), and append the routing prefix P to it.
2. Encrypt the quantity created in step 1 with using the secret encryption key K, and compute the MD5 message digest over the encrypted value.
3. Take the left-most 64 bits of the MD5 digest and set bit 6 (the left-most bit is numbered 0) to zero. Save the generated value as next entry of the sequence of interface identifiers I_i.
4. Take the right-most 64 bits of the MD5 digest computed in step 2 and save them in stable storage as the history value J_i to be used in the next iteration of the algorithm.

Figure 1 illustrates the flow of information for generating a sequence of addresses. The length of encryption key should be selected long enough so that it cannot be disclosed by the brute force attacks.

3   Implementation of One-Time Receiver Address

We have implemented the mechanism of one-time receiver address described in previous section into the Linux system which support IPv6 protocol stacks with extensions developed by USAGI project[14].

3.1   Implementation of One-Time Addresses on Receiver Side

It is not efficient to assign a lot of addresses to a network interface, but a receiver may be accessed from more than one sender, and it needs to manage sequences of

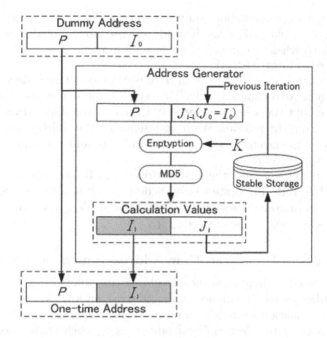

Fig. 1. Generation of a sequence of interface identifiers

addresses for all potential sender. We have implemented the following 3 features for the address sequence management.

1. Initial Address Generation:
   When a request of key exchange is sent to a receiver from a sender via a key server, the receiver exchanges the secret encryption key K with the Diffie Helman algorithm and starts generation of address sequence with the key K, a random initial interface identifier I_0 and routing prefix P obtained from a router advertisement(RA). Then, the receiver tests duplication of the initial address A_1 on its local network. If any collision detected with other nodes, the initial address is discarded, and new address sequence is generated by alternating the initial interface identifier I_0. Unless the duplication detected, the initial address A_1 is assigned to the network I/F, and the dummy address $< P : I_0 >$ is sent to the sender.

2. Alternation of Addresses
   In order to avoid the linkage by the attacker, a sender uses different addresses of receiver for every transaction. The receiver generates a range of addresses $A_i \cdots A_{i+r-1}$ (r: length of range) as described in 2.2, and assigns it to the network interface for accepting the transactions. Assigned addresses are managed with a manner similar to the sliding window algorithm in TCP, i.e. the next address A_{i+r} is drawn from the sequence when the transaction, which uses the address A_i, is finished. The used address A_i is removed from the interface, but generally it is not easy to detect the end of transaction. In

our current implementation, only the end of TCP session is detected by receiving a FIN flagged packet. The address used for the other type of sessions are removed when the unused time exceeds a limit.

3. Duplicated Address Detection

Although 128bits' address space in IPv6 is extremely large, the same address may be generated coincidentally. The receiver can detect the duplication of its address but the sender has no way to detect the duplication unless it is informed from the receiver. We have integrated the collision avoidance into the address management so that the sender is told the duplicate address before it use the one.

The receiver examines the next address A_{i+r} before it is attached to the network I/F. If the duplicate address is detected, it is not used and the ICMP information message is sent for stopping the sender from using it, and the address is stepped to the next A_{i+r+1}.

3.2   Implementation of One-Time Addresses on Sender Side

A sender also needs individual sequences of one-time addresses for each receiver, but those addresses aren't assigned to the network interface of the sender. They are used for destination address with which transactions are established. Therefore it is important to select different addresses for each transactions in order to avoid continuous use of the same address. Transactions may be established by many different applications, and it is not acceptable to change application programs. The address selection mechanism must be transparent to application programs. If human friendly identifiers, DNS names for example, were used in stead of direct network layer addresses, such mechanism could be implemented as a name resolver. We have developed an one-time address resolver, and integrated into address resolver library. Address sequences are maintained by a daemon program, and a service library communicates with the daemon program. The standard library(glibc-2.4) used for name resolution in Linux system is designed so that it can extend easily. More than one services can be specified in the configuration file(/etc/nsswitch.conf), and used in turn. The daemon program resolves a name as follows, and even if it failed, ordinary services like NIS, DNS, etc. are used as usual.

- When an address of a receiver is requested, the daemon program checks whether the address sequence, which corresponds to the receiver, has already been generated or not. If the sequence exists, the next address is drawn from the sequence and passed to the service library. If it doesn't exist, the daemon starts to generate a sequence of address. At first, the daemon requests the public key, which is used for the secret encryption key K, and the receiver's dummy address $< P : I_0 >$. Then it generates a sequence of addresses as described in 2.2, Finally it returns the initial address A_1 from the address sequence to the service library.
- If a duplicate address is detected on the receiver, it is told by the ICMP message from the receiver. The daemon, which is informed the duplication, deletes the address from the sequence.

– In the sender side, it is not required to detect the end of transaction. The daemon passes one after another the addresses from the sequence to the service library when they are requested.

4   Experimental Evaluations

We have configured an experimental network which is connected to the real IPv6 networks by using an IPv6 over IPv4 tunnel. The proposed one-time address works well and co-exists with normal addressing mechanisms. When we use a name registered for one-time address, the value of destination address changes for each sessions, while normal IPv6 site can be accessed with its DNS name simultaneously.

Because the overhead of our one-time address is loaded on the end points, we have measured it by the nodes connected to the same segment. Table 1 shows the RTT between sender(Pentium D 2.8GHz, 2GB memory) and receiver(AMD Athlon 64 1GHz, 2GB memory) using `ping6`. The difference between the normal address on the original kernel and the proposed one-time address on the modified kernel is at most hundreds micro seconds, and it is negligible compared to typical Internet transfer delay time.

Table 1. Difference of RTT of Between Original Kernel and Extension Kernel

Sequence Number	1	2	3	4
Normal address on original kernel(ms)	1.115	0.151	0.149	0.150
standard deviation	0.414	0.007	0.009	0.009
One-time address on modified kernel(ms)	1.291	0.190	0.191	0.192
standard deviation	0.310	0.011	0.015	0.009

5   Conclusion

In this paper we propose a mechanism for using one-time receiver address in IPv6 for providing unlinkability against eavesdroppers. In our system, the sender and receiver generate identical sequence of addresses independently by using a secret encryption key exchanged in advance. The sender uses novel address from the sequence when it initiates a transaction, and the only receiver can follows the change. We have implemented the proposed mechanism on the Linux system. The prototype system can hide relation between transactions with small overhead.

References

1. Goldberg, I.: Privacy-enhancing technologies for the internet, II, five years later. In: Federrath, H. (ed.) Designing Privacy Enhancing Technologies. LNCS, vol. 2009, pp. 1–12. Springer, Heidelberg (2001)
2. Kent, S., Seo, K.: Security architecture for the internet protocol. RFC 4301 (December 2005)

3. Dierks, T., Rescorla, E.: The transport layer security (TLS) protocol. RFC 4346 (April 2006)
4. Atkins, D., Stallings, W., Zimmermann, P.: PGP message exchange formats. RFC 1991 (August 1996)
5. Pfitzmann, A., Hansen, M.: Anonymity, unlinkability, undetectability, unobservability, pseudonymity, and identity management – a consolidated proposal for terminology (July 2007), http://dud.inf.tu-dresden.de/Anon_Terminology.shtml
6. Droms, R.: Dynamic host configuration protocol. RFC 2131 (March 1997)
7. Narten, T., Draves, R.: Privacy extensions for stateless address autoconfiguration in IPv6. RFC 3041 (January 2001)
8. Thomson, S., Narten, T.: Ipv6 stateless address autoconfiguration. RFC 2462 (December 1998)
9. Goldschlag, D., Reed, M., Syverson, P.: Onion routing. Communications of The ACM 42(2), 31–41 (1999)
10. Waters, B.R., Felten, E.W., Sahai, A.: Receiver anonymity via incomparable public keys. In: CCS 2003. Proceedings of the 10th ACM conference on Computer and Communications Security, Washington D.C., USA, pp. 112–121 (2003)
11. Bricklin, D.: Friend-to-friend networks (August 2000), http://www.bricklin.com/f2f.htm
12. Chothia, T., Chatzikokolakis, K.: A survey of anonymous peer-to-peer file-sharing. In: Enokido, T., Yan, L., Xiao, B., Kim, D., Dai, Y., Yang, L.T. (eds.) Embedded and Ubiquitous Computing – EUC 2005 Workshops. LNCS, vol. 3823, pp. 744–755. Springer, Heidelberg (2005)
13. Diffie, W., Hellman, M.E.: New directions in cryptography. IEEE Trans. of Information Theory 22(6), 644–654 (1976)
14. WIDE Project: USAGI project – linux IPv6 development project, http://www.linux-ipv6.org/

A Comprehensive Approach to Detect Unknown Attacks Via Intrusion Detection Alerts

Jungsuk Song[1], Hayato Ohba[1], Hiroki Takakura[2], Yasuo Okabe[2],
Kenji Ohira[1], and Yongjin Kwon[3]

[1] Graduate School of Informatics, Kyoto University
oaktree@net.ist.i.kyoto-u.ac.jp, hayato@net.ist.i.kyoto-u.ac.jp,
ohira@net.ist.i.kyoto-u.ac.jp
[2] Academic Center for Computing and Media Studies, Kyoto University
takakura@media.kyoto-u.ac.jp, okabe@i.kyoto-u.ac.jp
[3] Information and Telecom. Eng., Korea Aerospace University
yjkwon@tikwon.hangkong.ac.kr

Abstract. Intrusion detection system(IDS) has played an important role as a device to defend our networks from cyber attacks. However, since it still suffers from detecting an unknown attack, i.e., 0-day attack, the ultimate challenge in intrusion detection field is how we can exactly identify such an attack. This paper presents a novel approach that is quite different from the traditional detection models based on raw traffic data. The proposed method can extract unknown activities from IDS alerts by applying data mining technique. We evaluated our method over the log data of IDS that is deployed in Kyoto University, and our experimental results show that it can extract unknown(or under development) attacks from IDS alerts by assigning a score to them that reflects how anomalous they are, and visualizing the scored alerts.

1 Introduction

Due to the popularization of the Internet and local networks, security and privacy threats to the computer systems and networks are growing. In order to fight against these cyber attacks, many security techniques have been studied in the last decade, which include cryptography, firewalls and intrusion detection systems(IDSs), etc. Among these techniques, IDS[1] is becoming increasingly important in maintaining proper network security.

Although the existing IDSs that investigate raw traffic data have contributed to the construction of a higher-level security architecture, they still have weakness in detection of an unknown attack, i.e., 0-day attack. In addition, since they trigger too many false positive alerts, it is very difficult that IDS operators discover such an attack from the usual false positive alerts. Because of this, the ultimate challenge in intrusion detection field is how we can exactly identify such an attack.

On the other hand, skillful attackers devise diverse artifice to hide their activities because recent progress of security devices, including IDS, makes the attackers difficult to evade such security devices. In addition, the situation where

I. Cervesato (Ed.): ASIAN 2007, LNCS 4846, pp. 247–253, 2007.

anyone can easily acquire many IDS products and free software, e.g., snort[2], enables attackers to examine their behavior easily. Because they can control response of IDS by carefully analyzing its detection mechanism, and thus they can write attack codes to induce misjudgment of IDS operators or to evade security devices without difficulty. In many cases, however, they cannot hide their activities completely, so that IDS raises false positive alerts. Different from usual false positive ones, various types of alerts which have no relevancy among them appear simultaneously and frequently. Therefore, it is possible to identify something new activities from these usual false positive alerts. This paper presents a novel approach that is quite different from the traditional detection models based on raw traffic data. The proposed method can extract unknown activities from IDS alerts by applying data mining technique.

We evaluated our method over the log data of IDS that is deployed in Kyoto University. Our experimental results show that it can extract unknown(or under development) attacks from IDS alerts by assigning a score to them that reflects how anomalous they are, and visualizing the scored alerts.

The rest of the paper is organized as follows. In section 2, we give a general survey of the intrusion detection field. In section 3 we present our approach, and experimental results and their analysis are given in section 4. Finally, we present concluding remarks.

2   Related Work

As IDS has played a central role as an appliance to effectively defend our crucial computer systems or networks, large organization and companies have deployed different models of IDS from different vendors. Nevertheless, there is a fatal weakness that they trigger an unmanageable amount of alerts. Inspecting thousands of alerts per day and sensor[3] is not feasible, specially if 99% of them are false positives[4]. Due to this impracticability, during the last few years a lot of researches have been proposed to reduce the amount of false alerts, by studying the cause of these false positives, creating a higher level view or scenario of the attacks, and so on[5].

T. Bass firstly introduced data fusion techniques in military applications for improving performance of next-generation IDS[6]. Giacinto, et al. performed alert clustering which produces unified description of attacks from multiple alerts to attain a high-level description of threats[7]. In [8] Treinen, et al. used meta-alarms to identify known attack patterns in alarm streams, and used association rule mining to shorten the training time.

3   Extraction of Unknown Activities

In this section we present our method to extract unknown activities from IDS alerts, and to assign a score that reflects how anomalous they are. Our extraction process consists of four major parts; Data Preparation, Feature Extraction, Extracting Representative Points, and Scoring.

3.1 Data Preparation

In many researches based on data mining and machine learning techniques, they have usually used insufficient training data(with raw traffic data) to construct intrusion detection models. In other words, they have collected data instances within a certain period of time and generated the attack signatures or the normal patterns by calculating relationships among the instances. However, there are several problems that are unacceptable for actual network management. For example, they cannot represent current situation of the network and such insufficiency may trigger too many alerts to be inspected by IDS operators. Since new types of attack and normal activities are emerging everyday, it is difficult to accurately detect them by using only certain days' training data. In addition, most of the alerts are not attacks(i.e. false positive)[4]. As a result, IDS operators may not realize presence of an unknown attack by auditing such false positives.

In order to cope with these problems, we consider the multiple training data, in which each training data consists of IDS alerts of a day and any sets of the data are used to calculate the relationship, and the following feature extraction and normalization processes are applied to each training data. In addition, we regard all the training data as normal data because our ultimate purpose is to detect completely unknown attacks that are different from the well-known attacks, and never observed previously. After all, it means that we can obtain our training data easily without any preprocessing for generating good training data(i.e. correctly labeled training data) like traditional approaches.

3.2 Feature Extraction

In order to compute similarity between alerts, we need to define features like those of KDD Cup 99 data. In the existing researches they have used only the basic features that are recorded by IDS. However, the basic features can not contain enough information to extract attacker's ingenious conduct. Furthermore, there are two many redundant features such as protocol type, detection time and so on.

Therefore, in this study we consider the features as follows. First, only the following information is used as the basic features that are given in IDS alerts.

– **source address, source port, destination address, destination port**

Second, we calculate the following additional features that are extracted based on "incident ID" of IDS alerts. The "incident" indicates a group of the alerts that are considered as correlated attacks by IDS. Thus, if two instances(i.e. alerts) have the same incident ID, they become members of the same incident group.

– **num_same_incident**: the number of alerts with the same incident ID as the current alert.
– **num_alert** : the number of different kinds of alerts within an incident group where the current alert belongs.
– **kind_sequent_alert** : kinds of the alerts that appear after the current alert.

In case of "num_same_incident" feature, it is effective in detection of the attacks that consist of a large number of simultaneous connections such as DDoS attack and Probing attack. In case of a heavy DDoS attack(or Probing attack), they make the tremendous number of the same pattern alerts that is different from that of normal traffic. On the other hand, the rest two features are designed from empirical result that normal traffic or already-known attack often forms a constant patterns of alert combination. When new combination of alerts appeared or excessive combination occurred at the same time, it can be regarded as a high risk attack or new attack(or attack under development).

3.3   Extracting Representative Points

Our approach assigns a score to each alert of the testing data in order to represent degree of its abnormality. However, since this assignment process requires comparing the alerts of the training data with those of the testing data, utilization of all alerts within the training data causes very high time complexity. Therefore, in order to reduce the time complexity of the proposed method, we extract the representative points from the training data. In extraction of the representative points, we use LBG algorithm[14]. Its extracting process is described as follows. The Euclidean distance is used for the distance calculation in it.

- Initialization: Regard all the points in the training data as members of an initial cluster.
- The following steps are repeated l times.
  - Selection: Select two points from each cluster at random, and regard them as new representative point.
  - Assignment: Assign each point to the closest representative point (generation of cluster).
  - Updating: Replace every cluster's representative point with the average of its members.
  - Iteration: Repeat Selection and Updating until there is no change for each cluster.

As a result, 2^l representative points are obtained.

3.4   Scoring

In this procedure we assign a score to each alert in order to reflect how anomalous it is. To this end, we first measure the distance between the representative points and the alerts of the testing data. We find out the closest representative point from each alert, and then regard the distance between the point and the alert as its score. Note that we regard all alerts of training data as normal event if some of them represent actual attacks. As a result, the alerts that have higher scores are mostly likely to be unknown attacks and those with lower scores are most likely to be normal traffic or already-known attacks. After the scoring process is finished, security analyst investigates what malicious activities happened on his networks based on the scores.

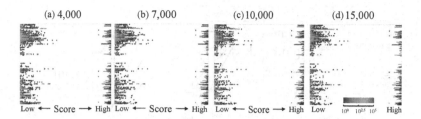

Fig. 1. Variation of the scored alerts according to the number of the representative points

4   Experimental Results and Their Analysis

We evaluated our system under the following conditions. First of all, to obtain IDS alerts, we used SNS7160 IDS system[9] that is actually deployed at the boundary of Kyoto University. We then prepared IDS alerts of a month(August, 2006)[1] as the training data, and regarded all of them as the normal data. Note that there are 30 different sets of the training data that consist of IDS alerts of a day. The total number of alerts in the training data was about 6,400,000, and there were 500 types of alerts based on signature ID. The total number of the representative points extracted in the training phase was about 15,000. As the testing data, we used IDS alerts collected on November, 2006[2].

We first investigated how well our scheme can extract unknown activities from IDS alerts. To this end, we visualized a score of each alert as shown in Figure 1. In Figure 1, the vertical axis indicates signature IDs. The horizontal axis means the score of the alerts, and it increases according to the right side. The different colors mean the number of the alerts that have the corresponding score(blue: 10^0, green: $10^{2.5}$, red: 10^5). The bar chart(the right side of each Figure) means the total number of the alerts that have the same signature ID. Second, we need to investigate whether our approach is sensitive or not with respect to the number of the representative points extracted from the multiple training data. For this experiment, we changed the number of the representative points; 4,000, 7,000, 10,000 and 15,000. As the results of Figure 1, the score of the alerts is almost unchanged; especially at the points that have higher score. Therefore, it can be concluded that our approach is not sensitive to the number of the representative points. In addition, we could identify that its the most right side points(i.e. the points that have the highest score) correspond to the unknown activities as described below.

Figure 2 shows that IDS detected 5 different exploit codes. Parenthesized numbers represent how many times the same exploit code or shellcode were observed, and thus the first 4 exploit codes were observed for the first time. In addition, we can observe that the first 4 codes adopt 2 shellcodes, and each session trig-

---

[1] Many exploit codes have been developed aiming MS06-040.
[2] New malware "Allaple[13]" was released.

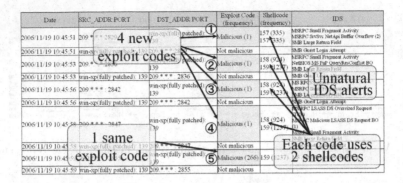

Fig. 2. Example of unknown activities

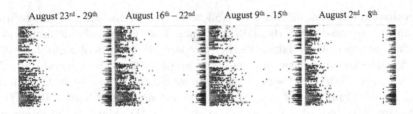

Fig. 3. Variation of the scored alerts according to 4 different training data

gered 3 or 4 different alerts at the same time. For example, the first session was detected as the latest attack "MSRPC SrvSvc NetApi Buffer Overflow (2)" to MS06-040[10] while old attack "SMB Large Return Field" to MS05-027[11] and "IDS Evasion"[12] were also included. However, these combinations of the alerts are unnatural because in case of an usual attack IDS reports only one alert with respect to it. This means, therefore, that attackers are developing their exploit codes that are combined by the existing exploit codes, so that the multiple alerts were recorded by IDS because different shellcodes raise different alerts. Later, it was identified that these activities were caused by Allaple worms[13].

In general, attackers carefully examine their well-crafted attack codes through a long period when they attack the victim host(s). Thus, the training data with short period of time is insufficient to extract their malicious activities from the testing data because their activities are also included in the training data; that is, there are few differences between the training data and the testing data. For demonstration, we prepared 4 different training data that consist of IDS alerts of a week; August 23rd-29th, 16th-22nd, 9th-15th, and 2nd-8th, and the testing data of a day; August 30th. The experimental results are shown in Figure 3. From Figure 3, we can observe that in case of the latest training data(i.e. August 23rd-29th) there are few alerts of a high score. While as we search retroactively, the number of the alerts that have higher scores gradually increases. This means that if we used only the latest training data to extract something new malicious attacks, we overlook presence of them. We should, therefore, use long enough interval of training data in order to identify something new malicious activities. In fact, we observed development of new attacks to MS06-040 since August 11st to 30th.

5   Conclusion

In this paper, we have focused on extracting unknown malicious activities from IDS alerts. In order to extract such activities effectively, we have proposed a novel approach that is based on data mining technique. Unlike the traditional methods that try to detect new attacks from only one training data with raw traffic data, the proposed method detects unknown attacks by applying the multiple training data that consist of IDS alerts. We have evaluated the proposed method over the log data of IDS that is deployed in Kyoto University, and showed that it has capability to extract unknown(or under development) attacks from IDS alerts. Furthermore, the stability of the proposed method with respect to the number of the representative points makes our approach more promising.

References

1. Denning, D.E.: An intrusion detection model. IEEE Transactions on Software Engineering, SE 13, 222–232 (1987)
2. http://www.snort.org/
3. Manganaris, S., Christensen, M., Zerkle, D., Hermiz, K.: A Data Mining Analysis of RTID Alarms. Computer Networks 34(4), 571–577 (2000)
4. Julisch, K.: Clustering Intrusion Detection Alarms to Support Root Cause Analysis. ACM Transactions on Information and System Security 6(4), 443–471 (2003)
5. Zurutuza, U., Uribeetxeberria, R.: Intrusion Detection Alarm Correlation: A Survey. In: Proceedings of the IADAT International Conference on Telecommunications and Computer Networks (December 1-3, 2004)
6. Bass, T.: Intrusion detection systems and multisensor data fusion. In: Communications of the ACM, pp. 99–105. ACM Press, New York (2000)
7. Giacinto, G., Perdisci, R., Roli, F.: Alarm Clustering for Intrusion Detection Systems in Computer Networks. In: Perner, P., Imiya, A. (eds.) MLDM 2005. LNCS (LNAI), vol. 3587, pp. 184–193. Springer, Heidelberg (2005)
8. Treinen, J.J., Thurimella, R.: A Framework for the Application of Association Rule Mining in Large Intrusion Detection Infrastructures. In: Zamboni, D., Kruegel, C. (eds.) RAID 2006. LNCS, vol. 4219, pp. 1–18. Springer, Heidelberg (2006)
9. Symantec Network Security 7100 Series
10. http://www.support.microsoft.com/kb/921883
11. http://www.microsoft.com/technet/security/bulletin/MS05-027.mspx
12. http://www.sans.org/resources/idfaq/rpc_evas.php
13. http://www.sophos.com/security/analyses/w32allapleb.html
14. Linde, Y., Buzo, A., Gray, R.M.: An Algorithm for Vector Quantizer Design. IEEE Trans. on communications 28(1), 84–95 (1980)

Combining Heterogeneous Classifiers for Network Intrusion Detection

Ali Borji

School of Cognitive Sciences,
Institute for Studies in Theoretical Physics and Mathematics,
Niavaran Bldg. P.O.Box 19395-5746, Tehran, IRAN
borji@ipm.ir

Abstract. Extensive use of computer networks and online electronic data and high demand for security has called for reliable intrusion detection systems. A repertoire of different classifiers has been proposed for this problem over last decade. In this paper we propose a combining classification approach for intrusion detection. Outputs of four base classifiers ANN, SVM, *k*NN and decision trees are fused using three combination strategies: majority voting, Bayesian averaging and a belief measure. Our results support the superiority of the proposed approach compared with single classifiers for the problem of intrusion detection.

Keywords: Intrusion Detection, Combined Classifiers, PCA, Misuse Detection, Anomaly Detection.

1 Introduction

With the rapid development in the technology based on Internet, new application domains in computer network have emerged. As networks grow in both importance and size, there is an increasing need for effective security monitors such as network intrusion detection systems to prevent illicit accesses. Intrusion detection systems provide a layer of defense which oversees network traffic to identify suspicious activity or patterns that may suggest potentially hostile traffics.

One promise for network intrusion detection is the abnormal access pattern that is generated by scans. Sources that attempt to access an unusual number of uncommon or non-existent destinations, or propagate an irregular number of failed connections are often deemed suspicious [1].

An intrusion detection system (IDS) attempts to detect attacks by monitoring and controlling the network behavior. While many existing IDSs require manual definitions of normal and abnormal behavior (intrusion signatures), recent work has shown that it is possible to identify abnormalities automatically using machine learning or data mining techniques. These works analyze network or system activity logs to generate models or rules, which the IDS can use to detect intrusions that can potentially compromise the system reliability.

Numerous approaches based on soft computing techniques such as artificial neural networks and fuzzy inference systems are proposed in the literature for the purpose of

I. Cervesato (Ed.): ASIAN 2007, LNCS 4846, pp. 254–260, 2007.

intrusion detection. In [2] two hierarchical neural network frameworks, serial hierarchical IDS (SHIDS) and parallel hierarchical IDS (PHIDS), are proposed. BPL and RBF are two important learning algorithms used in these neural networks. Authors have shown that BPL has a slightly better performance than RBF in the case of misuse detection, while the RBF takes less training time. On the other hand RBF shows a better performance in the case of anomaly detection. In [3], authors proposed ANNs and support vector machine (SVM) algorithms for ID with frequency-based encoding method. In the chosen DARPA data set, they used 250 attacks and 41,426 normal sessions. The percentage of detection rate (%DR) they archived were between 43.6% and 100% while percentage of false positive rate (%FPR) varied from 0.27% to 8.53% using different thresholds. An in depth review of several anomaly detection techniques for identification of different network intrusions are brought in [4].

In [5], authors have proposed an experimental framework for comparative analysis of both supervised and unsupervised learning techniques including C.45, multi-layer perceptron (MLP), K-nearest neighbor (KNN), etc. The best result they attained was 95% DR and 1% FPR using C.45 algorithm.

In [6] a set of fuzzy rules are generated that can distinguish anomalous connections using only normal samples. Their approach uses genetic algorithms to evolve a set of rules. In [7], SVM was used as an analysis engine which does some preprocessing on the input data. Fuzzy logic is then used as a decision making engine.

It is well known that principal component analysis (PCA) is the most popular feature reduction and data compression method. It has also been applied to the domain of ID [8]. In [9], neural network principal component analysis (NNPCA) and nonlinear component analysis (NLCA) are proposed to reduce the dimension of network traffic patterns. Their approach is based on comparing information of the compressed data with that of the original data. In [10], PCA was used to detect selected denial-of-service and network probe attacks. The authors analyzed the loading values of the various feature vector components with respect to the principal components.

In [11], an ensemble method for intrusion detection is used. They have considered two types of classifiers; ANN and SVM. Another ensemble method is proposed in [12]. In their method, each member of the ensemble is trained on a distinct feature representation of patterns and then the results of the ensemble members are combined. In this paper we propose a new combining classifier approach to intrusion detection by considering a set of heterogeneous classifiers. Four different base classifiers perform classification over an input pattern. Results are then combined using three combing methodologies.

The reminder of this paper is organized as follows. Problem of intrusion detection is defined in more detail in section 2. Section 3 explains the datasets and brings the results of single classifiers. Our proposed method for classifier combination and its results are shown in section four. Finally section five, draws conclusions and summarizes the paper.

2 Intrusion Detection

Intrusion detection process is a software or hardware product that detects illicit activities, which are defined as attempts to compromise the confidentiality, integrity, availability, or to bypass the security mechanisms of a host or network. There exist mainly two categories of intrusion detection techniques: anomaly detection and signature recognition (misuse detection). Signature recognition techniques store patterns of intrusion signatures and compare those signatures with the observed activities for a match to detect an intrusion. The misuse detection, first attempts to model specific patterns of intrusions to a system, then systematically scans the system for their occurrences. Since the knowledge of the intrusions has to be known before the modeling, this method is mostly used to detect well-known intrusions. Although many existing intrusion detection systems are based on signature recognition techniques, anomaly detection techniques are better to detect novel intrusions or new variants of known intrusions. Anomaly detection creates a profile of typical normal traffic activities or user behaviors, then it compares the deviation between the profile and the input activity with a preset threshold to decide whether the input instance is normal or not. The preset threshold can be adjusted to meet desired performance. Signature recognition techniques may be more accurate in detecting known intrusions. Also many known attacks can be easily modified to present many different signatures. Hence, signature recognition techniques and anomaly detection techniques can be used together to complement each other by monitoring the same activities and generating their own results regarding the intrusiveness of the activities. Anomaly detection addresses the problem of detecting novel intrusions. Usually, it cannot provide detailed information about the attacks. A well designed intrusion detection system should have the ability to detect both misuse and anomaly attacks.

It is important to establish the key differences between anomaly detection and misuse detection approaches. The most significant advantage of misuse detection approaches is that known attacks can be detected fairly reliably and with a low false positive rate. Since specific attack sequences are encoded into misuse detection systems, it is very easy to determine exactly which attacks, or possible attacks, the system is currently experiencing. If the log data does not contain the attack signature, no alarm is raised. As a result, the false positive rate can be reduced very close to zero.

However, the key drawback of misuse detection approaches is that they cannot detect novel attacks against systems that leave different signatures behind. Anomaly detection techniques, on the other hand, directly address the problem of detecting novel attacks against systems. This is possible because anomaly detection techniques do not scan for specific patterns, but instead compare current activities against statistical models of past behavior. Any activity sufficiently deviant from the model will be flagged as anomalous, and hence considered as a possible attack. Furthermore, anomaly detection schemes are based on actual user histories and system data to create its internal models rather than predefined patterns. Though anomaly detection approaches are powerful in that they can detect novel attacks, they have their drawbacks as well. For instance, one clear drawback of anomaly detection is its inability to identify the specific type of attack that is occurring. However, probably the most significant disadvantage of anomaly detection approaches is the high rates of false alarm.

3 Intrusion Detection Using Single Classifiers

3.1 Dataset

In the 1998 DARPA intrusion detection evaluation program, an environment was set up to acquire raw TCP/IP dump data for a network by simulating a typical U.S. Air Force LAN. The LAN was operated like a real environment, but being blasted with multiple attacks. For each TCP/IP connection, 41 various quantitative and qualitative features were extracted. Of this database a subset of 494021 data were used, of which 20% represent normal patterns. The four different categories of attack patterns are:

a. **Denial of Service (DOS) Attacks:** A denial of service attack is a class of attacks in which an attacker makes some computing or memory resource too busy or too full to handle legitimate requests, or denies legitimate users access to a machine. Examples are Apache2, Back, Land, Mail bomb, SYN Flood, Ping of death, Process table, Smurf, Syslogd, Teardrop, Udpstorm.

b. **User to Superuser or Root Attacks (U2Su):** User to root exploits are a class of attacks in which an attacker starts out with access to a normal user account on the system and is able to exploit vulnerability to gain root access to the system. Examples are Eject, Ffbconfig, Fdformat, Loadmodule, Perl, Ps, Xterm.

c. **Remote to User Attacks (R2L):** A remote to user attack is a class of attacks in which an attacker sends packets to a machine over a network–but who does not have an account on that machine; exploits some vulnerability to gain local access as a user of that machine. Examples are Dictionary, Ftp_write, Guest, Imap, Named, Phf, Sendmail, Xlock, Xsnoop.

d. **Probing (Probe):** Probing is a class of attacks in which an attacker scans a network of computers to gather information or find known vulnerabilities. An attacker with a map of machines and services that are available on a network can use this information to look for exploits. Examples are Ipsweep, Mscan, Nmap, Saint, Satan.

3.2 Single Classifier Recognition

In our experiments, we performed 5-class classification. The (training and testing) data set contains 11982 randomly generated points from the five classes, with the number of data from each class proportional to its size, except that the smallest class is completely included. The normal data belongs to class 1, probe belongs to class 2, denial of service belongs to class 3, user to super user belongs to class 4, remote to local belongs to class 5. A number of 6890 points of the total data set (11982) was randomly selected for testing and the rest for the train. Smaller number of training patterns than test patterns is because the intrusion detection method must learn from few learning samples the characteristics of the intrusions.

3.2.1 ANN

The set of 5092 training data is divided into five classes: normal, probe, denial of service attacks, user to super user and remote to local attacks, where the attack is a collection of 22 different types of instances that belong to the four classes described in section 2, and the other is the normal data. In our study we used two hidden layers with 20 and 30 neurons respectively and the networks were trained using standard back propagation algorithm.

3.2.2 SVM

The same training test (5092) used for training the neural networks and the same testing test (6890) used for testing the neural networks were used to validate the performance of SVM. Because SVMs are only capable of binary classifications, we will need to employ five SVMs, for the 5-clas classification problem in intrusion detection, respectively. We partition the data into the two classes of "Normal" and "Rest" (Probe, DoS, U2Su, R2L) patterns, where the Rest is the collection of four classes of attack instances in the data set. The objective is to separate normal and attack patterns. We repeat this process for all classes. Training is done using the RBF (radial bias function) kernel option.

3.2.3 Decision Trees

The decision tree is constructed during the learning phase, it is then used to predict the classes of new instances. Most of the decision trees algorithms use a top down strategy, i.e from the root to the leaves. Two main processes are necessary to use the decision tree: the building process and the classification process. The same dataset as ANN and SVM were used for building and verifying decision trees. C4.5 algorithm with normalized information gain was used in tree building.

3.2.4 *k*NN

In *k*NN, an input pattern is classified by a majority vote of its neighbors, with the pattern being assigned the class most common amongst its k nearest neighbors. Training patterns are saved in memory. Then in classification a majority vote determines the class label of a test pattern. In our experiments we used Euclidean distance to find the nearest neighbors. Using a cross-validation experiment we found k=3 the most sailable value for k. Results showing the performances of four single classifiers discussed above is summarized in table one.

Table 1. Intrusion detction performacne using four heterogenius classifiers

Classification Method Performance	ANN	SVM	Decision Tree	kNN (k=3)
Detection Rate (DR)	98.45%	99.5%	95.5%	88.9%
False Positive Rate (FPR)	3.57%	2.9%	1.2%	4.1%

4 Combing Classifiers for Intrusion Detection

The ensemble method proposed for solving the Intrusion Detection problem can be illustrated as follows. First each trained classifiers over the same training set is used independently to perform attack detection. Then the evidences are combined in order to produce the final decision. The approach based on classifier combination may also attain effective attack detection as the combination of multiple evidences usually exhibits higher accuracies, i.e. lower false positives, than individual decisions. In addition, the generalization capabilities of pattern recognition algorithms allow for the detection of novel attacks that is not provided by rule-based signatures.

In order to illustrate combination approach, we used three simple fusion techniques: the majority voting rule, the average rule and the "belief" function. These fusion techniques compute the final decision from the set of decisions of an ensemble made up of K classifiers. The "majority voting rule "assigns a given input pattern to the majority class among the K outputs of the classifiers combined. The "average rule" assigns a given input pattern to the class with the maximum average posterior probability, the average being computed among the K classifiers (this rule can be applied if classifiers provide estimates of posterior probabilities, like multi-layer perceptron neural networks). The third fusion rule is based on the computation of a "belief" value for each data class given the set of outputs of the K classifiers. Belief values are based on estimates of the probabilities that a pattern assigned to a given data class actually belongs to that class or to other classes. These probabilities can be easily computed from the confusion matrix on the training set. The classification is then performed by assigning the input pattern to the data class with the maximum "belief" value. For more details about the above combination methods the reader is referred to [13].

Results of combining classifiers to recognize intrusions using three combination approaches are shown in table 2.

Table 2. Intrusion detection performance using combination of four disticnt classifiers

Combination Method / Performance	Majority	Bayesian Average	Belief
Detection Rate (DR)	99.18%	99.33%	99.68%
False Positive Rate (FPR)	1.20%	1.03%	0.87%

5 Conclusions

Our results show the effectiveness of classifier combination in providing more reliable results, as the final decision depends on the agreement among distinct classifiers. In particular better results have been obtained by the fusion rule based on the "belief" function paradigm because it takes into account the different discriminative power provided by the considered feature sets. Other combination schemes should be devised to further improve the presented figures. In addition, more extensive testing is required to compare IDSs based on pattern recognition tools with traditional IDSs. With respect to the capability of ensemble learning approaches of providing a better trade-off between generalization capabilities and false alarm rate, it can be concluded that combination reduces the overall error rate, but may also reduce the generalization capabilities. This aspect should be further investigated in order to deploy effective IDSs based on pattern recognition.

References

1. Roesch, M.: Snort: Lightweight intrusion detection for networks. In: Proceedings of the 13th Conference on Systems Administration (LISA 1999), pp. 229–238 (1999)
2. Zhang, C., Jiang, J., Kamel, M.: Intrusion detection using hierarchical neural networks. Pattern Analysis and Machine Intelligence Research Group, Department of Electrical and Computer Engineering, University of Waterloo, Canada (2004)
3. Wun-Hua, C., Sheng-Hsun, H., Hwang-Pin, S.: Application of SVM and ANN for intrusion detection. Comput. Oper. Res. 32(10), 2617–2634 (2005)
4. Lazarevic, A., Ertoz, L., Kumar, V., Ozgur, A., Srivastava, J.: A comparative study of anomaly detection schemes in network intrusion detection. In: Proceedings of the Third SIAM Conference on Data Mining (2003)
5. Pavel, L., Patrick, D., Christin, S., Rieck, K.: Learning Intrusion Detection: Supervised or Unsupervised. In: Roli, F., Vitulano, S. (eds.) ICIAP 2005. LNCS, vol. 3617, pp. 50–57. Springer, Heidelberg (2005)
6. Gómez, J., González, F., Dasgupta, D.: An immuno-fuzzy approach to anomaly detection. Fuzzy Systems. In: FUZZ 2003. 12th IEEE International Conference on Fuzzy Systems, vol. 2, pp. 1219–1224 (2003)
7. Yao, J., Zhao, S., Saxton, L.: A study on fuzzy intrusion detection. Data Mining, Intrusion Detection, Information Assurance, and Data Networks Security 2005. In: Dasarathy, B.V.(ed.) Proceedings of the SPIE, vol. 5812, pp.23–30 (2005)
8. Oja.: Principal components, minor components, and linear neural networks. Neural Networks 5(6), 927–935 (1972)
9. Kuchimanchi, G.K., Phoha, V.V., Balagami, K.S., Gaddam, S.R.: Dimension reduction using feature extraction methods for Real-time misuse detection systems. In: Proceedings of the 2004 IEEE Workshop on Information Assurance and Security, West Point, NY, pp. 195–202 (2004)
10. Labib, K., Vemuri, V.R.: Detecting and visualizing denial-of-service and network probe attacks using principal component analysis. In: Third Conference on Security and Network Architectures, La Londe, France (2004)
11. Mukkamala, S., Sung, A.H., Abraham, A.: Intrusion Detection Using Ensemble of Soft Computing Paradigms. Journal of Network and Computer Applications 28, 167–182 (2005)
12. Didaci, L., Giacinto, G., Roli, F.: Ensemble Learning for Intrusion Detection in Computer Networks. In: Workshop su apprendimento automatico: metodi ed applicazioni (2006)
13. Xu, L., Krzyzak, A., Suen, C.Y.: Methods for combining multiple classifiers and their applications to handwriting recognition. IEEE Trans. Systems, Man and Cybernetics 22, 418–435 (1992)

Managing Uncertainty in Access Control Decisions in Distributed Autonomous Collaborative Environments

Petros Belsis[1], Stefanos Gritzalis[1], Christos Skourlas[2], and Vassilis Tsoukalas[3]

[1] Department of Information and Communication Systems Engineering,
University of the Aegean, Karlovassi, Samos, Greece
[2] Department of Informatics, Technological Education Institute, Athens, Greece
[3] Department of Industrial Informatics, Technological Education Institute, Kavala, Greece
{pbelsis, sgritz}@aegean.gr, cskourlas@teiath.gr,
vtsouk@teikav.edu.gr

Abstract. Coalitions of autonomous domains gain constantly interest during the last years due to the various fields of their potential application. A lot of challenges of both academic as well as of practical nature are related with their deployment. Among else, the distributed nature of a coalition demands special focus in respect to security management. In this paper we argue about the necessity for adjustable security mechanisms towards the security management of multi-domain environments; we describe an approach that allows determination of preferences when defining access control permissions over the shared objects. We handle such preferences by encoding access control constraints using fuzzy relations and we describe a prototype security architecture that implements the basic principles of our approach.

1 Introduction

In various collaborative environments (such as ministries in e-government environments, interconnected medical domains etc), there is a need for joint access over shared resource among different organizations. The aim of these collaborative environments is to increase the capability of the participating domains to respond in various challenges without demanding excessive times. Achieving interoperability, retrieving efficiently knowledge assets in the distributed environment and managing security are among the main research challenges when building similar infrastructures; still the developed security mechanisms lack when it comes to their capability to be adaptive.

We present a method that incorporates extensions to multi-domain security models and allows determination of preferences in handling access control decisions over the shared resources for the participating domains. We describe in the framework of ongoing research work the modular components of our prototype architecture that implements policy based access control enforcement; another feature is that it allows reasoning over access requests by incorporating in the calculations fuzzy constraints. The rest of the paper is organized as follows: section 2 presents related work in context, outlining in brief differentiations from our approach; section 3 discusses some basic principles for access control enforcement in multi-domain environments.

I. Cervesato (Ed.): ASIAN 2007, LNCS 4846, pp. 261–267, 2007.

Section 4 presents our approach that allows determination of preferences in access control decisions for shared objects in the federated domain, using fuzzy constraints. Section 5 presents the prototype architecture that enables access control enforcement in collaborative environments. Section 6 concludes the paper, evaluating the implementation status of our approach and providing directions for further work.

2 Related Work

Barker and Stuckey [1] use constraint logic programming to express multiple access control policies; in their work they do not provide support for multiple access control restrictions, such as limitations to access objects at certain locations. In addition there is no support for determination of preferences over the access constraints.

Bonatti et al [5], propose an algebra for the creation of an access control policy out of simpler policies. In their model their language's expressiveness is analysed with respect to first order logic. They show that their language's formal semantics are equivalent to first order logic formulations. A global policy is composed out of simpler ones; in our approach instead we enable a policy bridging mechanism enabling interoperation between the constituent policies. We also define a novel technique that allows determination of preferences over specific requests or actions over the shared workspace.

In [6] a scalable solution to enable formation of coalitions over ad-hoc environments is proposed. A distributed service registry is utilized to enable interoperation between different autonomous wirelessly interconnected domains. In this approach, the management of the coalition is performed using information codified in the registry, which plays similar role as in our approach; still the proposed approach does not allow the flexibility to manage access requests that are not explicitly defined in advance.

3 Access Control Solutions for Multi-domain Environments

The Role Based Access Control (RBAC) model [2] has proved so far to be the most prominent security model; RBAC parameters can be encoded as policy expressions and can be codified in policy languages. The recorded policies are further loaded and interpreted dynamically; accordingly the policy enforcement modules reason over specific access requests. Thus, we have also adopted a policy driven approach in order to simplify and automate security management.

Considering permissions as a set of Boolean constraints associated with a given role, we can represent the security policy using constraints, each one consisting of a triplet of the following variables: the role variable, the permissions and the assets (objects) which the role is allowed to access. In a multi-domain environment where different domains share their assets, the problem of assigning privileges to roles can be cast to specifying generalised constraints (that contain tuples with RBAC variables from different domains) which have to be jointly satisfied. Typically an access control decision is defined by a tuple (Role, Object, Permission) where R is one of the available roles in the system, O is the requested object and P is an access permission (in the UNIX© system for instance access permissions can be represented as w, r, x for write, read and execute permissions respectively). The evaluation of allowed requests - and therefore the system's access control operation - may rely on decomposition of RBAC related tasks which can furthermore be evaluated on the basis of appropriate logic expressions. Thus, in order to evaluate a state <authorised(john, write, o)|true> a number of sub-goals may be evaluated, such as: <ura(john,R_1, date)>, active(john, R_1), senior_to(R_1, R_2), pra(write,o, R_2, date)> where ura, pra, senior_to, correspond to typical RBAC expressions (user-to-role assignment, permission–to-role assignment etc)[1].

In a multi-domain environment we can consider that security tuples may be expanded so as to contain the role which originated the request, the corresponding role to the target domain, the requested object and the permission under request. Considering that all the tuples cannot be defined always in advance as new organizations join or leave, an alternative approach may rely on defining a way to express preferences over the shared objects, which define the criticality of the object and thus the willingness of a domain to share or not the resource.

4 Determining Fuzzy Relations for the Access Control Model

Access control problem formulations can be easily encoded by means of appropriate constraint representations; this is mainly due to the constraint nature of the RBAC model. Therefore allowed accesses can be represented as tuples of RBAC variables. In multi-domain environments it is not easy to describe all the possible access combinations in advance, since due to the dynamic nature of the environment new systems join and new roles and shared assets are continuously contributed to the shared environment. Security management -in contrast to the single domain paradigm- within the federated framework is much more complicated, since it is not feasible to always determine in advance all the allowed accesses. The inherent uncertainty in managing access control in these environments [11] may be treated using fuzzy relations which allow determination of the degree of satisfaction of a specific statement.

Since all the possible access combinations in multi-domain environments cannot be defined in advance and access constraints may not be evaluated on basis of Boolean expressions, fuzzy constraints may be used instead; thus, we may extend the notion of access constraints and associate them with a degree of satisfaction, expressed on a [0, 1] scale. By utilizing soft constraints it is possible to treat access control problems by encountering preferences expressed as values (k-tuples) that can be assigned to a set of variables. Therefore we can assign to each tuple a level of preference $\mu_e(u_1, ...,u_k)$ which assigns a value in a totally ordered set [0,1] [4]. Instead of an ordinary Constraint Satisfaction Problem (CSP) we can incorporate in our calculations fuzzy metrics, transforming the problem to fuzzy CSP's. More specifically, as a fuzzy CSP we can consider a list of variables $(x_1, ...x_k)$, a list of finite domains of values $(D_1,....,D_k)$ and a list of fuzzy constraints $(c_1,.......,c_k)$. An instantiation $v^* \in D$ is considered as a perfect solution if all individual constraints are satisfied. An instantiation $v^* \in D$ is a best solution if the degree of joint satisfaction of all the constraints is maximal possible C $((c_1,c_2,..c_k)\underline{v}^*)$. We consider that these preferences are encoded in a fuzzy relation R that associates each k-tuple $(u_1, ...,u_k)$ with a level of preference

$P(u_1, ..., u_k)$. $P_R(u_1, ..., u_k)$, $>P_R(u'_1, ..., u'_k)$ means that $(u_1, ..., u_k)$ is preferable $(u'_1, ..., u'_k)$. $P_R(u_1, ..., u_k)=0$ means that tuple $(u_1, ..., u_k)$ fully violates the constraint while $P_R(u_1, ..., u_k)=1$ means the constraint is fully satisfied.

We will show the applicability of our approach with an example. Considering that we want to express preferences for two available roles, R_1 and R_2 and two shared assets A and B and with 'w' and 'r' we define the two allowed permissions for these assets, we can model the problem as a fuzzy CSP (FCSP) with variables R (role), O (object) P (permission) with value-domains $\{R_1, R_2\}$, $\{A, B\}$, and $\{w,r\}$ respectively.

We consider different combinations of domain variables encoded in a matrix as constraint representations (Table 1). In our case we consider two constraints that define the degree of preference for a combination of values for two (or more in a general case) problem variables. The first constraint associates roles with a preference to access the shared objects, the second associates the given objects with different types of permissions. Combinations which are totally unacceptable are not presented in Table 1 still they are encountered as not acceptable combinations during the computation of preferences.

Table 1. Encoding domain preferences by means of fuzzy constraints

Constraint	Satisfaction	R (role)	P (permission)	O (Object)
	0.8	R_1		A
	0.2	R_2		A
C_1	0.7	R_1		B
	0.1	R_2		B
	0.3		W	B
C_2	0.1		W	A
	0.4		R	B
	0.3		R	A

The legitimacy of an access request may be calculated using the preference constraints and by calculating a degree of total satisfaction for the possible combinations of values for all the problem variables. We can introduce at this point two useful metrics in order to estimate the most appropriate combinations: the appropriateness $a_i(v)$ of a value $v \in D_i$ for a variable x_i is evaluated on the basis of the degree of the best possible joint satisfaction of the constraints referring to x_i and is defined as

$$a_i(v)=\max\{C((c_{i1},..,cih),\underline{v}) \mid \underline{v} \in D_{i1}, \times ... \times D_{ik-1} \times \{v\} \times D_{ik+1} .. \times Dih\} \qquad (1)$$

and the difficulty of a variable, which can be computed according to the following formula [3]:

$$d_i = \sum_{v \in D_i} a_i(v) \qquad (2)$$

The difficulty metric can be used as an estimation of the most critical parameter, which should be instantiated first. While seeking for combinations that satisfy most the defined preferences, we utilize as a tool the aforementioned metrics. Therefore, we calculate first the difficulty of the variables under examination and accordingly we

Instantiate the one which achieves the higher degree, which means that is the most critical and should be instantiated first. For this value according to equation (1) we choose the most appropriate value which maximizes the degree of satisfaction.

As an application scenario, we can consider the case where we have two domains that cooperate and want to share resources. In order the coalition to enable access to the shared resources, we need to establish a remote privilege management mechanism. We establish a role mapping approach which allows –under certain circumstances – access over shared resources [9][10]). The main idea behind this approach is that roles with many privileges and a high position in the role hierarchy are more likely to be granted access permissions over shared objects, even if these permissions have not been explicitly defined. We first calculate the difficulty for the variables R, O, P that participate in the two defined constraints by identifying the domain values and their degree of preference. For the role R variable as it can be seen from table 1 we have two possible instantiations and the maximal values for each instantiation, according to equation (1) are: 1 for R_1 and 0.2 for R_2, achieving thus a value of d=1.2. For variable O (object) we have as maximal values from Table 1, 0.8 for object A and 0.7 for B giving thus a value d=1.5 (for the difficulty). Similarly for the P variable (permission) we achieve for the possible values a difficulty of d=0.7. Therefore we instantiate first the Object variable assigning the value with higher preference: A. Accordingly, from the remaining variables according to equation we proceed by considering only the remaining combinations that contain this selected value A for the instantiated variable. The next variable to be instantiated is Role and as most appropriate value is R_1 which satisfies better the constraint. In a similar manner we conclude that the most preferred access action is read over the shared object. Therefore the most preferable allowed tuple is $<R_1, DB_1, r>$. We have in brief thus showed that by encoding preferences we can define which accesses are most preferred over which objects and for specific roles with higher privileges and a position higher than others in the role hierarchy.

5 Access Control Enforcement Architecture

We have proceeded in implementing a prototype that implements the basic operational principles of our model. The policy management architecture consists of the following modules (Fig. 1):

- The authentication module which evaluates the user credentials and provides through a single-sign-in procedure a SAML [8] assertion that allows interaction with all the modules within the coalition framework.
- The Policy Decision Point (PDP) that evaluates the requests according to the given policy.
- The Policy Enforcement Point (PEP) that actually implements access control enforcement.
- The policy mapping repository that stores all the necessary information to allow policy interoperation.
- The constraint solving module that loads the constraints and calculates the degree of satisfaction for a given constraint and facilitates the policy decision for requests that their legitimacy is not defined in advance.

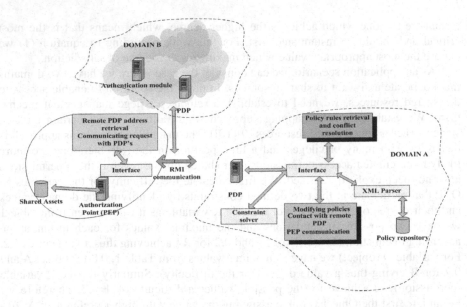

Fig. 1. Generic access control enforcement system architecture

An example usage scenario operates as follows: A user (originating in domain B) logs in the system and acquires an authentication credential which is issued as a SAML compliant assertion and which is recognizable by all the domains and allows interaction within the coalition framework; thus the operation of the framework is based on a single sign-on process which simplifies the authentication procedures for all the participating domains. In order to acquire access to shared resources, the request is formulated through the PEP interface which is implemented entirely in Java. The PEP operates using software modules that are partially provided by the XACML framework [7] and other modules that we developed for use in our multi-domain framework; accordingly, the PEP creates a XACML request (encoded in XML form). The request is sent to the PDP for further evaluation. The PDP software module is also built in Java. It primarily invokes a XACML compatible parser and isolates the access request message payload. Next it checks the request against the local policy (stored in the policy repository) to determine if the request should be authorized. In case the request comes from a role that originates in a remote domain, the PDP queries the coalition management registry and identifies whether the remote role is invoked in the coalition. This is done by sending a request to the cooperating PDP's using the Java RMI protocol. Last, the PEP receives a XACML reply message from the PDP's and enforces the decision.

6   Conclusions

Policy management in distributed collaborating environments is a challenging task, confronting with various research and technical challenges. We have presented a method that allows determination of preferences over access constraints for coalitions of autonomous systems and have tested the validity of our approach through a prototype implementation. Specific attention has been given to the design principles of our prototype architecture so as to retain an interoperable and scalable character.

We have tested the validity of the approach by directing requests from three different domains (subnets) where each domain comprised of a three level hierarchy, with three roles for each domain. The initial performance results of the prototype were very promising. We are currently working on expanding the functionality of our prototype architecture, especially by integrating different commercial constraint solvers.

References

1. Barker, S., Stuckey, P.: Flexible Access Control Policy Specification with Constraint logic programming. ACM Trans. Inf. Syst. Secur. 6(4), 501–546 (2003)
2. Sandhu, R., Ferraiolo, D., Kuhn, R.: The NIST model for role-based access control: towards a unified standard. In: RBAC 2000. Proceedings of the Fifth ACM Workshop on Role-Based Access Control, pp. 47–63. ACM press, New York (2000)
3. Ruttkay, Z.: Fuzzy constraint satisfaction. In: Proc. 3rd IEEE International Conference on Fuzzy Systems, pp. 1263–1268 (1994)
4. Dubois, D., Fargier, H., Prade, H.: The calculus of fuzzy restrictions as a basis for flexible constraint satisfaction. In: Proc. IEEE International Conference on Fuzzy Systems, pp. 1131–1136. IEEE Computer Society, Los Alamitos (1993)
5. Bonatti, P., di Vimercati, D.C.S., Samarati, P.: An algebra for composing access control policies. ACM Trans. Inf. Syst. Secur (TISSEC) 5(1), 1–35 (2002)
6. Mukkamala, R., Atluri, V., Warner, J.: A Distributed Service Registry for Resource Sharing among Ad-hoc Dynamic Coalitions. In: Proc. of IFIP Joint Working Conference on Security Management, Integrity, and Internal Control in Information systems. LNCS, Springer, Heidelberg (2005)
7. XACML Extensible access control markup language specification 2.0, OASIS Standard (March 2004), available at http://www.oasis-open.org
8. Hughes, et al.: Technical Overview of the OASIS Security Assertion Markup Language (SAML) V1.1.OASIS, http://xml.coverpages.org/saml.html
9. Joshi, J.B.D., Bhatti, R., Bertino, E., Ghafoor, A.: Access Control Language for Multi-Domain Environments. IEEE Internet Computing 8(6), 40–50 (2004)
10. Belokolsztolszki, A., Eyers, D., Moody, K.: Policy Contexts: Controlling Information Flow in Parameterised RBAC. In: POLICY 2003. Proc. of the 4th Int. Workshop on Policies for Distributed Systems and Networks, pp. 99–110. IEEE Press, Los Alamitos
11. Hosmer, H.: Security is fuzzy!: applying the fuzzy logic paradigm to the multipolicy paradigm. In: Proceedings on the 1992-1993 Workshop on New Security Paradigms (Little Compton, Rhode Island, United States), pp. 175–184. ACM Press, New York

On Run-Time Enforcement of Policies

Harshit Shah[1] and R.K. Shyamasundar[2]

[1] Dep. Informatica & TLC, Univ. of Trento, Italy
shah@dit.unitn.it
[2] School of Tech. & Comp. Science, TIFR, Mumbai, India
shyam@tcs.tifr.res.in

Abstract. Monitoring untrusted code for harmful behaviour is an important security issue. Many approaches have been proposed for restricting activities and the range of untrusted code. Among these, run-time monitoring is a promising approach for constricting run-time behaviour of programs. In this paper we describe a method of containing the effects of untrusted code with respect to a specified policy. We use a guarded command like language for specifying policies that could monitor system calls, APIs or library routines of the underlying system. We also discuss a system call monitoring architecture for an operating system like Linux. We provide semantics of the language in terms of Security Automata and also discuss how pure past temporal properties can be automatically compiled into policies in guarded command language. This allows users to specify policies in terms of logical formulae and automatically generate monitoring algorithm for the same in terms of guarded commands. We show how simple modifications allow us to specify constraints on the overall behaviour of a group of processes.

1   Introduction

Software is a very important and very complex component of computer systems. A user does not have a thorough understanding of most of the code running on his machine. In such a scenario, code containing malicious payload becomes a serious threat [14]. Such a piece of code tricks the unsuspecting user into believing that it adds functionality to the device. In [18], Ken Thomson showed how a seemingly harmless compiler could be loaded with harmful content that would open a backdoor to the system.

The amount of damage that can be incurred by malicious code can be huge. It can perform a range of nasty activities from corrupting a system to obtaining complete control over it. The situation becomes worse when one considers mobile platforms that have limited capabilities (which also come at a price). It therefore becomes important to make sure that these capabilities are not abused and to also provide mechanisms that ensure that untrusted code does not breach user's expectations. Achieving this objective is not easy. It is difficult to check code for malicious content. Code writers use a high level of sophistication to make sure that the unwanted behaviour goes undetected. It is impractical to expect the end

I. Cervesato (Ed.): ASIAN 2007, LNCS 4846, pp. 268–281, 2007.

user to carefully examine and execute untrusted code so as not to compromise system security.

Run-time monitoring of code comes across as a promising approach to constrain activities of a running program. In such scenarios, a user typically writes a policy which is then used to instrument code (to insert checks at appropriate places) or which is compiled into a separate monitor. Many specification languages and monitoring mechanisms have been proposed. Some of the specification languages are platform specific (e.g., for Linux) while some are specific to a programming language (e.g., Java). In order to achieve platform independence, it has been proposed to abstract the underlying system. The policy specification can then be provided in terms of the abstraction [19]. Often, policy specification becomes difficult and user requires good amount of knowledge about the specification language to ensure that he has written the correct policy.

In order to make specification easier, we use a simple Guarded Command Policy Specification Language (GCPSL) to specify security policies that have to be enforced on untrusted code. GCPSL has the advantage that it describes the actions that monitor has to perform and the state information it has to maintain to enforce the policy. When untrusted code is executed, the actions performed by the code are monitored. At any point of time, if the code is about to violate a security policy, then the execution is terminated. We show the connection between pure past temporal specification and GCPSL. This helps us to automatically generate monitoring algorithm for a policy specified as a temporal logic formula (with past temporal operators). We discuss a sample monitoring architecture for system calls and extend the specification language to allow formulation of policies constraining the behaviour of a set of processes. The rest of the paper is organized as follows: section 2 provides the syntax and semantics of the (GCPSL), section 3 describes a system call monitoring architecture, in section 4 we outline the extension to GCPSL to handle a set of processes, in section 5 we show how temporal constraints can be compiled into monitor specification in GCPSL, in section 6 we discuss the state of the implementation, section 7 describes related work and section 8 presents the conclusion.

2 Guarded Command Policy Specification Language

Guarded command language [4] is a well founded and structured formulation widely used for a variety of specification and applications. A guarded command is of the form $G \rightarrow S$ where G is a proposition and S is a statement. When G evaluates to true, S is executed. Guarded command language also contains conditional and repetitive structures as shown below:

if	**do**
$G_0 \rightarrow S_0$	$G_0 \rightarrow S_0$
$G_1 \rightarrow S_1$	$G_1 \rightarrow S_1$
$\ldots$	$\ldots$
$G_n \rightarrow S_n$	$G_n \rightarrow S_n$
fi	**od**

In each case, more than one guard could evaluate to true at a time. In this case, one of the statements is chosen non-deterministically. Thus, non-determinism is an intrinsic property of guarded command language. When none of the guards evaluate to true, execution is aborted.

GCPSL, like guarded command language, is a list of guarded commands. To ensure determinacy, the guards must be mutually exclusive (i.e., at most one guard can evaluate to true at a given time). However, to allow for easier specification of policies, we do not require that the guards be mutually exclusive. Whenever more than one guard evaluates to true, we execute the instructions following the first true guard. Here, we assume that the policies are written at the level of system calls, library routines or APIs i.e., a policy imposes constraints on how these calls can be used by untrusted code. State variables keep track of current state of execution of code and are updated upon witnessing relevant actions (in this case, method calls with actual arguments).

2.1   Syntax of GCPSL

A policy in the language consists of two sections; first part (which is optional) is used to declare state variables and the second part is a list of guarded commands. The syntax is shown below.

state:
$\quad\quad var\_type_1 \; state\_var_1 = initial\_value_1;$
$\quad\quad \vdots$

command:
$\quad\quad (method\_call_1(x,y,z)) \wedge (condition_1 \vee condition_2) \rightarrow statement_1; \ldots ;$
$\quad\quad (method\_call_2(w)) \wedge (condition_3) \rightarrow$ **terminate**;
$\quad\quad \vdots$

default: skip | terminate;

State variable declaration consists of the keyword "state" followed by a series of variable declarations. The state variables have to be initialized to some value so that a unique start state can be determined. Guarded command list consists of the keyword "command" followed by at least one guarded command and the "default" action is either skip or terminate. Each guarded command consists of a guard followed by one or more statements. A guard can be a boolean combination of conditions: it could be an event denoting method call/s (with the name of the call and a list of arguments) or a comparison of expressions (involving only constants, state variables and formal arguments to the current method call). Statements can either update the state variables and allow the action or terminate the program under supervision or skip updation and allow the aciton. State variables are updated after the actual method call returns. Statements can use the return value of the call through the keyword "result". The "default" declaration tells what should be done when none of the guards evaluate to true.

Example 1. Consider a policy which states that processes cannot write more than 80KB (total) into files. This policy could be specified as:

state:

   int *written*=0;

command:

   (write(*fd, buff, num_bytes*)) $\wedge$ (*written* < 80000) $\wedge$
       (*written* + *num_bytes* $\leq$ 80000) $\rightarrow$ *written*= *written* + **result**;
   !(write(*fd, buff, num_bytes*)) $\rightarrow$ **skip**;

default: terminate;

2.2 Semantics of GCPSL

We provide semantics using *security automata* as defined in [16]. The security automaton is a 4-tuple $\langle Q, \Sigma, \delta, Q \rangle$. The set of states Q is the set of values that the state variables can take. Suppose that the state variable declaration is as shown below:

state:

   var_type_1 $s_1 = c_1$;

   ⋮

   var_type_n $s_n = c_n$;

Let **val** be a function that takes as input a variable and returns the set of values (of appropriate type) that it can take. Then the set of states Q can be defined as:

$$Q = \mathbf{val}(s_1) \times \cdots \times \mathbf{val}(s_n).$$

The initial state is the set of initial values that are assigned to state variables (i.e., $\langle c_1, \cdots, c_n \rangle$). The alphabet Σ is the set of monitored method call events. It is defined as:

$\Sigma = \{$method_call$(v_1, \cdots, v_n) \mid$ method_call$(x_1, \cdots, x_n)$ is a method call with
       formal arguments $x_1, \cdots, x_n$ and $\forall 1 \leq i \leq n.\ v_i \in \mathbf{val}(x_i)\}$

We now define the transition function. Consider the command section of a policy as defined below:

command:

   $guard_1 \rightarrow statement_1$

   ⋮

   $guard_m \rightarrow statement_m$

Let G be a function that evaluates each guard on current state and current input symbol and returns the index of the first guard that evaluates to true (if none of the guards evaluates to true, it returns 0). G is defined as:

$$\text{G}: Q \times \Sigma \rightarrow \{0, \cdots, m\}$$

Let F_i be the partial function associated with the statement part of guarded command i. This function captures the way in which statement i updates the state. We use function G to select appropriate function F_i on a given $\langle$input state, symbol$\rangle$ pair. We then define the transition function in terms of F_i. Formally,

$$\forall 1 \leq i \leq m.\ \text{F}_i : Q \times \Sigma \rightarrow Q \text{ and}$$

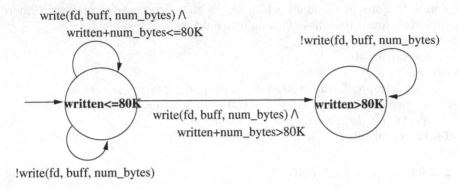

write(fd, buff, num_bytes) ∧
written+num_bytes<=80K

!write(fd, buff, num_bytes)

written<=80K

write(fd, buff, num_bytes) ∧
written+num_bytes>80K

written>80K

!write(fd, buff, num_bytes)

Fig. 1. Automaton for example 1

$\forall q \in Q$ and $\forall a \in \Sigma$, $F_0(q, a) = q$
(if specification has "**default**: skip") and
$\forall q \in Q$ and $\forall a \in \Sigma$, $F_0(q, a)$ is not defined
(if specification has "**default**: terminate")

Thus, $\forall q \in Q$ and $\forall a \in \Sigma$, $\delta(q, a) = F_{G(q,a)}(q, a)$.

Figure 1 shows the security automaton (reduced to 2 states) for policy shown in example 1.

3   A Sample Monitoring Architecture: Monitoring System Calls Without Program Instrumentation

System calls constitute an important programming aid. They abstract away low level hardware details from the programmer. All access to underlying hardware is made through these system calls (which are provided by the operating system through libraries). Thus, system calls form an important boundary at which we can monitor program actions.

Monitoring system calls at run-time can be done without modifying untrusted code. System calls are made by generating an interrupt (e.g., `int 80x` on Linux/i86). This transfers the control to kernel mode. The service for this interrupt uses a system call table (set by the operating system) that is looked up (using the value in register eax as index) and control is transferred to code for the appropriate system call in kernel space. The process is shown in fig. 2.

Since all the necessary information is already maintained by the operating system, we only have to intercept system calls inside the kernel and check whether they should be allowed. To make this decision, the kernel module consults a user space monitoring module. The user space module allows user to specify policies, compiles them and then takes a decision based on information provided by the kernel module (figure 3).

For example, consider a policy that no file in "/bin" can be written into. To enforce this policy, we write the following specification:

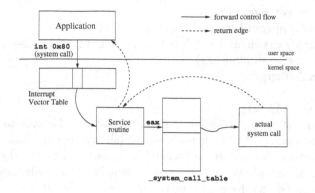

Fig. 2. System call architecture in Linux

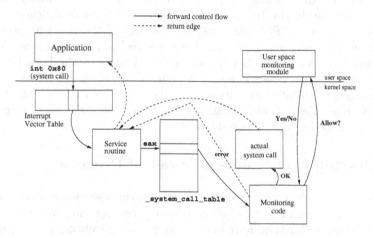

Fig. 3. System call monitoring architecture in Linux

commands:
> (open(*file_name, access_mode*)) ∧ (file_path(*file_name*)=="/bin") ∧
> ((*access_mode*==O_WRONLY) ∨ (*access_mode*==O_RDWR))
>   →**terminate**;

default: skip;

The "file_path()" function takes a file name and returns the absolute path of the file. This function is not a system call or a library routine but such functions can be used to make specification easier. Based on the target platform, the run-time enforcement mechanism implements the necessary functionality. The policy can be easily compiled into user space module of the monitor. The kernel module signals the user space module when relevant system calls are made (along with state information and arguments). Shown below is a part of C code (for user space component) compiled from the GCPSL policy shown above:

```
action = get_event();
if ( (strcmp(action.call_id,"open") &&
(file_path(aciton.arg_1,"/bin")) && ((action.arg_2==O_WRONLY) ||
(action.arg_2==O_RDONLY)) )
    signal(deny);
else
    signal(allow);
```

The "action" structure contains information about the system call (name, arguments, etc.) passed by the kernel module (shown by edge labeled "Allow?" in fig. 3). Whether the system call should be allowed or not is decided by the code fragment shown above and the reply is sent back to the kernel module via signal() function (shown by edge labeled "Yes/No" in fig. 3).

In the monitoring architecture, kernel mode provides good insulation to the in-kernel module that intercepts the system calls. The state variables could also be maintained inside the kernel (and hence be safe from modification by user space code). Since GCPSL captures the working of the monitor, it is easily compiled into the user space module that takes decisions regarding actions. The monitoring framework does not require major changes in the kernel code or a reboot when the user policy changes. The drawback of the architecture is that the decision is taken after execution enters kernel mode and the switch is very time consuming. Care should be taken to ensure safety of the user space module from interference by malicious code.

4   Enforcing Constraints on a Set of Processes

The monitoring architecture described in the previous section enforces run-time constraints (specified in GCPSL) on individual processes. However, there are certain cases where restrictions have to be imposed collectively on a set of processes. Here, we provide extension to GCPSL so that specification of such collective constraints becomes easy.

Consider a mobile phone game that can have multiple instances running on the platform. The user interacts with other online players through messages. However, since messages cannot be sent free of cost, user wants to limit the number to MAX_MESSAGES (some pre-defined constant). Once the limit is reached, user should be asked each time before sending a message. To handle such policies, we equip the GCPSL with extra constructs that allow us to handle a set of processes. We partition the state variables into two sets namely, "global" and "local". For the example mentioned above, we could write a policy as follows:

state:
    global:
        int num_msg=0;
    local:
        int $asked$=0;

command:

    (**send_message**(*remote_host*)) $\wedge$ (*num_msg*<MAX_MESSAGES) $\to$ *num_msg*++;

    (**ask_user**(*msg*)) $\wedge$ (*num_msg*==MAX_MESSAGES) $\to$ *asked*=1;

    (**send_message**(*remote_host*)) $\wedge$ (*num_msg*==MAX_MESSAGES)

        $\wedge$(asked==1) $\to$ *asked*=0;

    !(send_message(remote_host))$\to$ **skip**;

default: terminate;

Thus, GCPSL can be easily adapted to enable a user to specify policies over multiple processes. It is important to note that global state variables should be locked before access to ensure that concurrent execution does not corrupt them. Also, in some cases, like the example mentioned above, the global state of the monitor may have to be persistent. In the example above, if 2 sessions of the game use up the MAX_MESSAGES limit set by the monitor, then any session that may be invoked later should always have to ask before sending a message. Thus, for example, a monthly limit on the number of messages that can be sent without permission can be set. When the month is over, the global state of the monitor has to be reset again. We do not include this in specification. The local state variables pertaining to individual game sessions can be created when the process starts and can be removed when the process terminates. Thus, the extension to the GCPSL can be easily handled by the system call monitoring architecture described in the previous section with minor changes to the kernel module.

4.1 Semantics

Let us assume that we are given a policy to enforce on a set of processes $P_1, P_2, \cdots, P_p$. Also, each process has its own copy of local state variables (we tag local variables with the process name).

Suppose that the policy has state variable declaration as:

state:

    global:

        var_type_1 $g_1 = c_1$;

        $\vdots$

        var_type_n $g_n = c_n$;

    local:

        var_type_1 $l_1 = c_1'$;

        $\vdots$

        var_type_n $l_{n'} = c_{n'}'$;

Then, the set of states is given by

$$Q = \mathbf{val}(g_1) \times \cdots \times \mathbf{val}(g_n) \times \{\mathbf{val}(l_1) \times \cdots \times \mathbf{val}(l_{n'})\}^p.$$

Initial state is given by $\langle c_1, \cdots, c_n, \{c_1', \cdots, c_{n'}'\}^p \rangle$.

The alphabet is given by

$$\Sigma = \{\langle P_i, \text{method\_call}(v_1, \cdots, v_k)\rangle \mid \text{method\_call}(\mathrm{x}_1, \cdots, \mathrm{x}_k) \text{ is a call}$$

        with formal parameters $x_1, \cdots, x_k$ and for $1 \le i \le k$. $v_i \in \mathbf{val}(x_i)$

        and $\mathrm{P_i}$ is the process which made the call$\}$

Consider the command section of a policy as defined below:

command:

$$guard_1 \rightarrow statement_1$$

$$\vdots$$

$$guard_m \rightarrow statement_m$$

Let G be a function that evaluates each guard on current state and current input symbol and returns the index of the first guard that evaluates to true (or returns 0 when none of the guards is true). G is defined as:

$$G: Q \times \Sigma \rightarrow \{0, \ldots, m\}$$

Let F_i be the partial function associated with the statement part of guarded command i. This function captures the way in which statement i updates the state. We use function G to select appropriate function F_i on a given $\langle$input state, symbol$\rangle$ pair. We then define the transition function in terms of F_i. Formally, $\forall 1 \leq i \leq m$. $F_i : Q \times \Sigma \rightarrow Q$ (and F_0 is defined the same way as before).

The information about which process performed corresponding action is needed to update the local state variables pertaining to that process. For updation of global state variables, this information is discarded. The transition function can therefore be written as:

$$\forall q \in Q \text{ and } \forall a \in \Sigma, \ \delta(q,a) = F_{G(q,a)}(q, a)$$

5   From Pure Past Temporal Logic to GCPSL

GCPSL policies describe the operation of the run-time monitor in terms of states and allowed actions. Many policies enforce temporal restrictions on the actions (e.g., library routines, system calls, etc.) of an untrusted program. These restrictions can sometimes be difficult to capture through such a detailed specification of monitoring mechanism as GCPSL. Temporal logic is better suited for specification of such policies. Temporal logic formulae are more convenient when complex policies are composed by conjunction/disjunciton of several simple policies. A composition of simple policies could lead to a huge number of guarded commands in GCPSL. A separation of concerns can therefore be achieved if users can specify such complex policies in temporal logic which could then be compiled into GCPSL (which, as we have seen in section 3, can be easily compiled into user space component).

Since the monitoring architecture presented in section 3 relies on GCPSL policies to make run-time decisions (which are compiled into the user space component of the architecture), we will see how conversion of pure past temporal logic formulae into GCPSL policies can be done so that they can be incorporated without any change in the architecture.

As we are concerned with security policies that can be monitored during execution, we focus our attention on *safety properties* which stipulate that the execution never enters a forbidden state. Every past formula is interpreted on a finite sequence of states $\sigma = s_0, \cdots, s_n$ (where S is the set of states and each $s_i \in S$). The formula is built from a set of atomic propositions AP and logical and temporal connectives. A labelling function $l : S \to 2^{AP}$ tells which propositions are true in a particular state. The syntax for pure past temporal logic is as follows:

$$\varphi: = p \mid \neg\varphi \mid \varphi \vee \varphi \mid \varphi\,\mathcal{S}\,\varphi \mid \mathcal{Y}\varphi$$

Here, $p \in AP$ is an atomic propostion, $\mathcal{S}$ is the "since" operator and $\mathcal{Y}$ is the "yesterday" or the "previous step" operator. Other operators can be expressed in terms of these as follows:

$\mathcal{O}\varphi \equiv \mathbf{T}\,\mathcal{S}\,\varphi$ ($\mathcal{O}$ - once in the past)

$\mathcal{H}\varphi \equiv \neg\mathcal{O}\neg\varphi$ ($\mathcal{H}$ - always in the past)

Let $p \in AP$ be an atomic proposition and $\sigma = s_0, s_1, \ldots, s_n$ (each $s_i \in S$) be a finite sequence of states. Let σ_x denote the prefix sequence $s_0, s_1, \ldots, s_x$ of σ. The satisfaction relation is defined by:

$\sigma \models p$ iff $p \in l(s_n)$

$\sigma \models \neg\varphi$ iff $\neg(\sigma \models \varphi)$

$\sigma \models \varphi \vee \psi$ iff $(\sigma \models \varphi) \vee (\sigma \models \psi)$

$\sigma \models \varphi\,\mathcal{S}\,\psi$ iff $\exists j, 0 \le j \le n . \sigma_j \models \psi$ and

$\qquad\qquad \forall i, j < i \le n . \sigma_i \models \varphi$

$\sigma \models \mathcal{Y}\varphi$ iff $n > 0$ and $\sigma_{n-1} \models \varphi$

A sequence σ satisfying a formula is called the model of the formula. All safety properties expressible in temporal logic can be represented as $\mathcal{H}\varphi$ where φ is a past LTL formula [12]. The models of such a safety formula are infinite sequences of states $\sigma = s_0, s_1, \ldots$ such that

$$\forall i \ge 0 . \sigma_i \models \varphi$$

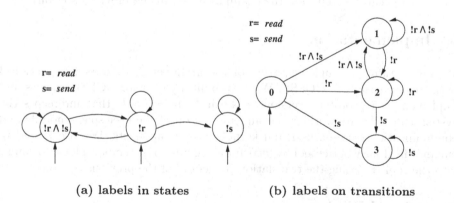

(a) labels in states   (b) labels on transitions

Fig. 4. Automaton for $\mathcal{H}(send \to \neg\mathcal{O}(read))$

In [17], authors present an efficient approach for converting a formula in pure past temporal logic into a finite state automaton. This paves the way for converting temporal restrictions on program actions into guarded command statements. The simple idea is to have an enumerated state variable that can range from 1 to i if there are i states $(q_1, \cdots, q_i)$ in the automaton. For each state and a transition going out of it, we take conjunction of index of the state and the label on outgoing transition as the guard and update the state variable to the index of the state reached via the transition. We set the "**default**: terminate" to indicate a violation.

For example, consider the policy that a message cannot be sent after a file has been read. Let *send* and *read* be the propositions that correspond to **send**() and **read**() method invocations. Then, the policy can be stated in pure past LTL as $\mathcal{H}(send \rightarrow \neg\mathcal{O}(read))$. The automaton produced for this formula is shown in fig. 4(a). The same automaton with labels moved to transitions is shown in fig. 4(b). Thus, the state variable would be declared as:

state:

int $q=0$;

Consider state 0 in the automaton shown in figure 4(b). Since it has 3 outgoing edges, we add a guarded command for each edge as follows:

$(q{=}{=}0)\wedge(!\mathsf{send}())\wedge(!\mathsf{read}())\rightarrow q{=}1;$

$(q{=}{=}0)\wedge(!\mathsf{read}())\rightarrow q{=}2;$

$(q{=}{=}0)\wedge(!\mathsf{send}())\rightarrow q{=}3;$

Continuing this way, we add guarded commands for each outgoing transition from each state and use the default condition to signal violation. Note that the GCPSL policy obtained this way could be longer than what one would write directly using GCPSL. But, complex policies are easer to specify in pure past temporal logic and the translation can be made automatic. The most important aspect of the conversion is mapping of the propositions in the formula to the actions in the guards. To enforce restrictions on a set of processes, we would require a larger set of atomic propositions to incorporate information about the process that performs an action. But guarded command specification can handle it better (as can be seen from the example stated in the previous section).

6   Implementation

We are working on implementation of the architecture described in section 3 with the extensions to GCPSL. We have built a parser for GCPSL policies and implemented a prototype version of the in-kernel module that intercepts the system calls. We are working on implementation of the user space module and communication between user and kernel space components. We also intend to enhance flexibility of the tool by incorporating pure past temporal logic formulae into the tool (by using the translation procedure of the previous section).

7   Related Work

In [19], Uppuluri and Sekar propose a specification language called Behavioural Monitoring Specification Language (BMSL) to specify constraints on program behaviour. They also describe how abstraction can be used to specify policies by grouping system calls into categories. This makes the task of policy specification easier and the policies portable across platforms. The authors also show how more involved policies can be obtained by refining generic policies. Policies in

BMSL can be easily translated into guarded commands. Our approach allows specification of constraints for a set of processes and can even take advantage of the abstraction mechanisms mentioned in [19]. A similar approach for specifying software wrappers for commercial off-the-shelf components was presented in [8]. The specification language proposed in [8] also uses abstraction but is much more complex and often leads to lengthier policies. In addition, the approach uses databases to store and share information among wrappers.

Substantial amount of research has been done on run-time enforcement of security policies. In [9], authors provide a theoretical classification of security policies that can be enforced by different mechanisms (e.g., static analysis, execution monitoring and program re-writing). The authors show that the class of properties that can be monitored at run-time is co-RE (i.e., a policy violation can be detected in finite amount of time but execution that conforms to policy goes on forever). In [16], Schneider presents a theoretical study of execution monitors (mechanisms that monitor program execution and terminate the program before it can violate a security policy) and shows that they can only enforce safety policies. Schneider also presents a *security automata* model of an execution monitor (and also shows that the same can be coded in guarded command language).

Many tools provide system call interception (e.g., [1] and [3]). In [15], author proposes an interactive policy generation tool for monitoring system calls. The specification language is very simple and not as expressive as the guarded command language. A policy in their framework just states whether a particular system call (with specific arguments) should be allowed. The system allows for interactive policy generation through training runs. If a particular system call is not covered by the policy, then the tool asks the user to make a decision (which can be added to the policy). The tool does not allow specification of policies that restrict the order in which system calls are made. Also, the tool cannot constrain the amount of resources used by a process as shown in example 1 in section 2. Another tool called "syscalltrack"[1] allows monitoring of system calls through a simple specification language. On observing a monitored system call (with appropriate arguments), it either allows the call (with logging) or returns an error. Both the tools mentioned above cannot specify policies for a set of processes.

In [13] different models of monitors were proposed which were more powerful than execution monitor in that they could suppress or insert program actions or could truncate execution. It was also shown that edit automata (which can truncate, suppress and insert actions) could enforce any property on execution (even if it were not a safety property). A specification language and a run-time monitoring system called Polymer [2] was also provided for monitoring of Java programs. In this framework, every policy extends an abstract policy class. One has to define security relevant actions (method invocations) and then the policy provides various suggestions (e.g., skip, insert actions, replace action, etc.) when these actions are performed. Different mechanisms for composing policies are also

---

[1] available at http://syscalltrack.sourceforge.net/index.html

provided in [2]. Instead of writing complex policies directly in Java, one could use GCPSL to specify an edit automaton and then compile it into a Polymer policy. By including actions in the instruction part of the guarded commands, one can easily specify an edit automata policy. For example, the specification can be changed as follows:

(Guard)→ terminate;
OR
(Guard)→ {action}*;
            update state | skip;

Thus, whenever a guard is true, either the execution is terminated or sequence of actions is performed and is followed by a possible change of state.

In [7], authors propose a model for run-time monitoring (called *Shallow History Automata*) that tracks only the execution history and does not remember the order of events. Although less powerful than security automata, SHA can enforce some important security policies. In [5], security automata implementation of Software based Fault Isolation (SFI) was discussed and prototypes for x86 and JVML were provided in SAL (Security Automata Language). The language is just a text based representation of security automata with macro definitions in the beginning. The author also presents PSLang (Policy Specification Language) and PoET (Policy Enforcement Toolkit) for in-line monitoring of Java code. In this approach, the untrusted program is instrumented with proper checks so that the modified program does not violate security policy. In [6], author presents Naccio framework for policy enforcement through in-line monitoring. Naccio allows user to specify policies in a platform independent way by providing abstract system interface (the interface, however, is not very easy to use).

All specification languages mentioned so far are platform specific (except Naccio). GCPSL can be seen as a simple way for specifying monitoring algorithm in a platform independent way. Other approaches for run-time monitoring of Java code have been proposed in [11,10] (these approaches were mainly aimed at checking program correctness). In [20], a tool for sand-boxing of untrusted applications is presented.

8   Conclusion

We have described how GCPSL can be used for easy specification of policies. Through a simple extension, GCPSL can enforce a policy collectively on a set of processes. Validation of GCPSL policies is achieved through security automata semantics. The most important objective was to provide a simple specification language that allows a rich set of policies to be formulated and validated. A *separation of concerns* can be achieved by specifying policy in terms of pure past temporal logic and then automatically producing monitoring instructions (guarded commands). A robust system call monitoring architecture for enforcing GCPSL policies was described. GCPSL can be easily modified to incorporate other models of enforcement like suppression, insertion or edit automata (by allowing corresponding actions in the statement part of the guarded command).

References

1. Acharya, A., Raje, M.: MAPbox: using parameterized behavior classes to confine untrusted applications. In: SSYM 2000. Proceedings of the 9th conference on USENIX Security Symposium, Denver, Colorado, p. 1. USENIX Association, Berkeley, CA, USA (2000)
2. Bauer, L., Ligatti, J., Walker, D.: Composing security policies with polymer. In: Proceedings of ACM SIGPLAN Conference on Programming Language Design and Implementation (2005)
3. Chari, S.N., Cheng, P.-C.: Bluebox: A policy-driven, host-based intrusion detection system. ACM Trans. Inf. Syst. Secur. 6(2), 173–200 (2003)
4. Dijkstra, E.W.: Guarded commands, nondeterminacy and formal derivation of programs. Communications of the ACM 18(8), 453–457 (1975)
5. Erlingsson, U.: The Inlined Reference Monitor Approach to Security Policy Enforcement. PhD thesis, Department of Computer Science, Cornell University (2003)
6. Evans, D.: Policy-Directed Code Safety. PhD thesis, Dept. of Electrical Engg. amd Computer Science, Massachusetts Institute of Technology (February 2000)
7. Fong, P.W.L.: Access control by tracking shallow execution history. In: Proceedings, IEEE Symposium on Security and Privacy, 2004, pp. 43–55 (May 2004)
8. Fraser, T., Badger, L., Feldman, M.: Hardening COTS software with generic software wrappers. In: Proceedings of the 1999 IEEE Symposium on Security and Privacy, 1999, pp. 2–16 (1999)
9. Hamlen, K., Morrisett, G., Schneider, F.: Computability classes for enforcement mechanisms. Technical Report 2003-1908, Department of Computer Science, Cornell University (2003)
10. Havelund, K., Rosu, G.: Efficient monitoring of safety properties. International Journal on Software Tools for Technology Transfer 6(2), 158–173 (2004)
11. Kim, M., Kannan, S., Lee, I., Sokolsky, O.: Java-mac: a run-time assurance tool for java. In: 1st International Workshop on Run-time Verification, vol. 55 (2001)
12. Lichtenstein, O., Pnueli, A., Zuck, L.D.: The glory of the past. In: Parikh, R. (ed.) Logics of Programs. LNCS, vol. 193, pp. 196–218. Springer, Heidelberg (1985)
13. Ligatti, J., Bauer, L., Walker, D.: Edit automata: Enforcement mechanisms for run-time security policies. International Journal of Information Security 4(5), 2–16 (2005)
14. McGraw, G., Morrisett, G.: Attacking malicous code: a report to the infosec research council. Software, IEEE 17(5), 33–41 (2000)
15. Provos, N.: Improving host security with system call policies. In: SSYM 2003. Proceedings of the 12th conference on USENIX Security Symposium, Washington, DC, p. 18. USENIX Association, Berkeley, CA, USA (2003)
16. Schneider, F.B.: Enforceable security policies. ACM Trans. Inf. Syst. Secur. 3(1), 30–50 (2000)
17. Shah, H., Shyamasundar, R.K.: Efficient automata generation for pure past LTL. Technical report, School of Technology and Computer Science, TIFR (2007)
18. Thomson, K.: Reflections on trusting trust. Communication of the ACM 27(8), 761–763 (1984)
19. Uppuluri, P., Sekar, R.: Experiences with specification-based intrusion detection. In: RAID 2000. Proceedings of the 4th International Symposium on Recent Advances in Intrusion Detection, pp. 172–189. Springer, Heidelberg (2001)
20. Wagner, D.: Janus: an approach for confinement of untrusted applications. Technical Report CSD-99-1056, University of California, Berkeley (1999)

Static vs Dynamic Typing
for Access Control in Pi-Calculus[*]

Michele Bugliesi, Damiano Macedonio, and Sabina Rossi

Dipartimento di Informatica, Università Ca' Foscari, Venice
{michele,mace,srossi}@dsi.unive.it

Abstract. Traditional static typing systems for the pi-calculus are built around capability types that control the read/write access rights on channels and describe the type of the channels' payload. While static typing has proved adequate for reasoning on process behavior in typed contexts, dynamic techniques have often been advocated as more effective for access control in distributed/untyped contexts.

We study the relationships between the two approaches – static versus dynamic – by contrasting two versions of the asynchronous pi-calculus. The former, APɪ, comes with an entirely standard static typing system. The latter, APɪ@, combines static and dynamic typing: a static type system associates channels with flat types that only express read/write capabilities and disregard the payload type, while a dynamically typed synchronization complements the static type system to guarantee type soundness.

We show that APɪ@ can be encoded into APɪ in a fully abstract manner, preserving the respective behavioral equivalences of the two calculi. Besides yielding an interesting expressivity result, the encoding also sheds light on the effectiveness of dynamic typing as a mechanism for access control.

1 Introduction

Static typing systems have long been established as an effective device to control the interaction among processes in the pi-calculus and related calculi [8,9,13,14]. In these systems the communication channels are viewed as resources, and their types define the capabilities needed to use them. Thus, for instance $\mathsf{rw}\langle S\,;T\rangle$ is the type of a channel where one can output at type T and input at type S (provided that T is a subtype of S). The nested structure of the types makes it possible to control the way that capabilities are delivered and made available. To illustrate, a process knowing the name (or channel) a at the type $\mathsf{rw}\langle\mathsf{r}\langle S\rangle\,;\mathsf{rw}\langle S\,;S\rangle\rangle$ may output on a a full-fledged channel (with payload type S) and be guaranteed that any (well-typed) process inputing on a will only be reading on the channel received. This form of type-based control yields powerful techniques to reason on the behavior of processes in typed contexts: in fact, by putting enough structure on the types of the shared channels, one may gain strong control on the interaction of a process with any typed context. Unfortunately, these techniques do not scale well to general, potentially untyped, contexts.

---

[*] Work partially supported by M.I.U.R (Italian Ministry of Education, University and Research) under contract n. 2005015785.

I. Cervesato (Ed.): ASIAN 2007, LNCS 4846, pp. 282–296, 2007.

To address this shortcoming, [2] introduces a variant of the (asynchronous) pi-calculus, named APɪ@, in which the ability to control the use of channels relies on a combination of static and dynamic typing. The types of channels are still formed around capabilities, but in APɪ@ they only exhibit the "top-level" read/write capabilities, disregarding the types of the values transmitted. Given this simple type structure, the type system is much less effective in providing control on the use of channels. To compensate for that, APɪ@ includes a new form of output construct, noted $\bar{a}\langle v@B\rangle$, that relies on a type coercion to enforce the delivery of v at type B. A static typing system guarantees that v may indeed be assigned the coercion type B, while a mechanism of dynamically typed synchronization guarantees that v is received only at supertypes of B, so as to guarantee the type soundness of the exchange.

As argued in [2], the new typing system succeeds in its goal to provide reasoning methods for typed processes in arbitrary contexts. Indeed, [3] shows that the processes of APɪ@ may be implemented as low-level principals of a cryptographic process calculus based on the applied pi-calculus [1], while preserving their behavioral invariants. The present paper complements the work in [2,3] by investigating how the combination of static and dynamic typing in APɪ@ impacts on the ability to control the behavior of processes with respect to traditional systems relying solely on static typing, as in APɪ.

In particular, we show that there exists a sub-type preserving encoding of APɪ@ into APɪ which is fully abstract, i.e., preserves the dynamically typed equivalences of APɪ@ in all APɪ contexts. The encoding is interesting in two respects. First, it yields a non-trivial, and in some respects surprising, expressivity result connecting dynamic to static typing. Secondly, it establishes a connection between APɪ and the fully abstract implementation developed in [3]. In particular, it allows us to isolate the fragment of APɪ for which the implementation of [3] is fully abstract.

Plan of the paper. Section 2 reviews the two calculi involved in the encoding. Sections 3 and 4 detail the encodings and outline the proof of full abstraction. Section 5 concludes with final remarks. An extended version of the paper, with more details on the proofs, is available as a technical report [4].

2   Static and Dynamic Typing in the Pi-Calculus

We presuppose two countable sets of names and variables, ranged over by $a, b, \ldots, n, m$ and $x, y, \ldots$, respectively; u, v range collectively over names and variables whenever the distinction does not matter; $\tilde{u}, \tilde{T}, \tilde{A}$ denote (possibly empty) tuples of values, and static and dynamic types, respectively; the notation $\tilde{v}@\tilde{A}$ is a shorthand for the tuple $v_1@A_1, \ldots, v_n@A_n$; a corresponding convention applies to $\tilde{v} : \tilde{A}$. Syntactically, APɪ and APɪ@ differ only in the form of the communication primitives, and in the structure of the types. The productions are as follows:

APɪ – *Static Typing*
Processes $P, Q ::= \mathbf{0} \mid P|Q \mid (\nu n : S)P \mid !P \mid [u{=}v]P; Q \mid \bar{u}\langle \tilde{v}\rangle \mid u(\tilde{x}).P$
Types $S, T ::= \top \mid \mathsf{r}\langle \tilde{T}\rangle \mid \mathsf{w}\langle \tilde{T}\rangle \mid \mathsf{rw}\langle \tilde{S}; \tilde{T}\rangle \mid X \mid \mu X.T$

APɪ@ – *Dynamic Typing*
Processes $P, Q ::= \mathbf{0} \mid P|Q \mid (\nu n : A)P \mid !P \mid [u{=}v]P; Q \mid \bar{u}\langle \tilde{v}@\tilde{A}\rangle \mid u(\tilde{x}@\tilde{B}).P$
Types $A, B ::= \top \mid \mathsf{r} \mid \mathsf{w} \mid \mathsf{rw}$

Table 1. Typing and subtyping rules

Subtyping in APi (we write $S <: T$ if $\emptyset \vdash S <: T$).

$$\frac{\Sigma \vdash \tilde{U}_w <: \tilde{T}_w <: \tilde{T}_r}{\Sigma \vdash \mathsf{rw}\langle \tilde{T}_r; \tilde{T}_w \rangle <: \mathsf{w}\langle \tilde{U}_w \rangle} \qquad \frac{\Sigma \vdash \tilde{U}_w <: \tilde{T}_w <: \tilde{T}_r <: \tilde{U}_r}{\Sigma \vdash \mathsf{rw}\langle \tilde{T}_r; \tilde{T}_w \rangle <: \mathsf{rw}\langle \tilde{U}_r; \tilde{U}_w \rangle} \qquad \frac{\Sigma \vdash \tilde{T}_w <: \tilde{T}_r <: \tilde{U}_r}{\Sigma \vdash \mathsf{rw}\langle \tilde{T}_r; \tilde{T}_w \rangle <: \mathsf{r}\langle \tilde{U}_r \rangle}$$

$$\frac{\Sigma, \mu X.T_1 <: T_2 \vdash T_1 \{ \mu X.T_1/X \} <: T_2}{\Sigma \vdash T_1 <: T_2} \qquad \frac{\Sigma, T_1 <: \mu X.T_2 \vdash T_1 <: T_2 \{ \mu X.T_2/X \}}{\Sigma \vdash T_1 <: T_2}$$

Typing of communication in APi and APi@

(APi-IN)
$$\frac{\Gamma \vdash u : \mathsf{r}\langle \tilde{T} \rangle \quad \Gamma, \langle \tilde{x} : \tilde{T} \rangle \vdash P}{\Gamma \vdash u(\tilde{x}).P}$$

(APi-OUT)
$$\frac{\Gamma \vdash u : \mathsf{w}\langle \tilde{T} \rangle \quad \Gamma \vdash \tilde{v} : \tilde{T}}{\Gamma \vdash \bar{u}\langle \tilde{v} \rangle}$$

(APi@-IN)
$$\frac{\Gamma \vdash u : \mathsf{r} \quad \Gamma, \langle \tilde{x} : \tilde{A} \rangle \vdash P}{\Gamma \vdash u(\tilde{x}@\tilde{A}).P}$$

(APi@-OUT)
$$\frac{\Gamma \vdash u : \mathsf{w} \quad \Gamma \vdash \tilde{v} : \tilde{B}}{\Gamma \vdash \bar{u}\langle \tilde{v}@\tilde{B} \rangle}$$

APi is a standard version of the asynchronous pi-calculus with matching, denoted by the construct $[u = v]P; Q$, and recursive capability types á la [8,9][1]. We use the shorthand $\mathsf{rw}\langle \tilde{T} \rangle$ to mean $\mathsf{rw}\langle \tilde{T}; \tilde{T} \rangle$. APi@ replaces the input and output forms from APi with new constructs that make explicit the types at which values should be exchanged. As anticipated, the types are reduced to the simplest structure that only exhibits the capabilities for reading and writing.

Typing and Subtyping. In both calculi, the subtype relations $<:$ are partially complete pre-orders with a meet operator $\sqcap$ and top type $\top$. In APi the subtype relation is defined as in [8,9], with the standard extensions needed to handle the presence of recursive types, cf. Table 1. In APi@ subtyping is generated by the axioms $\mathsf{rw} <: \{\mathsf{r}, \mathsf{w}\} <: \top$. *Type environments*, ranged over by $\Gamma, \Gamma' \ldots$, are finite mappings from names and variables to types. We write $\Gamma \vdash P$ to mean that P is well typed in Γ. The type environment $\Gamma, \langle u : T \rangle$ is $\Gamma, u : T$ if $u \notin dom(\Gamma)$; otherwise it is the type environment Γ' such that $\Gamma'(v) = \Gamma(v)$ for $v \neq u$ and $\Gamma'(u) = \Gamma(u) \sqcap T$ if $\Gamma(u) \sqcap T$ is defined. Subtyping is extended to type environments as expected: $\Gamma <: \Gamma'$ whenever $dom(\Gamma) = dom(\Gamma')$ and for all $v \in dom(\Gamma)$ it holds $\Gamma(v) <: \Gamma'(v)$.

Operational Semantics. The dynamics of APi is expressed by the usual labeled transition system of the asynchronous pi-calculus. On the other hand, in order to express the dynamics for APi@, the input/output labels of pi-calculus are extended with a type capability in order to force the synchronization at the desired type. In Table 2 we report the rules for synchronization: the remaining rules are standard, and common to the

---

[1] In fact, in [8,9] the types are not recursive; however, as far as we see, the generalization is harmless for the results relevant to our present endeavor.

Table 2. Labeled Transitions

(APi-IN)	(APi-OUT)	(APi-OPEN)

$$(\text{APi-OPEN}) \quad \dfrac{P \xrightarrow{(\tilde{c}:\tilde{T})\bar{a}\langle\tilde{v}\rangle} P' \quad b \in \{\tilde{v}\} \setminus \{a,\tilde{c}\}}{(\nu b:S)P \xrightarrow{(b:S\cdot\tilde{c}:\tilde{T})\bar{a}\langle\tilde{v}\rangle} P'}$$

$$\dfrac{}{a(\tilde{x}).P \xrightarrow{a(\tilde{v})} P\{\tilde{v}/\tilde{x}\}} \qquad \dfrac{}{\bar{a}\langle\tilde{v}\rangle \xrightarrow{\bar{a}\langle\tilde{v}\rangle} 0}$$

(APi-COMM)

$$\dfrac{P \xrightarrow{(\tilde{c}:\tilde{T})\bar{a}\langle\tilde{v}\rangle} P' \quad Q \xrightarrow{a(\tilde{v})} Q' \quad \tilde{c} \cap fn(Q) = \emptyset}{P\,|\,Q \xrightarrow{\tau} (\nu\tilde{c}:\tilde{T})(P'\,|\,Q')}$$

(APi@-IN)	(APi@-OUT)	(APi@-OPEN)

$$(\text{APi@-OPEN}) \quad \dfrac{P \xrightarrow{(\tilde{c}:\tilde{C})\bar{a}\langle\tilde{A}@\tilde{v}\rangle} P' \quad b \in \{\tilde{v}\} \setminus \{a,\tilde{c}\}}{(\nu b:B)P \xrightarrow{(b:B\cdot\tilde{c}:\tilde{C})\bar{a}\langle\tilde{v}@\tilde{A}\rangle} P'}$$

$$\dfrac{}{a(\tilde{x}@\tilde{A}).P \xrightarrow{a(\tilde{v}@\tilde{A})} P\{\tilde{v}/\tilde{x}\}} \qquad \dfrac{}{\bar{a}\langle\tilde{v}@\tilde{A}\rangle \xrightarrow{\bar{a}\langle\tilde{v}@\tilde{A}\rangle} 0}$$

(APi@-COMM)

$$\dfrac{P \xrightarrow{(\tilde{c}:\tilde{C})\bar{a}\langle\tilde{v}@\tilde{A}\rangle} P' \quad Q \xrightarrow{a(\tilde{v}@\tilde{B})} Q' \quad \tilde{A} <: \tilde{B} \quad \tilde{c} \cap fn(Q) = \emptyset}{P\,|\,Q \xrightarrow{\tau} (\nu\tilde{c}:\tilde{C})(P'\,|\,Q')}$$

two calculi, we omit them for the lack of space. Notice how in APi@ the labels carry extra information about the types at which names are exchanged. More interestingly, however, these rules show the fundamentally different nature of the interaction between processes: in APi the receiver acquires the names emitted at the read type of the transmission channel, while in APi@ the type $\tilde{B}$ is decided by the sender. In addition, processes of both calculi may synchronize with a τ transition when exhibiting complementary labels that, in the case of APi@, are required to agree on the type of the values exchanged, as in $a(\tilde{v}@\tilde{A})$ and $\bar{a}\langle\tilde{v}@\tilde{A}\rangle$.

The notion of observational equivalence is based on the usual notion of reduction barbed congruence and is mediated by the type capabilities that the contexts possess on the names shared with the processes. It relies on the notion of *configuration*: a configuration is a pair of the form $\mathcal{I} \rhd P$, where $\mathcal{I}$ represents what contexts know of the names shared with P: remarkably, P may know those names at more precise types than $\mathcal{I}$, as $\mathcal{I} \rhd P$ is a well-defined configuration only if there exists $\Gamma <: \mathcal{I}$ such that $\Gamma \vdash P$.

Definition 1 (Type-indexed Relation). *A type-indexed relation $\mathcal{R}$ is a family of binary relations between processes indexed by type environments. We write $\mathcal{I} \models P \,\mathcal{R}\, Q$ to mean (i) that P and Q are related by $\mathcal{R}$ and (ii) that $\mathcal{I} \rhd P$ and $\mathcal{I} \rhd Q$ are configurations.*

Definition 2 (Contextuality). *A type-indexed relation $\mathcal{R}$ is contextual when:*

1. *$\mathcal{I}, a : A \models P\,\mathcal{R}\,Q$ implies $\mathcal{I} \models (\nu a{:}A)P\,\mathcal{R}\,(\nu a{:}A)Q$*
2. *$\mathcal{I} \models P\,\mathcal{R}\,Q$ implies $\mathcal{I}, a : A \models P\,\mathcal{R}\,Q$ for $a \notin dom(\mathcal{I})$*

3. $\mathcal{I} \models P \,\mathcal{R}\, Q$ and $\mathcal{I} \vdash R$ imply $\mathcal{I} \models P|R \,\mathcal{R}\, Q|R$

The definition of barbs is based on the actual capability of the context $\mathcal{I}$ to see barbs. The notation $\mathcal{I}^r(a) \downarrow$ indicates that $\mathcal{I}$ (hence the context) has a read capability on the name a, i.e., $\mathcal{I}(a) <: r$, only in that case the output action performed by the process is observable by the context. Moreover we denote by $\Longrightarrow$ the reflexive and transitive closure of $\xrightarrow{\tau}$.

Definition 3 (Barbs). *Given a configuration $\mathcal{I} \triangleright P$, we say that*

1. $\mathcal{I} \triangleright P \downarrow_a$ *if and only if $\mathcal{I}^r(a) \downarrow$ and $P \xrightarrow{(\tilde{c}:\tilde{C})\bar{a}\langle\tilde{v}@\tilde{A}\rangle}$.*
2. $\mathcal{I} \triangleright P \Downarrow_a$ *if and only if $P \Longrightarrow P'$ and $\mathcal{I} \triangleright P' \downarrow_a$.*

The definition above is given for APɪ@; the corresponding definition for APɪ is just as expected.

Definition 4 (Typed Behavioral Congruence). *Typed behavioral congruence is the largest symmetric, contextual and type-indexed relation $\mathcal{R}$ such that $\mathcal{I} \models P \,\mathcal{R}\, Q$ implies*

1. *if $\mathcal{I} \models P \downarrow_a$ then $\mathcal{I} \models Q \Downarrow_a$*
2. *if $Q \xrightarrow{\tau} Q$ then there exists Q' such that $Q \Longrightarrow Q'$ and $\mathcal{I} \models P' \,\mathcal{R}\, Q'$.*

The typed behavioral congruence is denoted as $\approx$ in APɪ and as $\approx_@$ in APɪ@.

3   A Correct Encoding

We define our encoding in terms of two related, but independent mappings, for type environments and processes, respectively. The encoding of processes maps typing judgements in APɪ@ to processes of APɪ: indeed, in our first formulation of the encoding, we define it directly by induction on the structure of processes, as the syntax of APɪ@ contains enough information to guide the generation of target code. In the final formulation, however, it is technically more convenient to refer to typing judgements to ease the definition. The encoding of type environments, in turn, maps the capabilities (types) of the observing APɪ@ contexts into the corresponding capabilities of APɪ contexts. This allows us to establish our full abstraction theorem in terms of the type-indexed relations of behavioral congruences in the two calculi.

In this and the next sections we give the encoding for the monadic fragment of APɪ@. In Section 5, we briefly discuss how the approach can be generalized to the polyadic calculus.

First attempt. We start with a relatively simple approach, which almost work, but not quite. The idea is to represent each name n in APɪ@ as a 4-tuple of names $\underline{n} = (n_{rw}, n_r, n_w, n_\top)$, where each component of the tuple corresponds to one of the four types at which a synchronization may take place on n. Thus, an APɪ@ synchronization on n at, say, the type w, will correspond in APɪ to a synchronization on n_w. Clearly, this idea must be applied systematically, hence exchanging a name in APɪ@ will correspond to exchanging a tuple in APɪ. Thus the output $\bar{u}\langle v@A \rangle$ is translated into the output $\overline{u_A}\langle \underline{v} \rangle$ that emits the 4-tuple of names that represent v. The input prefix requires a little more

Table 3. Encoding functions (with $Q = u(\tilde{x}).P$)

$$\text{READ}_l \langle Q \rangle \stackrel{def}{=} u(\tilde{x}).\text{TEST}_l \langle Q \rangle$$

$$\text{TEST}_l \langle Q \rangle \stackrel{def}{=} l(z).[z = \mathsf{t}]\text{COMMIT}_l \langle Q \rangle \oplus \text{UNDO}_l \langle Q \rangle ; \text{ABORT}_l \langle Q \rangle \qquad z \text{ fresh}$$

$$\text{UNDO}_l \langle Q \rangle \stackrel{def}{=} \bar{l}\langle \mathsf{t} \rangle | \bar{u}\langle \tilde{x} \rangle$$

$$\text{COMMIT}_l \langle Q \rangle \stackrel{def}{=} \bar{l}\langle \mathsf{f} \rangle | P$$

$$\text{ABORT}_l \langle Q \rangle \stackrel{def}{=} \bar{l}\langle \mathsf{f} \rangle | \bar{u}\langle \tilde{x} \rangle$$

$$R_1 \oplus R_2 \stackrel{def}{=} (vi : \mathsf{rw}\langle \rangle)(\bar{i}\langle \rangle \mid i().R_1 \mid i().R_2) \qquad i \text{ fresh}$$

care, as in APι@ the process $u(x@A).P$ may synchronize with any output on u at a type $B <: A$. In fact, given the translation of the output construct we just outlined, it is easily seen that the behavior of the input form $u(x@A).P$ corresponds precisely to the input guarded choice[2] $\Sigma_{B<:A} u_B(\underline{x}).P$. Combining these intuitions with the encoding of guarded choice from [11] yields the following definition.

$$\langle\!\langle \bar{u}\langle v@A \rangle \rangle\!\rangle \stackrel{def}{=} \overline{u_A}\langle \underline{v} \rangle$$

$$\langle\!\langle u(x@A).P \rangle\!\rangle \stackrel{def}{=} (vl : \mathsf{rw}\langle \top \rangle)\left(\bar{l}\langle \mathsf{t} \rangle | \prod_{B<:A} \, ! \text{READ}_l \left\langle u_B(\underline{x}).\langle\!\langle P \rangle\!\rangle \right\rangle \right)$$

$$\langle\!\langle (v n)P \rangle\!\rangle \stackrel{def}{=} (v \underline{n})\langle\!\langle P \rangle\!\rangle$$

$$\langle\!\langle [u = v]P; Q \rangle\!\rangle \stackrel{def}{=} [u_\top = v_\top]\langle\!\langle P \rangle\!\rangle; \langle\!\langle Q \rangle\!\rangle$$

Just as in [11], the encoding of input runs a mutual exclusion protocol, installing a local lock on a parallel composition of its branches. The protocol is implemented by the processes in Table 3, which we inherit, essentially unchanged, from [11] (as in that case, $\oplus$ denotes internal choice). The branches $\text{READ}_l \langle - \rangle$ concurrently try to test the lock after reading messages from the environment. Every branch can 'black out' and return to its initial state after it has taken the lock, just by resending the message. Just one branch will proceed with its continuation and thereby commit the input. Every other branch will then be forced to resend its message and abort its continuation.

Unfortunately, the re-sending of messages is problematic for type preservation. To see why, notice that a APι@ process may have just the read capability on a channel in order to perform an input, while its encoding must also be granted a write capability in order to run the mutual exclusion protocol. The typing failure would not arise if we dropped the type r, and worked with just three types: indeed, for this fragment of APι@ the encoding we just illustrated may be shown to be type-preserving and fully abstract. In the general case, we need to move the responsibility of running the mutual exclusion protocol from the (encoding of the) input process to some other process possessing the required capabilities. We discuss how that can be accomplished below.

Fixing the typing problem. The solution is inspired by [3] and based on representing channels as processes that serve the input and output requests by a client willing to synchronize: given a name n, we write $\text{CHAN}(n)$ for the server associated with n.

---

[2] For uniformity with the notation adopted for names, we write $\underline{x}$ to note a quadruple of variables used to store name representations.

Table 4. A correct encoding of processes

Channel Servers

$$\text{CHAN}(n) \stackrel{def}{=} \prod_{A\in\{rw,r,w,\top\}} !\, n_{r@A}(h).\text{CHOOSE}(n, A, h)$$
$$\text{CHOOSE}(n, A, h) \stackrel{def}{=} (vl : rw\langle\top\rangle)\left(\bar{l}\langle t\rangle \mid \prod_{B<:A} !\,\text{READ}_l\left\langle n_{w@B}(\underline{z}).\bar{h}\langle\underline{z}\rangle\right\rangle\right)$$

Clients

$$\{\!|\, 0\, |\!\} \stackrel{def}{=} 0$$
$$\{\!|\, \bar{u}\langle v@A\rangle\, |\!\} \stackrel{def}{=} \overline{u_{w@A}}\langle\underline{v}\rangle$$
$$\{\!|\, u(x@A).P\, |\!\} \stackrel{def}{=} (vh : rw\langle\mathbb{T}_A\rangle)\left(\overline{u_{r@A}}\langle h\rangle \mid h(\underline{x}).\{\!|\, P\, |\!\}\right) \quad \text{where the name } h \text{ is fresh}$$
$$\{\!|\, P\,|\,Q\, |\!\} \stackrel{def}{=} \{\!|\, P\, |\!\} \mid \{\!|\, Q\, |\!\}$$
$$\{\!|\, (va:A)P\, |\!\} \stackrel{def}{=} (v\underline{a}:\mathbb{S})(\{\!|\, P\, |\!\} \mid \text{CHAN}(a))$$
$$\{\!|\, [u=v]P; Q\, |\!\} \stackrel{def}{=} [u_{r@r} = v_{r@r}]\{\!|\, P\, |\!\}; \{\!|\, Q\, |\!\}$$
$$\{\!|\, !P\, |\!\} \stackrel{def}{=} !\{\!|\, P\, |\!\}$$

Complete Systems

$$\{\!|\, P\, |\!\}_{\mathcal{I}} \stackrel{def}{=} \{\!|\, P\, |\!\} \mid \prod_{a\in dom(\mathcal{I})} \text{CHAN}(a)$$

Each exchange on n in the source calculus corresponds to running two separate protocols. For input, a client willing to input on n at type, say A, sends a read request (in the form of a private name) on the name $n_{r@A}$. In the write protocol, a process willing to output on n and type $B <: A$ sends its output on $n_{w@B}$. Collectively, each name n from APi@ is thus translated into the 8-tuple $\underline{n} = (n_R, n_W)$, where the components $n_R = n_{r@rw}, n_{r@r}, n_{r@w}, n_{r@\top}$ are the names employed in the input protocol to communicate the input requests at the corresponding types, while the components $n_W = n_{w@rw}, n_{w@r}, n_{w@w}, n_{w@\top}$ serve the same purpose for the output protocol. Thus, for instance, the output $\bar{n}\langle v@rw\rangle$ corresponds to the output $\overline{n_{w@rw}}\langle\underline{v}\rangle$ and synchronizes only with $n_{w@rw}(\underline{x})$. The input $n(x@rw).P$, in turn, sends a request $\overline{n_{r@rw}}\langle l\rangle$, where l is a private channel on which the client waits for CHAN(n) to reply back a (tuple of) value(s). The server CHAN(n) is granted read and write access to all the names n_W and n_R, so that it may safely run the mutual exclusion protocol that mimics the synchronizations in the source calculus. Indeed, CHAN(n) is the only process with read capabilities on n_W and n_R while clients will, at their best, have write capabilities on these names: as a result, no client may interfere with the protocols that other clients run with the channel server.

The definitions in Table 4 formalize these intuitions: each APi@ process corresponds, via the encoding, to a set of clients of the protocols described above: the relevant clauses are those for the input and output forms, while the remaining cases are defined homomorphically. Two remarks are in order, however. For the case of matching, it is enough to compare just one of the components of the tuple representing the source-level names, as long as the components are chosen consistently. For the case of restriction, notice that creating a new name corresponds to allocating a channel server associated to the name, so that the translated processes may synchronize via the name created, using the server. In fact, to mimic all the synchronizations of the source processes, we must allocate channels for all the free names that occur in the source process and that the source process may share with the environment. That is accomplished by the final clause in the definition of the encoding.

Table 5. Encoding of types

Client types

$$\mathbb{T}_{rw} \stackrel{def}{=} (\mathbb{R}, \mathbb{W}) \quad \mathbb{T}_r \stackrel{def}{=} (\mathbb{R}, \top) \quad \mathbb{T}_w \stackrel{def}{=} (\top, \mathbb{W}) \quad \mathbb{T}_\top \stackrel{def}{=} (\top, \top)$$

$$\mathbb{R} \stackrel{def}{=} (T_{r@rw}, T_{r@r}, T_{r@rw}, T_{r@\top}) \quad \mathbb{W} \stackrel{def}{=} (T_{w@rw}, T_{w@r}, T_{w@rw}, T_{w@\top})$$

$$T_{r@rw} \stackrel{def}{=} \mathsf{w}\langle \mathsf{w}\langle \mathbb{R}, \mathbb{W}\rangle\rangle \qquad T_{w@rw} \stackrel{def}{=} \mathsf{w}\langle \mathbb{R}, \mathbb{W}\rangle$$
$$T_{r@r} \stackrel{def}{=} \mathsf{w}\langle \mathsf{w}\langle \mathbb{R}, \top\rangle\rangle \qquad T_{w@r} \stackrel{def}{=} \mathsf{w}\langle \mathbb{R}, \top\rangle$$
$$T_{r@w} \stackrel{def}{=} \mathsf{w}\langle \mathsf{w}\langle \top, \mathbb{W}\rangle\rangle \qquad T_{w@w} \stackrel{def}{=} \mathsf{w}\langle \top, \mathbb{W}\rangle$$
$$T_{r@\top} \stackrel{def}{=} \mathsf{w}\langle \mathsf{w}\langle \top, \top\rangle\rangle \qquad T_{w@\top} \stackrel{def}{=} \mathsf{w}\langle \top, \top\rangle$$

Server types

$$\mathbb{S} \stackrel{def}{=} (\mathbb{R}_S, \mathbb{W}_S)$$

$$\mathbb{R}_S \stackrel{def}{=} (S_{r@rw}, S_{r@r}, S_{r@w}, S_{r@\top}) \quad \mathbb{W}_S \stackrel{def}{=} (S_{w@rw}, S_{w@r}, S_{w@w}, S_{w@\top})$$

$$S_{r@rw} \stackrel{def}{=} \mathsf{rw}\langle \mathsf{w}\langle \mathbb{R}, \mathbb{W}\rangle\rangle \qquad S_{w@rw} \stackrel{def}{=} \mathsf{rw}\langle \mathbb{R}, \mathbb{W}\rangle$$
$$S_{r@r} \stackrel{def}{=} \mathsf{rw}\langle \mathsf{w}\langle \mathbb{R}, \top\rangle\rangle \qquad S_{w@r} \stackrel{def}{=} \mathsf{rw}\langle \mathbb{R}, \top\rangle$$
$$S_{r@w} \stackrel{def}{=} \mathsf{rw}\langle \mathsf{w}\langle \top, \mathbb{W}\rangle\rangle \qquad S_{w@w} \stackrel{def}{=} \mathsf{rw}\langle \top, \mathbb{W}\rangle$$
$$S_{r@\top} \stackrel{def}{=} \mathsf{rw}\langle \mathsf{w}\langle \top, \top\rangle\rangle \qquad S_{w@\top} \stackrel{def}{=} \mathsf{rw}\langle \top, \top\rangle$$

Type Environments

$$\{\!|0|\!\} \stackrel{def}{=} \mathtt{t} : \top, \mathtt{f} : \top \qquad \{\!|\Gamma, v : A|\!\} \stackrel{def}{=} \{\!|\Gamma|\!\}, (\underline{v}) : T_A$$

The new version of the encoding solves the typing problem of our initial attempt. Table 5, details the encoding of types. Typewise, a read capability on n in APi@ corresponds in APi to a write capability on all the names in $n_\mathbb{R}$, while a write capability on n corresponds to a write capability on the names $n_\mathbb{W}$. With each type A in APi@ we associate a corresponding tuple of types T_A, as in $\mathbb{T}_{rw} = (\mathbb{R}, \mathbb{W})$ or $\mathbb{T}_w = (\top, \mathbb{W})$ where $\mathbb{R}$ and $\mathbb{W}$ are the client types associated to the names employed in the read/write protocols (according to the convention that $n_{r@A} : T_{r@A}$ and $n_{w@A} : T_{w@A}$) and $\top$ is the representation of the top type in APi@. Notice that clients are only granted write capabilities on the channels involved in the protocols, while the channel servers know the same names at the lower types $\mathbb{R}_S$ and $\mathbb{W}_S$ which grant them full access to those names.

Based on these definition, we may now prove that the encoding preserves the expected properties about typing:

Theorem 1 (Typing and subtyping preservation). *For all types A, B in APi@, $A <: B$ implies $T_A <: T_B$ in APi. Furthermore, whenever $\Gamma \vdash P$ in APi@, then there exists $\Gamma' <: \{\!|\Gamma|\!\}$ such that $\Gamma' \vdash \{\!|P|\!\}_\Gamma$ in APi.*

Also, we can show that the encoding is sound, in the sense made precise below.

Theorem 2 (Soundness). *Let $\Gamma <: I$ and $\Gamma' <: I$ be two type environments such that $\Gamma \vdash P$ and $\Gamma' \vdash Q$ in APi@. Then $\{\!|I|\!\} \models \{\!|P|\!\}_\Gamma \approx \{\!|Q|\!\}_{\Gamma'}$ implies $I \models P \approx_@ Q$.*

The converse direction of Theorem 2 does not hold. The problem is that the properties of the communication protocols are based on certain invariants that are verified by the names and the channel servers allocated by the encoding, but may fail for the names created dynamically by the context. Below, we show that this failure breaks full abstraction (i.e., the converse of Theorem 2).

Failure of full abstraction. Take the following two APi@ processes

$$P \stackrel{def}{=} a(x@\text{rw}).x(y@\text{rw}).\overline{x}\langle y@\text{rw}\rangle$$

$$Q \stackrel{def}{=} a(x@\text{rw}).\mathbf{0}$$

As shown in [2], one has $I \models n(y@\text{rw}).\overline{n}\langle y@\text{rw}\rangle \approx_@ \mathbf{0}$ for all I such that n:rw $\in I$. From this, one easily derives $a : \text{w} \models P \approx_@ Q$. Now take the encoding of the two processes (we omit the type for readability, as they are irrelevant to the present purposes):

$$\{P\} = (\nu h)(\overline{a_{r@\text{rw}}}\langle h\rangle \mid h(\underline{x}).(\nu k)(\overline{x_{r@\text{rw}}}\langle k\rangle \mid k(y).\overline{x_{w@\text{rw}}}\langle y\rangle))$$

$$\{Q\} = (\nu h)(\overline{a_{r@\text{rw}}}\langle h\rangle \mid h(\underline{x}).\mathbf{0})$$

We show that the equivalence we just established for P and Q does not carry over to their encodings. In particular, let $I = a : \text{w}$, so that $\{I\} = \underline{a} : \mathbb{T}_\text{w}$, and assume $\underline{a} : \mathbb{T}_\text{w} \models \{P\}_I \approx \{Q\}_I$. Let also $\mathbb{S}$ be the server type defined in Table 5. Then, by contextuality, one would have:

$$\underline{a} : \mathbb{T}_\text{w}, \underline{b} : \mathbb{S} \models \{P\}_I \mid \overline{a_{w@\text{rw}}}\langle \underline{b}\rangle \approx \{Q\}_I \mid \overline{a_{w@\text{rw}}}\langle \underline{b}\rangle$$

On the other hand, this equivalence is easily disproved. In fact, on the one hand we have:

$$\{P\}_I \mid \overline{a_{w@\text{rw}}}\langle \underline{b}\rangle \Longrightarrow\approx (\nu k)(\overline{b_{r@\text{rw}}}\langle k\rangle \mid k(y).\overline{b_{w@\text{rw}}}\langle y\rangle)$$

with

$$\underline{a} : \mathbb{T}_\text{w}, \underline{b} : \mathbb{S} \triangleright (\nu k)(\overline{b_{r@\text{rw}}}\langle k\rangle \mid k(y).\overline{b_{w@\text{rw}}}\langle y\rangle) \downarrow_{b_{r@\text{rw}}} .$$

This is because $\underline{b} : \mathbb{S}$ implies that $b_{r@\text{rw}} : \text{rw}\langle\text{w}\langle\mathbb{T}_\text{rw}\rangle\rangle$, hence the context has visibility of the output action by the process. On the other hand, clearly,

$$\underline{a} : \mathbb{T}_\text{w}, \underline{b} : \mathbb{S} \triangleright \{Q\}_I \mid \overline{a_{w@\text{rw}}}\langle \underline{b}\rangle \not\Downarrow_{b_{r@\text{rw}}}$$

as Q never attempts to output on b, and correspondingly its encoding makes no requests on any of the components in $\underline{b}$. Thus, it follows that $\underline{a} : \mathbb{T}_\text{w} \not\models \{P\}_I \approx \{Q\}_I$ as we anticipated.

4   A Fully Abstract Encoding

To recover full abstraction, we need to protect the clients generated by the encoding from direct interactions on context-generated names such as the one illustrated above. To accomplish that, we adopt a solution inspired by [3], which relies on a *proxy* service to filter the interactions between channel servers, clients and the context. The *proxy* introduces a separation between *client names*, used by the context and the translated processes to communicate, and the corresponding *proxy names*, generated within the system and associated with system generated channels which are employed in the actual protocols for communication.

The proxy server is a process, noted PROXY, that maintains an association map between client and server names in order to preserve the expected interactions among

Table 6. Fully Abstract Encoding of APi@ into APi

Proxy

$$\text{Proxy} \overset{def}{=} (vt:\text{TBL}[\top,\mathbb{S}])\,(\text{Server}(t)\mid\text{TABLE}(t,[\,]))$$
$$\text{Server}(t) \overset{def}{=} \textstyle\prod_A \,!\,p_A(h,z).(vr:\text{rw}\langle\top,\mathbb{S}\rangle)\big(\text{LOOKUP}(z,t,r)\mid r(x,\underline{y})[x=\text{t}]\overline{h}\langle y\rangle;\,(\overline{h}\langle y\rangle\mid\text{Chan}(y))\big)$$

Clients

$$\langle\!\langle\,\mathbf{0}\,\rangle\!\rangle_\Gamma \overset{def}{=} \mathbf{0}$$
$$\langle\!\langle\,\overline{u}\langle v@A\rangle\,\rangle\!\rangle_\Gamma \overset{def}{=} \text{Link}_\Gamma\,(u,\underline{x})\,\text{IN}\,\overline{x_{w@A}}\langle v\rangle$$
$$\langle\!\langle\,u(y@A).P\,\rangle\!\rangle_\Gamma \overset{def}{=} \text{Link}_\Gamma\,(u,\underline{x})\,\text{IN}\,(vh:\text{rw}\langle\mathbb{T}_A\rangle)\big(\overline{x_{r@A}}\langle h\rangle\mid h(\underline{y}).\langle\!\langle\,P\,\rangle\!\rangle_{\Gamma,y:A}\big) \qquad \text{with } h \text{ fresh}$$
$$\langle\!\langle\,P\mid Q\,\rangle\!\rangle_\Gamma \overset{def}{=} \langle\!\langle\,P\,\rangle\!\rangle_\Gamma\mid\langle\!\langle\,Q\,\rangle\!\rangle_\Gamma$$
$$\langle\!\langle\,(va:A)P\,\rangle\!\rangle_\Gamma \overset{def}{=} (v\underline{a}:\mathbb{T}_A)\langle\!\langle\,P\,\rangle\!\rangle_{\Gamma,a:A}$$
$$\langle\!\langle\,[u=v]P;\,Q\,\rangle\!\rangle_\Gamma \overset{def}{=} [u_{r@\Gamma}=v_{r@\Gamma}]\langle\!\langle\,P\,\rangle\!\rangle_{\Gamma,\langle u:\Gamma(u)\rangle,\langle v:\Gamma(v)\rangle};\,\langle\!\langle\,Q\,\rangle\!\rangle_\Gamma$$
$$\langle\!\langle\,!P\,\rangle\!\rangle_\Gamma \overset{def}{=} \,!\langle\!\langle\,P\,\rangle\!\rangle_\Gamma$$

Complete Systems

$$\langle\!\langle\,P\,\rangle\!\rangle_\Gamma^* \overset{def}{=} \langle\!\langle\,P\,\rangle\!\rangle_\Gamma\mid\text{Proxy}$$

clients. The read and write protocols follow the same rationale as in the previous encoding, with the difference that in the new version of the encoding a client must obtain the access to the system channel with a request to Proxy before being able to start the input/output protocols. The interaction between clients and Proxy is now as follows: the client presents a name to the proxy, and the proxy replies with the corresponding server name. When Proxy receives a client name for the first time, it maps it to a fresh name, and allocates a channel server for the new proxy name.

The definition of the proxy server is reported in Table 6. Server is a process always ready to serve client requests along the four channels p_A, one for each $A \in \{\text{rw}, \text{r}, \text{w}, \top\}$. These channels are known to the clients and to the context at the type $p_A : \text{w}\langle\text{w}\langle\mathbb{T}_A\rangle,\mathbb{T}_A\rangle$, while the Server is granted full access rights on them. After receiving an input on p_A, the Server starts a search on the association table and replies with the requested system name. If the client name was not known to the proxy, a fresh proxy name is created, the association table extended with the new pair, and a channel server for the newly created proxy name allocated. We omit most of the largely obvious details of the implementation of the association table, and describe it in terms of the following macros.

- TABLE$(t, \mathcal{T})$ is a process parameterized over a structure $\mathcal{T}$ representing the table, and $t : \text{TBL}[\top,\mathbb{S}]$ is the reference to the table, i.e., a name providing access to the table's entries. We organize $\mathcal{T}$ as a list of pairs that map channel names to server names: we write $(n,\underline{k}) \in \mathcal{T}$ when n is associated to the tuple $\underline{k}$, and $n \in dom(\mathcal{T})$ to say that there exists $\underline{k}$ with $(n,\underline{k}) \in \mathcal{T}$. Initially, the list $\mathcal{T}$ is empty (cf. Table 6).
- LOOKUP(n, t, r) is a process employed by the proxy to access the table referenced to by $t : \text{TBL}[\top,\mathbb{S}]$. Here, $n : \top$ is the (client) name to be looked up in the table, and $r : \text{w}\langle\top,\mathbb{S}\rangle$ is the reply channel where to report back the result of the search. The result, in turn, comes as a pair that comprises the proxy names associated with the client name together with a boolean flag that says whether a new entry was created

in the table as a result of the search. Thus, $\text{LOOKUP}(n, t, r)$ replies on r the pair $(x, \underline{k})$ where $\underline{k}$ is the tuple associated with n, and x is t iff $\underline{k}$ was created freshly for n. This information is used by the remaining component of the proxy to allocate a new channel server for newly created proxy names, and to forward the proxy names to the requesting clients.

Operationally, we define the behavior of the macro processes by means of the following two ad-hoc internal reductions:

(Table-Lookup-Found)

$$\frac{(n, \underline{k}) \in \mathcal{T}}{\text{LOOKUP}(n, t, r) \mid \text{TABLE}(t, \mathcal{T}) \xrightarrow{\ \tau\ } \overline{r}\langle \mathsf{t}, \underline{k} \rangle \mid \text{TABLE}(t, \mathcal{T})}$$

(Table-Lookup-NotFound)

$$\frac{n \notin dom(\mathcal{T}), \quad \underline{k} \text{ fresh in } \mathcal{T}}{\text{LOOKUP}(n, t, r) \mid \text{TABLE}(t, \mathcal{T}) \xrightarrow{\ \tau\ } (\nu \underline{k} : \mathbb{S}) \left(\overline{r}\langle \mathsf{f}, \underline{k} \rangle \mid \text{TABLE}(t, [(n, \underline{k}) :: \mathcal{T}]) \right)}$$

On the client side, the interaction with the proxy server requires a new initialization step to link the name available to the client with the corresponding proxy name associated with it. This init step is accomplished as follows:

$$\text{LINK}_\Gamma \ (u, \underline{x}) \text{ IN } P \ \stackrel{\text{def}}{=} \ (\nu h : \mathsf{rw}\langle \mathbb{T}_A \rangle)(\overline{p_A}\langle h, u_{r@r} \rangle \mid h(\underline{x}).P) \quad \text{with } A = \Gamma(u)$$

To link the client name u (in fact, the component names in $\underline{u}$) with a corresponding proxy name, the client selects the first component in $\underline{u}$ on the proxy channel dedicated to serve the link requests, and waits for the proxy to reply on the channel h. Notice that the definition of the link process is parameterized on the context Γ, which helps recover the type that then guides the selection of the appropriate channel p_A used in the interaction with the proxy. To make this parametrization meaningful, the new encoding is given by induction on typing judgements. The other important difference with respect to the original definition in Table 4 is that the case of restriction is now defined purely homomorphically, as the allocation of the channel server is delegated to the proxy. For the same reason, the encoding of complete system does not need to allocate any channel for the free names shared with the context. It does, instead, require the presence of the proxy server to filter the synchronizations between clients.

Typewise, there are only few differences with respect to the original definitions in Table 5. Indeed, the exact same types work with the new translation of clients, while a two remarks are in order for the types employed in the definition of the proxy. First, the channels p_A are made available to the clients (and the context) at the types $\mathsf{w}\langle \mathsf{w}\langle \mathbb{T}_A \rangle, \mathbb{T}_A \rangle$, with $A \in \{\mathsf{rw}, \mathsf{r}, \mathsf{w}, \top\}$, that only grant write access. Correspondingly, we have a new encoding of type environments:

$$(\Gamma) \stackrel{\text{def}}{=} \{ \Gamma \} \cup \{ p_A : \mathsf{w}\langle \mathsf{w}\langle \mathbb{T}_A \rangle, \mathbb{T}_A \rangle \}_{A \in \{\mathsf{rw}, \mathsf{r}, \mathsf{w}, \top\}}$$

with $\{ \Gamma \}$ as in Table 5. Lower types, preciselythe types $\mathsf{rw}\langle \mathsf{w}\langle \mathbb{T}_A \rangle, \mathbb{T}_A \rangle$, are instead available for type checking the proxy definition.

As for the type $\mathsf{TBL}[\mathsf{T}, \mathbb{S}]$ employed in the definition of the TABLE macro, T and $\mathbb{S}$ are the types of the entries in the table, while we assume the following ad-hoc typing rules for the LOOKUP and TABLE macro processes:

(T-Lookup)

$$\frac{\Gamma \vdash t : \mathsf{TBL}[\mathsf{T}, \mathbb{S}], n : \mathsf{T}, r : \mathsf{rw}\langle \mathsf{T}, \mathbb{S}\rangle}{\Gamma \vdash \mathsf{LOOKUP}(n, t, r)}$$

(T-Table)

$$\frac{\Gamma \vdash t : \mathsf{TBL}[\mathsf{T}, \mathbb{S}], n_1 : \mathsf{T}, \underline{k_1} : \mathbb{S}, \ldots n_l : \mathsf{T}, \underline{k_l} : \mathbb{S}}{\Gamma \vdash \mathsf{TABLE}(t, [(n_1, \underline{k_1}) :: \cdots (n_l, \underline{k_l})])}$$

Based on these definitions, we can show that the encoding has the desired properties of type and subtype preservation.

Theorem 3 (Typing and subtyping preservation). *For all types A, B in* APı@*, $A <: B$ implies* $\mathbb{T}_A <: \mathbb{T}_B$ *in* APı*. Furthermore, whenever $\Gamma \vdash P$ in* APı@*, then there exists $\Gamma' <: (\![\Gamma]\!)$ such that $\Gamma' \vdash (\![P]\!)^*_\Gamma$ in* APı*.

Furthermore, the presence of the proxy now makes the encoding fully abstract.

Theorem 4 (Full Abstraction). *Let $\Gamma <: I$ and $\Gamma' <: I$ be two type environments such that $\Gamma \vdash P$ and $\Gamma' \vdash Q$. Then $I \models P \approx_@ Q$ if and only if $(\![I]\!) \models (\![P]\!)^*_\Gamma \approx (\![Q]\!)^*_{\Gamma'}$.*

Below we outline the full abstraction proof. Before doing that, it is instructive to look at how the new encoding solves the problem with the example discussed in Section 3. In that case, the encodings of the two processes

$$P \overset{def}{=} a(x@\mathsf{rw}).x(y@\mathsf{rw}).\overline{x}\langle y@\mathsf{rw}\rangle$$
$$Q \overset{def}{=} a(x@\mathsf{rw}).0$$

are distinguished by any context that sends a fresh name on a and retains full access to the components of that name, because any such context may observe the read request made by the encoding of P.

The presence of the proxy solves the problem as now the encoding of P makes its request not on the name received by the context, but rather on the proxy name that is associated with the context name. Thus, if b is the name send over the channel a, we have:

$$(\![P]\!)_\Gamma \mid \overline{a_{w@\mathsf{rw}}}\langle \underline{b}\rangle \Longrightarrow \approx \mathsf{LINK}_\Gamma\ (b, x)\ \mathsf{IN}\ (\nu k)(\overline{x_{\mathsf{r@rw}}}\langle k\rangle \mid k(y).\overline{x_{\mathsf{w@rw}}}\langle y\rangle)$$

where now

$$\underline{a} : \mathbb{T}_\mathsf{w}, \underline{b} : \mathbb{S} \triangleright \mathsf{LINK}_\Gamma\ (b, x)\ \mathsf{IN}\ (\nu k)(\overline{x_{\mathsf{r@rw}}}\langle k\rangle \mid k(y).\overline{x_{\mathsf{w@rw}}}\langle y\rangle)\ \Downarrow_{b_{\mathsf{r@rw}}}$$

as the context has no read access on the components of the proxy name $\underline{x}$ associated with b.

Proof of Theorem 4 (outline). The proof is difficult and rather elaborate, especially in the "if" direction (*soundness*), which as usual requires the following properties of operational correspondence:

- If $P \Longrightarrow P'$ then $(\![P]\!)^*_\Gamma \Longrightarrow K$ with $(\![I]\!) \models K \approx (\![P']\!)^*_\Gamma$.
- If $(\![P]\!)^*_\Gamma \Longrightarrow K$ then there exists P' such that $P \Longrightarrow P'$ and $(\![I]\!) \models K \approx (\![P']\!)^*_\Gamma$.

The "reflection" direction, stated by the second item above, is subtle, because our encoding is not "prompt" [11]. Note, in fact, that it takes several steps for the encoding of a process to be ready for the commit action that corresponds to the APɪ@ synchronization on the channel. As it turns out, however, these steps are not observable and can be factored out in the proof by resorting to a suitable notion of (term-indexed) *administrative* equivalence, noted $\approx_A$ and included in $\approx$. The definition of $\approx_A$ draws on a classification for the reductions of the translated processes into *commitment* steps, corresponding to synchronizations in the APɪ@ processes, and *administrative reductions*, corresponding to the steps that precede and follow the commitment steps. Then two processes are equated by $\approx_A$ only if they are behaviorally equivalent and, in addition, they can simulate each other's commitment transitions in a 'strong' way. The relation $\approx_A$ can be used to prove the following variant of operational correspondence:

Lemma 1 (Operational Correspondence). *Let $I \rhd P$ be a configuration in APɪ@ and $\Gamma <: I$ such that $\Gamma \vdash P$. Then:*

1. *If $P \xrightarrow{\tau} P'$ then $(\![P]\!)_\Gamma^* \Longrightarrow H$ with $(\![I]\!) \vDash H \approx_A (\![P']\!)_\Gamma^*$.*
2. *If $(\![I]\!) \vDash H \approx_A (\![P]\!)_\Gamma^*$ and $H \xrightarrow{\tau} K$, then either $(\![I]\!) \vDash H \approx_A K$ or there exists P' such that $P \xrightarrow{\tau} P'$ and $(\![I]\!) \vDash K \approx_A (\![P']\!)_\Gamma^*$.*

Proof. (Sketch). The first item (i.e., the "preservation" direction) follows routinely. For the second item, the first case occurs when the move from H is an administrative step, while the second corresponds to the case when H is finally prompt to commit on a synchronization reduction that reflects a source-level synchronization.   □

The proof of soundness requires a further preliminary lemma:

Lemma 2 (Barb Correspondence). *Let $I \rhd P$ a configuration in APɪ@ and $\Gamma <: I$ such that $\Gamma \vdash P$. Then there exists I', $h \in dom(I')$ and $C[\cdot]$ such that*

1. *If $I \rhd P \downarrow_a$ then $(\![I]\!), I' \rhd C[(\![P]\!)_\Gamma^*] \Downarrow_h$*
2. *If $(\![I]\!), I' \rhd C[(\![P]\!)_\Gamma^*] \Downarrow_h$ then $I \rhd P \downarrow_a$.*

Proof. Choose $I' = h : \mathsf{rw}\langle \mathbb{T}_\top \rangle$ and $C[-] = \mathrm{LINK}_\Gamma(a, \underline{x}) \text{ IN } \overline{x_{r@A}}\langle h \rangle \mid -$ □

Relying on Lemmas 1 and 2, we have:

Theorem 5 (Soundness). *Let $\Gamma <: I$ and $\Gamma' <: I$ be such that $\Gamma \vdash P$ and $\Gamma' \vdash Q$. Then $(\![I]\!) \vDash (\![P]\!)_\Gamma^* \approx (\![Q]\!)_{\Gamma'}^*$ implies $I \vDash P \approx_@ Q$.*

Proof. Let $\mathcal{R}$ be the type indexed relation defined as follows: $I \vDash P \, \mathcal{R} \, Q$ whenever $(\![I]\!) \vDash (\![P]\!)_\Gamma^* \approx_@ (\![Q]\!)_{\Gamma'}^*$. Show that $\mathcal{R}$ is barb preserving, reduction closed and contextual.   □

In the "only if" direction (*completeness*), the proof follows, more directly, by coinduction. However, the definition of the candidate relation requires some care, as we need to keep track of the states reached by PROXY as a result of the interactions with its clients. We note $\mathsf{E}_\mathcal{T}[-]$ a context representing that state, for an arbitrary list $\mathcal{T}$, and define:

$$\mathsf{E}_\mathcal{T}[-] \overset{def}{=} - \mid \prod_{(n,\underline{k}) \in \mathcal{T}} \mathrm{CHAN}(k) \mid (\nu t : \mathrm{TBL}[\top, \mathbb{S}]) \, (\mathrm{SERVER}(t) \mid \mathrm{TABLE}(t, \mathcal{T})).$$

Thus $\mathsf{E}_\mathcal{T}[(\![P]\!)_\Gamma] = (\![P]\!)_\Gamma^*$ at the initial state when $\mathcal{T} = [\,]$. Then we have:

Theorem 6 (Completeness). *Let $\Gamma <: I$ and $\Gamma' <: I$ be two type environments such that $\Gamma \vdash P$ and $\Gamma' \vdash Q$. Then $I \models P \approx_@ Q$ implies $(\!| I |\!) \models (\!| P |\!)^*_\Gamma \approx (\!| Q |\!)^*_{\Gamma'}$.*

Proof. (Sketch). Let $\mathcal{R}$ be the type indexed relation such that

$$(\!| I |\!), a_1 : T_1, \ldots a_n : T_n \models C[\, \mathsf{E}_{\mathcal{T}}[(\!| P |\!)_\Gamma]\,]\ \mathcal{R}\ C[\, \mathsf{E}_{\mathcal{T}}[(\!| Q |\!)_\Gamma]\,]$$

whenever (i) $I \models P \approx_@ Q$, (ii) $\Gamma <: I$ and $\Gamma \vdash P$, (iii) $\Gamma' <: I$ and $\Gamma' \vdash Q$ (iv) $a_i \notin dom((\!| I |\!))$, and (v) $C[-]$ is an evaluation context that binds the $\underline{k}$ in $\mathcal{T}$ and such that $(\!| I |\!), a_1 : T_1, \ldots a_n : T_n \vdash C[-]$. The proof follows by showing that $\mathcal{R}$ satisfies the properties of the administrative equivalence. The most difficult part is the proof that $\mathcal{R}$ is reduction closed, as the processes reached by $C[\, \mathsf{E}_{\mathcal{T}}[(\!| P |\!)_\Gamma]\,]$ after an arbitrary number of reductions will, in general, have the form $C'[\, \mathsf{E}_{\mathcal{T}'}[K]\,]$ with K a derivative of $(\!| P' |\!)_\Gamma$, for some P', rather than $(\!| P' |\!)_\Gamma$ as required by $\mathcal{R}$. We rely on an up-to technique to factor out the administrative steps required to close the relation on two terms with the required format. □

5 Conclusions

We have given a fully abstract encoding of APɪ@ into APɪ. In its present form, the encoding only applies to the monadic fragment of APɪ@, and requires the presence of recursive types in APɪ. In fact, the same technique would work for the polyadic calculus, as long as we can count on a finite bound on the maximal arity. In that case, every APɪ@ channel may be associated to different tuples of names, one for each possible arity. Similarly, we could do without recursive types in APɪ, as in the original formulation of [8,9] by assuming a finite bound on the number of cascading re-transmission via other names. In fact, the dynamic types of APɪ@ allow any channel to communicate its own name: in the general case, this requires (or at least it appears to require) types with arbitrarily deep nesting, viz, recursive types.

The encoding is interesting as it shows how the dynamically typed synchronization of APɪ@ may be simulated by a combination of untyped synchronizations on suitably designed channels, and it allows us to identify precisely the subclass of the static types of APɪ that correspond to the dynamic types of APɪ@. On the one hand, the recursive structure of the static types that emerges from the encoding shows that the dynamic types of APɪ@ offer limited access control mechanisms, as they only provide ways to control the use of the top-level capabilities associated with names. On the other hand, it is precisely because of its limited expressive power, that the dynamic typing system may be used effectively in arbitrary, untyped contexts, as shown by their secure implementation described in [3].

Types and advanced techniques for behavioral observation have been used extensively in the analysis of distributed computations and open systems. Types have been employed to describe resources and their usage [5,6,7,10,12] and typed equational theories have been studied to characterize the observational properties of processes [2,8,9,14]. In particular, the type systems introduced in [5,6], for Ambient calculus, and in [7], for KLAIM calculus, guarantee the delivery of resources at the expected type by resorting to type coercion on outputs. As in APɪ@, the soundness of these systems is given by a combination of static and dynamic typing. Future work may include extending our present results to other calculi such as Ambients and KLAIM.

References

1. Abadi, M., Fournet, C.: Mobile values, new names, and secure communication. In: POPL, pp. 104–115. ACM Press, New York (2001)
2. Bugliesi, M., Giunti, M.: Typed processes in untyped contexts. In: De Nicola, R., Sangiorgi, D. (eds.) TGC 2005. LNCS, vol. 3705, pp. 19–32. Springer, Heidelberg (2005)
3. Bugliesi, M., Giunti, M.: Secure implementations of typed channel abstractions. In: POPL, pp. 251–262. ACM Press, New York (2007)
4. Bugliesi, M., Macedonio, D., Rossi, S.: Static vs dynamic typing for access control in pi-calculus (extended version). Technical Report CS-2007-5, Dipartimento di informatica, Università Ca' Foscari di Venezia (2007), Also available at: http://www.dsi.unive.it/~mace/ASIAN07.pdf
5. Coppo, M., Cozzi, F., Dezani-Ciancaglini, M., Giovannetti, E., Pugliese, R.: A mobility calculus with local and dependent types. In: Middeldorp, A., van Oostrom, V., van Raamsdonk, F., de Vrijer, R. (eds.) Processes, Terms and Cycles: Steps on the Road to Infinity. LNCS, vol. 3838, Springer, Heidelberg (2005)
6. Coppo, M., Dezani-Ciancaglini, M., Giovannetti, E., Pugliese, R.: Dynamic and local typing for mobile ambients. In: IFIP TCS, pp. 577–590. Kluwer Academic Publishers, Dordrecht (2004)
7. Gorla, D., Pugliese, R.: Resource access and mobility control with dynamic privileges acquisition. In: Baeten, J.C.M., Lenstra, J.K., Parrow, J., Woeginger, G.J. (eds.) ICALP 2003. LNCS, vol. 2719, pp. 119–132. Springer, Heidelberg (2003)
8. Hennessy, M.: A Distributed Pi-Calculus. Cambridge University Press, Cambridge (2007)
9. Hennessy, M., Rathke, J.: Typed behavioural equivalences for processes in the presence of subtyping. Mathematical Structures in Computer Science 14(5), 651–684 (2004)
10. Hennessy, M., Riely, J.: Resource access control in systems of mobile agents. Information and Computation 173(1), 82–120 (2002)
11. Nestmann, U., Pierce, B.C.: Decoding choice encodings. Information and Computation 163(1), 1–59 (2000)
12. Nicola, R.D., Ferrari, G.L., Pugliese, R., Venneri, B.: Types for access control. Theoretical Computer Science 240(1), 215–254 (2000)
13. Pierce, B.C., Sangiorgi, D.: Typing and subtyping for mobile processes. Mathematical Structures in Computer Science 6(5), 409–453 (1996)
14. Pierce, B.C., Sangiorgi, D.: Behavioral equivalence in the polymorphic pi-calculus. Journal of the ACM 47(3), 531–584 (2000)

A Sandbox with a Dynamic Policy Based on Execution Contexts of Applications

Tomohiro Shioya, Yoshihiro Oyama, and Hideya Iwasaki

The University of Electro-Communications
shioya@ipl.cs.uec.ac.jp, {oyama, iwasaki}@cs.uec.ac.jp

Abstract. We propose a sandbox system that dynamically changes its behavior according to the application's execution context. Our system allows users to give different policies, each of which specifies permitted system calls, depending on the user functions in which the target application is executing. The target application can be given less privilege than would be possible with other single-policy sandbox systems. We implemented the sandbox by using LKM (Loadable Kernel Module) of Linux that intercepts the system call issued by the application process. We experimentally demonstrated the effectiveness of the sandbox.

1 Introduction

A *sandbox system* is a security system that securely executes applications by confining them in a special environment called a *sandbox*. Much literature has been devoted to showing the usefulness of such systems [5,9]. Sandbox systems monitor the behavior of applications and prevent operations that are against the intention of users. Usually, users of a sandbox specify the privileges of programs for operating each resource, and give specifications to the sandbox system. A set of specifications is called a *policy*. When an application in a sandbox attempts to access a resource, the sandbox system checks its privilege regarding the operation in the policy. If the policy allows the operation, the sandbox lets the application execute the operation. Otherwise, it causes the operation to fail. Although sandbox systems do not prevent malicious code exploiting vulnerabilities in an application, they can minimize the range of harmful effects caused by attacks. Although there are various sandbox systems, this study focuses on sandbox systems based on system call interception.

Unfortunately, most sandbox systems, e.g., Janus [5] and Systrace [9], have a limitation that prevents them from providing sufficiently secure confinement; only a single policy is applied to an application from the start to the end of the execution. For example, let us consider sandboxing a server program. Suppose that the server reads the password file in the user authentication part of the program and does not need the password file in other parts. Suppose also that the authentication part is very small and is not frequently executed. Users who attempt to protect the server with an existing sandbox must choose one of two extreme alternatives: allowing or denying the operation to read the password

I. Cervesato (Ed.): ASIAN 2007, LNCS 4846, pp. 297 311, 2007.

file throughout the execution of the server. Thus, users are obliged to allow
the operation. Consequently, malicious code that has taken over a part of the
server would be able to read the password, in spite of the sandbox protection.
This kind of always-or-never execution control is too coarse-grained to guarantee
highly secure sandboxing.

In this paper, we propose a sandbox system that enables users to switch between different policies dynamically so that an adequate policy can be applied
to each execution context. Here, an *execution context* means a chain of user-
defined function calls which lead to the current execution point. The proposed
sandbox decides whether a resource access is allowed according to the policy
associated with the current execution context. Because resources are generally
accessed through system calls provided by the operating system, "resource access" can be restated as "execution of a system call" or "issue of a system call".
The sandbox controls the behavior of the target application by monitoring and,
if necessary, denying the execution of system calls. This work is a step towards
a highly secure sandbox system that conforms well to the principle of the least
privilege [10]. We implemented the system on Linux and conducted experiments
including detection of attacks against a modified version of the Qpopper POP
server.

The proposed system has the following advantages:

- It provides finer-grain access control than many existing sandbox systems
  based on system call interception. Moreover, it makes mimicry attacks [12]
  harder because an attacker must create a fake execution context, i.e., stack
  frames, to evade the detection by the sandbox.
- It does not incur a large runtime overhead. The overhead of our system
  observed from the client side was almost 4% in the Qpopper experiment,
  which is a permissible level.

The contributions of this study are as follows:

- It describes a design and implementation of a sandbox system that enables
  users to associate different access control policies with different execution
  contexts.
- It shows experimental results including detection of an exploit against a
  realistic server and a measurement of runtime overhead.

This paper is organized as follows. Section 2 shows a motivating example.
We describe the design of the system in Section 3. Section 4 explains how to
describe a dynamic policy that depends on execution contexts. We describe our
implementations in Section 5. Section 6 discusses the experimental results. This
work is compared with related work in Section 7. Section 8 concludes this paper.

2   Motivating Example

We explain the basic idea through an example of a POP server. A POP server
executes various operations including creating sockets, establishing connections,

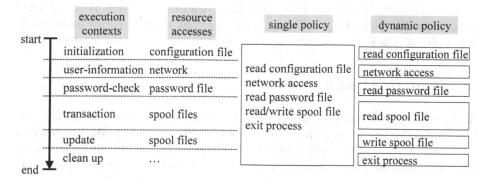

Fig. 1. Execution contexts, resource accesses, and policies of POP server

reading the password file, and reading and writing mail spool files. The entire execution of a POP server can be partitioned straightforwardly according to its execution contexts (or states). Figure 1 shows an example of partitioning. Our key observation is that the set of operations to be executed and the set of resources to be accessed are closely related to the execution context. For example, configuration files are accessed only in the initialization context and a mail spool file is updated only in the update context. Hence, resource accesses can be controlled in a fine-grain manner by associating a different set of privileges with each execution context.

Let us consider protecting a POP server with a sandbox system that allows only a single policy from the start to the end of the execution. A problem is that the policy must allow *all* resource accesses that may be performed at least once during the entire execution, as illustrated in Fig. 1. The policy is so coarse-grained that a set of excessive privileges is given for each execution context. For example, in the partitioning in Fig. 1, the POP server reads the password file only in the user-information context. However, the sandbox system always allows the read operation. If malicious code were to penetrate any part of the server, it would obtain access to the password file. How to address this problem is crucial design point. An effective approach is to apply different policies to different execution contexts.

Another design is the handling of dynamically provided information. The accessed resource often depends on such information provided at runtime as user input via a network. In the POP server example, the mail spool directory is dynamically determined on the basis of the user name sent in the user-information context (i.e., /var/spool/*user_name* is accessed). Suppose that a user attempts to protect the POP server with a sandbox system in which all accessed resources must be statically specified. The sandbox will allow the server, whether or not it supports dynamic policy switching, to read and update all spool files under /var/spool during transaction and update contexts. Thus, an attacker who takes the control of the server can modify or delete a spool file of any user, irrespective of the user being served at the time of the attack. While the server is in the update context for *user_name*, the privilege for updating /var/spool/*user_name* is sufficient.

We solve these problems with an enhanced sandbox system that supports dynamic policy switching and the inclusion of dynamically provided information into policies. The enhancement goes well with the principle of the least privilege.

3   Sandbox Design

The proposed sandbox system dynamically applies different policies to the target application process on the basis of its execution contexts. We use a *chain of user-defined function calls* which lead to the current execution point as an approximation of a context of the point. Let us consider the following example where main calls f and then g, f calls h, and both g and h call k.

```
main() { ... f(); ... g(); ... }
f() { ... h(); ... }
g() { ... k(); ... }
h() { ... k(); ....}
k() { ... }
```

The context during the execution of h's code is h–f–main, and that of the execution of g's code is g–main. For the execution of k, if it is called from h, its context is k–h–f–main, while if it is called from g, its context is k–g–main.

As a practical example, let us consider Qpopper 4.0.4, a widely used implementation of a POP server. Qpopper 4.0.4 defines such functions as pop_init, pop_user, pop_pass, pop_list, and pop_updt. Each of these functions implements an execution context of the POP server. For instance, pop_init and pop_updt respectively implement the initialization and update contexts of the server. Thus, a chain of function calls that leads to one of these functions can be regarded as an execution context of the function.

There are two reasons why we adopted a chain of user-defined function calls as an approximation of a context. First, since an application program is generally

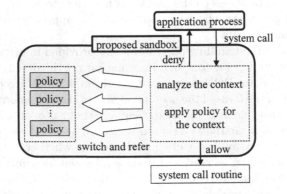

Fig. 2. Basic design of the proposed system

coded using many functions, each of which implements some related parts within the application, it is quite natural to use these user-defined functions in the approximation of a context. Second, this approximation makes it easy to write context-dependent policies, as will be described in Sect. 4.

Figure 2 shows the basic design of the sandbox. The user is required to give the policy of the target application in advance. The sandbox system intercepts each system call issued by a target application process to analyse the current execution context, i.e., the chain of user-defined function calls, at the moment of the system call and to determine whether it is allowed or not according to the policy of the context. If the sandbox judges that this system call is allowed, it lets the process proceed to the service routine of the system call in the OS kernel; otherwise it denies execution of the system call by returning an error to the application process.

4   Description of Dynamic Policy

In the proposed system, each sandboxed application has its own policy that is dynamically applied on the basis of the execution context of each system call. The policy is expected to be prepared by the application developers, because they would surely understand the internal structure, i.e., which functions are defined and which system calls or library functions are called from these functions. Thus, they should have no trouble in describing the application's policy.

The policy must give a list of allowed system calls or library functions with their argument patterns for every function of interest defined in the source code of the application. To begin with, we focus on system calls in the list; library functions in the list will be explained in Sect. 4.4. By default, system calls that do not appear in the list are denied at the execution points within the corresponding user-defined function. Conversely, those in the list are allowed to execute in the function. The rest of this section explains how to describe policies for a concrete policy definition for Qpopper 4.0.4, part of which is shown in Fig. 3.

4.1   Basics of Policy Description

A policy file has two sections divided by the %% line. The first section contains #include and #define directives as is often seen in a normal C file, whose meanings are the same as C's pre-processor. The second section contains the body of the policy definition. The objective of the first section is to define macros and types that are used in the policy definitions in the second section. For example, the first line of Fig. 3 states that <fcntl.h> has to be included, because this file has definitions of O_RDONLY on line 11, and O_RDWR and O_CREAT on the 29-th line. Similarly, <sys/socket.h> defines AF_INET and SOCK_STREAM, and <netinet/in.h> have definitions of INADDR_ANY and the structure sockaddr_in. Line 5 includes "popper.h", a header file in the source code of Qpopper. This file is also necessary because it defines the type named POP used in the body of the policy definition.

```
1 #include <sys/fcntl.h>
2 #include <netinet/in.h>
3 #include <sys/socket.h>
4 ...
5 #include "popper.h"
6 #define SERV_TCP_PORT 110
7
8 %%
9
10 main() {
11   open("/dev/null", O_RDONLY, 0);
12   socket(AF_INET, SOCK_STREAM, 0);
13   bind(_,
14       *(struct sockaddr_in *){sin_family: AF_INET,
15                           sin_port: htons(SERV_TCP_PORT),
16                           sin_addr.s_addr: htonl(INADDR_ANY)},
17       sizeof(struct sockaddr_in));
18   fopen("/dev/null", "w+");
19   ...
20 }
21
22 pop_init(POP *p) {
23   gethostbyname(p->myhost);
24   ...
25 }
26
27 pop_pass(POP *p) {
28   >sleep(_);
29   >open(concat("/var/spool", p->name), O_RDWR | O_CREAT, 0666);
30   ...
31 }
```

Fig. 3. Part of a policy file for Qpopper

The first line of the second section (line 10 in Fig. 3) starts a policy definition of a user-defined function named `main`. Lines 11–17 list the allowed system calls during the execution of `main`. By default, each system call in this list is allowed to execute only when it is called *directly* from `main`. This means that its execution within a descendant function called from `main` is blocked by the sandbox system Conversely, each system call with the ">" mark in front of its name is allowed to be called directly or indirectly from the user-defined function that lists allowed system calls. In other words, callee functions inherit the permission of the system calls with the ">" mark from their caller functions. This mechanism is called *policy inheritance*. Examples of the usage of ">" can be seen in the definition of `pop_pass` on lines 28 and 29. The policy inheritance mechanism enables us to choose a restricted number of user-defined functions that most approximate execution contexts and to specify allowed system calls and library functions for each of them. Since it is not necessary to give the policy of *every* user-defined function, time and effort for describing policy definitions can be saved.

The description of allowed system calls can include an argument *pattern*. The special pattern "_" means that any actual parameter is accepted. A literal like 0 or "/dev/null" means that the actual parameter has to exactly match the literal. Macros that are defined in the first section of the policy file can be used as literals. Also we can use special built-in macros like `htons` and `inet_addr`, whose meanings are the same as those defined in the standard C library (libc).

4.2   Specifying a Structure

Some system calls accept as their arguments complex structures. For example, the second argument of the `bind` system call is a pointer to `struct sockaddr_in` for assigning an Internet address to a socket. To specify a pattern for such structures, we can use a special notation using "{...}", as shown on lines 14–16. This notation means a structure body, in which pairs of member name and associated value (literal) are listed. In the example of `bind`, its second argument has to be a pointer to a `sockaddr_in` structure whose `sin_family`, `sin_port`, and `sin_addr.s_addr` members are `AF_INET`, `htons(SERV_TCP_PORT)`, and `htonl(INADDR_ANY)`, respectively.

4.3   Getting Runtime Information

As described in Sect. 2, an application often wants to dynamically decide the resources to access by using runtime information. For the POP server example, the server must be able to access the spool directory of an authenticated user, e.g., `"/var/mail/shioya"` if the user is `shioya`, but it is unnecessary to access to other users' spools, e.g., `"/var/mail/iwasaki"`. Thus, a mechanism that restricts the access of the sandboxed POP server to only the authenticated user's spool directory is required.

In the policy description, runtime information can be obtained by using a formal parameter of a user-defined function. For example, the policy of `pop_pass` (lines 27–31) states that the `open` system call is allowed only when all of the following conditions are satisfied.

- The first argument is `"/var/spool"` concatenated with the string in the `name` member of `p`, where `p` is the `pop_pass`'es actual parameter of the type POP, and
- The second argument is 0.

Note that `concat` means a string concatenation operator which can be used in the policy file.

4.4   Listing Library Functions

Many application programs use such library functions as `gethostbyname` and `fopen` instead of directly using system calls. These library functions provide their respective facilities, but their implementations are within a black-box. Thus, it is too severe a task for the application developers to list all system calls that could be (directly or indirectly) called from the library functions they use. For example, `gethostbyname` could open `/etc/hosts`, consult the NIS server, or consult the DNS server on the basis of the configuration file `/etc/nsswitch.conf`.

To cope with this problem, library functions can be included in the list of allowed functions for a user-defined function. Examples can be seen on lines 18 and 23 in Fig. 3.

To do so, the sandbox system needs policies for library functions that include lists of system calls used by them. Figure 4 shows an example of the policy

```
 1 #include <sys/fcntl.h>
 2 #include <netinet/in.h>
 3 #include <sys/socket.h>
 4
 5 %%
 6
 7 gethostbyname(char* name) {
 8   open("/etc/nsswitch.conf", O_RDONLY, _);
 9   open("/etc/hosts", O_RDONLY, _);
10   socket(AF_INET, SOCK_DGRAM, IPPROTO_IP);
11   connect(_,
12           *(struct sockaddr_in){sin_family: AF_INET,
13                                 sim_port: htons(53),
14                                 sin_addr.s_addr: inet_addr("192.168.65.8"),
15           sizeof(struct sockaddr_in));
16   ...
17 }
18
19 fopen(char* path, "r") {
20   open(path, O_RDONLY, _);
21 }
22
23 fopen(char* path, "w") {
24   open(path, O_CREAT | O_WRONLY | O_TRANC);
25 }
```

Fig. 4. Part of the policy file for `gethostbyname` and `fopen`

of `gethostbyname` and `fopen`. Similar to the case of the policies of sandboxed applications, they are expected to be prepared by the developers of the library and provided together with the library code itself.

5   Implementation

We implemented the sandbox system on Linux 2.6.8. The following four approaches were considered for this implementation.

1. User-level implementation
   (a) A method that rewrites the source code of the target application.
   (b) A method that uses the `ptrace` system call.
2. Kernel-level implementation
   (a) A method that rewrites the kernel code.
   (b) A method that uses loadable kernel module (LKM).

Method 1-(a) inserts check codes just before each invocation of a system call. The codes check the policy of this execution context and determine whether the system call is allowed or not. Although this method can be implemented only at the user level, doing so is still complicated and difficult.

Method 1-(b) uses `ptrace` to intercept a system call issued by the application process. When the sandbox process intercepts a system call, it checks the context-dependent policy. Although it is easy to implement, it imposes significant overhead because of the use of `ptrace`, and this lowers the efficiency of the target application.

Method 2-(a) directly rewrites the kernel codes so as to monitor the issues of system calls by the target application process. Although its efficiency is high, it depends on the kernel version too much.

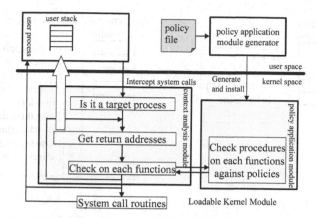

Fig. 5. Implementation of the proposed system

Method 2-(b) dynamically inserts kernel modules (codes) into the kernel after Linux starts up. Though this method also depends on the kernel version, it is easier than method 2-(a) to follow version updates, because it does not rewrite the kernel code itself. Thus, we chose this approach.

Figure 5 shows the overall structure of the implementation of the sandbox system. The system consists of two LKMs. One is a *context analysis module* that is independent of the target application, and the other is a *policy application module* that depends on a target application. The policy application module rewrites the system call entry table in the kernel space, which is used in the dispatch of a system call request, to intercept the system calls of the target application process. Because the behaviour of the policy application module depends on the policy of the target application, we automatically generate this module as an LKM from the description of the policy.

As shown in Fig. 6 (a), each entry of the table contains a pointer to the corresponding service routine of the system call. __NR_open is the identifier of the open system call, so the __NR_open-th element of the table is a pointer to the default service routine of open in the kernel, namely sys_open(). Suppose that the policy of some target application allows the call open in user-defined functions f, g, and h and the module for this policy is loaded into the kernel. Then the entry for open is rewritten to the just-loaded function that checks the context and determines whether it is allowed or not.

The sandbox system works as follows.

Before startup of the system:

1. A policy application module is generated from the policy file of the target process.
2. The policy application module that has been just generated and the context analysis module are loaded within the Linux kernel. As a result, the system call entry table is updated.
3. The sandbox system starts.

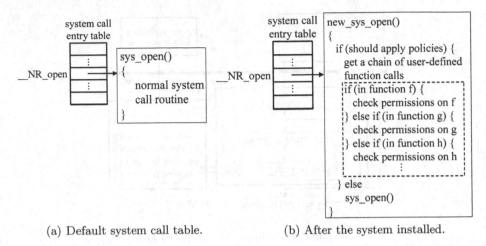

(a) Default system call table.   (b) After the system installed.

Fig. 6. Flow of the proposed system after it intercepts system calls

After startup:

1. When a process of the target application issues a system call, it goes into the kernel and executes the processing function of the system call that is registered in the system call entry table.
2. The processing function checks whether the process that issued the system call is one of the targets of the sandbox or not. If not, the process proceeds to the default service routine of the system call, e.g., `sys_open()`, and returns from the kernel.
3. The processing function then investigates the chain of user-defined function calls by using the context analysis module.
4. For each user-defined function in the chain (from the top of the stack to the bottom), the processing function checks whether the system call with the current actual parameter is allowed to execute in the user-defined function. If so, the process proceeds to the default service routine of the system call; if not, it checks the next user-defined function.
5. If none of the user-defined functions in the chain allows an execution of the system call, the process returns from the kernel with an error.

To obtain the chain of user-defined functions, the context analysis module investigates the stack frame in the user space of the target process (Fig. 7 (a)). A stack frame contains its return address and the link to the caller's stack frame. By consulting the application's symbol table (Fig. 7 (b)) that contains symbol names and their start addresses, the module can know the function name of the return address in a stack frame. Thus, it is possible to obtain the chain by successively following the links in a stack frame.

Attackers may try to modify return addresses and force target applications to execute malicious codes in stack or heap spaces. The sandbox can refuse system calls by malicious code because the stack frames are rewritten with unknown return addresses.

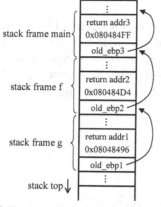

(a) User stack and stack frames.

start address	symbol name
...	...
0x08048464	g
0x080484cf	f
0x080484df	main
0x080485b0	–
...	...

(b) Symbol table.

Fig. 7. Obtaining the chain of user-defined functions

6   Experimental Results

We conducted the following experiments.

- Two experiments using Qpopper 4.0.4: one was to verify that the sandbox could detect an attack and the other was to check the overhead of the sandbox.
- An experiment using a micro benchmark.

The experiments were done on a PC with 3.0-GHz Pentium 4 and 1-GB of main memory running Linux kernel 2.6.8.

6.1   Detection of Attacks

We inserted an intentional vulnerability into the transaction state of Qpopper. In this state, Qpopper accepts a LIST command. If an argument, a message number, is given, Qpopper issues a response with a line containing information for that message. If a negative value is given as the argument, the server returns a "no such message" error. For the experiments, we rewrote the code of Qpopper and inserted a vulnerability that opened the password file if a negative argument is given to a LIST command.

We ran the Qpopper server in the sandbox system with a policy in which accessing the password file is restricted only in the user-information state. We attacked Qpopper by giving a negative argument to a LIST command and made sure that the sandbox system could block the attack with a permission error. Of course, Qpopper could open the password file in the user-information state. Through this experiment, we confirmed that the system could apply dynamic policies based on execution contexts.

6.2   Overhead

First, we measured the execution times of a micro benchmark. The micro benchmark repeated the same operation 10,000 times and we calculated the time for executing the operation once. The operation consisted of opening a file and immediately closing it. We gave a policy of `main` in which both opening and closing the file would be allowed in any execution context by putting the ">" mark in front of `open` and `close`.

```
main() {
  >open(_, _, _);
  >close(_);
}
```

If `open` or `close` are called in the context of f_n—$\cdots$—f_1—`main`, i.e., the length of the chain of user-defined functions is n, the sandbox system will analyze $n + 1$ stack frames. We measured execution times for $n = 0, 1, \ldots, 5$. Note that the case $n = 0$ roughly approximates the behaviour of a sandbox with a single policy, because the system need not investigate successive stack frames.

Next, we measured the client-side response time, time between client's sending a request and receiving the first reply message of the request, for USER, LIST, and RETR commands to the Qpopper server. In this experiment, client PC and server PC were interconnected by a single switch through 1000 Base-T Ethernet. The client PC was equipped with a Pentium III 930-MHz CPU, 256-MB memory, and its operating system was Linux 2.4.27.

We repeated the same operation 1,000 times and calculated the averages. The dynamic policy for the Qpopper application contained a list of user-defined functions whose abstraction levels were sufficiently high, and hence the policy was very compact. We did not give a policy to user-defined functions whose abstraction levels were low. We used policy inheritance to specify system calls that the functions needed for their execution.

These experiments were done on the following three configurations:

1. Applications run on the normal kernel without the proposed LKMs.
2. Applications run on the normal kernel loaded with the proposed LKMs. However, the applications do not run in a sandbox.
3. Applications run in a sandbox on the normal kernel loaded with the proposed LKMs.

The un-sandboxed applications and the sandboxed applications have an overhead to check the necessity of applying a policy. In addition, the sandboxed applications have extra overheads to analyze the execution context and apply the policy associated with the context.

Table 1 shows the results of the micro benchmark. The extra overhead of the sandboxed program ($n = 5$) was 180% compared with the case without the proposed system. Although this overhead was not small, the extra overhead compared with the case $n = 0$, an approximation of a single-policy sandbox, was 44%. We regard that this overhead are permissible by the following two reasons.

Table 1. Results of micro benchmark (μsec)

without proposed system	with proposed system						
	un-sandboxed	sandboxed					
		$n = 0$	$n = 1$	$n = 2$	$n = 3$	$n = 4$	$n = 5$
1.75	1.88	3.40	3.79	4.04	4.26	4.57	4.91

Table 2. Results of client-side response time of Qpopper (μsec)

command	without proposed system	with proposed system	
		un-sandboxed	sandboxed
USER	24.0	24.3	25.0
LIST	11.0	11.2	11.3
RETR	21.8	21.9	22.6

- In exchange for this overhead, a sandboxed application by the proposed system has higher security.
- As will be seen in the results of the client-side response time of Qpopper, this overhead is small enough compared with the network latency between a client and a server.

Table 2 shows the results of the Qpopper. The overhead of the un-sandboxed Qpopper was within 2 %, and that of the sandboxed Qpopper was almost 4%, compared with the normal Qpopper. These results show that the overhead of the proposed sandbox is not a serious problem because of the network latency.

7   Related Work

Many studies have been devoted to sandbox systems based on system call interception. Unlike our system, many do not support dynamic policy switching [1,5,8,9].

Several sandbox systems or sandboxing mechanisms that can dynamically switch policies exist. SubDomain [2] is a sandbox system that can switch policies when a target process calls an **exec** system call or a special system call **change_hat** that is inserted in the source code of a target application. Thus, the application code must be modified to switch policies at program points except the invocation of **exec**. Kurchuk et al. [7] extends a single-policy sandbox system Systrace [9] to support dynamic policy switches. Their application code must be modified. To switch policies, an application must call a special function **systrace_setpolicy**. Moreover, an application must call a special function **systrace_setstate** to tell the state of the application to the sandbox. In contrast to these systems, our system does not require the user to modify the application code.

There are several researches on intrusion detection systems using system call information and stack information. VtPath [3] is an intrusion detection method that checks the list of the current stack frames when a system call is invoked. The system judges that an anomaly has occurred if the transition between the current list and the previous list does not conform to the normal behavior pattern learned in advance. An intrusion detection system based on finite-state automaton (FSA) [11] is also a learning-based system that detects intrusions by using the information on system calls and stack frames at the time of system call invocation. VtPath and FSA-based systems focus on detecting malicious manipulation of a control flow, and they ignore system call arguments. On the other hand, our system focuses on preventing malicious resource accesses that often occur after control flow manipulation. In addition, our system inspects more information than their systems do, including system call arguments.

Wagner et al. [12] studied mimicry attacks that disguise themselves as normal programs and circumvent detection by security systems. Mimicry attacks can deceive security systems that are straightforwardly implemented using system call interception [4]. Attackers against our system have difficulty succeeding with mimicry attacks, because they must create mimic stack frames (execution contexts) before invoking the system calls. As described in Kruegel et al.'s paper [6], an elaborate analysis is needed to create a successful mimicry attack.

Java Stack Inspection [13] enables dynamic policy switches in Java sandboxes. In this framework, a resource access policy is determined according to the content of the stack. A resource can be accessed if the stack contains a frame for a code part permitted to access the resource. Since a Java application runs on a virtual machine, it is not difficult for a security mechanism to obtain the state of a target application and control resource accesses. Our work differs from Java in that it achieves dynamic policy switches in the context of sandboxing native code.

8   Conclusion

We proposed and implemented a sandbox system that can apply dynamic policies in accordance with the execution contexts of the target application processes. This sandbox system can give privileges to a target application that are more in keeping with the principle of the least privilege, compared with existing sandbox systems with a single policy. It uses a chain of user-defined function calls as an approximation of an execution context and switches the policy on the basis of its execution context. Thus, it provides fine-grained control to guarantee highly secure sandboxes. One of our future tasks is to develop an automatic policy generation system from source codes of target applications.

References

1. Acharya, A., Raje, M.: MAPbox: Using Parameterized Behavior Classes to Confine Untrusted Applications. In: Proc. 9th USENIX Security Symposium, pp. 1–17 (2000)
2. Cowan, C., Beattie, S., Kroah-Hartman, G., Pu, C., Wagle, P., Gligor, V.: SubDomain: Parsimonious Server Security. In: Proc. 14th Systems Administration Conference (LISA 2000) (2000)

3. Hanping Feng, H., Kolesnikov, O.M., Fogla, P., Lee, W., Gong, W.: Anomaly Detection Using Call Stack Information. In: Proc. 2003 IEEE Symposium on Security and Privacy, pp. 62–75 (2003)
4. Forrest, S., Perelson, A.S., Allen, L., Cherukuri, R.: Self-nonself Discrimination in a Computer. In: Proc. 1994 IEEE Symposium on Research in Security and Privacy, pp. 202–212 (1994)
5. Goldberg, I., Wagner, D., Thomas, R., Brewer, E.A.: A Secure Environment for Untrusted Helper Applications. In: Proc. 6th USENIX Security Symposium, pp. 1–14 (1996)
6. Kruegel, C., Kirda, E., Mutz, D., Robertson, W., Vigna, G.: Automating Mimicry Attacks Using Static Binary Analysis. In: Proc. 14th Conference on USENIX Security Symposium, pp. 161–176 (2005)
7. Kurchuk, A., Keromytis, A.: Recursive Sandboxes: Extending Systrace to Empower Applications. In: Proc. 19th IFIP International Information Security Conference, pp. 473–487 (2004)
8. Peterson, D.S., Bishop, M., Pandey, R.: A Flexible Containment Mechanism for Executing Untrusted Code. In: Proc. 11th USENIX Security Symposium, pp. 207–225 (2002)
9. Provos, N.: Improving Host Security with System Call Policies. In: Proc. 12th USENIX Security Symposium, pp. 257–272 (2003)
10. Saltzer, J.H., Schroeder, M.D.: The Protection of Information in Computer Systems. Proceedings of the IEEE 63(9), 1278–1308 (1975)
11. Sekar, R., Bendre, M., Dhurjati, D., Bollineni, P.: A Fast Automaton-Based Method for Detecting Anomalous Program Behaviors. In: Proc. 2001 IEEE Symposium on Security and Privacy, pp. 144–155 (2001)
12. Wagner, D., Soto, P.: Mimicry Attacks on Host-Based Intrusion Detection Systems. In: Proc. 9th ACM Conference on Computer and communications security, pp. 255–264 (2002)
13. Wallach, D.S., Balfanz, D., Dean, D., Felten, E.W.: Extensible Security Architectures for Java. In: Proc. 16th ACM Symposium on Operating Systems Principles, pp. 116–128 (1997)

Author Index

Lecture Notes in Computer Science

Sublibrary 1: Theoretical Computer Science and General Issues

For information about Vols. 1–4494
please contact your bookseller or Springer